Derek Annable (Boy

60 YEARS BEHIND T

CW00530060

To Dez a Pearl

Also by the same author

Frank Franklyn's African Adventure

Frank Franklyn's Africa

Derek a Brenda

Derek Annable
(Boy Racer)

60 Years Behind the Wheel

First published in the United Kingdom 2006 by
Derek Annable
Mount View, Rhosgoch,
Amlwch, Anglesey, LL66 0AR

To order this book direct from the author, please write to the above address or fax your order to +44 (0)1248 410143.

ISBN 0–9549732–1–6 paperback

A catalogue record for this book is available from the British Library.

Design, origination and editing by
Aardvark Editorial, Harleston, Norfolk

Printed and bound in Great Britain by
The Charlesworth Group, West Yorkshire

Contents

List of Photographs

Preface

I have tried with all honesty to record my life in motorsport, although it is difficult to rely solely on one's memory for recalling the finer details of the events of so many years. Nevertheless, being someone who never throws anything away, my house is filled with documents and mementoes going back fifty years, and the records so carefully stored for all these years have been the basis of my book. To this source of hard information are added my own personal memories, thoughts and feelings, and the resultant combination reflects a bygone world and culture, as well as the thrusting brashness of modern motorsport.

Some people may question what I have written, and if there are minor errors of memory, I will stand corrected. As for myself, I am an open book and were somebody to point out a forgotten foible or peccadillo, I should reply, 'Yes; why not!'

Life should be lived to the full, and with passion; passion in its broadest sense, involving strong emotions and great enthusiasm. This I have tried to do. As you read this book, I hope you will yourself feel the passion for life and for motorsport unfold and evolve, carrying you through the twentieth century and beyond in the tale of one man's life.

Derek Annable

Foreword

Carla Pittau, *Heaven & Hell Racing*

'Grandad' Derek Annable … a bit of a legend. Sixty years in motorsports, his name offers a new definition of 'heart like a wheel'.

This is a man who truly dedicated his whole life to motor racing, and to prove it he has sampled most types from behind the wheel. Although he came to drag racing later in life, his passion for the straight quarter mile proved to be a mature, long-lasting love.

He sampled several drag racing classes – from Sportsman, all the way to Top Methanol dragster – campaigning, among other cars, his street legal Chevrolet Camaro, his wife's BMW, an Altered with nitrous oxide, and finally the dragster.

The world of drag racing is truly amazing. It perhaps differs from other types of motorsport in that competing racers will help each other in the pits to their last nut and bolt – being happy only if they defeat the other party fair and square, on the track. However, although this world is a wonderful place, it is not perfect, and at times there were rifts and problems which needed discussion and, on occasion, direct action to resolve.

Derek is a man who does not compromise with truth – he will stand up every time for what he thinks is right and will never be afraid if his voice is the only dissenting one.

We have not always agreed on things, but any disagreement was always discussed with the greatest degree of civility and respect for each other. I can recall at least one occasion when his was the only vote against a proposed merger of two sportsman racers associations and, along with everyone else, I disagreed with him at the time. The details are not relevant here, but I will say that his view was proved, if not dead-on right, then very near the mark.

There is not enough space here to paint an accurate picture of this man – you will have to read the book to make up your own mind – but Derek has proved to all of us that it isn't just the thrill of the race that he values, he also really cares about the future of drag racing and believes it should expand, grow, and bring excitement and enjoyment to many more people in the future.

May I race you again, Derek; I know it would be a very enjoyable race.

Foreword

Claire Meaddows, *Wild Bunch Race Coordinator/Treasurer*

When Derek told me he was writing a book about his life in motorsport, I was very excited to hear more about his racing experiences; but little did I know how much insight it would give into the life of this remarkable man, who is truly passionate about motorsport and drag racing in particular.

Derek is an honest man who always speaks his mind. Even when this sometimes lands him in 'hot water', he still has the courage of his convictions. I respect him greatly for repeatedly showing himself true to what he believes in; and I admire him for his campaigning letters, constantly trying to promote drag racing with the sport's best interest at heart, and always encouraging others around him.

Despite now being a pensioner, Derek's enthusiasm, motivation and competitive spirit still keep him young at heart, as he is a 'boy racer' by nature. This has always driven him on to achieve the best he could out of any vehicle he raced, nothing less!

I'm sure the reader will be fascinated and amazed to hear of Derek's single-seater racing days in the early 1950s through to his more recent drag racing exploits in bracket racing and his involvement with the Wild Bunch Nostalgia Drag Racing Club. And learning of the great support of Derek's amazing wife Brenda (who has triumphed over ill health and shared many ups and downs throughout their long happy marriage) is a great inspiration and clearly shows why racing is their 'life force'. A truly great partnership. The Wild Bunch were recently proud to have the honour of presenting them with a lifetime achievement award for their contributions, commitment and dedication to motorsport. They, in turn, presented a new award for couples contributing to drag racing, thereby continuing their legacy.

Throughout Derek's life, his perseverance, sportsmanship and determination have enabled him to succeed in many things and, since his retirement, he has gone on to achieve many more of his goals in drag racing, with Brenda by his side. This book will be an inspiration to young and old alike to follow their own dreams.

Acknowledgements

This book is a team effort. I am the driver, with a pen instead of a steering wheel in his hand. Now, the team:

Chris Hartnell and Claire Meaddows. What can I say! Chris is the leader of the Wild Bunch, and Claire is one hell of a lady. The statistics lady: 'No errors, Derek!' Thank you Claire.

Pam Robinson, who is my sister and a late arrival. Without her illustrations, the book would have been lacking.

Lynne Annable, my daughter, who has been the linchpin of all my scribblings.

Then there is Brian Staines, the genius with a camera.

John Turner, the quiet man who has put up with my rants and raves. Without him the cars wouldn't have raced. Thank you, John.

Next is Desmond Hammill. He controlled my emotions, and from this came the written word. Desmond, to me, you are my mentor.

Now the final member of the team. Annabel Ackroyd, the rock who has helped Derek 'Grandad' Annable to indulge his ego!

One hell of a team which has no equal.

Derek Annable

Glossary of Terms

alcohol: methanol when used as fuel in an engine.

altered: a car based on a known body type but changed or radically customised.

blower/supercharger: a crank drive air-to-fuel moisture compressor. It increases atmospheric pressure in the engine, giving extra horsepower.

bracket: the upper and lower ET index limits on a class.

breakout: running faster than the index in handicap racing.

burnout: spinning the driving wheels in water prior to the run. This heats and cleans them, giving better traction.

Christmas tree: the starting lights controlled by the timing computer.

ci (cubic inch) or **cc (cubic centimetre):** a measure of engine capacity.

deep stage: a driver is deep staged when, after staging, he/she rolls forward a few inches further, causing the pre-stage light to go out. The vehicle is nearer the finish line but is dangerously close to a red light. In some classes, the act is illegal.

dial-in: in handicap racing, the time the racer considers is the most consistent he can achieve.

dialled in: a vehicle is said to be dialled in when driver and crew are happy it will run consistently.

doorslammer: a full-bodied car with operable doors.

eliminations: a tournament-style competition where the losers are eliminated and the winners progress until only one winner remains.

ET: elapsed time. The total time taken to travel from start line to finish line.

flopper/fuel coupe: a Funny Car.

foul: an infringement of a rule during a run. This may be pulling a red light, crossing a lane boundary, or running under an index.

headers: fine-tuned exhaust system, routing exhaust from engine. Replaces conventional exhaust manifolds.

heads-up: non-handicap racing, where both competitors start together.

hemi: an engine, which has a hemispherical-shaped cylinder-head chamber.

holeshot: an advantage gained by a quicker reaction time on the start line.

in pre-stage: a racer is in pre-stage when the front wheel has interrupted the first light beam just before the start line. Full stage is only inches ahead.

in stage: a racer is in stage when the front wheels have interrupted both light beams at the start line (see also deep stage).

index: an elapsed time establishing the limit for a handicap class.

light up (tyres): generally too much power is used, causing the tyres to spin in smoke instead of gripping the track.

methanol: pure methyl alcohol produced by synthesis; primarily associated with Top Methanol or Alcohol dragsters and Funny Cars.

NHRA: National Hot Rod Association. Major US drag racing governing body.

nitro: nitromethane, the ultimate fuel specially produced for drag racing. A result of a chemical reaction between nitric acid and propane.

nitrous: nitrous oxide. Gives added horsepower when injected with fuel into the engine as it contains accessible oxygen.

qualifying: before eliminations begin, racers must qualify. If a field is too large, only the quickest qualifiers will make up the number in the elimination.

reaction time or **rt:** the time it takes a racer to react to the green starting light. Measured in thousandths of a second. The rt counter begins when the last amber flashes and stops when the vehicle clears the stage beams.

s/c: supercharged

slick: smooth tyres with no tread, giving maximum traction of rubber to track.

staging lane: designated assembly area for competitors, also known as the pairing lanes, where competitors are paired prior to racing.

stock: standard factory appearance.

street legal: a car or bike, which could or does qualify for an MOT and can run legally on the road.

supercharger: *see* blower/supercharger.

terminal speed: the speed through the finish line.

trackbite or **traction compound:** a liquid that is sprayed onto the track, providing added grip or traction when dry.

wheelie bars: bars with small wheels protruding from the rear of some vehicles, preventing excessive front wheel lift.

WT: no time recorded.

CHAPTER 1

Naissance

We were an average middle-class family. My brother and sister enjoyed listening to Violet Carson on the radio, our father got up early to go to work, and mother worked hard for our respectability. The summers were hot and the winters were cold, with snow at Christmas.

All this came to an end when Neville Chamberlain met Hitler, and within six short months our father had joined the army. Before he went away, he called my brother and me into his study and told us, 'When you feel the urge for a girl ...' (we were only 8 and 9 at the time) '... don't do it with a respectable girl – find a lass of the world.'

Life went on with mother in charge. We children went to the local schools – my sister to the girls' school and my brother and I to Alderley Junior School. Many of our friends were sent to the USA to avoid the war. One friend, Stockdale, actually had relatives there but, with the brutal glee of ignorant childhood, he was still labelled a coward for going.

One morning in late 1940, my mother started packing suitcases and told me I was being sent to a school in Shropshire. The next day I was put on a train with a Mr Price. My mother kissed me and said, 'Mr Price will take you to the school.' I liked Mr Price; he was a Welshman who had fought in the First World War with the Welsh Guards and was too old to fight this time.

When we arrived at the school in Shropshire, Mr Price took all the suitcases to my dormitory, shook my hand and said, 'You're a man now.' I don't know whether that helped or not, but I certainly didn't feel particularly manly. The juniors were very friendly, but the prefects had their own rooms and were distant and aloof. Within a matter of hours, I had passed from the warmth and security of family life to one of cold, emotionless self-sufficiency, and it took most of the first term to settle in – I won't go into the torments I went through. Mr Price took me home for the holidays.

The second term was more enjoyable. The prefects were showing their authority and some were brutal, but my house was 'York' and we had a kindly housemaster. There were walks every Sunday up the local mountain and I made a few friends among the other new juniors.

Every morning we would march to the dining room for breakfast, sit down and wait for the food to be brought to us. On the first morning of the new term, the boys on my table noticed there was a new lady in charge of the waitresses. We lost all interest in food; she was tall, slim, with curves where they should be, dark-skinned and with jet-black hair. Can you imagine thirty 10- and 11-year-olds off their food for two weeks?

The manageress only served food to the top tables where the masters and head boy sat. We wondered how we could get her attention to come down to the main hall. Every table had a junior master in charge – we should persuade him there was something wrong with the food. Every Friday it was fish, so we kept some fish in the dormitory all week, then smuggled it into the dining room. It worked! For weeks afterwards, there were creaking beds in the dormitory. When our house prefect found out what we had done with the fish, six of us were thrashed with his leather slipper. Matron felt sorry for us but there was nothing she could do. Never mind – it was his last term at the school; maybe Hitler's army would capture him and thrash him with an iron rod.

Matron was like a second mother to us. Cut fingers or running noses, the orders were to go and see matron, and one winter we all needed her. The rules were that all dormitory windows had to be open and there was also no heating. We weren't allowed any extra clothing, so the floor mats were used as supplementary bed covers. Then the snows came. Every morning for a week, there were two inches of snow on our beds and the floor. We put the snow through the fourth-floor windows where we slept and prayed for summer. The weakest boy became ill and passed the virus on to us. Matron was giving us all sorts of medicine, one of which was foul and tasted of chloroform and tar, but we all survived and sent matron a birthday card.

The years 1941 and 1942 were good ones. The house teams won many cups for rugby, cricket and other sports. My brother joined me at the school but he was put into a different house from me. The tuck shop was our main meeting place, burning bread on a toasting fork over an open fire. Christmas 1942 was spent at home amid a great family gathering, with all our relatives present for Christmas Day and Boxing Day. One of them, our Uncle Alf, worked at A.V. Roe, making Lancaster bombers. He was a lovely man.

The spring term of 1943 was a landmark. York's housemaster had retired and one of the new teachers was appointed in his place. At the same time, the headmaster transferred a junior master from Denton house to be our assistant housemaster. We had heard from the boys in Denton that this master was strange, and we soon found out what they meant by that.

Once a week was bath night. Matron supervised the young ones as they went to bed early, but the middle school had to share the same bath water one by one until the water was cold, and only then was fresh water supplied. Bath night went on for hours, and the last in line soon found out how strange our new assistant housemaster was. He would come out of the prefects' room, go into the bathroom and start taking his clothes off, order the boys out of the bath and make us stand there naked in the room, which by now was full of steam. He then stood naked in the bath of hot water and lathered himself with his own bar of soap – we boys had to share one bar and make it last for weeks. Hedgehog (a name given to him by the boys of our dormitory because his private parts were covered by a mass of black spiky hair) would foam that area of his body until it vanished from sight. Next, one boy was ordered to get a bucket of clean warm water and pour it over him until all the soap suds had gone.

We were blessed in that Hedgehog didn't do this every bath night, but the fear was there. Matron knew there was a problem, because boys who reported sick were checked for lice and the evidence began to emerge.

One boy hadn't had a bath all term and was showing signs of stress. His best friend was Bruiser Bellis, who was York house's boxing champion and, although small, he could floor boys twice his size with one punch. One bath night in the summer term, Bruiser Bellis volunteered to be last boy to have a bath when we knew Hedgehog was going to make one of his surprise visits to the bathroom. Things were very quiet, which was strange as Hedgehog always shouted his orders. Bruiser Bellis came out with the bucket and filled it from the hot water tap, which came direct from the boiler in the basement and on bath night always had a good head of steam. The screams from the bathroom could be heard in the quadrangle. Hedgehog left at the end of the summer term to join the navy – maybe.

The war against Hitler had reached a bad stage. Many of the boys' fathers were killed on active service, and families were being wiped out by German bombing. Young Taylor had lost his father when a U-boat sank his ship, which was on escort duty with an Atlantic convoy in late 1943. At roll call, young Taylor went missing. A search of the school proved fruitless; he couldn't be found, so we all went to bed.

Our dormitory was in the roof space, with windows opening onto a stone ledge, all of 50ft above ground. In the middle of the night, we were woken by talking. It was Bonzo. He was a well-loved master who smoked the most foul-smelling weed. He never slept; all night he could be seen walking around the school grounds. After five minutes of this, the three boys who slept under the windows stood on their beds and looked out. Bonzo was talking to someone on the roof – it was young Taylor.

By now, a prefect had come into our room. He climbed onto the ledge to reach up to the boy but he was frozen to the spot with fear. Being a school which looked after its own, no fire brigade or police were called. Mattresses, bedding, cardboard boxes, all were thrown out of the dorm windows to be piled up below where young Taylor was stuck on the roof; even the swimming pool cover was put on top of this pile of mattresses and so on, which had grown to at least 10ft high. The gym master now took charge; he was so strong he could climb up a rope one-handed. After what seemed like hours, he managed to secure a rope around the boy and lower him to the ground. There were two heroes that night, Bonzo and the gym master, and we were all proud to be part of a team – a secret team. No press were called and parents were told little. Bars were put on the windows and lessons carried on as usual.

One school holiday at the end of 1943, I had my first experience of driving. The local ladies in my home village of Alderley Edge were arranging an American Day for the GIs at Burtonwood base in Warrington and our house was chosen for the officers' reception. This was because we had two large rooms and the house was far enough away from the main road to make it private.

General (Pistol-packing) Patton was on a goodwill tour of the area and he would try to attend our celebration, if time permitted. Because of a less-than-warm reception from some people to a speech he made in nearby Knutsford, he drove straight to our house. When he got out of the staff car, you could see his mood was pretty grim – fire was coming out of his mouth. Well, to a 12-year-old it looked like fire. Mother told me later it was a large cigar he was smoking. All the ladies surrounded him and they went inside. The general's car was nice but what interested me were the Jeeps. Three were on escort duty and I started talking to the driver of one, when out of the house came Patton, to collect his famous pearl-handled pistols from the staff car.

'Hi, boy, do you like that Jeep?'

I replied, 'Yes, sir,' and stood to attention as I was taught at school.

'Good. Driver, let this young man have a drive in the Jeep. Show him how everything works; I shall be going to Burtonwood in an hour.'

I sat in the driving seat. With the pedals being on the floor, I could just reach them. The young American driver, who came from Texas, said, 'We'll stay in first gear. That's the clutch, forget the brake peddle, I'll use the handbrake to stop us,' and off we went down the drive. Since I hadn't let the clutch out all the way, it was a bumpy ride. Five miles per hour came up on the speedo, and then we had to stop because of a large crowd on the main road. General Patton thanked all the ladies of Alderley Edge and was driven to Burtonwood where a plane was waiting to take him back to the USA. The D-day landings started in June the following year and Patton was soon in the thick of it.

That drive in the Jeep was the start of Derek Annable, boy racer. I later passed my driving test at the first attempt on my seventeenth birthday, although the lady examiner was more interested in the radio and the cream and maroon Park Ward Drophead 1936 Bentley she was sitting in than my driving. She did ask, 'how fast does it go?'

I said, 'I don't know.'

'Put it into second gear and take us to fifty miles per hour.' This I did.

'Very nice', she said. 'I enjoyed that, what a lovely car. Oh, you've passed; you can drive home on your own.'

Meanwhile, the school holidays over, it was back to my friends and some cold days and nights in our dormitory. At least I had something to brag about. Even our housemaster was impressed when I told him about General Patton's visit to our house.

The year 1944 drifted on, and new masters started and left. One particular new master who started at the school towards the end of the year had a lasting impact on us; this was the music teacher who lived in the town. He transformed the choir – the Welsh would have been proud of it. We travelled to other schools and gave concerts. Now, every boy in the school wanted to play the piano. A new music room was formed, with cubicles in which old upright pianos were installed, donated by parents and other music lovers. We in the choir began to feel like the privileged few; our church was full of visitors on open days and choir practice took priority over other lessons and sport. After six months, all music lovers within the school were on the crest of a wave.

Suddenly this started to change. Boys who had piano lessons were going for short spells in the school sanatorium with nervous problems, and many gave up the piano lessons. We in the choir found the music teacher a perfect gentleman, although sometimes he was a bit free with his chubby hand on your knee, but the trouble started when boys had private lessons at his house – for us, this was a good excuse to get out of the school's perimeter wall and into the town. All the time he was at the school, we thought he was married, but when we had private lessons no lady ever appeared. Other boys, not in the choir, told us his hand went a little higher than the knee. If you got up and said you were going back to school, no problem, you were free to leave. Others who stayed were quiet for weeks and reported to matron.

The end of the war in Europe came. I gave up the choir and spent all my free time on my forthcoming exams. The results were fair but no chance of university. I left school the following year, much to the disgust of my demobbed father. On the last day of term, I packed my suitcases and walked to the railway station, never looking back. I knew the words of Mr Price were true.

Now, when I drive southeast across Shropshire, I see the mountain, all 407m high, and hidden behind it are the town and six years of my life, the ghosts of my youth. Did we walk to the top every Sunday and return to school before curfew? Yes we did. No time to stop and look at all the pretty girls in the town. A Shropshire lass is pretty beyond belief … dreams, all dreams.

Whether the school is still there, I don't know. Bad memories meant no return. The good memories, though, are many: Bonzo with his flowing robes, cigarette smoke everywhere, sports day, parents' day, and songs we made up ('Pennington is a Naughty Boy'), and last but not least that dark-skinned beauty who was in charge of the dining hall. Where is she now? I hope she found happiness, because without her that school would have broken your will to live.

We drift through time not knowing where our future will take us, but this book tells the story of what did happen to me, after my father returned home from the war. Nearly six years is a long time, people change, relationships have to be rebuilt and it can be hell. Mother found it hard to adjust.

CHAPTER 2

Awareness

For my father, who had spent five years fighting Hitler's various armies in the deserts of North Africa and Arabia, sand, heat and sun were not on his agenda; neither were cold and snow – mountains were. In the dead of night, he bundled us all into an old pre-war Buick and we set off for our annual holiday. We stayed in a remote part of North Wales – high mountains with their tops hidden in mist, raging waterfalls, ravines that looked as though Satan had carved them out of the granite. There were five buildings; one was called the Wasp's Nest and was next to a hotel, the others were gift shops. What intrigued me about the Wasp's Nest was the dark young gypsy girl who sat outside. The sign said: 'Your fortune told for two shillings.'

My brother and I joked who was to be first. As it turned out, to joke about the powers she possessed was foolish. I paid my two shillings and sat down on a stone seat. She took my hand and turned the palm upwards.

She said, 'Your future is obscured. There has been pain but this is over. There are people, famous people – one man of now, followed by one man and one woman in the distance. I see wheels, heat; everything is blurred like a plane diving through the sky.'

'What else?'

'Many children.' She then walked inside and closed the door.

Our holiday over, father put us children to work, with the promise that at the end of three years we could have money to pursue any sport of our choice. My brother went into farming and I started work with the local builder.

Because of my brother's interest in farming, we met a young man who lived on a farm in the next county. Strangely, he drove about the farm in a Sherman tank. His father had also bought him an old American Jeep. The tank laid a track around one field, with hairpin bends, fast corners and slow corners, and this lad then drove the Jeep around the circuit with a stop-watch around his neck. We didn't know what his father's job was, although he always wore a white coat – he could have been a vet. My brother said, 'How could he be a vet? Have you seen the bag he carries? It's full of drills and pliers.' We agreed he used them to take out horses' teeth. Life should be fun.

In the third year, to ensure fulfilment of our father's promise, it was work and more work. Rationing was still the order of the day for the British people, and hotels and restaurants would pay good money for fresh extra foodstuffs. That is how I got involved with the egg run. Three times a week (never before one o'clock in the morning), I made weekly deliveries which were often in excess of 500 dozen fresh free-range eggs to high-class restaurants – always through the back door. At this time the Mafia started to show an interest in the UK, and many famous people from America became its frontmen. On the egg run I saw them taking their girlfriends to the West End restaurants I supplied. I imagined George Raft eating a soufflé made with eggs I delivered to his favourite watering hole. The excitement! Did he carry a gun? Who were his bodyguards? Police once raided the Colony Club.

Six months of little sleep was causing me to miss work and my father began to suspect that I had a second job. No more egg runs.

The big day came for us and the cheques were handed over. With mine I went out and bought an HRG sports car (registration LKL 999) in British racing green. It was agreed the brothers Annable were going into mud trials. The first meet was at a farm three miles from ours. On our arrival we learned that we were second off behind an up-and-coming young man called Colin Chapman with his later famous Lotus 7.

From now on, we spent the winter travelling the length and breadth of Buckinghamshire and North Wales with the HRG to compete in these mud trials. The method was to let the rear tyres down to 5–10lbs pressure, with my brother bouncing over the rear wheels. One hiccup, and he ended up face down in the mud as I pounded off.

Colin arrived at one meet with his new car, incorporating a super-light chassis and so on. Sorry, but in the mud game, grip is required through weight over the rear wheels. To overcome this, Colin brought a 15-stone friend whose job it was to bounce on the rear of the car. This worked until he drove through the second farm gate and onto the step climb: bang, bang on the rear suspension with 15 stone on it, and it broke. Was this to be the future of all Chapman cars?

Being the man he was, Colin Chapman produced some great cars. The power-to-weight ratio factor was all important, and Colin's genius was to take a humble 1500cc engine, fit it into a lightweight frame, put four wheels on it and make it go at 200 miles per hour. He learnt lessons in the mud racing days that enabled him to produce a car which had no rival and is still surviving today.

Racing in mud trials had its own problems though. On the journey home, with our car covered in the best farmyard manure, everybody wanted to race us as a laughter factor.

One night while having a drink at the Fitzroy Club in Marlow, two of the hale and hearty types from the rowing club said, 'Derek why don't you go circuit racing?'

Young Platt, who had an MG sports car, said, 'No, Derek, why don't you and I race as a team in the RAC rally? Norman Jameson will be your navigator.' The next morning I applied for my RAC licence and entered the HRG for the rally. It was a nightmare – never to be repeated!

Our group set off from High Wycombe heading west. The HRG was a very spartan car – cold, with hard suspension – and the discomfort increased as we drove for hour after hour. Norman was a good navigator until we arrived in the Welsh mountains stage of the rally, then everything went wrong. The torch battery gave up. No spare battery. It was pitch dark, the mist was closing in and we were lost. Every road we travelled, the other competitors were going the opposite direction. By now, Norman was fast asleep. Headlights were coming towards me, which turned out to be three cars. I slammed the brakes on, turned into a farm entrance and followed the three cars in hot pursuit. Thank God it was starting to get light and I could see their race numbers – let them do the work.

Dawn broke as we approached Bristol – what relief, the last section lay ahead. Torquay was the finishing line so no need to worry; I knew this road well, I could let the others charge off. Feeling hungry, I gave Norman a dig in the ribs. Time to eat the last of our sandwiches and pull over for some human relief. The nearby signpost said 'Exeter 80 miles', so having had our comfort stop, we set off at top speed. Could we make up the time lost in the Welsh mountains?

Then, as we left Exeter, the most amazing thing I have even seen, or will ever see again, happened. One competitor's car was up a bank and stuck in the hedge. Both driver and navigator were asleep in the grass. Another competitor was parked on the footpath. What was wrong? I should have remembered they were popping the same pills as me! Benzedrine.

The signpost said 'Torquay 25 miles'. Why was a dog on top of the signpost? We turned the next corner and an elephant ran out in front of us. 'Torquay 10 miles', a monkey dropped out of the trees in front of the car – I swerved. Where was the monkey? How I drove to the finishing line is a miracle. Of 40 hours without sleep, 34 of those were driving the car. Those blasted tablets some buddy got for me – were they what he said? Then the finishing line and the end of the rally. Norman helped me up to the hotel bedroom at the Palm Court and I slept until I heard young Platt and Norman telling me the dinner dance had started an hour ago and an RAC official was annoyed I was missing.

That was my first and last rally. Circuit racing, being more civilised, became the driving force for me in motorsport from 1949 onwards. Now to join a motor club and go racing was easier said than done. The clubs required new members to be proposed and seconded, plus an RAC race licence. By chance, I met a young man connected with circuit racing who introduced me to a Bentley driver who was a member of the British Automobile Racing Club (BARC), the club I wanted to join. My application for membership was accepted – now Derek Annable could race.

At the ripe old age of 19 I would be racing the HRG at Goodwood against Bentleys, Aston Martins and SS Jaguars. For one reason or another I missed many of the early Clubman meetings. One private members' meeting which I did enter at Goodwood racing circuit was set for 12 August 1950. This brought out a big field of pre-war cars: Jaguar 100s, Alfa-Romeo s/c dropheads and many Frazer-Nashes. Also included in the entry list were new cars: one Healey and a Jaguar XK120.

I arrived early that morning, pitted my HRG and signed on. Then it was a practice session all morning, with racing to start at 2pm. My event, a five-lap handicap, was the last race of the day, and when it was called out I was lined up on the second-to-last row of cars. To my right was D. Parker in his Frazer-Nash PF1 861; to my left was N.A. Bartlett in his HRG, KLD 447, and alongside him J.I. Bremmer in the third HRG, GRE 134. The three rows of cars in front of me were beginning to leave the start line, some as much as one and a half minutes ahead. How could I catch them? I decided I'd pass them in five laps.

The starter's flag was now raised in front of our row of cars. He was looking at his stopwatch. Don Parker in his Frazer-Nash had the starter's flag above his right-hand front wheel, which gave him a slight advantage – he could look forward over the bonnet of his car. Us three HRG drivers had to twist our heads to the right and watch for the flag to come down. Even today, I ask myself, did Don Parker jump the starter's flag? Boy, was he quick off the line that day.

The starter's flag came down. We raced head to tail for the first lap, and then Don Parker's Frazer-Nash started to pull away. On lap four Mrs C.K. Mortimer driving her 2½-litre Healey passed me. That lap, she made fastest lap of the day, at 1 minute 53 seconds. The winner of our race was C.J. Hamilton in a 4½-litre Invicta, who was three seconds ahead of the second-placed man, Don Parker in the Frazer-Nash. Where did I finish? Well, I did finish!

This was when a thin, gaunt man came across to me and said, 'Why don't you race five hundreds?' That was a Formula 3.

'Can't afford it', I said.

To this, Ken Gregory said, 'There is no such thing as can't; we'll work something out.'

At that time most racing drivers were sons of the ruling classes and their fathers were multimillionaires. Consequently, I had great respect for Ken. He had a full-time job which was most demanding and he worked long hours for little money. I sometimes joked, 'Don't you ever eat?' No reply, just a smile from him. We never talked family, instead we exchanged telephone numbers.

Winter that year was hard, as I was between jobs. My brother and the farming industry had problems with milk prices, and pork wasn't in demand. Our father did his own thing, leaving us to survive the best we could. Lack of income forced me to sell the sports car.

My mother and father always put on a good show at Christmas, and relatives from far and wide stayed with us for Christmas Day and Boxing Day – we had an abundance of food and drink. What to do on New Year's Eve? Why not go to the Albert Hall? Mother bought the tickets and off I went. What a building, when you enter the main hall, the heavens open up and you are transported through space and time. A medieval cathedral – not for the bishop's throne, but for all of God's music. I saw the New Year in and left early.

In the meantime, because I'd used the family car to go to the Albert Hall, my father decided it was time for me to have transport of my own again, so off we went to London and the used car lots which specialised in sports cars for the road and racing. My luck wasn't in this time and I was hugely disappointed, but not my father. Then the owner of the car lot came over to see us. He spoke to my father for what seemed like hours – well, to me it did.

Without warning, my father turned round and said to me, 'Derek, Sidney Allard is selling his race sports car, get back in the Bentley.'

All I could muster was, 'Yes, Dad!' Then 'Crasher Annable' (a name given to him from the days he was a speedway biker at Belle Vue, Manchester from 1922/1929) raced off in the direction of Sidney Allard's factory.

What a journey that was! I closed my eyes and prayed. When I opened them, we had arrived – and there it was. An Allard J2 – one beautiful car. Sidney was a genius with no equal and my respect for this man has lasted more than fifty years. After much haggling, my father agreed to buy it, but the car had to be delivered to the farm at no extra cost. The car was duly delivered, and now it was time to try it on the roads around Marlow. (John Peskett is now the proud owner of the Allard J2, KXC 170, and is restoring the car to its former glory. He hopes to race it at Prescot Hill Climb during 2007/2008.)

I must say the Allard was a bit of a handful. The torque from the V8 engine meant you could drive in top most of the time. On a wet road, too much throttle and the back end would break away. I entered it for the

Easter Monday meeting at Goodwood circuit, but we didn't race because although there were 20 cars entered for my event, only 10 of them could take part. Never mind. I was down to race at the fifth members meeting on Saturday 21 April, so back home I went to look forward to it.

When I received the official programme for the April meeting at Goodwood, what I read made up for any disappointment I went through at Easter. John Coombs was racing a Jaguar XK120, A.P.R. Rolt was racing Rob Walker's blue Delahaya, Ken Watkins was in an Allard and J. Goodhew in a Lagonda. Now *there* was a field to beat – all the big names were in my event, number 4.

I made sure the Allard was well prepared for the April meeting. Platt's Garage checked everything and fine-tuned the engine. You can imagine my excitement as I gently drove the car south to Goodwood. Earl Marsh would be there to greet us. Now we would see what I could do on that circuit with the extra power under the bonnet. Through the main gateway I went, across the track and into the pits, a very happy young man.

Some more surprises awaited me. Mike Hawthorn was driving a Riley in event 5, a handicap race. Miss Bode was racing her HRG and Sir Samuelson had his trusted Healey. Then there were the Bentley boys, H.J. Wilmshurst, R.H.B. Mason, J.H. Bailey and J.A. Williamson, all lined up in a special section of the pits which was reserved for them. Those pre-war Bentleys – what monsters and a joy to see.

Practice went well for me, now it was time for all drivers to go to the ballot for their starting positions. This was the way drivers were given their grid number in five-lap scratch races for non-s/c cars over 3000cc. A quick lunch and it was my turn to race. What a race! I kept bringing my lap times down by a second a lap – this car was quick. Okay, the Jaguar XK120s were lapping four to five seconds quicker than me, but I knew that with more practice, I could get my lap times down to 1 minute 50 seconds and under, the times the XK120s were running.

One man I was determined to beat in our race was John Coombs, who was driving his blue Jaguar XK120, and this I did. He moaned and whinged that the car wasn't producing enough power. Why, John? You sold Jaguars from your garage in Guildford, so your preparation should have been better. And maybe I was just the better driver on the day.

I sang all the way home, 'John's blue car was beaten by the Red Flash. All he could see was the flash, flash from my twin exhausts.' When I arrived home, my father opened a bottle of champagne and we celebrated. A few months earlier, John Coombs had tried to sell a Jaguar XK120 to my father and he, in his wisdom, had refused to buy it. 'There you are, my son, we bought an Allard for half the price of a Jaguar and in time you will win. Well done and money well spent!'

Sports car racing was enjoyable but most of the drivers were turning to single-seater race cars. The one I was interested in had a motorbike engine at the rear of the car and was affordable. Then one morning the phone rang. It was Ken Gregory.

'I have found a sponsor. Come down to south London with your cheque book; the car's ready, trailer and all.'

Ken always amazed me. Here was a man who could move mountains, and who one day might restructure motor racing and change it forever. Others will follow, but their driving force would be money. Ken, however, had a love for the sport. He would never be rich in money, but in the end would be richer in satisfaction than all the multimillionaires put together.

I couldn't wait for the first race meeting at Brands Hatch in my all-white Cooper JAP. But what was I to tow the trailer with? All my money had gone on the race car and trailer, although the sponsor's money would pay for that year's racing. Being the time of year when my brother spent all his days with the hundreds of piglets charging around the fields, I asked if I could use his old Jeep. Reluctantly he agreed, and off I went to Brands Hatch.

Being a rookie, I was told on arrival: 'You pit over there. Unless you can run the circuit in 60 seconds, don't bother taking the car off the trailer.' Later in the day I found out they couldn't run the circuit in 70 seconds, never mind 60 seconds. I didn't have a crew, so I shouted to the spectators, 'Any strong volunteers?' One young lady dashed forward with her friend and push-started the car for me. I have a photo of that first push-start hanging on the wall at home, fifty years on. After two laps, the chain broke, we put the car on the trailer and returned home. I had forgotten to bring a centre punch and hammer to put a new link in the chain.

At this time in my motor racing career, there was a young man with curly hair who was making an impact in motorsport. He did not race at our level, but spent most of his time testing cars for the major motor manufacturers. It must have paid well, for he had gold around his neck and on both wrists. Little did I know that one day our paths would cross with advantage to all. His name was Stirling Moss.

The big sports car race of the year was the Tourist Trophy in the Isle of Man. Because of problems with my car – a new engine – I couldn't drive, so I asked Peter Scott Russell to be the pilot at the Isle of Man. This would leave me to prepare the car and run in the engine. The night before the race, I had decided to get up at 3am and drive the Allard around the bike TT circuit for four hours to loosen up the engine for Peter. It paid off – he won. Peter never knew this. I got back into bed before he woke up at 8am. He did say,

'Strange, Derek, the car seemed hot and the engine heat was perfect for racing. Good idea of yours to park the car in the sun yesterday evening!'

Now it was time to travel south again; the sixth members' meeting for sports cars was at the Goodwood circuit. The Allard was entered in event 5, a five-lap handicap race. There were five Jaguar XK120s and three Allards, including mine, entered in the 3½-litre engine class, and making up the numbers for this class were the two smaller engined Healeys of F.A. Spiller and J.B. de Edwards.

Practice went well. Again my lap times were 1 minute 54–55 seconds, with all three Allards running within one or two seconds of each other. So we were given a 5-second lap start on the Jaguars, 25 seconds in total. With that advantage, I should be able to keep ahead of them, but could I catch and pass the Healeys of Spiller and Edwards?

We all lined up on the start line for our event. The Healeys went off nearly a minute before me but I managed to get ahead of the other Allards. On the first lap all the cars were spread out around the circuit. It was much the same on the second lap. I was now in third place, catching the Healey of Spiller and edging closer on every corner. At the end of the third lap, I was in a position to pass, which I did during lap four. Now there was only the green Healey of de Edwards to pass and he was still four seconds ahead of me. Coming out of the last corner before the finishing line, we were alongside each other and crossed the line together. We waited half an hour before the RAC stewards gave their ruling. I had lost the race by .025 of a second. I call that close racing! Never mind – none of the Jaguars were in the first four finishers. Also, much to my delight, I had broken my best lap time to date, with a 1 minute 50 second lap. This I would never better, as the Allard was sold before the start of next season's racing.

What a year. Never the winner, but after most meetings I went home with a profit. The sport divided itself into blokes like me, and the others. I was an enthusiast of motorsport – they were like an American football team, always in a huddle. The best race of the year was the Silverstone 100 miles. I still hadn't got a crew together. By now the other drivers were fed up with me shouting, 'Any volunteers?' This time I picked out a pretty girl walking around the pits and asked her to find me three strapping lads to push the car to the start line. She said, 'I'll do better than that, I'll go and get my sisters.' Ten minutes passed – nobody. How can I push this car back onto compression and then push-start it? One minute to go to practice session. I took my helmet off, got back into the car and closed my eyes. Suddenly the car started to move slowly forward. I looked around and all I could see were bosoms!

We had a good practice session and did well in the race; sixth position out of 20-plus cars was a good result. All the prize money was spent buying champagne cocktails for Beverley and her three sisters who made it possible.

The last race of the year was the finals at Brands Hatch, the Open Challenge on 23 September 1951, but I still had no crew. All the local boys in our village were only interested in football and going to dances where Joe Loss was playing 'In the Mood'. One of the friends I'd made in the racing world was Frank Hobart from Australia. I knew he would be at Brands Hatch for the finals, so, being an optimist, off I went with trailer loaded. The car was spot on, as the JAP engine had been rebuilt by the factory. My brother's Jeep was doing its best, firing on all four cylinders going downhill. Why did it only fire on three when you went uphill?

Everybody involved in the championship was at Brands. Frank Hobart met me in the pits and he agreed to crew. A quick check on the car, good feeling – winner this time. Then, at the bottom end of the pits, I saw the curly head of Stirling Moss, with some new type of race car which had rubber bands for its rear suspension and a double knocker Norton engine. Number 7 was on the front of the car. My number was 666, so no chance of a win then!

This assumption proved wrong. Stirling's prototype car was quick alright, but in the finals it was half a lap ahead when all the spokes in the rear wheels went through the tyres. I came third in my Cooper JAP and these points made me runner-up in the 500 Championship for the year 1951. It had been hard work, with many thousands of miles spent towing the trailer with my race car on, but the result made it worthwhile. I can't remember who the winner was; Don Parker had broken away from the main pack but a young man called B.C. Ecclestone was hot on his heels.

B.C. Ecclestone … ah ha, that's Bernie, the great man who now runs Formula One through his company FOA. Although he raced 500 cars in the 1950–52 period, he never became a member of the British Racing Drivers Club (BRDC) until 1989. This was an honorary membership. Then, in 1996, he became a BRDC gold medal winner. Money speaks volumes. Could it be that, in 1950, the son of a Suffolk trawlerman didn't fit into the criteria of the club at the time? He was a likeable lad, a bit nervous and kept himself to himself. Like Don Parker, he was small, and both had worked hard to get the money together for them to race Cooper JAPs. In the early 1950s, the money boys were everywhere and were very selective. Now, more than fifty years on, Bernie Ecclestone can buy them all out while he is eating his breakfast and still have enough money left over to last him a thousand years. The blazer brigade stand in awe of him and have lost many past battles against his empire. Well done, Bernie.

During 1951, Ken Gregory had proposed me for membership of the Steering Wheel Club, the watering hole of all the famous racing drivers past and present. I had been there as a guest on many occasions, but to be a member was a dream come true. My first visit to the Steering Wheel Club on my own would be mid-week, when the club was quiet and I could relax, so off I went, drove the 30 miles to London, parked the car and went in. I was greeted by a lot of noise from the top end of the bar. Three young drivers were laughing at a lady who was having difficulty sitting on the bar stool as her legs were very short. Then the three drivers' attention was turned to her rings, one of which must have been three to four carats and very expensive. Their jibes went on:

'Is it glass?'

'No, she must have stolen it.'

One voice sounded familiar so, as they had their backs to me, I asked the barman who was doing the talking. His reply was, 'That one is Stirling Moss, the others are Peter Collins and friend.'

Thoughts of my school days flashed before me, painful thoughts.

'Annable, what's the matter?'

'Sir, I can't get on the stool.'

'Did you hear that, boys. Annable can't get on the stool, his legs are too short.'

The whole class laughed, then the master turned to Johnson the house bully and said, 'Johnson, I expect Annable's legs to be long enough to sit on that stool next time he comes to a class of mine.'

All day I had hidden in the toilets. Can you imagine the fear a nine-year-old boy was going through, in a school far from home?

So I left the club, sat in the car for half an hour and then drove home.

There was no racing for me that weekend so I decided to spend Saturday night in London with a visit to the Steering Wheel Club, knowing the three racers of such ungentlemanly conduct would be racing somewhere in the world. First, I went to the Windmill where Ken Gregory's girlfriend was one of the performers – all very enjoyable. Show over, I went straight to the Steering Wheel Club as my table was booked for 9pm. While I was eating, the lady Stirling and company had ridiculed walked in with a distinguished-looking gentleman. He went over to a table and started talking business with three men, leaving the lady at the bar. When my meal was finished, I introduced myself to her and apologised for the torment she was put through the other evening. She said, 'I am Lita Rosa and sing with the Ted Heath Band. He is over there talking business with those gentlemen. His interest in motorsport goes beyond watching. If costs can be worked out, there will be a race car.'

She thanked me for the apology and I promised it wouldn't happen again if I was in the club at the time. We shook hands – kissing isn't my style! Ted Heath and Lita Rosa became frequent visitors to the Steering Wheel Club, and Lita and I always exchanged smiles and a wink. She still sported that diamond. Happy days.

Having sold the Cooper JAP to an up-and-coming driver whose father ran the biggest fleet of taxis in London, the new year dawned for me with two options: build my own car, or buy one with a Welsh pedigree. I opted for the Welsh car, warts and all. The car was delivered complete with a bottle of chilled champagne, instruction book for parts and stress factors on the main chassis points. I wasn't sure we'd bought well, as the Kieft factory was a bit of an unknown then. Only one man could check the race car out – Ken the wizard. Getting him away from his beloved workshop was like pulling teeth. Three bottles of malt whisky did the trick and that night we drank nearly two! We agreed I would get the car to his workshop, leave it there for two weeks and it would be ready for the first race of the season.

Time now to start racing. JAP had brought out a new state-of-the-art engine which was producing horsepower nearly on a par with the Nortons. A white-haired gentleman delivered the new engine to the wizard's workshop and the first race meeting at Brands Hatch was up to my expectations; the car performed well with a lap record and lasted to the end of all the races without any major problem. We had three weeks to the next meeting to fine-tune the engine and the car to 100% reliability as the European season was about to start.

Late one evening, the factory phoned me. They were unable to have a car ready in time for a driver who would be racing in Europe, and would I loan my car to him? If I said yes, I could race one of the factory team cars at Silverstone. Ever the opportunist, I said 'yes'. The factory collected the car and passed it on to the driver.

The managing director phoned me and we went over the insurance details on the car. He then told me who the driver was and I went into a state of shock. It was Stirling Moss. No one had built a car he couldn't break, whereas I could race my car all season and finish 90% of the races. Some drivers' attitude was 'win at all costs', and the car suffered. But against this, I was to be a factory team driver at the main meeting at Silverstone. Thus started the Stirling Moss/Derek Annable episode.

My racing was now on hold. What would I drive for the rest of the season? Then Ken phoned. 'Would you like to go as crew with your car to the Luxembourg Grand Prix at Findel?'

A quick check of my passport, and I said 'Yes.'

'Be at Dover tomorrow, leave your road car there and travel in Stirling's race truck with the crew. The hotel is booked.'

I was told, many years on, that you could get ten people into a mini. Stirling's race truck was big enough for the car, spares and equipment – but not human beings. On the main road to Brussels, one of the crew tried to climb onto the roof because of the smell of bodies inside the cab. Our driver must have been blind – cars and vans in front he never saw, and double white lines he ignored. I asked him, 'What were you looking at?' His reply was, 'That truck.' That truck was nearly half a mile in the distance. It was with relief that we arrived at the hotel Ken had booked for the crew and me.

Not interested in watching somebody else drive my car, I stayed in Luxembourg on race day. Stirling was first in heat 2 and only sixth in the final because of a magneto short, or so they said. Surely the car should have been better prepared? Next day we all returned to the UK with our blind driver, I collected my road car at Dover and drove home. To be fair, Stirling did split the prize money with me. He could be generous to the people who furthered his racing career.

The car (Annable's car) was entered to race at Eifelremen, Nurburgring in the 500cc race. Ken phoned me: 'Derek, please help. Stirling doesn't like going to race meetings on his own and I am not well enough to travel with him.'

I told Ken, 'Yes, my friend, I shall get him off your hands for a couple of days. You need a bit of a break.'

Jaguar Cars had arranged for Stirling to use an XK120 to go to Germany. Off we set. Don't ask me about the journey, I shut my eyes and hoped for the best. Stirling came second to Rudi Fischer's Ferrari in the HWM he was driving. Not a good day in my Kieft for him, he retired when second because a rear hub sheared off the axle shaft. I say again, who prepared the car? They were not very professional. My agreement with the factory now came to an end as they were building a new car for Stirling. To my benefit, the Annable car had been improved with some of the better bits from Stirling's original Kieft car which had been a write-off at the Bois de la Cambre race meeting. I put my JAP engine back into the car, repaired the broken parts and started racing again.

This was to begin at the 500 International on Whit Monday, 2 June 1952. It was being held at the Goodwood motor circuit. The first race was to start at 1.30pm, and mine was during the late afternoon which gave me time to watch the others run. The main opposition to me at this meet came from Don Parker in a Kieft JAP, Les Leston in a Leston Norton and Bicknell in a Revis JAP. The joker in the pack would be Ken Carter who was driving a Cooper Norton, the new model – or was it!

The BARC were in charge of this event, the 500 Club had had to stay on the sidelines and let the club take charge. Again, starting positions were set by practice times, this put me on the third row with Don Parker. It was an overcast day and it looked like there could be rain during our race. However, I was good in the wet, having proved it many times, and only Stirling was quicker on a wet track. Time to take my position on the grid.

I made a good start – believe it or not, I left the line before Don Parker – but seven laps is a long way for these little cars and anything can happen. Some of the drivers thought the way to win was to force your opponent off the circuit. In those days there were few officials around the circuit and on some parts there weren't even spectators to see what was happening.

Lap after lap I diced with the front runners. Don and I kept changing positions; now we were starting to pass the leaders. By lap six there was only Don Parker, myself and Bicknell in contention, with the others starting to trail in our wake and fast losing ground. On the last lap Don nearly lost it and Bicknell went past, taking me with him. As I had predicted, second place was going to be mine, then suddenly Don came storming past and, on the last corner, went into the lead and in doing so made the fastest lap – 77.28mph. His race average was 75.29mph. Watch out Stirling, Don could take the championship from you and your third BRDC gold star would be lost. Don was in good form and could win Silverstone in a couple of weeks' time.

I was to drive a factory car at Silverstone but I was still bothered. I had agreed Stirling Moss was to race my car, the 'Annable car' he kept calling it, at Silverstone. Stirling has many shortcomings, his greatest is that he won't listen to other people's advice. Restraint isn't in his vocabulary. I was anxious that he would do damage to my car.

On my return home my mother, bless her heart, suggested I go to North Wales for a few days. In my youth the family had spent many holidays there and I had good memories. I packed my bags and off I went. June and July is the best time to explore the Welsh mountains as the tops can still have snow on them. Forget the Swiss Alps, the Snowdonia forest area around Betws-y-Coed and Capel Curig is superior. The smell of the pine trees, mist from the waterfalls – pure heaven.

Most nights I phoned my mother to let her know I was alright. One night when I phoned, she said, 'Derek, Ken has been on the phone. Stirling needs your car for the 500cc race at Silverstone on 19 July. Come home quickly and get the car ready to take to Martin's garage so the engine can be changed.'

No wonder Ken was a nervous wreck. Stirling was ruthless with every-body around him, except me. Why? Maybe it was because of something that had happened when I went with Stirling to a European race meeting.

We were travelling through the Swiss Alps in a car the Ford Motor Company had lent Stirling for the week (right-hand drive model). He was his usual self, driving as if everybody knew the car was being driven by the racing driver Stirling Moss. In the distance, I could see a farm cart full of hay being drawn slowly out of a field by a horse, but whether Stirling could see it I don't know. His foot was hard down on the floor, and we were at top speed. The horse kept coming out of the field, its driver sitting on the loaded cart. Stirling was still at top speed. It was as if everything went in slow motion. The horse and cart came onto the main road to go in the opposite direction to us, and Stirling still had his foot hard down. 'For Christ sake, lift off and brake!' I yelled. But no, we drove full speed into the hay cart. The Ford Zephyr was a write-off.

I let him have the full force of my temper. 'You stupid bastard, you nearly killed us, why the hell didn't you lift off?' No answer. If he had argued, I would have knocked his bloody head off and put him into the local hospital for a month. We left the car on the roadside, walked to the nearest railway station and caught a train home – a two-day trip.

When I got back home from North Wales, I arranged for the Kieft to be taken to Martin's garage and phoned the factory. Cyril Kieft was always a gentleman and a man who could be trusted. 'Sorry about this Derek', he said. 'You can drive a factory team car at Silverstone. Your race number will be 24. Leave everything to us, just turn up at Silverstone with your kit and RAC licence. We should have a factory car ready with all the various modifications Stirling requires by the 27 July, but in case there are any problems, we will enter your car at the Fairwood Aerodrome GP as back-up. Sorry, but you will miss a drive there.'

The British GP at Silverstone was the big one. Every Formula 3 (500cc) driver would be there – Peter Collins, Don Parker, Eric Brandon, Les Leston. Stirling had a new engine, a short stroke Norton, to put into my car. The race would be between Don Parker and Stirling. Practice was good and the factory car performed well. On one lap I tucked in behind Stirling and got into his slipstream down the straight, much to his annoyance as it was he who had perfected this technique. I knew if I could hold him on the corner the man could be rattled and select first instead of top as he came out of the turn, because he had done this in other races. No such luck here. The new Norton powered him away.

The heats went well, giving me a midfield position on the start line for the finals. Don Parker and Stirling had the race to themselves because of their speed down Hanger Straight, while the rest of us (20+ cars) enjoyed passing and repassing, lap after lap, and the leaders started to overtake the back markers. Suddenly my race ended when the rear wheels collapsed; I just made it to the pits. Stirling won when Don Parker's primary chain broke. I thanked Cyril Kieft and Ken for the ride, left early and went home.

My car was entered for Stirling to drive at the Namur Grand Prix in Belgium on 20 July. I heard from other drivers that the front suspension broke in the finals, but Stirling did come first in the heat. The champ was becoming more demanding of the people around him, to the point where people and relationships were being sacrificed. Then came the GP at Fairwood Aerodrome, Wales. The records show Stirling Moss wrote off his second Kieft race car in heat 2. What a man. History will show there were two Stirling Moss Kiefts – well, bits of them – which others would own. At the same meeting, in the F3 invitation race, my car – in his words, 'Annable's now tired car' – came third for him. But it did get him second place at Prescott Hill Climb the next day, 28 July 1952. Was it a record time?

At Fairwood, meanwhile, before the invitation race, I came third in heat 3, thanks to Stirling's double knocker Norton engine which he allowed me to fit into my Kieft car. This was in gratitude for the use of my race car at the Silverstone Grand Prix.

Thus my 'tired' car had done both Stirling and me proud that weekend, giving much pleasure to many young enthusiasts in South Wales, people like Brian Jenkins from Swansea, who has been a fan of Kieft race cars all his life.

At the beginning of August, the Moss camp were turning their attention to the John Cooper works cars. Cyril Kieft was to become redundant to their greater plans for the future, and the great man had to make a decision. In his own words: 'I had finally decided there was no future in the Kieft. There'd never been one as good as our prototype, so I returned to Coopers for the rest of my 500 career, resigned my directorship of Kieft and that was that.'

Annable's 'tired car' was raced by Stirling Moss on 4 August 1952 at the August sprint, Brands Hatch GP, and the Daily Telegraph Trophy. Results were: second in heat 4; second in the final of the August sprint; first in heat 3, also a lap record 71.43mph; retired in the final when the engine threw a rod after leading for 15 laps. My car was a world beater, the driver threw a rod because he had over-revved or missed a gear.

Thus ended the Stirling Moss/Derek Annable episode except for one personal problem which arose. At this period the Moss girlfriend was Sally Weston (Biscuit Weston, so she said). Although the young lady was a relative of the great Garfield Weston she never had any money: 'Derek, lend me a fiver until my cheque comes in the post.' No matter. It was as plain as the nose on your face she had decided Stirling was going to be the first Mr Sally Weston and they were going to play happy families. He thought the world of her; why? I didn't know. She was pretty and, to say the least, a bit podgy, so not my cup of china tea.

Ken Gregory had moved into Stirling's flat in Kensington and gave up his own flat in Hampstead on the grounds that, 'it is easier to manage Stirling's business affairs.' Sorry, Ken. A flatmate who worked at the RAC gave Stirling respectability and helped his career, which he needed because of his many sexual affairs. No woman was safe. When one models one's lifestyle on Errol Flynn the film star, added to youth with little knowledge of life, situations can develop not of our making. Sally Weston and others had to be kept at bay. Who was left holding the fort with the media? Kenneth Gregory. To progress in any business you have to be squeaky clean, whether you like it or not, and motorsport is a business that has high standards which have been handed down from one generation of great drivers to the next. This must not be tarnished.

The phone rang, 'Derek, there is a girl in Maidenhead who thinks she is having Stirling's baby. Can you go and talk to her? This is the address.'

The next evening I went round to her parents' house, knocked on the door and this stunning young girl stood there. Oh no, I knew her from the party scene. She asked me in. 'No, Dee,' (let's call her that), 'let's go for a drink.'

Off we went to the local steak house on the Reading Road. Did I say steak? Horse steaks! As we drove she asked, 'Has Stirling sent you?'

I said, 'No.'

'Derek, I'm pregnant.'

I asked her, 'What makes you think it is Stirling's baby?'

'Believe me, Derek, it is.'

'Do your parents know you are pregnant?'

'No. I want an abortion. Can you help?'

'Sorry, Dee, No.'

I never saw Dee again. When you think certain F1 drivers were boasting about collecting girls' knickers and hiding them in their race cars, taking them out at the end of the season and counting who had the most, no wonder women are now getting their own back on the male species. And good for them.

In mid-August my Kieft racing car was returned to me. Now I could get it back into shape for the remaining Clubman meetings. It took six days of hard work to put my single knocker Norton back in, check the rubber bands on the rear suspension, replace most of them, clean off the green water paint on the bodywork back to the white (my colours) paint-work, paint the tyres with black tyre paint, and polish all the track and steering arms until you could see your face in them like a mirror. I took the car to Snetterton circuit and raced against some real people, enjoyed a beer, loaded the car on the trailer and returned home.

The last Clubman meeting was at Brands Hatch. There was a record lap of 71.43mph to take from a certain gentleman, so I decided to have a go and knock it on the head. The previous week I had rejected an offer from Frazer-Nash sports cars to become one of their drivers: the car on offer for 1953 had flipped earlier in the year and killed the driver, although they promised the problem had been sorted out.

But before going for that lap record at Brands Hatch, there was the last sports car race of the year, the News of the World International Car Race at the Goodwood circuit. This was for sports cars, and was a nine-hour race starting at 3pm on Saturday 16 August 1952 and ending at midnight that night. The entry list read like a *Who's Who* of motorsport.

During the week prior to the race, I had been to the Goodwood circuit for special practice sessions with the Leonard Cooper MG 1500cc sports car. I was comfortable in the car and managed some quick times. We practised the Le Mans-type start, where the driver sprinted across the track, jumped into the car, started the engine and then off you went after the faster cars. I was to be number two driver, but on the race day Leonard decided I should be number one driver. As he said, 'Derek, you are in good physical shape and you are the only one who can outsprint Stirling Moss and thus give the slower cars a chance.'

This was to be a big mistake. At the best of times, the car was a pig to start – it started first time for Leonard, but for me the battery didn't have enough punch. If the engine didn't fire the first time, it never would. But, a driver never argues with the owner/entrant, so I became number one driver.

Now it was time to race. There were 30 sports cars lined up, with the drivers ready to sprint across the track to them. Off we went. I reached my car first, at least three seconds ahead of Stirling. Oh no! My car, number 36, wouldn't start. The battery sounded flat. When the engine did fire, I was last to leave the start line. Soon after that the car was retired from the race and the whole team were gutted. Records show that the C-Type Jaguar, driven by Stirling Moss and Peter Walker, finished fifth.

My next race would be in my beloved Kieft JAP at Brands Hatch. I took a quick look at the list of competitors for each of the heats. Don Parker wasn't in my heat. Frank Hobart, a young lad I knew who was into Norton bikes, was going to crew for me and tweaked the engine. A good heat and the car performed well. Fifteen of us lined up for the finals with Don in pole position and off we went. After three laps it started to rain, and in the wet there was only one man who could beat me – Stirling Moss. In my JAP Cooper days on a wet track, I had taken out Eric Brandon, Alan Brown, Don Parker and others. Now, competitors were spinning off on every corner. Halfway through the race a brown shape could be seen in the spray. It was difficult to know whose car it was, but then it started to slide and it was Don Parker's Kieft. How did Don Parker win so many races?

Well his Kieft was the lightest race car because of the work he did to bring the overall weight down. Others were too lazy. It was all down to the power-to-weight ratio, and Don, being a slight man, weighed two stone less than me! Anyway, Don won the race and I was credited with the fastest lap in the wet. Sorry, Don, wherever you are. I couldn't resist the leg pull!

This was a very satisfactory end to the season's racing. For myself, I had reached a crossroads. Goodbye to Formula 3 (500cc), no need for an RAC race licence, the end of my racing driver status. Don and Stirling could fight it out for top driver in Formula 3, they were safe at the front of the pack, but midfield it was a jungle. At every meeting, new young drivers were coming into our class of racing, and they were ruthless to the point that somebody was going to get killed. Entry into the corners was more like American stock car racing than circuit car racing UK. Biff! Bonk!

Kieft and Cooper cars didn't give the driver any protection against a sideways impact. You could have your legs trapped in an accident, and if the car rolled, your upper body would take the full force – goodbye sweetheart. If a driver complained, all hell broke out; you were classed as a sissy and the pack would take it out on you at the next meeting. Not just one car trying to put you out at the corner, but two and sometimes three was the order of the day. Their response was, 'It's good fun old boy. We'll never win, so let's enjoy ourselves.' Never argue with the Douglas Bader types in any kind of sport.

Thus my direction was away from motorsport at that time. I told myself that maybe, one day in the future, I would come back and prove that gentlemen can still win races. Although it was the end of the Derek Annable/Stirling Moss relationship and it would be nearly fifty years before we met again, I followed his motor racing career with interest up to his near-fatal accident in 1962. Stirling's record of wins in every class of motorsport was impressive. Very few drivers, either past or present, could equal it.

But to me, Stirling Moss is an enigma. If he was such a brilliant driver, why didn't he pass Fangio and win the World F1 Championship? There are so many questions left unanswered about his career. Could it be that, like every all-rounder in life, he was a jack of all trades and master of none? Should Stirling Moss have focused all his energy on Grand Prix racing? I say no, he enjoyed racing any car which was offered to him. He sat in it and found a new challenge, then went out to win.

Maybe pressure from his parents and others, plus the lack of a good Grand Prix car (British) at the time stopped him putting all his energy into Grand Prix racing. Did he think that to fulfil his destiny he must win in a British racing green car!

Having at times in telling this tale been a little uncomplimentary towards Stirling Moss, let me now set the record straight in the old-fashioned 'marks out of 10' fashion by comparison with the other greats of the period, 1948–1968, which, but for the accident, he would have completed.

1   *Was Stirling Moss a great Formula One driver?*
     No! Fangio was in a class of his own; even Hawthorn and Collins were on a par with Stirling. 8/10
2   *Was Stirling Moss the best 500cc/Formula Three driver?*
     No! Don Parker was a far better driver and his love for that class of car was total. 7/10
3   *Was Stirling Moss the best rally driver?*
     No! Paddy Hopkirk was a genius and concentrated all his energy on one discipline, rally driving. Stirling wouldn't make the same commitment. 7/10
4   *Was Stirling Moss the best FI/sports car/saloon car driver?*
     No! Jim Clarke was the most complete driver of those two decades and, to date, has no equal. My own view is that Clarke was probably the greatest racing driver of all time. He once said to someone, 'Why don't the others go as fast as me?' Those are the words of a true master of his sport and a gentlemen. 9/10

This gives us a grand total of 31/40. On reflection, I don't believe the results of my marking. Stirling came out tops of all the drivers in motorsport who I marked for greatness. This makes him, taking four disciplines, the most complete driver of the twentieth century.

The Annable brothers with Uncle Albert, 1936. Derek in the car (© Derek Annable)

Left and above: *Derek, aged 6 (© Derek Annable)*

Front row, from left: *Grandad Lyons, Grandma Annable, Auntie Bessie, Uncle Alf.* Back: *Joyce (cousin), Derek (© Derek Annable)*

House cups 1945. Champions: York House, Wrekin College, Shropshire. Derek (front row, right) was in the winning house

York House, Wrekin College, Shropshire. End of term 1945. Derek, 3rd row, standing eighth from left

1945: House champions 1st XV, Wrekin College Top row from left: Sheriton, Bailey, Williams, Salt, Roberts, Evans, Hayward Middle row from left: Parsons, Murray, Timmis (capt.), Stewart, Woolley Bottom row from left: Holmes, Jones, Heath

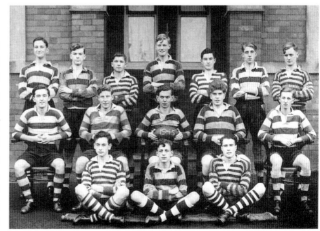

*1945: House champions 2nd
XV, Wrekin College*
Top row from left: *Passmore,
Elstone, Button, Wheatley,
Rhodes, Tilley, Stephenson*
Middle row from left:
*Tomson, Waterworth, Kenyon
(capt.), Wiltshaw, Evans*
Bottom row from left:
*Braithwaite, Hallworth,
Hogg*

*Derek 1948,
Franklyn, Alderley Edge*

Above, right and
below: *Franklyn,
Alderley Edge*

*The lodge where General
Patton's Jeep stopped*

*Brand's Hatch. Ken
Gregory pushing a
Cooper JAP
(photo: © unknown)*

*Spanish Grand Prix,
1950, from left: Stirling,
unknown, Derek,
Francis, Ken
(photo: © unknown)*

*Derek, HRG No. 31,
Goodwood, 12 August 1950
(© C. Guy Griffiths)*

Derek, HRG No. 31, Goodwood,
12 August 1950
(© C. Guy Griffiths)

1951/52: Derek, Kieft JAP 500
(© Motor Racing Pictorial)

1950/51: Derek, Cooper JAP
500 (© C.N.W. Norman)

1950/51: Derek in the
Allard, outside Blounts,
his home
(© Derek Annable)

Derek, Allard, Silverstone 1951 (© C. James Brymer)

Left and below: *Derek, Allard No. 61, Goodwood, 21 April 1951 (© C. Guy Griffiths)*

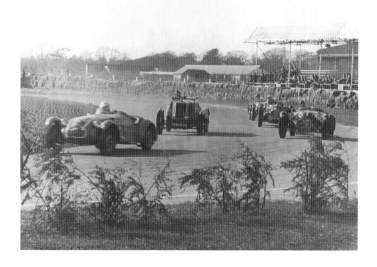

*1951: Derek in
Allard, Silverstone
(© James Brymer)*

*Goodwood, 1952: Derek,
white Kieft (No. 42), second
row (© Popperfoto)*

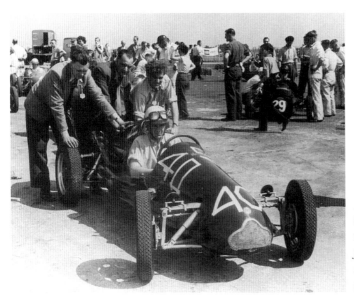

*1952: Derek and his
Cooper Norton
which was bought
for Ken Gregory to
race with Derek
(© Guy Griffiths)*

Don Parker (No. 28) being chased by Stirling Moss (No. 7) who was driving Derek Annable's car. (Photograph of original painting by Roy Pratt. Commissioned by Brian V. M. Jenkins)

Fairwood, 26 July 1952
(© T. Cyril Jenkins)

Raith Corner, Scotland, 1952: Charles Headland just before a crash in which he was thrown out of the car only to have it land on top of him. He was lucky – he escaped with a few bruises (© Bill Henderson)

Mike Hawthorne who became an overnight success after winning two races at the Easter Goodwood meeting (© Brian Jenkins)

Fairwood, 26 July 1952: The winner – George Wicken (© T. Cyril Jenkins)

1952: Stirling Moss in the new ERA, a car that was dogged by problems (© Autosport)

CHAPTER 3

Boy Racer

I married Brenda on 4 July 1953. Our first child came onto the scene in 1954 and more followed, with all the restraints a family brings. Now living in the northwest of England, our transport was a Ford Zephyr. Always the boy racer, I decided to have a Raymond Mays head fitted to improve the horse-power and up the speed. This it did at the expense of the bottom end – piston rods through the side of the engine. Good idea Raymond, but some-body forgot the bottom end wouldn't take the strain.

Year after year I set myself a challenge. One was to better my times between Manchester and Liverpool. Brenda's Mini was the perfect car for ducking and diving through the traffic at the start line in Salford, blasting along the East Lancs Road, then through the traffic to the finishing line in Liverpool.

Next on the agenda was the drivers' road between Manchester and Holy-head, as we were on the move to Anglesey which was to become our home for the next forty years. Many quiet years followed until I had to work in the Shrewsbury area. This meant travelling down every Monday morning at 5am and returning home on Friday evening. Thus was born the Bangor to Shrewsbury challenge on the A5, 110 miles of mountainous roads with a long straight through Shropshire. Driven comfortably, it took two hours. Could this be reduced to one and a half hours at an average speed of approximately 70mph? The rule was never to let your speed drop below 50mph and always, where possible, drive the car at top speed. Every corner through the mountains had a maximum speed which the Mini could reach with ease, but the problems were the straights, on which our Mini was 10–20mph below the speeds of larger cars.

Over many years, my wife and I perfected the technique and had brought the time down to 1 hour 37 minutes. Any activity on the 110-mile route by other traffic and particularly farmers' tractors caused a hazard, therefore a quiet road was required. But when? Answer, three o'clock in the morning and under darkness. Extra lights were fitted to the Mini and the inside was stripped down to be 30lbs lighter. With Brenda following in the back-up car (some five minutes behind), the Mini was 140lbs lighter in total. Could this give us the edge we needed?

I left Bangor at 3am. The weather was perfect – dry, no wind, air temperature 55°F. The extra lights made the drive a pleasure. When I passed through Bethesda, the moon lit up Carnedd Dafydd, all 3000ft of her. Either side of me were granite walls which had been cut out of the mountain, their tops pointing to the heavens. Then, there it was, Llyn Ogwen, with the mist rolling off the water and across the road I was travelling on. Within it were white reflections from my headlights; my God, it was sheep crossing the road, with their eyes flashing back at me like a warning of doom. I swerved to the left with brakes full on, lifted off and was through, my heart pounding in my chest like a steam engine.

Now it was downhill to Betws-y-Coed. Don't forget the sharp right turn after crossing Waterloo Bridge. The Mini took fast corners with ease, a driver's dream. One left-hand bend followed by a short straight, then a right-hand bend, another left and right, sheer joy. All the time the car was passing through the ghost-like mist coming from the trees that cloaked the mountains around me. Is heaven like this?

The light from the moon was so intense I switched off the headlights and glided along. Then I saw a light. What was it, an oncoming car? No, it was the lights from a chapel. As I passed I could hear the voices of the early morning choir breaking the silence with their rendering, in Welsh, of 'Land of my Fathers'. This forced me on to achieve what Brenda and I had worked for, the Bangor to Shrewsbury run in one and a half hours.

As I crossed the bridge over the Alwen River, the signpost caught in my headlights read 'Corwen 1 mile'. The clear air must have been oxygen-rich as the engine had never pulled so well. The halfway stage was completed in just over three-quarters of an hour. On the straight, the car cut through the still air at what must have been 6–8mph above its normal speed, and the result was that brake fade was becoming a problem. The corners over the mountains had nearly worn the shoes out and the clutch had also taken a hammering. From now on, many long bends had to be taken in top gear instead of third, thus the exit was slower. Suddenly, the water tower was picked up in the headlights – Shrewsbury and the finishing line. I hit the brakes and stopped. With a shilling in my hand, I jumped out of the car, ran to the phone box, checked the stopwatch – 1 hour and 29 minutes – and phoned home – success!

Never again could we repeat the Bangor to Shrewsbury run. The police were getting more vigilant and new speed limits were being imposed. Even the quiet roads had a new hazard: heavy trucks day and night. The Mini was sold and a dual purpose, business/pleasure vehicle was bought. Many quiet years followed.

On my retirement in 1989 we bought a small filling station in Moelfre,

Anglesey. This was to become the focal point of my motorsport reawakening for the next fifteen years. The garage had room for two cars in the workshop and three pumps delivering leaded and unleaded fuel and derv. Off we set for a bright new future! The business was a reasonable success; it paid the bills and supplied us with fuel at no extra cost (after VAT adjustments).

We needed a change of car and it had to be quick because of the mileage travelled to keep our various business activities going. Brenda's dress shop required two visits a year to Harrogate, plus a further two to the NEC in Birmingham. My wife's customers required the best, like John Charles and Bernshaw ball gowns and wedding dresses.

The pressure was on, but what would fit the bill? Yes, the only car which could outrun the police was a 2-litre Cosworth Ford saloon. Thus we bought a beautiful white 2-litre Ford Cosworth Sapphire from a local dealer, which had been transport for the managing director of Ford at Dagenham. It should be quick!

The following week we had to make a visit to Birmingham, so I booked a room at the Chesford Grange, Kenilworth, and off we went. Brenda loved staying there; the food was to her liking. After a good night's rest and breakfast, we drove to the NEC, parked the car in the main car park and caught the shuttle bus to the Fashion Hall. After nine hours of hard buying, we returned to the car park. Where was Brenda's Cosworth? Just an empty space. We stood there in a state of shock. Then we asked the car park attendant what had happened.

'Sir, a low loader arrived, the driver said you had instructed him to take the car away for repairs, then he signed this release form.'

The police were called and after much form filling we were taken back to our hotel in one of their cars. The driver of the police car said, 'Sir, your Cosworth was stolen to order and will be halfway across Europe by now.'

What a miserable Sunday. The car stolen, and inside were all the keys for our shop and garage businesses. Then there was still one more day of buying at the NEC to complete.

On the Monday morning, the hotel laid on a minibus to take us and our luggage to the NEC. After four hours of further buying we caught the train home. Our son met us at Bangor station and drove us the 25 miles to our house, lit us a fire and left.

There we sat in front of a glowing coal fire. Brenda said, 'Derek, I can't take much more of this.'

'I know dear. What would you like to eat?'

'Derek, what is wrong with you? I wish I was dead and you ask me what I'd like to eat! You're a nut. How about a hot curry?'

'Yes, darling. It will be ready in half an hour. And it was.

We replaced the stolen Cosworth with a rather slow Rover. Then, one day in February 1994, our daughter Lynne showed me a car sales magazine and asked, 'Dad, of all these cars, which would you choose?'

There was a section of American cars. One stood out, a Chevrolet Camaro Z28, colour red, fitted with a blower and it was right-hand drive. 'That's the one, Lynne.'

My daughter said, 'It's a race car, not a road car – 200mph, 400hp etc. Why?' My answer was, 'It's the most beautiful car I've seen in forty years.' End of story. But no, it wasn't!

The Rover saloon we owned was so sluggish it was getting on my wife's nerves. One evening she said, 'Why don't we change it for an American car?' When we got married in 1953, we had a clapped-out 1936 Buick the Americans used during the war. One night the headlights went out and we hit a wall and were nearly killed. We hadn't had an American car since then.

I phoned the dealer advertising the Camaro and to my surprise he still had the car. The next day we set off for Bournemouth in my wife's Rover, booked into a local hotel and arranged for the dealer to bring the Camaro around the next morning. The seven-hour drive had tired us so we went to bed early with a couple of nightcaps after a gorgeous meal.

The great day dawned. At eleven o'clock in the morning the car should have been at the front door of the hotel. No car. Twelve o'clock, still no car! Then we got a phone call. The dealer had had trouble getting the car to start but he would be over in half an hour. We decided to go to our room which was at the front of the hotel and wait. Then came an almighty rumbling sound, the hotel windows rattled, and the noise got louder and louder. We looked out of the window and there it was. By now, the guests were flocking out of the hotel to admire this red monster; the driver blipped the throttle, the thunderous roar was magic.

With mounting excitement, we got into the car and went onto the Bournemouth bypass for a demo. Brenda became bored and complained, 'Can't this car go any faster?'

The dealer's response was, 'I can't drive it any faster, it's too powerful.'

'Stop the car', my wife ordered. 'Get out and let me drive.' The engine revs mounted, then smoke came from the rear tyres – 55mph came up in first gear, 95mph in second gear (the box was automatic). We must have been travelling at 120mph on two-thirds throttle before Brenda lifted off.

'I'll have it', I said to the dealer.

A cheque for £5,000 plus our Rover car was agreed. The Camaro was to be delivered to North Wales. I said to the dealer, 'We are going home at ten o'clock in the morning. I want all the paperwork, tax, MOT and warranty agreed before we leave.' The dealer had had this car on his books for over a year and we found out later that he needed the money. The bank cleared our cheque and back home we went with the promise of delivery in three days. High noon on Thursday, and around the corner and onto our garage forecourt the Camaro arrived on a low loader. The red monster was unloaded and the Rover was loaded for its journey back to Bournemouth.

Friday morning, I decided to try the Z28 for myself. Yes it was powerful, but where was the 200mph and the 400hp? I didn't fancy taking the engine out and having it tested on a Dyno. Mark Holdsworth (who had been a bike racer) suggested we took it to Santa Pod and he would test it. The following weekend we set off for the Pod, and Mark was to follow in his van.

Did I say follow? We waited at the Pod for two hours – no Mark. In the end, I signed on and took the car down the strip myself. I hadn't a clue how the start lights (Christmas tree) worked and how to launch the car down the strip. The first run completed, I went to the tower for my timing ticket. The driver in the other lane was 25 years old and his reaction time was .850. Mine was .650. If a 63-year-old man was $^2/_{10}$ of a second quicker on the lights, it was worth considering racing. All this time my wife was talking to the bikers, with their pony tails and leathers. Drinks all round in the bar and a promise we would be back.

Mark Holdsworth arrived at the Pod as the RWYB (Run What You Bring) meeting was finishing. His excuse? 'One of the tyres on the van burst, I hadn't any money for the repair job so I left an IOU with the garage. I will pay them on the way home out of the money you promised me.' I gave him his petrol money and £10 for his time and that was that. Brenda and I were glad to get back home. It had been a long day.

The subject of what to do with the Camaro Z28 arose many times. We finally decided to take it down to the next RWYB meeting at the Pod to work on the lights and my reaction times. If they were good, then we would become members of the Santa Pod Racers Club (SPRC) and enter the car in the remaining championship meetings and Brenda would be crew chief. The meeting went well, although the auto box didn't shift with ease. On the journey home the auto box wouldn't stay in, but as we drove over the bridge to Anglesey, first gear was okay. It was with relief that we arrived at our garage.

The next day confirmed our worst fears. The clutches in the auto were burnt out. Who would we get to repair it? One firm in Atherton, Lancs, said they could repair it if we brought the car in the next day, so off I went on the 120-mile journey in first gear. Three and a half hours later, I arrived, parked the car and went into reception. I gave them the details of the car but after a quick check under the bonnet by the foreman, he said, 'Sorry, sir, we can't help you. There's a man in Bolton who repairs American cars.' They gave me his address and directions to get there, but when I started the Camaro and shifted into drive, nothing happened. The auto box had collapsed.

The garage agreed to make arrangements to transfer the car to Fred Whittle's workshop in Bolton. They drove me to the nearest railway station and I caught a train home. Why are trains more reliable than cars?

On Tuesday morning Fred phoned me and explained the engine had to come out, then the auto box, and so it went on. I thought, is he rebuilding the whole car? 'Hold on, Fred, prices please.'

His answer was, 'The strip-down will take three days. Come up to my workshop on Saturday and I will have some prices.'

Before Friday arrived, Fred was back on the phone. 'Mr Annable, it's worse than I thought. The main bearing's gone and the heads need to be taken off to inspect for any damage to the piston liners.'

'Take the heads off', I said. 'I will be at your workshop in the morning and I still want some prices.' By now my wife was going spare.

'What have we bought? I'll sue that dealer, he's sold us a load of rubbish.'

'Yes, Brenda, he has, but he didn't know we were taking the car to Santa Pod to test it. If he had known, he would have refused to sell the car to us. Calm down, Fred Whittle seems an honest man.'

To cut a long story short, Fred Whittle's shopping list was:

1. Recondition and fit a TH350 auto box
2. New torque converter; including a special bracket from engine to rear axle to support the TH350 box
3. Trans AM heads fitted with extra valve springs. Bore out the heads to take these springs. New piston rings (the cylinder liners were OK)
4. Renew all crank bearings (small and big end), assemble and road test the car.

Cost £3,500. What could I do? The car was in bits all over his workshop.

This wasn't the end of the story. After three months of bullying from me, Fred said, 'I don't need your work; get your car out of my workshop.'

'How, Fred, in a council dust cart? The car is in bits, thanks to you.'

I came to the conclusion that I should never pay anybody upfront for a job, whatever their reasons. Anyway, the car was tested in the hope I could race it at the last meeting at Santa Pod and again Fred Whittle came up with the numbers – the blower wasn't producing the poundage. 'I'll have to send it down south for an overhaul', he said – cost £1,250. By now I had been through a baptism of fire and was streetwise. I knew B&M Blowers in the USA would supply me with a new blower for US$800.

Now, how to get the work on the Camaro finished and the car back to

Anglesey? This is where Brenda played a key role. My wife is good at dealing with the ladies, so she spoke to Fred's wife. 'Sorry, Mrs Whittle, if my husband upset Mr Whittle. You see, the Camaro is my car, not my husband's. When Fred is in a good mood, could you please ask him when he can start work on the car again.' Mrs Whittle agreed to my wife's request and said she would phone back in the evening.

Two weeks after that phone call, the Camaro was ready for us to collect from the Whittle workshop, so off we went with £1,000 in cash. I was to drive the Camaro back to Anglesey, with Brenda following in the BMW. When we arrived at the workshop, I sat in the BMW and left Brenda to deal with Fred. Money paid, he brought the Camaro from the back of the workshop and parked it in the road. Now I surfaced, got into the Camaro and off we went, in convoy, back to Wales. OK, the old blower was still on the car but B&M Blowers had promised delivery of a new one in early 1995, which we would be fitting on the engine ourselves.

The Camaro didn't make the last meet at Santa Pod, so a very old and tired BMW 7 series was my race car. Never mind; lessons had been learned. From now on, all future work on our race cars was carried out at our garage, not by some so-called expert.

Oh yes! The last meeting at Santa Pod, I was entered in the Provisional Championship. My first round of the day's racing was against Phil Evans who many racers said was the greatest bracket racer ever. He had been champion many times during the last twenty years. I cut a good light and forced him to break out (quicker than his dial-in) and won.

During the afternoon's racing, Brenda arranged to buy Fay Fischer's Altered, including trailer, for £5,500. This was to be an investment for future racing. The car was worth in the region of £7,500, plus the trailer. Thus was born the Thunder and Lightning drag racing team for 1995. The Camaro was to race in Street ET at all the major meetings for the National Championship and then, after a year's practice with the ex-Fay Fischer Altered, we would go for the Modified Championship in 1996. These were to be exciting years, with many challenges for us, and the future looked good. Also, offers to crew were coming in from racer friends. What more could anybody ask?

All that winter we planned a strict cost-cutting exercise on parts purchased and put into store for next year's first meet – the Easter Thunderball 1995. Nearly £4,000 had been paid to Fred Whittle, plus a further £950 on the blower and the spares required to keep us competitive.

Having bought Fay Fischer's 1923 Model T Altered (Lucky Fisch), it was paramount we kept to a planned budget. Any major engine blow-up in 1995 could put an end to that year's racing. At our age, time was against us – we wouldn't be able to recover from any financial set-back.

CHAPTER 4

Renaissance (1995)

Christmas was over and it was time to start planning our race programme. However, before this could be set into motion, we had to undertake our annual buying expedition for my wife's dress shop, Dreams Come True. This meant staying in Harrogate and visiting all the designer stands at the Fashion Show Centre, placing forward orders with firms like John Charles and Bernshaw for the evening wear section of the shop. After that, the day wear for spring and summer was ordered from Freemans (not the catalogue people); their range always sold well. After two days of hectic buying and little rest, back to the shop we went.

One lady, who worked for the local Welsh-language newspaper, said to my wife on her return, 'Brenda, you and your husband live in the fast lane – both lanes, cars and business.' She wrote an article for the paper about our life. Little did we know that she was dying of cancer, and three months after the article was published, she passed away.

I risk my life racing and accept the risk, but that lady, through no fault of her own, had her life taken away. In her last months she loved to sit in our shop in Caernarfon looking at the gorgeous clothes hanging on the many rails, but she never bought any. Like us, she was too set in her ways – the clothes were for the young ones. We pass this way only once, and we still grieve for our friend's passing.

The Thunder and Lightning team were going to have a busy schedule racing the Camaro and the BMW 635, which we had bought at the end of the previous year to replace the old BMW 7 series. Also the ex-Fay Fischer Altered would require testing. The first testing session for this car was on a cold day in mid-March at the York Raceway track. Try taking an open race car down the quarter-mile strip with snowflakes drifting down in front of you. After two hours of this we put the car onto the trailer and went back to Wales.

The first race meeting of the season was a night race at Santa Pod Raceway before the end of March. Night racing – why not give my wife's BMW 635 an airing? It had better headlights than the Camaro and was more comfortable. We entered it for the first round of the SPRC Divisional Championship, otherwise known as the Saturday Nite Special, on 25 March.

Because of the distance from home of all the raceways, the Pod being the furthest (250 miles), we always stayed overnight at a bed and breakfast, or a Travelodge. This time we stayed at the Travelodge and were on the track before nine o'clock on the Saturday morning. We had the car scrutineered, then waited for the track to be prepared for racing. All racers were allowed a practice session in the morning, followed by three qualifying runs in the afternoon.

The Street ET qualifying list was posted. Position one, car 109, Steven Harrington, ET (elapsed time) 14.029, 99.52mph; position two, car 613, Derek Annable, ET 16.356, 85.89mph; position three, car 138, Tim Coldwell, ET 17.170, 80.16mph. This gave Steven Harrington a bye into the semi-finals, meaning I would be up against Tim Coldwell in the first round.

Racing didn't start until dark. At 6pm, Tim and I lined up under what was called the tower. With our headlights full on we moved forward together. I pre-staged first, then Tim Coldwell moved through pre-stage and into stage, which caught me out. As I staged, the lights came down, one amber, second amber and then the third. Tim must have pulled a near perfect light because he was off before me. I did catch him, but the race was his. In the finals, he was given a win because Steven Harrington pulled a red on the start lights (Christmas tree). He had wasted a whole day's effort by going off the line too early. Brenda and I said our goodbyes and off we went on our 250-mile journey, arriving home at midnight.

Our garage, Action's, and the dress shop, Dreams Come True, took priority for the next two weeks, and then it was time to plan for the Easter Thunderball at Santa Pod. This was the first round of the IHRA/UK National Championship and there would be Top Alcohol dragsters competing for the British and European Crown. The Camaro, sporting its new blower, was entered in Street ET, the bracket we wanted to win, but problems with the auto box meant we had to race the BMW. Since it was a three-day meeting, we decided to stay at the Hind Hotel in Wellingborough, which was offering special rates for the racers and a free evening meal thrown in on the first night. We drove down on Friday afternoon, booked into the hotel, enjoyed the meal and retired early. The other racers at the hotel would be drinking into the early hours of Saturday morning.

The next day, I enjoyed a 7am breakfast. Everything we needed for the day was loaded into the BMW and off we went. The Street ET pits were in the usual waterlogged part of Santa Pod – no hard standing for the Cinderellas of drag racing. The car was scrutineered and signed on, and we checked the official programme. There were 12 cars in my class: Keith Milne and Ian Turnbull (Plough Garage) had entered two Chevrolet Chevelle Ss, with Ian's being the quickest. Steven Harrington and Tim Coldwell were also entered, and I plotted revenge.

It was practice for all cars on Saturday, followed by qualifying on Sunday. The BMW is the perfect car for Street ET as it is so reliable, capable of 16-second passes all day. Sunday was a similar story and I became top qualifier. Phil Walker in his Pontiac Firebird 'Royal Ragtop', was number two, followed by Colin Catlin in his Ford Escort MK 3, with Paul Hudson well down the list of qualifiers.

Monday morning, we booked out of the Hind Hotel and dashed to the Pod. Our class, Street ET, was first out at 10am. Having taken the car off the track we had to go through scrutineering again, but thank goodness Amos Meekins was up and about. He passed the car again and I was ready for racing. The weather didn't look good, the sky was heavy with storm clouds and it was cold. Our class of cars were called out to the fire-up road and, within minutes, we were paired off and racing. Keith Milne and Tim Coldwell went through to the next round, followed by me and Phil Walker, who had just knocked out Paul Hudson who was driving his Ford Capri MK 3. The last two cars to make the quarter-finals were driven by Martin Lewis and Lance Richards.

Street ET would be out racing again at 11.30am. One heavy shower delayed things a little, but the track crew soon had the surface dry and it was our turn to race again. This time my opponent was Keith Milne. He pulled a better light than I did and it was time for me to go home. We stayed to watch the first round of Top Alcohol cars, had some lunch and then left Santa Pod. As we were leaving, the heavens opened and the meeting was cancelled. I did collect 575 points, making me fourth in Street ET.

We would be back at Santa Pod in a fortnight's time for the second round of the SPRC Divisional Championship and the Camaro should be ready for that.

Drag racing was taking up more of our time and this caused problems in our Dreams Come True business from April onwards. Anglesey relies heavily on trade from people on holiday, the caravan parks are open and business in North Wales is brisk, so with Brenda away every other weekend, we had to arrange for part-time help in her shop. This post our daughter filled. Now my wife could relax and enjoy our weekend motor racing.

A room was booked at the Rushton Travelodge and off we went in the Camaro to contest another round of the Saturday Nite Specials. The last one had started in the dark, but this round the start would be in daylight; only the winners would be racing with their headlights on.

It was a small field of six cars, but the main players were racing: Turnbull, Harrington and Hudson. It was the usual morning practice, then time for afternoon qualifying again. I was number two qualifier and this time nobody had a bye in the first round. One interesting fact I noticed on the programme was that last year's winner of Street ET was now running her car in Super ET with times in the low 13s and high 12s. Now there is a top racer, Carla Pittau. She was always at the receiving end of other racers' jokes and John Price's jibes about 'Why is an Italian racing in this country, and isn't she doing well?'

Time to race, and Ian Turnbull was paired with Chris Orthodorcua who was driving his girlfriend's Ford Fiesta. Steven Harrington was paired with Gareth Mogford and I had Paul Hudson. Turnbull went through to the next round, Orthodorcua, the Big 'O', pulled a reaction time of .938 and broke out, then Harrington took out Mogford. This left Paul and me. Although I caught Paul at the finishing line, he ran a 17.01 on a 17.00 which was a near perfect dial-in. He did lose to Harrington in the next round by virtue of his car going slower by $\frac{3}{10}$ of a second. I had a good day's racing; the Camaro was running mid-14 seconds on a regular basis and was competitive. Nearly one thousand miles in two weeks and not even a misfire; that blower was delivering the poundage; I was even impressed with the work Fred Whittle had carried out on the top end of the engine. I had paid a price for it, but at the end of the day it was worth it!

Then back to the Travelodge, as Brenda had arranged for the Altered to be brought down to the Pod from Anglesey on Sunday morning for me to test at the Race What You Bring (RWYB) meeting. A quick wash and change and it was time for our evening meal. We finished our meal and went to bed – tomorrow was checkout time and an early start at the Pod.

Sunday morning was bright and dry. When we arrived at the track there must have been 80–90 street legal cars already fired up and ready to go and their numbers would double before midday. They could race all day for £10. Our Altered, being a quick race car, was allowed to take priority over the RWYB cars, so we should have two runs around lunchtime.

I signed in, paid my entry fee and returned to the pits. Our race car had arrived and was being unloaded. We jacked the car onto a pair of stands, fired the engine and spun the rear wheels to warm the transmission oils. After a couple of minutes we switched her off and the car was ready to race in the RWYB.

My first pass was a top end lift off 12.66 ET, 96.47mph. Brenda towed me back to the pits where we let the engine cool and had a quick lunch. We were then ready for my second pass. This was quick; the car reached 100mph at the eighth mile, again another lift off at the top end. This was real racing. We loaded the car back into the trailer and left for home. John

Turner drove the tow car, Brenda and I followed in the Camaro. It would be dark before we crossed the bridge onto Anglesey. The next time the Altered would be taken out of the trailer depended on us accepting an invitation to the Anglesey Farmer's Show in August in their car section.

The second round of the IHRA/UK National Championship was at York Raceway on 13/14 May, and it was time for John Turner to change the engine oil and check the engine. First was a leak down test and then replace the points and spark plugs, this would keep my launch crisp and the power equal on every run. As this was a two-day meeting, Brenda booked us in at the South Cave Travelodge. Our eating out would be at the Little Chef, where their Early Starter breakfast was always top quality and a reasonable price for those days. In the evening we indulged ourselves and drank our own wine, which we carried back with us in our suitcases. No wonder we were called the 'lotus-eaters' by Graham Beckwith, but we just enjoyed ourselves. York Raceway can be a bleak and cold place in both winter and summer, so we took extra clothing with us, just in case.

What a bumpy ride from the main road to the pits! The Camaro exhausts were hitting the ground. 'There aren't many racers here today, Brenda.'

'Do you blame them?' was her reply.

There were five cars in Street ET: Paul Hudson, Colin Catlin, Neimantos from Brighouse and Clayton from Bradford, and us. Thank goodness it wasn't raining. The car was checked out and passed by the club, then I signed on at the control tower and we were ready for what they called open testing. I tried the car out on the track which was still a little damp – there was too much wheel spin on the launch area.

After a hot dog lunch, it was time for official qualifying. I dialled in 14.85 and ran a 14.867, term speed 94mph, reaction .840. I would have to improve my reaction time. Second run ET 14.814, term speed 100mph, reaction .648. That's better, but I broke out (went quicker than my dial-in). On the third and final run for the day, I changed my dial-in to 14.80 and ran 14.860 – a good result. Sunday morning was a bright, dry day and the half-hour drive to the track gave Brenda the chance to eat the bacon bap I had bought her for breakfast. I had eaten the full works, the Early Starter, two rounds of toast and marmalade, washed down with three cups of tea. I never eat breakfast when I'm at home, only when I am racing.

Straight into qualifying at 10am, I kept my dial-in of 14.80 and ran a 14.846. That meant I was top qualifier and had a bye in the first round of racing.

The parade of custom cars over, it was time for the first round of racing. As Richard Lyons reported in the *Pennine Drag Racing Club News*, 'New PDRC member Derek Annable made the long trip over from Anglesey with his Thunder and Lightning Camaro to qualify N° 1 but lost in the second round to class winner Heartbeat Hauler who then disposed of N° 2 qualifier Paul Hudson's "Lost Cause" Capri.' Paul Hudson collected 725 points from this meeting, while I collected 475. This made us equal in the championship on 1050 points each after two rounds. It all hinged on the next round of the championship at the Pod on 27/29 May.

We went to work late on Monday morning. Most shops in Anglesey and Caernarfon don't open Monday because business is so slow, but this changes in August when the schools are on holiday. We still had ten championship (IHRA/UK and SPRC Divisional) meetings to take part in during the next five months, plus the Hot Rod Drags with the ex-Fay Fischer Altered. I suggested Brenda should reduce her workload by staying home when I was racing, or only open the shop for four days a week. Her answer was, 'Don't think I am going to stay at home while you could be killing yourself in that car. We close the shop on Monday and Tuesday every week.' With that answer, we could plan our racing programme with a vengeance. The IHRA/UK National Championship was our target, therefore both cars would have to be well prepared. The BMW 635 was to be back-up for my car, since we could not afford to miss one meeting.

The next challenge was the Main Event at Santa Pod on the 27/29 May. At this meeting we needed a good result, otherwise Paul Hudson would forge ahead. With accommodation booked for the weekend and the Camaro sounding good, we went on the long haul down to Wellingborough.

It was late when we arrived at the Hind Hotel. Brenda suggested we went to the residents' bar for a drink. As I was ordering our drinks, a short podgy man who was wearing an Anita Makala T-shirt turned to Brenda and said, 'Excuse me, madam, are you crew chief to the team Thunder and Lightning? My name is Jeff.'

'Hi Jeff, yes I'm Brenda. Have you seen us race?'

'Yes, I have seen your name on the side of the race car.'

After a couple of drinks, my wife asked Jeff to join us in the dining room. The conversation centred on Anita Makala, the Top Alcohol driver. Jeff was a fan of hers and he followed her to all the major races in Europe.

How nice it was to see my wife talking to someone who spoke her language. Jeff couldn't understand how a Marlow girl could live in North Wales. It's strange how everybody living within a radius of 30 miles of London feels they are a cockney. It was all 'bread and butter' and 'apples and pears' – I was lost! This lovely man paid for his own meal, then he wouldn't let us buy any drinks. He paid all evening, saying, 'No, Derek, it's my treat.' To this day, my wife feels we were freeloaders, but that isn't the case – when a generous person wishes to do this, it is an insult not to accept their generosity. We can't go around living life on a tit-for-tat basis.

Before the weekend was over we had made a friend who we would welcome in our pit at any time. We did see Jeff at the big meetings at Santa Pod during 1995 and 1996, but then we lost contact.

As usual, Saturday was set aside for practice all day. Sunday would be qualifying all classes, with two slots for Top Alcohol cars and three for Top Fuel. We had to get a good qualifying time before 12 noon when these cars came out. Any oil down would take hours to clean up, and we could end up with only one run in our class of cars. The paying spectators had come to see the Fuel Cars run, we were just a fill-in between the big boys and to keep the track warm for them.

Who was racing in Street ET with a chance to pass Paul and me on the points ladder? The big danger was Phil Walker, followed by Colin Catlin and Keith Milne – any one of these three could end up top dog at the end of racing on Monday. Practice was a struggle for me; the engine was off tune, with a misfire now and again. A couple of low 15 seconds, but when power came in on all eight cylinders, I did manage a 14.679, then the next run went back to low 15 seconds. Would Sunday's qualifying be any better? No it wasn't, except for the last run of the day, when I dialled in 14.89 and ran a 14.822. This meant I had broken out by nearly $7/100$ of a second and wouldn't count towards the qualifying list, so I ended fifth. Brenda said, 'Don't worry, Derek, everything will come together tomorrow, and you will win.' My wife can be an optimist.

A good night's sleep worked wonders. I felt in the mood to win and started cracking jokes at breakfast, much to the annoyance of the other guests in the dining room. During the short drive to the Santa Pod Raceway, my thoughts were on who I'd be facing in the first round, and instead of driving straight to the pits, I stopped at the control tower and checked the running order for the day. There, pinned alongside it, was our pairing list – car 252, Keith Milne, was my opponent. He had won our last encounter. Would it be my turn to win?

Street ET are always called out first on race day, so down the fire-up road went 12 cars and then into the pairing lanes. Keith and I were at the back of the queue. He had dialled in 15.25, mine was 14.89. His light would come on before mine, so I mustn't pull a red. We pre-staged and staged together, I could hear a misfire coming from his engine and off he went. I pulled a safe light and soon caught him and kept with him. I then turned the power on just before the finishing line and it was my win – sweet revenge some would say, but not my choice of words. He had lost the race because of a mechanical fault, not because of my driving skill.

As I pulled into the pits, Brenda said, 'You have Phil Walker in the next round.'

Phil and his Pontiac Firebird 'Royal Ragtop' – there is a racer who lives and breathes drag racing. He and his wife, Tracy, always leave the Travelodge at Rushden before 6am, no breakfast for them, and head off to the racetrack. What a lovely couple. He is one of the gentlemen of drag racing. If Brenda and I had turned up with a £200,000 Aston Martin, he wouldn't have been jealous.

Street ET's next round was in an hour's time, which would give me a chance to check the spark plugs. One spark plug did have a broken insulator. In went a new plug and down came my dial-in to 14.80. Now I was ready for Phil; this win I needed. Paul Hudson had gone through to the next round and was up against Ian Turnbull who was racing some very old American car which was running mid-17s. Paul should win and he did – Ian broke out big time and this gave Paul the win.

Now it was my turn. Phil and I staged together and we left the start line together. At the eighth mile he was a wheel ahead of me and our speeds were 75mph. Then my blower started to come in with a vengeance and Phil started to lose ground against my more powerful car. Over the finishing line we went, then the winner's light came on in my lane. I had won and was through to the semi-finals. My car had crossed the finishing line $^6/100$ of a second ahead of Phil's car.

This left three cars in the semi-finals, Colin Catlin, Paul Hudson and me. Colin had a bye, which meant Paul and I would shoot it out, with winner takes all (championship points). Time for lunch and to consider my dial-in. Leave it the same, which meant Paul would leave the start line two seconds before me. I mustn't pull a red. Lunch over, time to race. The Top Fuel cars which had gone out before us had made a big oil down on the track, and for nearly an hour we waited for it to be cleaned up and trackbite (a solution sprayed on the tarmac) to be put down and left to dry. Now we were called forward by the start line marshall. I let Paul stage first, which didn't seem to bother him. He had a good launch and I followed two seconds later. He was going well, would I catch him? The revs came up to 6000, then 6500, well into the red. Must change now or the engine would destroy. This I did and shot past Paul as we crossed the finishing line. When his winner's light came on I was gutted, and when I got back to the pits Brenda gave me a real rollicking. 'You broke out by $^3/1000$ of a second. Let's go home.'

We left the meeting before the finals of Street ET; later, we were told Paul Hudson won because Colin Catlin didn't show. Paul was now leading the championship with 2150 points. I was 375 points behind him and in second place. Paul didn't contest the next two meetings of the championship, but instead went on holiday to Kenya. This cost him the championship. He could never make up the lost ground and finished third behind Steven Harrington.

Back home in Anglesey, we needed to shift our priorities. Invitations to a fashion show we were holding had been accepted by the local ladies, the models were booked, and it would take all of Thursday to prepare the shop for the show on Friday. Time would be short to put the girls through their paces.

Our daughters would be helping on the day to dress the models. On Thursday, Brenda had to choose the bridal wear and ball gowns for the girls to wear the following day. One model was size 10, the others were sizes 14 and 18. Ann, the most petite of the three, would be showing off a lovely dress from the Bernshaw collection, followed by a bridal dress which we had specially imported from Germany. Jean was an average size 14, which gave us the greatest selection of clothes to choose from. Ronald & Joyce had delivered some spectacular bridal and evening wear from their After Six range, and Jean would be the belle of the ball. Now what was Mair going to wear? There was a problem here – she was a size 16 hip with a size 20 bust. While we tried to find appropriate apparel the shop floor was covered in wedding gowns which were the wrong size, shape, you name it. We then grasped the nettle; it had to be John Charles, whose ranges were generous. We phoned Griselda, a seamstress who lived in Pentraeth, and arranged for her to come to the shop. We would select two dresses for her to alter, get food and drink in from the Prince of Wales pub, turn the heating up and she could work all night taking in two size 20s below the bust line. Fortunately, Griselda agreed.

Clothes chosen, the models walked across the road to Paula's beauty parlour for the full treatment – hair, face and nails. The lady who owned the beauty parlour had been in business from her early teens and she was the tops. Brenda didn't get on with her, they were two powerful women on a collision course, but each needed business from the ladies of Caernarfon so there was a standoff. I took the models back to Bangor and reminded them I would be taking them to the shop at nine o'clock on Friday morning.

Friday morning dawned, and I took Brenda and our two daughters to the shop. Before I had time to take a second breath, I was ordered to go to Bangor for the models and be back in half an hour. Uh-oh, the stopwatch again! This meant the three models had to be in the shop within the ordered time. Thank goodness I was a racing driver and knew how to avoid the local speed traps and traffic cops, their headquarters being in Caernarfon.

My contribution to the show over, I beat a hasty retreat to our garage, which is over the bridge into Anglesey. There I spent the next six hours working on our two race cars. I also spent some time talking to the people on holiday as they walked past our garage and generally worried about how things were going at the shop. Fashion shows can be very stressful and should be kept to no more than three a year. Now it was time to go back to Caernarfon and find out if we had wasted our money. There would be buckets of tears from my wife and daughters if the show had been a disaster. But three happy ladies greeted me as I pulled up at the shop.

'Dad, fifty people attended the fashion show', one of my daughters said. The other daughter shouted from the changing room, 'And four ladies are coming back tomorrow to try some evening wear and bridal gowns on.'

'Good', I said. One bonus gained for all my family's hard work was a write-up in the local newspapers with a picture of Brenda and the models.

Time to take the models back to their homes in Bangor. On my return, three tired ladies had completed the task of restoring the shop to its normal state for business as usual on Saturday morning. The Annable family were soon back in their various homes in Anglesey. Straight to bed for Brenda, and the nightly update of my VAT returns for me, then bed too.

Surprise, surprise! Many of the Caernarfon ladies did come back to the shop on Saturday and try on the ball gowns and evening dresses. The till rang up a healthy £500 plus for the day.

Our next drag race meeting was on Saturday 10 June, so we now had to plan everything and book our accommodation for the weekend. We were taking two cars this time; our son Peter would be racing the BMW and me the Camaro. I hoped everything would go well for Peter, as this was his first drive in my wife's car.

We drove in convoy down to the Pod, signed on and were ready for the open practice. Peter decided to go against me on the first run, pulled a good light and ran a 16.294. Mine was 14.806. From now on he had to race against the other cars and test the opposition for himself, the learning curve in drag racing. A quick lunch and it would be the first session of qualifying. Peter and I left Brenda with some friends in the Santa Pod café – thank goodness she wouldn't be watching her son compete against the likes of Ian Turnbull and Steven Harrington. In fact, I would get them during the qualifying sessions.

Why this happened, I don't know, but I had Ian Turnbull in a slow Camaro on all three qualifying passes. The first run, he pulled a poor light and was way off on his dial-in. I dialled in 14.80 and ran 14.833. Second run I pulled a near perfect light, .542, and Ian again had a poor light, .837. I didn't watch the other drivers in the last qualifying session – I was too preoccupied watching Ian Turnbull working out some mathematical formula on what to dial in on the back window of his car. There it was, 17.40. Now let's see what happens. We staged together, the amber start lights came down and off I went. Out of the corner of my eye, I could see Ian had pulled a red (a foul), and the race was lost for him.

Brenda was watching Peter racing, and she was well pleased with his performance in qualifying. Now it was time for the pit marshall to come round with the pairing list. I had Steven Harrington who was making the SPRC Divisional Championship his own by leading after two rounds and was all fired up to win this round.

The first round of eliminations started. Now it was my turn to race. I pre-staged first and waited for Steven Harrington to move forward into pre-stage, but he just sat there. He had a habit of doing this, hoping it would unnerve his opponent. When he did move he went straight through into stage. I was expecting him to do this so I kept the revs up, lifted the pressure on the foot brake, staged and shot forward on the last amber. I pulled a red but so did Steven. My red was first by $5/100$ of a second, therefore I fouled first and Steven was the winner. He went on to win in the finals. The third round of the Divisional Championship was his, giving him a massive 1,000 point lead over the number two who was Ian Turnbull.

Our Peter was knocked out in the first round like his dad, so it was time to drive home. The next meeting would be in two weeks' time up at York Raceway. The Thunder and Lightning team were racing two cars again with father and son as drivers and Brenda as crew chief. She always liked the York meetings and would be keen to see one of us win.

Time for round four of the IHRA/UK National Championship for cars. Brenda and I booked into the Travelodge at South Cave, a few miles from Hull. Peter had towed his caravan to the track camping area. It was to be a five-car field. Philip Evans with his BMW (now there is a racer, some say the greatest bracket racer of all time, and I had beaten him last year), Colin Catlin in his Ford Escort MK 3 Turbo and Dave Allen driving a Ford Mustang. Making up the numbers were the Thunder and Lightning team of Derek and Peter Annable, Camaro and BMW 635 respectively.

Scrutineering completed, all cars were called to the fire-up lane for open testing. Brenda suggested that this would give me a chance to go through the water and practise burnout for when racing the Altered. This I did, but unknown to me my front wheels left some water on the start line and who was to follow me down the track? None other than Carla Pittau in her Camaro, 'Heaven & Hell'. When she launched, the car squirrelled all over the track and she nearly lost it. I got the biggest wigging ever from her. 'Derek, don't practise Modified car burnouts in a street car.'

All I could muster was a very quiet, 'Yes, Carla.' She is, when roused, a fiery lady and always a dedicated racer.

It is sad that the general public's awareness of our sport of drag racing is minimal. The quick cars are equal to any Formula One car. These cars have engines producing around 3000hp in the Alcohol class and up to 5000hp in the Top Fuellers. In both, the most competent drivers are ladies like Viveca Averstedt and Anita Makala. In drag racing, aggression doesn't enter the winning equation, and so ladies have the right temperament to win – calm, cool and fixed as one with the car. Believe it or not, they can take the G-force better than men. After a 4-G run at nearly 300mph, they get out of the car as if they were getting out of bed, whereas many a man has to be helped out of his car! Carla is in the mould of the top lady drivers and one day will reach the pinnacle of our sport.

Another racer at York Raceway was Mike Ellis. One day he would be involved with the Thunder and Lightning team when I raced the ex-Fay Fischer Altered, but this time he was racing his Rookie Racers car in Euro Street. There was a separate championship for these cars, his Street class and the Quick Class Euro Pro. There was some problem with his car because the engine wasn't a Rover car engine, so I suggested he came into Street ET and run in our championship for the rest of the year. He said he'd think about it.

For the first qualifying session my Camaro was a bit off tune, so I dialled in 15.28 but the nearest I could run to it was 15.377. This put me at the bottom of the list of qualifiers. You need to be within hundredths of a second of your dial-in to receive extra points and the championship was all about points. Brenda and I called it a day; we left Peter at the track and went back to the Travelodge. One good thing about staying at South Cave Travelodge was that there weren't any other racers staying there and we could relax with no one talking about drag racing. We could have a quiet meal and watch the rabbits digging holes in the lawn outside the Little Chef with the sun setting on the horizon. It was so peaceful.

Sunday morning and it was time to race. I had to do better in the qualifying session, which was up to lunchtime. This I did, and I became top qualifier with a 15.28 on a 15.28 dial-in, giving me a bye in the first round. Peter's first round was against Phil Evans, BMW against BMW, age and experience against youth. Which would prevail? Phil Evans won. Colin Catlin took out Dave Allan and went through to a bye into the finals, so I now had Phil Evans. There was plenty of time for Brenda to consider how I could win the semi-final against Phil, as Steve Munty, the track owner, was putting on a parade of custom cars for the paying public. This also gave Steve time to go and check the toilet blocks. York Raceway was on an old World War Two airfield and plumbing wasn't up to Savoy Hotel standards. Why should it be? He wasn't running the British Grand Prix with the Fédération Internationale de l'Auto-mobile (FIA) looking over his shoulder, and because of his efforts we had a track in the north of England. I, for one, enjoyed racing on it.

The call-out came over the public address. John Price was his usual happy self, making rude remarks about various racers. 'Next out', he said, 'are two racers with beards like Moses from the Bible, one in a BMW and the other, Grandad, all the way from Anglesey' – he always said 'Anglesey' as if I owned it – 'driving a Camaro. Ladies and gentlemen, you can't miss them; the cars they drive have whiskers blocking their view through the windscreen.'

I pulled a good light and soon caught Phil, held him to the last 50 yards and then passed him. Now it was me and Colin Catlin in the final, a turbo car against a supercharged car. Our dial-ins were close. The ambers would be coming down very close to each other. Would he try to launch on my ambers? This could be risky, many have tried it but few have succeeded.

We both staged together, which is the way of gentlemen. He was in the left-hand lane, and both cars being right-hand drive meant I couldn't see his light but he could see mine. I thought after the start that he'd got away quickly, he must have pulled a good light. I couldn't make up the lost ground before the finish and he crossed the line first. Phil Evans was waiting for me when I drove into the pits. 'That was Colin's race, Phil, his reactions were quick.'

To which Phil answered, 'Too quick, Derek. He pulled a red. You're the winner.'

I enjoyed collecting the trophy from Steve Munty. It was my first win this season. After that, it was getting late so we packed up and went home. The Camaro broke down as we travelled through Wales but a quick road-side repair by the RAC and we managed to get a sick bunny home. That win put me in the lead in the championship, with Colin Catlin now in second place. Paul Hudson had fallen back into third position.

John Turner checked the Camaro for faults on Monday morning. The problems which caused the car to break down coming home were, firstly, the points on the Mallory distributor must have ashed. To be safe, we must change them and the condenser. Also one of the wires to the coil could have come loose, which would cause the engine to cut out. The Cannonball at Santa Pod was our next race and with the mileage the car was clocking up every week it was time to change the engine oil and filters. I left John working on the car and went to the shop for Brenda. We had arranged a visit to the fashion houses in Manchester to collect and view some new stock which the agents said would fill a gap in our summer forward order.

When I arrived for work on Tuesday morning, John told me that some of the parts he needed wouldn't arrive until Wednesday afternoon, but he promised the car would be ready for me to test early Wednesday evening. Thank God for that. We had to leave for the Pod on Thursday afternoon, since the Cannonball is a three-day meeting with a 10am start on Friday.

Sure enough, the car was ready for me to test on Wednesday evening.

There was a spit-back in the blower intake which was quickly rectified – the timing was too far advanced. Both cars were now ready to drive down to the Pod in the morning. I would be driving the Camaro, John the BMW. This was necessary because Peter had decided to stay at the Pod in his caravan with his wife and family, so they could see him race. Brenda had booked us into the Hind Hotel in Wellingborough and John into the Travelodge at Rushden. He could then get the car to the track early for our son to be signed on and ready to race in the first session of qualifying. This would give him the practice he needed with the BMW because he wasn't used to an automatic gearbox.

Everything went according to plan, until it was my turn to qualify. It was a poor result, 15.88 on a 15.28 dial-in. My next run was even worse, so I let John play about with the engine and try to bring the power back. While all this was going on, our son was charging up the track every half an hour showing off to his wife who thought drag racing was only a bit of fun. Brenda said to me, 'Derek, am I crew chief?'

'Yes, you are, Brenda.' So she went over to our son and read him the riot act. This seemed to subdue the team's number two driver, whose qualifying times improved from then on.

The engine of the Camaro sounded better on Saturday morning and it was agreed that I should stay with my dial-in of 15.28. On the first run I managed 15.52, which put me twelfth, two from the bottom. I gave the car back to John for him to check the timing again.

The Street ET class had one final run so we changed our dial-in to 15.38 hoping the cooler air would give us more power, and it did. I ran a 15.48, which put me in third position behind top qualifier Colin Catlin and number two Steven Harrington. It was the end of our day's racing but the big cars would carry on until dark.

We chose an Indian restaurant for our supper. The food was delicious and we took our time over eating, then relaxed with a coffee and liqueur before we paid the bill and walked back to the Hind Hotel. The hotel was full of racers from Sweden, Denmark and Germany, so we went to bed early.

Sunday dawned and I ate an early breakfast, while Brenda packed the suitcases. We paid the bill by MasterCard, oh, those lovely plastic cards, so quick and easy! We use them to our advantage, paying off the full amount owed on both cards every month, thus getting a free overdraft for twelve months.

In eliminations, Street ET are always out first. We must find Amos Meekins, where was he? The other RAC scrutineer, Stuart Vincent, who was in the compound, wouldn't check my car, he thought I was too old to race and drag racing isn't for OAPs. Thank goodness I could see Amos coming through the pits. My bonnet up, he signed my pass and said, 'There you go, Derek. Go out and win for Brenda.'

I thanked him, closed the bonnet and put my helmet on, fired up the engine and joined the queue in the fire-up lane.

When I reached the pairing lanes, I could see Brenda was in lane two with Peter who was alongside Martin Lewis in his Nova SR 'Nova Blaze'. My opponent was Marie Isaacs in a Ford Capri. Peter and Martin were to race before me, so I didn't see the race but I could see the scoreboard – it was a win for Martin Lewis, much to the disgust of Brenda. A Nova had beaten her BMW!

Now it was my turn to race. Marie Isaacs pulled a red and it was a win for me, I was through to the quarter-finals. When I arrived back at the pits, there was one hell of a row going on between mother and son in which each was blaming the other. I heard Brenda say, 'Ok, you didn't hear what John Price said over the public address when you got bogged down on the start lane, but I did. He said "Young Annable, you'd better give the car back to your mother, she would win races with it!"'

This was the end of our two-car team; Peter resigned as number two driver. I lost in the next round of eliminations, so we all went home, with John driving the BMW and Brenda and me in the Camaro. The only reward for an expensive three days was 475 points towards the championships.

There were three weeks before the next race meeting, which would give us more time to put the finishing touches to our new ladies' dress shop in Benllech. The lease on the shop in Caernarfon Road had come to an end, and from our garage business in Moelfre, a shop two miles down the road would be easier to run and mean less travelling for Brenda.

Again it was the time of the year to make our visit to the NEC in Birmingham and forward order for next season. A ladies' dress shop can be very demanding. It requires new stock on an ever-increasing cycle. This time we were going to stay at a hotel-cum-caravan park outside Kenilworth.

Having endured an awful meal in the hotel restaurant, we wandered into the caravan park nightclub where a disco was in full swing. After a couple of minutes my wife's foot started to tap the floor, her body following the rhythm of the music. I nudged her, 'Brenda, should we join the dancers?'

'Derek, we're too old. Look, they're all young people.'

'Yes, they are. Let's show them how to dance to disco music. Are you game?'

'Yes, why not!' So Brenda and I launched into our dance routine.

What was wrong? Some of the young ones stopped dancing and stood there looking at us. Then the band started to up the beat. Brenda was unstoppable, we hadn't danced like this since the Barry White days. Nobody else was dancing, everybody stood there watching us.

The music stopped and two old people were surrounded by young people saying, 'We've never seen dancing like it! We're glad we came to this disco, you two have made our night, you are the greatest.'

We thanked the band and the other dancers and went to bed. What was the time? Dear me, it was 1am! We had to be at the NEC before 9am, fresh for a day's buying and the drive home.

The Thunder and Lightning drag racing team was now back to one driver and one car, but both cars had to be prepared for racing since the BMW was to be the back-up car again. As I was still leading the championship, I couldn't afford to miss any of the remaining rounds. Round six was the Alkymania at Avon Park Raceway on 22/23 July. Wendy Talbot, the secretary of the Avon Park International Racers Association (APIRA), had kindly sent us a list of guesthouses and other accommodation in the Stratford-on-Avon area. After a couple of phone calls, we chose Bank House in the village of Mickleton, which was only three miles from the racetrack. Friday and Saturday night were booked and we were ready to go.

The road from Anglesey to Stratford-on-Avon would be busy with holiday traffic so we set off early. We didn't want any hold-ups in Kidderminster at rush hour, since old American cars are prone to overheating in traffic, but we made good time and were in Mickleton by mid-afternoon. The Bank House was next to a pub serving bar food. This would be handy, with no long walks at night time. After the sun has set there is no drinking and driving for me – road and RAC competition licences are all-important.

Mrs Billington was a pleasant lady who was a native of Bramhall, Cheshire, having bought Bank House on her husband's retirement. From our bedroom window I could keep an eye on the Camaro which we had parked in the pub car park. The Billingtons, who had no parking space, encouraged their guests to eat at the pub and in return the landlord allowed Bank House guests to use his large car park for overnight parking.

After a good night's sleep and breakfast, which was so tasty that even Brenda partook, off to Long Marston we went. The thunder from the twin exhausts on the Camaro rattled the windows of this sleepy village and the local dogs were barking as we passed. Within minutes, we were driving into the pits where there was a big turnout. There must have been nearly a hundred cars and scores of bikes. We parked in the section reserved for Street ET. Everybody was there: Paul Hudson, Colin Catlin, Ian Turnbull, Steven Harrington, Phil Walker. Six people, including me, were after the car championship. Looking around, I said to Brenda, 'No wonder the meeting is called the Alkymania.' There were six Top Alcohol cars, and Barry Sheavills, the Turners, and Wilson in dragsters. Further down the pits were seven Pro-Modified cars, with Alan Packman, Dave Mingay, Englefield and Appleton all chasing points for their championship.

Time for the scrutineer to check my car. Mr Stockton passed it A1. His young son thought my Camaro Z28 was fabulous and kept asking if he could have a ride in it.

Saturday was practice; Sunday would be qualifying followed by eliminations. To save the motor I did one practice run against Marie Isaacs who was driving a Ford Granada. This time she asked if she could race against me and being a gentleman, I agreed. Where did she get these cars? One racer said he thought the cars were from the family workshop and that she borrowed them. A Ford Granada on a drag strip? What next? A Capri, yes, a Granada, no. But why spoil her fun? The lady from Devon had come a long way. Marie pulled a red, and therefore I won.

My practice run over, Brenda and I went over to the Super Gas pits to talk to Frank Mason, a Newcastle upon Tyne racer. Brenda got on well with his partner. Pitted next to Frank was Trevor Graves, the Bristol Doorslammer, who always took a lot of stick from John Price, the Santa Pod commentator, which went like this: 'How far down the strip will Trevor Graves get before the engine breaks again?' On my visits to the Pod, Trevor's car either breaks on the start or halfway down the track, with bits of the engine coming out of the exhaust pipes!

Further down the Super Gas pits was the beautiful Camaro of Terry Gibbs. One day this racer would become a promoter and run the Super Series on this raceway, and his wife Tina would become an RAC clerk of the course. For myself, I always feel that racers turned promoters are a bit like reformed smokers. Their approach to things is, 'I have given it up and you shouldn't do it', and 'when I was smoking (racing) I did it this way!' Never mind, it takes all sorts to make a world.

Time to go back to Mickleton, have a wash and try the pub food. The table was booked as we were told they get busy on a Saturday night. The meal was basic and generous in quantity, if not in quality.

When you're hungry, all you want is a plate of food and that is what we got. My wife kept saying, 'Those are big chips, Derek.'

I tried to explain to her that in Yorkshire, big chips are a delicacy. Ask Harry Ramsden, the fish and chip man. Her answer to this was, 'I am in Mickleton, not Yorkshire, and next time we will stay at the Chesford Grange Hotel.' 'Right, Brenda, let's check the car and go to bed. Tomorrow is another day and we have to leave early.'

Suitcase packed and breakfast over, we said our farewells to the Billingtons, got into the car and left. As we drove to Long Marston, Brenda kept saying, 'Those big chips ...'

I wondered what I could do to take her mind off last night, and there was the answer, a roadside fruit stall. Grapes, peaches and strawberries did the trick. Brenda sat there enjoying them, her face beaming with sheer joy. How she could eat all that fruit on top of a cooked breakfast, I don't know. I couldn't!

For the Street ET qualifying session I had dialled-in 15.48 at 92.830mph. There was no time for any more runs – our class were to go straight into eliminations. Who would I be racing? It was Mick Colley from Birmingham. Down the fire-up lane we went and turned right onto the track. He had the left-hand lane. We both pre-staged and staged together, but since he had the quicker car, I left half a second before him. At the eighth mile I was still ahead and held it to the finishing line, which I crossed first. We both broke out, he by .182 of a second, me by .297. His win.

That was me out first round. The only consolation was that Colin Catlin didn't show – car broken. Paul Hudson was also taken out first round, so the position at the top for me was unchanged. Phil Walker was the winner, which placed him in second position on points. Paul Hudson was now third. Steven Harrington was runner-up in the day's finals, so now he became the greatest threat to my lead. The next round of the championship was at York Raceway in three weeks' time. Would he come that far north? Last time he hadn't.

For months, I had been asked if I would display my race cars at the Anglesey Show and I finally agreed. However, only five miles into the journey there, there was a big 'clonk clonk' from the transmission and the Camaro came to an abrupt halt. The back wheels had locked up. Not a good day. At the show, the noise of my Altered and Paul Bland's Altered together, when we blipped engines, had upset the show's organisers and for months after the show, we suffered abuse from local farmers who didn't want cars like that in Anglesey. Never mind that we had put motorsport on the map in Anglesey. Soon after that, the Anglesey motorsport track was born.

The damage to the Camaro was serious. The crown wheel and pinion were broken, and we would have to order these parts and a spacer kit from the USA. Time was against us, since the next meeting in the IHRA/UK National Championship at York Raceway was on 12 August. The Camaro would be in bits for weeks. Brenda's BMW 635 would have to be my race car and it was ready to race – our planning was paying off. In the years when I raced Allards and Coopers, I wasn't in charge of my destiny because I was still a minor. In those days you had to be over 21 before you could sign contracts, and even Stirling Moss had this problem. His father cancelled a contract young Stirling had signed. Now I was in complete charge of my racing programme and would run it in the way that suited the Thunder and Lightning team. That day at the Anglesey Show was a nightmare, and I swore my cars would never go to any kind of farmers' meeting ever again. This holds good today.

There was very little time before the next round of the IHRA/UK Championship. This would force me to race the BMW because the Camaro was taking longer to repair than was first thought. The parts we required weren't listed. The North Star Nats were on 12–13 August at York Raceway, so our usual room was booked at South Cave Travelodge, the car was loaded with everything we needed for the weekend, and off we went full of hope for a win to make up for the bad results at Avon Park three weeks before.

When we arrived at the track the next morning, the pits were crowded. Thank goodness there was a vacant spot near the start line. There were seven cars in my class, with Phil Evans driving his 2½-litre BMW, Paul Hudson back trying to make up lost points and Colin Catlin having driven up from Bordon in Hampshire. Ian Armitage, the local boy, was looking strong in his El Camino, and all the way from Hornchurch in his Pontiac was Stephen Harrington. He was getting serious; a good result for him at York and the next meeting at the Pod and it would be winner takes all at the World Finals in September.

Everybody had two hours of open testing before the official qualifying session during the afternoon. The BMW was running mid-16s in testing, therefore in the first qualifying run I dialled-in 16.300 but the car went too quickly at 16.276. Brenda suggested trying 16.100 on the next run. Damn, the car went too slow this time, recording 16.377.

We decided to call it a day and save the car for Sunday morning's qualifying period, which for Street ET would be straight into eliminations. The weather and track conditions can change from day to day, so better to concentrate our efforts on the racing on Sunday.

When you are away racing, leisure time seems to pass in a flash. Before you know it, you are back at the racetrack. This weekend was like that and I was back in the fire-up road and entering the staging lane. I stayed with Saturday's dial-in and ran a 16.155. This made me number two qualifier behind Phil Evans. I must improve my performance on the last qualifying run, as a bye in the eliminations was up for grabs – a seven-car field meant the top qualifier would have a bye into the semi-finals. The last run of the morning and I made it, a 16.104 on a dial-in of 16.100. Brenda was jumping with joy – $^4/_{1000}$ of a second inside my dial-in, very few racers have ever been as close as that in a qualifying session. I was top qualifier.

It was time for lunch and to watch the parade of custom cars, followed by an exhibition by Steve Murty in his Pro Jet Ford Cargo, which is an awesome jet truck. The children in the stands loved it – a ten-ton truck racing up the drag strip at 150mph.

My bye run over, I checked the results of the races with Brenda. Harrington and Hudson had been knocked out in the first round, so in the semi-finals it was Phil Evans against me and Colin Catlin against Ian Armitage. Phil and Colin lost. Ian's Cher El Camino 'Heartbeat Hauler' would be my BMW's opponent in the finals. His car is quick and is always on the edge of the bracket, which is 13.50.

There we were staged and ready to race, my light would come down two and a half seconds before Ian's amber. Amber, amber, and I was off down the track, the white BMW pulling well. In my mirror I could see Ian was pounding up behind me and making ground fast on me. I thought, he must have pulled a good light, or did I pull a bad one? With a little over a second in time to the finishing line, my left foot caught the brake pedal and my brake light must have come on, because Ian banged his brakes on just before we crossed the line. He must have thought I was braking to avoid a breakout. He was wrong. I powered over the line and won by $^2/_{100}$ of a second.

This was one of the most exciting races I have ever taken part in. Ian Armitage was a great sportsman and a nice guy, and he never questioned whether my brake light came on as a deliberate act to confuse him. As George Beeken wrote in the *Pennine Drag Racing Club News* about that meeting, 'Street ET featured, among others, the two silent-running BMWs of Phil Evans and Derek Annable. Is this the future of Street Drag Racing, with Derek taking the Number 1 spot?' Further on he said, 'Derek Annable nicely took the Street ET Honours with a purring 16.36 in his BMW against the much noisier El Camino of Ian Armitage.'

This win secured my second place position behind Andy Holmes in the PDRC Championship. I had already won the club's Street Car Championship. We drove home well pleased with the weekend's racing. This was my sixth race out of eight in the IHRA/UK Championship, my maximum races allowed, with a total of 3950 points to my credit. It was up to the others to catch me in their remaining race. Paul Hudson and Stephen Harrington had one each, the Summer Nationals and the Word Finals, and the highest points from either would count towards their totals.

We still had problems with the Camaro, having been sent the wrong spacer kit. Racing would be in Brenda's BMW again, but the car was consistent with its times on the Santa Pod track and a much safer car to park outside the Hind Hotel on a bank holiday Saturday night in Wellingborough, where drunken brawls had happened on other weekend visits.

At some meetings at Santa Pod there were over 180 cars backed up with eight bike racers. The Summer Nationals this year were no exception; a quick look at the official programme showed there were entrants from many European countries. In the Top Alcohol class there were 20 of the fastest cars outside the USA, spearheaded by Anita Makala and Barry Sheavills. The race director was Jon Cross, with Carlo Gandoffi on the start line. When these gentlemen were in charge, the racers knew they would have a very professional and smooth weekend's racing.

In my class there were 12 cars, with Harrington, Hudson and Catlin hungry for points. Time for my first practice run to get the feel of the car. I ran a mid-16. Brenda posted a 16.30 on the car for my first qualifying run, which was to be against Colin Catlin. I was too quick by $^3/_{100}$ of a second, a breakout, which put me to the bottom of the pile. As there was such a big entry of cars and bikes, it was the end of Street ET's racing for the day. There was time to talk to the paying spectators who are allowed into the pits, most of whom could relate to my type of car. The Top Alcohol cars were for the real petrol heads. The main question we racers were asked was if they could race their family car, and if so where and when? That question answered, then came the big one: 'How expensive is drag racing?' My answer to this question never changed: 'As expensive as you want to make it. At a meeting like this in your family car, the cost would be £100 to £150. If you were to race a Top Alcohol car, the cost, without breakages, would be £1,000.'

Sunday dawned, our BMW had to be checked out again by Amos Meekins, who fortunately was up early and making himself a cup of tea. Amos passed my car and it went straight into the fire-up road. It was agreed I was to dial in 16.20. My opponent was Stephen Harrington. I don't know why, but he would sign himself Stephen at one track and Steven at another track. Anyway he had dialled in 14.00 and ran a 14.185. I pulled a better light and ran a 16.245 which made me top qualifier, with Bill Weston, who was driving his wife's Mustang, at number two. The rest struggled to get close to their dial-in and Phil Walker ended the day bottom of the pile.

Our racing over for the day, Brenda and I went to the track guardrail to watch the Top Alcohol cars in their qualifying session. There was some close racing, then what every racer fears happened. I now quote what Roger Gorringer wrote in *Drag Racing UK*:

Tragedy struck during qualifications when Britain's main hope and number two in the points chase Barry Sheavills lost his Torco Oils dragster to the top end barrier. It was a run-off between Barry and Micke Kagered to decide the rained off Hockenheim final; both cars got well crossed up with Barry ending up wrecking the whole car against the guardrail. He has vowed to try and rebuild the car ready for the World Finals in three weeks!

He did rebuild it and raced the car in the World Finals. This was the car we bought from Barry Sheavills at the end of the 1996 drag racing session – the complete works, engine and all – a five-second Top Alcohol dragster for me to move up to the ultimate in UK drag racing. Top Fuel cars were the ultimate in the USA and generally beyond the pockets of their poor cousins this side of the pond. At the time, nobody, not even Brenda and I, thought this would happen. We were always complaining the big cars spoilt our racing with the loss of track time because of oil downs. Me? A Top Alcohol dragster driver? Never! My doctor wouldn't allow it, but when the time came he did.

The Hind Hotel was full of European race teams, so we had a quick meal in the hotel restaurant and then retired to our bedroom, which was on the top floor away from all the noise, and watched TV for a couple of hours, before going to sleep.

For once we could take it easy and have a lazy breakfast because Street ET weren't out on the track until 12.30pm. This made a change. When we arrived at the pits, there would be no charging around in a panic, throwing suitcases out of the boot of the car and putting our race number on.

As we drove into the pits, Peter Catlin, Colin's father, greeted us. 'Brenda', he said, 'tell Derek he has Ian Turnbull in the first round.' Peter always spoke to my wife first. He was a very polite man and his wife, Joyce, always got on well with my wife. As I prepared the car for racing, my thoughts went into overdrive. Plough Garage again! I had to race the one who never smiled, Ian Turnbull. His partner Keith Milne always smiled and was a joy to race against. This was to be the slowest car, me, against the quickest car, Turnbull's. Brenda's BMW, 87mph, Turnbull's Camaro, 109mph. To date, it was two wins each from our four contests.

Because of track oil downs, racing was delayed by over an hour. When it was Street ET's turn to race, the tortoise (me) and the hare (Ian) were in the staging lanes. This time I decided to let Ian stage first, he didn't like it and he held back, but the start line marshall made him stage. Then I came on to stage quickly, it worked and I pulled a good light. Ian was having trouble catching me, and we crossed the line together. We both broke out but mine was the lesser, a win for me.

Some racers are never gracious, win or lose, but Ian kept going on about how he had problems on the start line. My only concern was championship points and who went through to the next round. The three contenders for the championship were through, Harrington, Hudson and myself. My next opponent was Wayne Hiscock in a Pontiac GTO and, as Mark Gredzinski wrote in *Custom Car*, the hot rod magazine:

Derek Annable, Senior, does double duty, driving a 'T' Altered and in this Street ET bracket fielding a white BMW 6 series. Not yer average drag match, Guv'nor! Derek qualified first but was beaten by Wayne Hiscock in a Pontiac GTO. Meanwhile Stephen Harrington in a GTO beat Paul Hudson's Capri, and in an all GTO final beat Wayne Hiscock 14.57 to a $1/100$ under 14.44.

Mark was right. Wayne beat me, yes, but not quite. The timing ticket shows I beat myself because I broke out by $9/100$ of a second!

With Paul Hudson going out in the quarter-finals like me, the points stood at 3950 for myself and 3325 for Harrington, and the World Finals would decide who won the trophy for 1995. Before this meeting I was entered in the Hot Rod Drags on the 9 September at Avon Park Raceway with the ex-Fay Fischer Altered, which would give me practice with the car for team Thunder and Lightning's assault on the Modified Car Championship in 1996.

Time to go home, but Brenda was holding court in the pits with a dozen race fans who were eager to hear her stories about being a crew chief. I said farewell to Phil Walker and Tracy. The Catlin family persuaded Brenda to get into the car, saying it would be midnight before we got home. At last my wife closed the car door and we left with shouts of 'See you at the World Finals, Grandad; please bring the Camaro to race.' It was indeed nearly midnight before we arrived home, since the bank holiday Monday traffic was intense.

When I arrived at work on Tuesday morning, John gave me some good news – the parts we needed to repair the Camaro's back axle would be delivered on Thursday morning and the car should be ready for me to test at the weekend. Brenda was already planning for the Hot Rod Drags, and our daughter had agreed to look after the shop. As the BMW was our tow car, we would stay with the Billingtons in Mickleton and leave the trailer in the pit area at Long Marston ready for racing. Colin Cripps, a friend of Brenda's, would act as guard.

I managed three runs over the weekend, and my best ET 10.852 and mph 124.703 earned me a write-up in *Custom Car*. To quote Mark Gredzinski, 'One of the nicest Ts on the track was Derek Annable's Altered, which is the ex-Fay Fischer car. This makes three cars on the strip for Derek.' All this and a quarter-page photo of the car. Some weeks later when we met Paul Fischer, Fay's husband, he said, 'Fay and I have raced that car for two years and never a mention from *Custom Car*. You buy it from us and are given half a page in the magazine!'

What a year! No sooner were we home than it was time to go racing again. The World Finals at Santa Pod was a three-day meeting, starting on Saturday. This meant travelling down in the now repaired Camaro on

Thursday morning. Today was Monday. We had three days to catch our breath and we would be off again.

The least said about the World Finals the better – it rained for two days, followed by more rain. We sat in the Camaro and watched the Santa Pod pit area turn into a lake. The meeting was cancelled and I was the IHRA/UK National Street ET Champion. Stephen Harrington was runner-up. Brenda and I had achieved what we set out to do way back in March; our planning had paid off, and we had the championship for 1995. As Gary Baldy wrote in *Drag Racing UK*,

> I have to make mention of the exploits of Derek 'Grandad' Annable who, in his first full season, became the national champ of Street ET, driving his wife Brenda's BMW. He didn't win events that often but he did go to all the early season races and racked up the points in steady fashion. The rest of the gang found the weather closed in on their late season attempts to catch him. Effort and commitment won the day here and considering Derek, like Carlo, is no spring chicken and the fact he lives on Anglesey island speaks volumes for his energy and enthusiasm. Well done, Sir!

About this time I was putting pen to paper. An article in the *Sun* prompted a couple of letters to Steve McKenlay, the motoring correspondent, one about drag racing's need for sponsorship, and the other about Derek Warwick retiring from the sport, in which I'd included a picture of my car. What happened? Stan Piecha must have seen the letters and got it wrong. He thought I raced a dragster around the streets of Manchester and Liverpool and sent a photographer from the *Sun* to take photos of me and the car outside our garage in Anglesey.

How could I race a car around corners when the only way to stop it was with a parachute? This proved to me the public's ignorance of our sport. Without realising it I had become the voice of drag racing, which kept me firing letters at the newspapers and other media to correct their ideas of drag racing. They thought we were drag queens running around dressed as ladies at some sort of party.

Every weekend from March until the end of September, we had raced one or the other of our cars and my wife was feeling the strain, therefore it was agreed we put our energy into improving my reaction times and 60ft launch times in the Altered. The Camaro wouldn't be raced again this year.

We took the Altered down to the RWYB meeting at Santa Pod on 7/8 October to work on my reaction times. On the first run I managed a .770 followed by a .411 (a red light). Soon afterwards, what we had travelled 500 miles for came up on the scoreboard: .536 followed on the next run by a

.521. A very tired crew chief was pleased with the results so we loaded the car into the trailer and went home.

The next RWYB meeting was at Avon Park Raceway on 21/22 October. This time it was the 60ft times, with a target of 1.700. Wendy Talbot was in charge of signing on and wished me luck, but I did struggle – the track was cold, making the car squirrel all over the strip. Our 60ft time was 1.800, speed 118.939mph. Second run: 60ft 1.769, speed 122mph. Because of a curfew, that was the end of my racing for the day. The local people living around the track had tried to close the track down because of the noise, but the judge in charge of the case had ruled they could only enforce a curfew. Saturday racing would be between 10am and 6pm, Sunday and bank holidays would be 11am to 5pm.

Sunday was a bright, cold day and the track was ready for racing by 11.30am. Street legal cars were out first, cars with slicks had to wait another hour before track conditions were good enough for the quicker of them. My first run was 1.751 for the 60ft, speed 121.036mph. After an hour's wait for the engine to cool, we would be ready for our second run. These cars run with a dry block, no coolant in the engine. Brenda towed me behind the BMW to the start line. After parking the BMW, she then brought me into pre-stage and left me to stage. It was a good run, 1.704 for the 60ft, speed 122.455mph. Time to go home.

Colin and I loaded the race car onto the trailer, leaving Brenda talking to Roy Wilding. Car secured, I thanked Colin and we started our journey home which would take over five hours. Brenda turned to me and said, 'Derek, you are racing with the Wild Bunch next year. Roy has agreed.'

On reflection, our first full season of drag racing had been a good year:

IHRA/UK National Champion in Street ET
Runner-up in the PDRC Championship
PDRC Class Winner in Street ET.

All very satisfactory. A couple of OAPs had achieved this and were still alive to tell the tale. Little did I know that this would be dwarfed seven years later, when I would have my most successful year behind the wheel.

Now it was time to relax and enjoy Christmas. It would soon be another year, and we must save hard for the start of the 1996 season of drag racing. The future looked good.

Derek becomes a family man

Brenda's dress shop in Bangor

The 'red monster' (Camaro)

Santa Pod 1994:
Derek in white BMW
in the World Finals

*Fay Fischer's 1923 Model T Altered – the
car Derek and Brenda bought*

Back to the shop we went (Dreams Come True, Caernarfon)

Carla Pittau, Street ET champion (© Carla Pittau)

Phil Walker in 'Royal Ragtop' was No. 2 qualifier (© Phil Walker)

Paul Hudson driving 'Lost Cause' (© Derek Annable)

Clothes for Brenda's fashion show
(© Brian Staines)

York: Derek and Peter in white BMW; Phil Evans in
brown BMW (© Derek Annable)

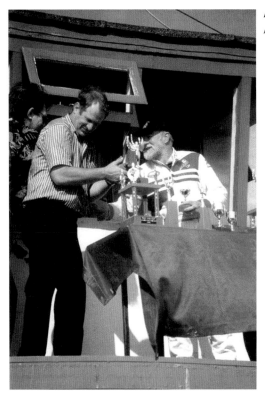

Derek collecting trophy from Steve Murty (© Derek Annable)

Martin Lewis, who knocked out our Peter, in 'Nova Blaze', Santa Pod

Derek and Brenda's dance routine of yesteryear (© Derek Annable)

Altered at Anglesey Show (© Derek Annable)

Santa Pod, Easter Thunderball: Derek racing the Altered in Modified Class
(© Colin Cripps)

PDRC class winner, Street ET. Dinner dance
prize-giving, Bradford (© York Raceway)

CHAPTER 5

1996

With Christmas over and the post back to normal, it was now time to try for some sponsorship money. I sent around 70 letters to a variety of companies, with most of them replying and returning my photos, although no offers of money. Some of the reasons given were: Marks & Spencer, 'we only sponsor people with disabilities'; Iceland, 'disabled children'; Manweb, 'had a community funding policy'; Parcelforce said, 'I must employ 25 people'; Carlsberg, Tetley, 'due to the drink/drive connotations they could not support motorsport and air sports'; Mars Confectionery, 'we only support health, youth and the elderly!'

While this was going on, Brenda and I went to the SPRC dinner dance and their trophy presentation on 27 January at the Hilton Hotel in Watford. It was snow and ice all the way from North Wales to Watford. We arrived in time for the club's AGM on Saturday afternoon. I was new to this type of meeting and as green as grass. I sat down next to a couple of gentlemen who didn't look like racers, they were dressed in smart lounge suits.

On the agenda was the points system for the new season's racing. To be able to put questions to the chairman, I had made a complete restructure of the points system written on the back of an envelope with my name and address on the front. The floor had put their views to the chairman, and it was then I realised who was sitting next to me – Steve Murty of York Raceway and Bo Meftah of Santa Pod. Steve was interested in my ideas, so I gave him my envelope and thought no more of it until the AGM of the PDRC at the end of February. At this meeting I sat next to Graham Beckwith who was the race and points overall championship coordinator and in his hand was the envelope I had given to Steve Murty at the SPRC AGM. To my amazement, Graham was putting to the meeting a new points system, item by item from the back of my old envelope, as if the ideas were his own. He didn't even say to me, 'Good idea, Derek'. So, my ideas were written into the rulebook, with Graham Beckwith taking the credit.

At the SPRC AGM on 27 January 1996 there was an item for discussion – it was sponsorship, or lack of it. This is when I got into hot water and was shouted down by the racers and bikers at the meeting. As I said, I had written to many firms trying to get financial help for the 1996 season. Some firms had expressed concern about the image drag racing projected in their magazines – four-letter words and excessive drinking – so big businesses were reluctant to have their good name tarnished because of that sort of behaviour. When I put this point to the meeting, three bikers had to be physically restrained. The chairman brought the meeting to an end, even then dozens of racers and bikers were still shouting at me. Why is it so many people who are looking for help cannot take any criticism and clean up their act?

The dinner dance went well and I picked up my trophy. Our son Paul had also driven down from North Wales to see me honoured. John Price gave me his usual 'Grandad' call and Jon Cross said, 'Well done, Derek.'

As we were leaving the dinner dance, Steve Murty came over to us and said to Brenda, 'Derek put his head in the lion's mouth this afternoon, ask him to keep out of the politics and enjoy his racing.'

Brenda turned to me and said, 'Derek, did you hear what Steve said?'

I replied, 'Thank you, Steve, but what you have said has made me more determined to get involved.' He smiled and left.

Over the years, people like Trevor Graves and others have never had a kind word to say about Steve Murty – they must have had their reasons. Me, I have found the Murty family 100% for drag racing and they have put many thousands of pounds of their own money into the sport, quite apart from any company money.

I had been through my baptism of fire and was stronger for it. As we were leaving the hotel on Sunday morning, Carla Pittau came over to me and said, 'Derek, take no notice of the bikers, we racers respect your views on the sport of drag racing. Up to now you are the only person who has had the guts to say what's wrong with it.'

Brenda thanked Carla and we drove home. There were more letters of rejection awaiting us but they had sent the photos back, so more sponsorship letters went off. Could I present a good case for UK firms to get involved in UK drag racing? Even today complete strangers come up to me and say, 'I remember that letter of yours all those years ago and I am sorry we couldn't help, my boss at the time didn't know what a drag racing car was but he does now!' A few kind words are worth more than money.

Time to consider the implication of Phil Evans' letter and check the proposed racing programme:

INFORMATION RELEASE FROM THE SANTA POD RACERS CLUB

Dear Member

On Friday 16 February 1996, Santa Pod Leisure Ltd and Santa Pod Properties Ltd, the operating company of Santa Pod Raceway, went into

Administrative Receivership. This means that the main creditor bank has decided to intervene with the financial affairs of the company and at the moment an appointee of the Receivers is running the company with a view to selling the facility as a going concern. It should be stressed that the company is not in liquidation but the bank has moved to protect its interests by forcing a move to new ownership of the company. Members of the executive committee of the Santa Pod Racers Club have been in contact with the Receiver to offer advice and assistance so that the potential transition to a new owner is carried out with the least disruption to the racing programme.

We had recently concluded a contract with Santa Pod Leisure Ltd, setting out the terms and conditions for the Club to organise the 1996 racing season. We were stressing to the Receiver that we can offer any potential new owner the organisational and race control expertise to enable the racing season to begin as scheduled. However there is obviously a good deal of confusion at the minute regarding specific details of promotion and financing for future meetings. We will try to keep you updated as much as possible and at the moment we are continuing to plan for the season opener at Easter.

On behalf of the Santa Pod Racers Club.

Philip Evans

It was agreed the Altered would race with the Wild Bunch and in the IHRA/UK National Championship and the Camaro would race at York Raceway and Avon Park if it didn't clash with any Wild Bunch meetings.

A leak down test on the Camaro engine showed we needed to change the camshaft. This time it had to be a roller cam and lifters. I wrote to Ashley Letts of Crane Cams asking for a discount on the parts, so we could improve on last year's achievements, and saying that the work would be done by students at the local technical college in order for them to gain experience on American engines for their diploma.

Mr Letts came up trumps, charging £500 (cat price £1,250) for the parts, freight, duty and VAT and shipped direct to us from the USA. Then I rang the principal of the college to give him the good news and arrange a date to take the car into their workshop. He assured me that the students were eager to start working on the car.

Before the Camaro was installed in their workshop, they had five students on the car mechanics course, and this increased week by week until they were turning away applicants. Never in North Wales had any student worked on a V8 engine. Word had got round and even young men in the Chester area were applying for the Anglesey course.

John Turner from our garage supervised the work with the college foreman on a three-day basis to fit in with their schedules. After six weeks, the work was completed and I went to collect the Camaro. When I arrived at the college, to my surprise all the students were coming out of the many buildings. I fired up the engine and drove out of the workshop to loud cheering – it made everybody's day. I had brought a little bit of excitement to the quiet island of Anglesey.

The following week a trip was arranged for the students who had worked on the car to watch the car race at Santa Pod. Unfortunately, two students pulled out because they couldn't afford the trip, and it had to be cancelled. I tried to persuade the principal to allow me to make up the cash shortfall but he wouldn't change his mind. Happily, some of the lads came later in the year to watch the car race at Santa Pod and went home full of pride and joy. Their work on the engine had given the car a win.

Most weeks I watched *Top Gear* on BBC2; there was Jeremy Clarkson going on about how quick the Ford GT90 was, 0–60 in three seconds, the car was this and that and that he was a great guy being able to drive a GT90. I couldn't resist writing the following letter to him:

Come on, Jeremy, try a man's car. My Altered (photo enclosed) on nitrous oxide (NO_2), laughing gas at the dentists, will reach 0–60mph in less than two seconds and cross the line (quarter mile) at 140mph.

Bring your Top Gear team to Santa Pod Raceway (Bedfordshire) and I shall bring my Altered from North Wales and give you the ride of your life, and I mean the ride of your life. Nothing will ever be the same again.

Yours sincerely

Derek Annable

His reply through John Wilcox of *Top Gear* was: 'Good idea, Derek.' Thus began a long-running correspondence between myself and Jeremy Clarkson/John Wilcox and *Top Gear* which is still lively today.

Anglesey is quiet at this time of the year and this gave us time to plan the race programme for the new season, which started with the Easter Thunderball at Santa Pod. It was agreed both cars were in tip-top condition, all that was needed for success was that I should get fit and lose some weight. So out into the garden I went, armed with a spade, to prepare the potato patch!

Colin Cripps, our crewman for 1996, sent us a couple of letters, the second with confirmation of the Drag Racing Nuts programme at the Santa Pod and Avon Park Raceways and details of the prize money. The support we racers were getting from the Drag Racing Nuts was considerable and welcome, they were a great bunch of people working hard to promote drag racing to British motorsport followers.

Easter was now with us and the ex-Fay Fischer Altered was entered in Mod ET. Pit passes had been sent to Colin who would be doing double duty, crewing for us and also filming the event with our camcorder. He couldn't be at the track until Saturday morning and the trailer wouldn't be safe in the pits overnight, so we booked into the Travelodge at Rushden.

The journey down to Rushden was tiring, the roads were busy with holiday traffic and six hours towing a trailer is no fun. Trailer and car parked, we went into the Little Chef for a meal. While we were eating, John Price walked in, sat down and ordered his usual half-pound double burger. Always the same food, breakfast, lunch and dinner, the man never changes, always cheerful.

Saturday morning was dry and cold. Colin had marked out a spot in the pit area for us and the three of us soon had the race car out of the trailer and passed by the scrutineers. It was straight into qualifying for the Mod ET racers. I was against Alan Golding, his car is quick, 10 seconds, and mine ran 11 seconds. My opponent in the second round was Simon Farmer, he pulled a red on the lights, I managed a good 60ft. That was the end of the day's racing for our class of car.

This was my first big meeting driving this type of car and all drivers are required to go through an upgrading assessment by an RAC steward. In charge of mine was John Ledster. I had to sit in the car (blindfolded) and talk through all the controls and start procedure, and the fire and safety switches. I could see John Ledster was well pleased, he endorsed my licence and that was that. Brenda and I, with Colin's help, put the race car into the trailer and drove back to the Travelodge.

Before dawn broke, I was woken by a loud rumbling noise. By my alarm clock, it was six o'clock, what the hell was going on? I looked out of the bedroom window, it was Phil Walker firing up his Pontiac Firebird. Tracy got into the car and off they went to the track. This would be the norm from now on when Phil and I were racing at the Pod. Every time this happened, he would come over to me and say, 'Derek, did I wake you up this morning?'

My answer would always be the same, 'You bet, Phil.'

Sunday qualifying for Modified ET cars started at 12 noon. My opponent was Pete Austin in his Plymouth 71 Cuda, 'Pinkie'. He dialled in 10.95 and ran a 11.17. This made him top qualifier. I had a poor reaction time and 60ft. My second run was against last year's champion Tony Guy, who broke out, but this time a good 60ft for me and I ran a 11.074 on a 11.04, making me the top qualifier ahead of Pete Austin. After two hours Al Golding went out and knocked me off the top of the pile. He ran $^5/_{1000}$ of a second within his dial-in.

Colin Cripps was having the time of his life with our camcorder and his camera. Brenda and I weren't. Two days we had been pitted with the other modified cars and in that time not one of the drivers, or their wives, had spoken to Brenda. This gang weren't very friendly. I hoped when I raced with the Wild Bunch they would speak to Brenda. The car went back in the trailer, with Colin on guard duty – he slept in a tent alongside our trailer.

Being our last night of eating at the Little Chef, it would be the best on offer. Who should walk in as we were drinking coffee but John Price. As he passed our table, he said, 'You are getting the handle of that car, well done.'

'Thank you, John, it is my crew chief who makes it possible.'

'Derek, you and the ladies, it must be your beard they like!'

Monday morning was the big day, my first race in front of the huge crowd on the banked area alongside the track at Santa Pod. I had raced a street car in front of large crowds but the Altered was a different beast. So it was to be early to bed and early to rise. Phil Walker wouldn't be waking me up this time, the BMW would be loaded up ready to go before he fired up his Pontiac.

As Brenda was preparing the BMW to tow me to the start line, Colin and I jacked up the Altered onto its stands and fired the engine, it sounded good. The pit marshall gave us the 10-minute sign. Brenda tied the towrope onto the BMW and off we went down the fire-up road and within seconds it was my turn in the first round of eliminations.

As Tony Guy and I moved out of the fire-up road, John Price was in full flow over the public address speakers. 'Here we have last year's champions racing each other. Street ET champion, Derek Annable, in the ex-Fay Fischer Altered against last year's overall champion, Tony Guy, in his Ford 1932 Model B. Tony has dialled in 10.254, Derek 11.04.'

We pre-staged and staged together. My lights came down, Tony's following three-quarters of a second later and off we went. He must have pulled a good light, catching me 50 yards before the finishing line and crossing it first. It was his win.

Colin helped Brenda and I to load up the trailer and secure the car and said he would be at Avon Park on Saturday. All the way home my wife kept saying, 'What went wrong?' I didn't know, the car seemed to lose power at the top end of the track. John Turner would have to check the engine on Tuesday morning. However, nothing was found to be wrong, I would have to think hard next time. One's dial-in is critical in bracket racing.

Brenda phoned me at the garage, Colin wasn't able to come to Avon Park on Saturday. This meant we would have to take the trailer off the track every evening, so Brenda booked us in at the Brymbo in Mickleton where there was enough space at the rear of the house for us to park the trailer.

The racing on Saturday was the first in the Wild Bunch series. This group of racers was funded by Roy Wilding, John Guthrie and several other drivers who were interested in slingshots, Altered and dragsters, mostly with a nostalgia theme. The membership list soon grew to 100 interested parties, and a partial season was held in 1995 with a total of four events.

The Trailblazer Nationals was the first round of the 1996 Wild Bunch series. As we arrived in the pits, we were greeted by Chris Hartnell and Claire Meaddows. Claire was a bubbly lady full of enthusiasm and both were very friendly. I knew there and then I would have to make a choice between racing in the IHRA/UK National Championship or the Wild Bunch series. Let's see the results position after two full meetings in each.

In Wild Bunch, you pair with another racer and give your dial-in to them. At this meeting it was Pete Dickenson, in my case it was 11.35, now can I run quicker or slower? A percentage is taken of four runs. In effect, you race against yourself, two cars on the track is for spectator interest and allows as many cars possible going through on the day.

In my first run I was paired with Bob Hancove who was racing an interesting small block Ford Prefect, he ran mid-15s, this time I ran an 11.374 which I backed up later with a 11.734. Percentage-wise, it was a poor result. On Sunday I made one more run and called it a day, we would be back in a fortnight's time for the Spring Shake-up, round two of the Wild Bunch series. Let's get the car home for John to check the engine; something was wrong. Roy Wilding helped me put the race car into the trailer and it was home James and don't spare the horses.

Easter was over and Anglesey had become quiet again. This gave Brenda time to relax before she started planning for our next race meetings; 27/28 April, back with the Wild Bunch; 5/6 May, York; 11/12 May, Avon Park.

The Camaro was ready to race and I was eager to test the new camshaft, the power should be up and no need to worry about over-revving. You can't bounce valves in a engine fitted with a roller cam, the engine blows up instead and the rods go through the side of the block. John found one spark plug had a cracked insulator, was this the problem?

The next meeting was the Volksfest on 27/28 April on the renamed track, now called the Shakespeare County Raceway. See what happens when a certain gentleman called Keith Bartlett of Santa Pod Raceways decides which way drag racing in the UK should go. Keith is a racer turned promoter. We were allowed to enter the Camaro in the Volksfest, John Turner would drive it down to the track early on Saturday morning, I would be towing the trailer with the BMW. To make a change we were going to stay at the Houndshill Hotel, which was only eight miles from the track. Two cars, one driver, this wasn't allowed at the Pod, but the APIRA, thanks to Wendy Talbot, had agreed I could race both cars, which set a precedent after nearly thirty years of racing.

After an uneventful journey, we arrived at the track, parked the trailer in the Wild Bunch pit area and waited for Colin. He arrived on time and took charge of the race trailer, so we went to our hotel.

Great, we were staying at the Houndshill Hotel (our nickname for it was Hound of the Baskervilles). That evening, while waiting in the bar for our turn to eat, I could see out of the corner of my eye something moving. My eyesight being 100 per cent, I wondered what it was and took a quick look – it was two men touching each other. I thought 'what the hell have I let us in for?' It was a good job my wife couldn't see what was happening.

Meal over, we said goodnight to the owner and his wife. I thought, 'shit, the bed will have to be wedged against our bedroom door.' I sat up all night but Brenda was snoring her head off. It was 2am before the last car left the car park and because of the footsteps up and down the landing it was dawn before I fell asleep.

When we went down for breakfast the next morning we were greeted by a man straight out of the Adams family. It was a good, grease-free breakfast with plenty of toast and tea. I was glad to leave for the day's racing. My wife said to me, 'Strange man, a bit scary.'

When we arrived at the track, Colin had already got the race car out of the trailer, quickly Brenda and Colin placed the jack under the back axle and lifted the car onto its stands. After warming the engine for a couple of minutes, I went and signed on.

My first race was against Roy Wilding – a race that nearly cost me my race licence. We pre-staged and staged together but I left the start line first. Out of the corner of my eye I could see Roy hadn't launched, he must be broke, so as I crossed the finishing line I started to turn into the right-hand lane. Roy nearly hit the back of my car. When you are strapped into an Altered, you can only see forwards and approx 45° to the left and right, you don't know what's happening behind you.

The race director came to my pit and started to read me the riot act and asked why I had endangered the other racer. Then Roy came over and calmed the situation down, saying, 'Derek, don't worry, I would have put the trans brake on.' If he had, it would have broken his gearbox. The race director said, 'If it happens again, you'll never race again.'

Let's wait for John to arrive. There it was, the Camaro coming towards me with John behind the wheel. He had made good time. Young Glenn Stockton, the chief scrutineer, checked the car and passed it fit to race. My first run was to get the feel of the car again, and at 3.11pm on Saturday 27 April 1996, the car made its quickest run since we had bought it – 14.725 at 98.255mph – the power was breathtaking. Well done you young men of Anglesey who, with John's help, had fitted the roller camshaft. This was indeed going to be a weekend to remember and look back on.

Half an hour after that run in the Camaro, I was sitting in the Altered being towed to the start line. A good burnout, I was against Dave Graham, my ET 11.165, that was better. Run over, there was no time to return to the pits, John had brought the Camaro down the fire-up road for me to race Street ET. It was a good run.

Time to change cars again, now it was the Altered that required my attention. The ET this time was 11.197, both runs at 122mph, this should give me a good result percentage-wise.

This is when Mike Ellis came over to Brenda and asked if I could become Rookie Racer number one for the rest of the year, and she agreed. From now on Mike Ellis would be towing me to the start line on all three tracks. We returned to the hotel, had a quick meal and retired early.

Sunday morning was warm with a gentle breeze, everybody should get some good times today. Street ET cars were out first, the Camaro was performing well, a couple of mid-14s, now John could take the car back to Anglesey.

Claire Meaddows told Brenda the Wild Bunch would have four slots in the afternoon and my opponent was Chris Hartnell (her boyfriend) driving 'Backdraft'.

After a 10-minute wait in the fire-up road, it was the turn of Chris and me to race. Chris is a hungry young man out to prove to everybody he is a good racer, and with a silver suit and gas mask he looked the part. We both had a short burnout and Mike brought me back in to pre-stage. This part of drag racing is one hell of a ritual. The man walks in front of the car with both arms above his head, pointing left or right or together if you are reversing in a straight line, the object being to bring the back tyres over the fresh rubber it has laid down in the burnout. Mike was good at this.

I won the first run against Chris, his 11.753 at 119.245mph, mine 11.471 at 119.150mph. It was a close race. Pete had our dial-in, the winner was the one closest to his dial-in.

Next time I was against Dominic Irving who was driving a rear-engined dragster. My ET 11.568, Dominic's 13.344, I was falling off my time given to Pete, so I had to go quicker in the last two runs, over half a second quicker. This I did, beating Calvin Evans driving 'Moon Eyes' by nearly one and a half seconds. The curfew came down on the track and it was time for prize giving.

Of the 11 participants, I was number one, with Calvin Evans number two. Brenda was happy, it was the team's first win of the year, she kept polishing the trophy all the way home.

The team's next race was the Open Nationals, at York Raceway, part of the IHRA/UK Championship in which I was contesting the Modified ET class. Because Mike Ellis and Colin Cripps wouldn't be at the York track until Saturday morning, we would have to park the trailer in the Travelodge car park. When we arrived, reception told us there had been cars, and even trucks, stolen from outside properties in the area. Being on the main road between Hull and Leeds, South Cave was ideal for a quick getaway. I didn't get much sleep that night and was a tired racer in the morning.

Thank goodness it was only a short journey to the track. Mike was there with his family and their caravan so I parked our trailer alongside it. The weather forecast for Sunday was heavy showers, therefore we had better make the best of today's racing as tomorrow could be a washout. There was a three-car field in my class, which didn't make for an exciting weekend. As there were points for the championship, this had brought Nigel Payne all the way from London.

Between them, Brenda and Mike had decided I should shake the car down with three runs and try for top qualifier, which would give me a bye into the finals. My first run was a 10.975 on a 11.14, too quick, so we changed my dial-in to 10.84 and I ran a 10.711, not my day.

It wasn't Martin Holgate's either, he was getting excessive tyre shake over the last eighth mile and had to lift off. Nigel Payne driving 'Sticky Situation' was looking strong and became top qualifier. I broke my jinx, running a strong 10.964 on a 10.84 dial-in and the car felt good.

Mike Ellis was doing double duty, crewing for us and racing 'Pink Panther' in Street ET. Colin Cripps was spending most of his time taking photos of the bikers for the *Drag Racing Nuts* mag. Being late afternoon we locked the trailer and drove back to the Travelodge, had a quick meal, watched television for a couple of hours and went to bed.

Sunday morning was bright, with heavy clouds in the distance. Breakfast over and luggage loaded into the BMW, off we went, no hurry this morning, racing didn't start before 11am.

I was against Martin Holgate. I felt confident of a win, this would be my day. Martin had a bouncy ride all the way down the track, my win. Now it would be Nigel Payne and myself in the finals. Suddenly the heavens opened, thunder followed by a heavy downpour washed out the track. For three hours, the PDRC members worked on the track, every time they dried it out the rain came back, and in the end the meeting was cancelled.

I got 220 points and Nigel Payne collected 270 points towards the championship. Our next meeting would be in five days at Shakespeare County Raceway. We thanked Mike and Colin and drove away from a very wet track, and, as often happens, half an hour after we left, the sun came out, so we were told, and it was a glorious evening.

We were looking for a place to stay when visiting the Stratford-on-Avon area. Fosbroke House in Bidford-on-Avon looked promising. It was run by Lyn and Don Newbury and the price was right. Brenda booked a room for two nights.

The Powertest 96 was a two-day meeting and a round of the championship. All the main contenders would be there, thank goodness we would have a full crew. After a traffic-free journey from North Wales, we were at Long Marston in good time, parked the trailer and left Colin and Mike on ground duty while we investigated Fosbroke House.

The weather forecast wasn't good, rain on and off. It was afternoon before I had my first qualifying run but it was a good run, ET 10.937, I was number three qualifier, 60 extra points. Pete Austin was number one – end of our day's racing.

During the lull in racing, I asked Mike to explain Rookie Racers to me; he did try, but I lost the plot early on. We agreed he would give me a full printout of Rookie Racers at the next drag racing meeting. Brenda wanted to try the restaurant Lyn had told us about, so we left the track early.

The following morning, racing started dead on time, Mike Benlley in his Ford Sierra was my opponent. Mike pulled a red and it was my race. Now it started to rain again with no let-up – end of racing. The points gained at this meeting placed me second behind Nigel Payne in the Mod ET section of the championship. A good result at the next meeting on the 25/27 May at Santa Pod and the Thunder and Lightning team would be taken as a serious force, not just a couple of OAPs having a bit of fun.

There was a letter from Jeremy Clarkson in Wednesday morning's post. In an article in the *Sun*, he had compared an elderly driver to a 17-year-old driver who was at least two times over the legal limit. In my letter I said perhaps the old bloke trying to turn right out of Park Lane into Hyde Park Corner was a tourist who had lost his way in London. I went on to explain that all old people deserve some degree of respect. His reply was:

13-5-96

Dear Mr Annable

Thank you for your letter. You were not the only one to say I'm talking rubbish but the whole point of a column is to be controversial. Next week, who knows, you may agree with everything I say.

Best wishes.

Yours sincerely

Jeremy Clarkson

ps Thanks for the picture.

Big things were happening in drag racing. There was a new self-appointed captain at the helm of the UK section of European drag racing, Keith Bartlett – chief exec of PRC:

I would like to take this opportunity of introducing Power Racing Communications, the new owners of Santa Pod Raceway, to existing race fans and offer a warm welcome to all spectators who are visiting Santa Pod for the first time.

Many of you are aware of my own role between 1990 and 1994 in developing the European Top Fuel challenge series across the whole of Europe through RRM (Real Racing Management). It was the next stage of RRM's plans to acquire a major racetrack facility to enable not only RRM's overall plans to progress, but to also play a major role in assisting the growth of European drag racing.

The timing of this acquisition is vital in view of the new 'FIA' 1996 professional European drag racing championships in its first year as we seriously need to look at bringing the racetrack's facilities and standards to a much higher level.

You only have to look at other circuit and racing facilities, such as Silverstone and Brands Hatch, to see what drag racing has to achieve not only to attract bigger commercial sponsorships, but to offer the general public a better day out, and improved facilities and amenities. During the 1990s drag racing in Europe and in particular England has seen the actual racing classes develop and become exciting racing, however for those classes to grow into large fields, thus attracting much wider media coverage and bigger spectator audiences, they in turn need larger sponsorship. This will only be achieved when corporate sponsors can visit drag races which offer facilities to justify their overall plan. That needs to happen if drag racing is to move up to the next stage of its development. The only way that I could see the way forward to control and organise the racing as it should be done was to purchase the Santa Pod Raceway and to seek to co-promote the races at Avon Park Raceway. This would instantly eliminate the political scraps between promoters and rival factions all looking to control drag racing without the knowledge or experience to be able to fill that commitment and obligation. Although most of the race fans have not been aware of the promoter's attitude towards the sport over the past five years, the results and consequences are there for all to see. The only way to take full control and organise the sport was to acquire the racetracks. This was the strategy at the end of 1994 when I resigned as president of the EFTA (European Top Fuel Association). By the beginning of 1996 that has been achieved with both Santa Pod and Avon Park Raceway.

However we have a long way to go. Both racers and spectators must try to understand that our development programme here at Santa Pod cannot be done over night, or indeed in one year alone. We need to complete an investment programme, which will exceed £1.5m in the next 15 months alone.

This will commence with a new £100,000 racetrack surface being laid in 1996 and hopefully in time for the 'Cannonball' in early July. At the end of this season we intend to install 5,000 grandstands (US style) as well as a new tower block (subject to planning consent) and major pit improvements for all classes.

In the meantime you can finally go to the toilets for free, after five years of paying for the pleasure of a pee!

Finally, may I take this opportunity on behalf of the directors of Power Racing Communications Ltd to welcome you all to the Main Event and hope you enjoy your time at Santa Pod Raceway. Have a good weekend.

See you at the track.

Keith Bartlett

Brave words! We shall see for ourselves at the end of next week how good the new surface is.

A pit pass and crew tickets were posted to Colin. We left early on Saturday morning because the bank holiday traffic could be heavy. We had a good journey and arrived at the Santa Pod pits before both Mike and Colin. To save time in the morning I signed on. Mike had arrived by now, his usual active self, charging here and there. 'Ok, you two leave it to me, go and enjoy a meal.'

Thank goodness we had booked three weeks ago, as Barry Sheavills, his crew and all the top racers were staying at the Travelodge.

This was the big one of the big meetings of the year, so we left early because I wanted to have the car in the first session of scrutineering. Stuart Vincent was in charge, but luckily for me he gave the job of checking our car to one of his juniors, who was a happy, friendly guy.

There were 14 cars in Mod ET. In the first session of qualifying I was against Ray Guy, my ET was a bit off. Because Mike Ellis was racing in Street ET, Brenda decided we should put the car back into the trailer and visit some of the other racers in their pits. First call had to be the Jens Nybo pit, he was a Top Fuel driver and Brenda always got on well with Jens, they were like kindred spirits and would talk for hours about life and its ups and downs. Jens was thinking of driving in the touring cars championship and giving up drag racing. Brenda kept saying to him, 'Why do you want to drive those dinky toys?!'

Next we went to the Wild Bunch pits – they were running five cars on an exhibition basis for Keith Bartlett. Chris and Claire were very excited but had found out Bartlett wasn't going to pay them, but in the end, under pressure from Brenda, he did.

Sunday morning was much the same as Saturday, one qualifying run, again against Ray Guy, bad run for me and I dropped down the ladder. We couldn't get the car to go quicker than 118mph, ET 11.15. Mod ET finished early so I sat in the car reading *Rookie Racers, Drag Racing Team 1996*.

ROOKIE RACERS – Drag Racing Team
1996 Season Plan and Timetable
Prepared for R.B. Enterprises by Mike Ellis

Mission Statement
To continue to introduce drag racing to a wider cross-section of both the motor racing world and the general public. To show that the entry level of drag racing to be one of the cheapest and potentially one of the easiest to succeed in. To show that as well as being one of the friendliest forms of motorsport, it is also the form of motorsport that allows the widest choice of car and modification.

History of Team
Rookie Racers was set up and sponsored by R.B. Enterprises in 1994, to compete in the 1995 season in the Euro Challenge Series, racing a modified X1.9 with a standard 1500cc engine. Another car 'The Pink Panther' (a 2 ltr Capri) was prepared and raced during the second part of the season. Rookie Racers' number one driver, Mike Ellis, finished 7th with over 2500 points and was the highest placed rookie driver in his class. Two other cars were purchased and are being prepared.

1996 Team
Rookie Racers plan to compete in four classes with up to 12 cars consisting of both Rookie Racers cars and owner-driver cars. Present plan covers the following classes:

Pro ET	Bob Duncan	Red Baron	(Racing Coach)
Mod ET	Derek Annable	Thunder and Lightning	(Number 1 Driver)
Street ET	Mike Ellis	Silver Bullet	(Team Manager)
	A.N. Other	Green Machine	
Euro Challenge	Rookie Racers' Cars	Pink Panther, Yellow Dart, White Diamond	

| | Owner-driver Cars | Blue Tube, Purple Haze, White Diamond, Black Dash, Golden Bolt |

Personnel

Roger Blake	Managing Director, R.B. Enterprises
Bob Duncan	Administrator
Mike Ellis	Team Manager

Marketing

A leading marketing company will be engaged in a partnership agreement.

Merchandising

A partnership agreement will be presented to Drag Racing Nuts to supply and sell Rookie Racers merchandising, a 50% split of net profits being proposed.

Insurance

Insurance will be placed with the RACMSA newly appointed brokers, Bradstock of Manchester, with additional coverage being arranged via Rookie Racers for both Rookie Racers drivers and others in drag racing.

Video

A partnership agreement will be presented to Image Wizard of London (the newly appointed PR company for Santa Pod and York raceways).

Photography

A partnership agreement with a Kodak Photo Shop will be sought. Jody Wynne-Jones will be asked to become official photographer.

Facilities

- A large covered pits area in conjunction with Sunbrella will be sought.
- Caravans and tents will be hired for drivers and personnel.
- Catering will be arranged on a fund-raising basis with a small catering company.

Operating Plan

Rookie Racers Owner-drivers

The current plan allows for up to 10 Rookie Racers drivers with their own cars racing and sponsored by Rookie Racers. The team already has eight owner-drivers committed and available.

Rookie Racers Cars

Two cars are already available to compete in the Euro Challenge series.
The Silver Bullet has been upgraded to compete in the Street ET Championship.

Team Members

The positions of team manager, racing coach and number one driver are agreed in principle. Contracts are being prepared and will be confirmed during February for a 1 March start-up date. Other positions are being arranged and will be announced later.

Rookie Racers Recruiters

Up to 12 recruiters will be engaged on a no-cost basis to expand the membership of Rookie Racers and to sell raffle tickets etc.

... and so it went on. It was full of good ideas, but they would be difficult to sell. I offered my help and support, but no money, to Mike.

It was breakout time for me on Monday, the car went quick, very quick.

My opponent pulled a near perfect light and broke out by less than me, putting me down to sixth place in the championship. Nigel Payne was still leading, having collected maximum points. We drove home thinking things could only get better.

We had ten days to relax and try to make some money, then it would be off again, this time Shakespeare County Raceway and the fourth round of the championship. Now I must write some letters, firstly to Carla Pittau of *ETRA News*, a publication for the ET Racers Association, thanking her for publishing my letter.

THE ETRA NEWS IS YOUR NEWS AND VIEWS
WE ARE PUBLISHING BELOW A LETTER RECEIVED FROM DEREK ANNABLE REGARDING HIS VIEWS ON RESTORING THE PUBLICATION DRUK.

ANYBODY WISHING TO RESPOND TO HIS INVITATION AND EXPRESS THEIR OPINIONS ON THIS CAN FAX OR CALL ON 01407-710645 (phone) 01248-853677 (fax) OR WRITE TO HIM AT THE FOLLOWING ADDRESS :MOUNT VIEW, RHOSGOCH, AMLWCH, ANGLESEY LL66 0AR.

Derek is a full member of SPRC/PDRC/APIRA/BRDC.

TO BE OR NOT TO BE:

Should the UK Racers/Crew/Supporters of our sport of DRAG RACING have a publication for UK consumption?

DRAG RACING UK has filled this role up to issue 25 – March 1996. For reasons better known to certain individuals, this publication is no more.

At the present time, I am fighting a lone battle to restore DRAG RACING UK for all racers. Any input from ETRA members, whether it be for or against restoring our publication, is welcome.

Thank you.

Derek (MOD 613)

I passed on the feedback received to the general secretary of the Santa Pod Racers Club (SPRC):

---

29 May 96

Dear General Secretary

Re: DRAG RACING UK

I am receiving feedback from Racers/Crew to my request in *ETRA News* (May 96 edition).

The up-to-date position is as follows: certain people who were contributors to the publication before it was axed, would be reluctant to become involved again. Whether it was because of their choice of names or other reasons, they were unfairly accused of taking sides by the various factions and had their privacy invaded with constant phone calls ...

We bracket racers require a stable publication to keep us informed, as was the format of DRUK. Next time there should be a better balance, with contributions from every bracket. I hear you say, 'the publication would be the size of a telephone book'. Not the case, each bracket would be allowed columns not pages. Cost could be reduced by publishing four summer editions (open season APR/SEP) and two winter editions (closed season OCT/MAR), total cost to racers and others, say £10–£12 per annum. Each club to decide how to collect revenue for distribution to members.

Please pass on to the main parties involved.

Thank you

Derek (MOD 613)

That done, I sat there and wondered why drag racing was such a bitchy sport. Could it be a smoke screen to cover up the many shortcomings of certain factions involved in running it? The jealousy among the racers didn't help either. This was old-style class warfare.

I decided I would concentrate the team's effort on racing the Camaro in Street ET and the Altered in the Wild Bunch series, thus giving Brenda more time in her shop, July and August being busy months on Anglesey.

The Summer Nationals was a Keith Bartlett ego trip; PRC were running the meeting with, as he said, 'The largest field of professional race cars ever seen at the Shakespeare County Raceway. I know that for all the people involved in this racing facility it is going to be an historic occasion and one that they have all been waiting many years to see.'

We would stay at Fosbroke House. Mike Ellis phoned to say he would crew for us and he was bringing two friends with him to sell raffle tickets for Rookie Racers. The winner would race the 'Pink Panther' at the Pod in July.

There was a 12-car field in Mod ET, which included the Guy brothers, Nigel Payne, Pete Austin and Al Golding – there would be some close racing and a bucket of points for the winner. We were first out on Friday morning, my opponent was Ian Hook driving a 34 Ford-FBR. We both broke out, this put us on the bottom of the qualifying list. My next opponent was Simon Farmer, he didn't show, good run for me, 11.06 on a 10.84. End of racing and time to relax.

Mike Ellis went off selling raffle tickets, so Brenda and I went to the Top Fuel pits to see Jens Nybo. He was chasing the front runner in the European Championship and sported TF 1, the champ's number. There they were, laughing and joking, most of the jokes were about me and my beard. Jens said to Brenda whilst pointing at me, 'I saw him race, not bad for an old man!' More laughter. The crowd loved Jens; when spectators tried to speak to other Top Fuel and Alcohol drivers they were ignored, but Jens always had a few words with everybody.

One good thing about staying at Fosbroke House is that it is away from the main road. No traffic noise to wake you up at five o'clock in the morning, so we slept well and had a good breakfast.

Mod ET were first out again, this time I was against Tony Guy, I pulled a red and broke out 10.726 on a 10.84 and 122.371mph, the quickest the car had run. It would be four hours before our class of car was out again so it was time for the pit walkabout. Brenda went to talk to Helen Curran who rode a Suzuki GSX in the 9.90 bike class.

The next port of call was the Street ET pits to ask Phil Walker and Tracy how life was treating them. Parked alongside Phil's car was Gareth Mogford's car, a 78 Chevrolet Camaro with Moonraker on the side of the car. Brenda looked once, then twice, and turned to Gareth and said, 'Who do you think you are, James Bond?' Everybody laughed.

I left Brenda talking to Phil and Tracy, it was time for me to race again. This time I was alongside Lee Huxley driving 'Top Banana'. It was a win for me, with the car breaking its own record with a 10.696. What made this possible was my 60ft 1.558 – now I was really getting the handle of this car. Mike Ellis towed me back to the pits with his headlights flashing, the team Thunder and Lightning/Rookie Racers were showing promise.

Race day Sunday would be an 11am start. Mod ET had to be in the fire-up road by 11.30, as we were always a slick turn round on this track. My burnout complete, Mike saw me back to the start line and in the right-hand lane was Mike Bennett. We staged together, amber, amber, amber and we were off. I reached the eighth mile just ahead of Bennett's car. Both cars were travelling at the same speed until 50 yards from the finish, then Bennett gave his engine a squirt of nitrous and the car shot forward, increasing its speed from 100mph to 140mph in a couple of seconds. Trying to keep up with him, I broke out and it was his win.

Brenda was gutted. Mike Ellis helped us put the race car on the trailer and we left – neither of us speaking all the way home. We decided that evening that the Camaro would be my race car for the next two races. The Altered would only race with the Wild Bunch from now on. We had raced the Altered in four meetings in the Modified class and not one racer's wife had ever spoken to Brenda; they were a funny lot. I was told later on, 'Derek, they resent you and Brenda because you can go out and buy any car you want, also you have never built one.' Oh, and another thing, 'when racing, you two stay in hotels and not at the track in tents.'

From now on, we were going to enjoy our racing and life in general. Brenda reduced the hours she spent in her shop and I did the same at the garage.

The meeting at York Dragway was uneventful, on Saturday I ran three 14.80s, then a 14.72. In the afternoon session, things began to improve, a 14.55 followed by a 14.43. What was happening was that the car was going quick and it finished the day on a 14.389 at 99mph. At the end of qualifying on Sunday morning, the car had run a 14.243 at 101mph, the magic ton. I lost in the first round of eliminations, by virtue of a poor reaction time, so home we went.

On the calendar we had marked down six races between the 6 July and 11 August, five with the Camaro and one with the Altered. In that time the longest we would be at home between races was five days. We would treat this period more as a holiday than racing. Three nights at the Hind Hotel in Wellingborough would be very restful, so we booked.

Off down the A55 expressway we went. It was hot inside the Camaro, I hoped we wouldn't meet any traffic hold-ups. The Cannonball at the Pod was going to be a Rookie Racers team effort. David Williams had won the raffle and would be driving Mike Ellis's Capri 'Pink Panther'. Two cars entered meant Dave and myself must not meet in the first round of eliminations, we would have to be very careful with our qualifying times. The Camaro went like a dream and we arrived in Wellingborough by mid-afternoon.

When we drove into the pits, we were greeted by Mike Ellis who pitted us alongside his car. First it was a photo session for Rookie Racers' drivers and cars, five cars in all, as Mike had sold the idea to three new driver-owners. Then we had a speech from Roger Blake of RB Enterprises who were Rookie Racers' sponsors. It had taken Mike Ellis over six months to sell his idea to the public. New cars were joining the team at every meeting.

My wife was taking a back seat at this meeting and only helping when required. With a 13-car field in Street ET, Phil Walker and Paul Hudson were all fired up and chasing for top points. There was a new driver, Liz Waller, sporting a Kia Pride LX Saloon. Mark Gredzinski reported in the next edition of *Custom Car*, 'a lady doing blistering 18 second quarters in her Kia Pride'. Liz was Colin Catlin's girlfriend. Colin wasn't competing this time due to some trouble with his Escort race car.

There had been changes in the SPRC, Sue Gandaffi had been forced to resign as club secretary because the club thought there was some incorrect use of club funds with the previous track owner. Lesley Digby was now the club secretary, and this wasn't popular with the Supergrassers and other racers. Troubled times lay ahead for the club. Phil Evans was left to try and calm things down. One good thing about this meeting was the choice of race director. It was Jon Cross who was now a full-blown international race director, you can't get higher than that. His assistant was Darren Prentice, so it was going to be a well-run meeting.

Amos Meekins passed my car A1 but there was some problem with the other Rookie Racers' cars, the rule book said no blacked-out windows. I ran a 14.40 and 14.30 in the first practice session and followed this up with a brace of 14.36s, one against Dave Williams and the other against Cliff Pullman.

In the first round of eliminations, I was against Dave Parrott, a nice lad who enjoyed his racing, who was driving a Ford Popular 100E in which he had installed a 3½-litre Buick engine. He broke on the line, so it was my win. My opponent in the next round was Martin Lewis driving his Nova. He dialled in at 17.00, my dial-in was 14.36. Being bracket racing, I had to wait on the start line for over two and a half seconds before I could start chasing him. We crossed the finishing line together and the winner's light came on in Martin's lane. I had lost by $^3/_{100}$ of a second, or as John Price in the tower said, 'the race was won on the start line'. Martin had pulled a better light, $^1/_{10}$ of a second better.

Mike Ellis was pleased, a quarter-page photo of 'Pink Panther' in *Custom Car*. The Thunder and Lightning team had raked in some points for Rookie Racers. We said goodbye to Mike and the other racers and went home.

Things were going to get hectic for the Thunder and Lightning team, the Bug Jam in two weeks, followed by a meeting every weekend for the next three weeks. We had been invited to race at the VW boys' meeting. The quicker cars could run 10-second passes, reaching 100mph in less than seven seconds. Their power plants were highly tuned Porsche engines.

We travelled down with the North Wales gang, headed by Dafydd Hughes. It was a one-day meet for me, two practice runs, a 14.65 and 14.64 followed by qualifying in the afternoon. In this session I was against car 354, my time 14.635 on a dial-in of 14.63 made me number one qualifier. Eliminations started at six o'clock and I was against a 19-second car, which had a 5-second start on me. It was disappearing into the sunset before I left the start line, yet both cars crossed the finishing line together. I had gone too quick by $^9/_{1000}$ of a second. That is drag racing! We wished Dafydd good luck with his racing and went home.

Round six of the Wild Bunch series was on 27 July, and the Altered was going to get an airing this time. And that's all it got, the event was rained off after two practice runs, one against Calvin Evans, the other Tony Hornby.

Next time I would drive the Camaro in the Dash for Cash at Santa Pod on 3/4 August. There was some big money to be won here, so the SPRC newsletter said, big field, big money. But when we arrived at the racetrack and looked around the pits, I thought they had cancelled the meeting. Where were the cars? Half a dozen here and there and in the distance a couple more. I had the track to myself for the first hour or so and, as it turned out, beyond.

We were staying at High View Hotel this time, so Brenda said, 'This is a waste of time, where are the hundreds of cars the club said would be here? Let's go and eat.' We made up for a boring day by having a curry feast.

Chinese people had taken over the High View Hotel. At this time the British government were handing back Hong Kong to China and Chinese businesspeople were flooding into the UK before the handover and snapping up any type of small business that was for sale. We were coming back to the Pod in five days' time so we booked a room for one night.

On race day everybody paid their money into a big pot. I won the first four rounds, now it was between Sarah Day driving the blue Hampster car and me in Thunder and Lightning. Everyone was rooting for Sarah. Off Sarah went and after what seemed like an hour I went after her car. Brenda was at the start line, everybody except her was shouting, 'Go on, Sarah, quicker Sarah, he is catching you, you must win.' When my win light came on, there was complete silence. People were shaking their heads in disgust because I had won the pot of money (the perception being that I was already rich!).

After four days at home, it was time to leave for the next two race meetings. Saturday we would be racing in the Bug Stock at Santa Pod, staying overnight in a motorway service area, followed by Sunday in the North Star Nats at York Dragway.

Here we were back at the Pod with typical British summer weather, rain and more rain followed by a few dry spells. It was nearly one o'clock before the practice runs could get started, and after an hour we went straight into qualifying. The Camaro was down on power but we managed a 14.81 on a 14.79. We were number one qualifier. My next run was against Rick Jolley and this time I broke out 14.56 on a 14.79, the power was a bit up and down. Brenda took a chance and put 14.70 on the back of the car.

I enjoyed the elimination, first round a win, second round a win against Gary Alce. We both broke out, me by the least. I followed this up with a win in the finals by $\frac{3}{100}$ of a second. My wife enjoyed the prize giving, and the later photo in the club newsletter of me receiving the cup. It was getting dark and we had a long drive to our overnight stop.

When we arrived at York Dragway the next morning, I could see Mike Ellis was already out, charging up the track in his 'Pink Panther'. Brenda went to talk to Jean Rownthwaite, the PDRC secretary, and then went to Dave Allen's pit. I was now ready to have a practice run against the 'Pink Panther', Mike loved it, trying to catch the Camaro. Colin Cripps was busy taking photographs and selling them to the racers.

After lunch it was Street ET eliminations, my opponent was Liz Waller who had dialled in 18.39, while mine was 14.70. We were held up by the weather, sitting in your car on the start line for half an hour isn't my idea of fun. When racing did start, I lost by $\frac{6}{1000}$ of a second to Liz. Brenda was upset and asked me why I always let the slower car win!

Mike said he would see us at the Summer Nationals at Santa Pod in two weeks' time. Dave Williams would be racing his girlfriend's car this time and Mike was racing the 'Pink Panther'. We thanked Mike and Colin and set off for home.

Four weeks of hectic racing and thousands of miles to and from the tracks were taking their toll. Brenda was looking tired and was smoking like a chimney. I arranged with our daughter to look after the shop for a week while her mother rested at home. The weather was warm with plenty of sunshine, so Brenda enjoyed some sunbathing.

Meanwhile, John and I checked out the Altered and fine-tuned the engine. Now I knew the car was ready to race, I booked a double room for three nights at High View Hotel.

Santa Pod here we come. My wife was her usual busy self, the rest had done her good. With the trailer parked in the pit area at the Pod and Mike to look after it, High View here we come. What a curry feast we had that evening

During breakfast, who should come into the dining room, but Paul and Fay Fischer. They didn't know what to say when they passed our table, 'Uh, good morning, Derek and Brenda. How are you?'

'Well, thank you Paul.' We finished our breakfast, and, on leaving, Brenda said to Fay, 'Derek is racing your old car tomorrow and is running some good times, see you both on the track.'

Fay Fischer was racing Lucky Fisch II in Super Pro ET and had a sponsor called the Big Bus Company of London and a crewman called Cliff Pett who had crewed for various top racers. He had never impressed me as a knowledgeable engine man. Fay Fischer was trying to make her mark in Super Pro ET and an engine man made the team look good.

When we bought the Altered from the Fischers, they didn't know I was going to be the driver. When Paul found out, he phoned Brenda and said, 'I don't want the other racers thinking we have forced an old-age pensioner to buy the car, I shall send Derek his cheque back.' Brenda was angry and never forgave Paul for that insult to me.

The Summer Nationals at Santa Pod are best forgotten. On Saturday I raced against Nigel Payne, no more racing that day. Sunday was the same, this time it was Simon Farmer who took the honours. It didn't get any better on the day of eliminations, I lost to Al Golding because I broke out first.

Drag bracket racing can be confusing to the paying public, as they can't understand why the car which crossed the finishing line first isn't the winner. When they pay £60 to watch a weekend's racing, they want to see the winner not some mathematical formula.

The only thing that turned a disaster into a pleasure was watching Phil Evans race his father's Singer Vogue in Street ET, now there is an old car. The record books show Phil had won many championships of yesteryear with this car. I can remember Phil saying to Brenda, 'Brenda, I would love to do what Derek is doing, driving street cars on the track, and the Altered and now a Top Alcohol dragster.'

Brenda replied, 'Why don't you, Phil, you are fifteen years younger than Derek and have more money than us.' He had no reply to that question. It all boils down to commitment, as Gary Baldy said. 'The Annables are 100% committed to the sport, come what may they will be there fighting their corner and nothing will stop them.' He was right, we race because life is a challenge.

The Altered was entered in two more meetings, The Hot Rod Drags with the Wild Bunch on 7/8 September and the World Finals at Santa Pod on 13–15 September. Brenda wanted the team Thunder and Lightning to finish the year on a high and I was determined she was going to be a happy lady. Most days of that week John and I brought the Altered out of the garage and tested it, much to the annoyance of the local people. You could hear that engine fire up two miles away. When we knew the performance of the engine couldn't be improved, the car was put onto the trailer, secured down and it was ready to race at the Hot Rod Drags.

When we arrived at the track on Friday evening, Colin was waiting for us. Instead of a tent to sleep in, he had a camper that the trailer could be parked alongside. This gave the team a professional look and Colin looked the part, sporting the team colours.

It was late on Saturday before the Wild Bunch cars had a run. I gave Pete Dickenson my dial-in 11.04 and paid the fee. No Mike this time, so Brenda towed me to the start line, a good run, 11.079. I needed a quicker run next time, a 11.00 would be perfect. After a two-hour wait, we went out again. This time the car picked up speed midway down the track, my ET was 10.846. Thank goodness the quick time was today. Now I shall set the car to run a brace of 10.80 and with luck we will go home with a trophy.

We were staying at Fosbroke House. Lyn and Don cooked us an evening meal this time, it saved walking to the pub, and Colin joined us, he bought the wine. After an enjoyable meal, the three of us sat in the lounge drinking coffee and talking Drag Racing Nuts. Colin told us about all the new ideas they had to help up-and-coming racers and the many championships they were going to sponsor next year. Time for bed and Colin left.

The weather on Sunday was perfect for drag racing, lots of oxygen. I had been paired against Mick White, we both ran good times, mine was a 10.895, then after an hour and a half I was out on the track again, this time my opponent was Paul Marsden. After a good burnout, Brenda brought me back to the start line, both cars staged together and the lights came down, a pro tree, green light on, we launched together. My head went back, it was a hard launch, Paul crossed the finishing line first, his win.

When I got back to the pits, Colin was all excited, 'Derek, your 60ft was a 1.059.' Only Top Fuel and Alcohol cars are quicker, my ET was 10.309, the quickest the car had ever been without nitrous. Even Fay Fischer had never had a 60ft and ET as quick as mine. This was a timing ticket to be treasured. It did spoil my chances of a trophy but what's a trophy compared to that timing ticket. I had joined the select few who had a sub-1.100 60ft launch.

We drove home well pleased with the day's racing. The World Finals were at Santa Pod at the end of the week, and with the car performing like this, it would be look out the Guy brothers, Nigel Payne and the other racers in the Modified class.

Now I was home, my first priority was to thank our daughter for looking after the shop and ask her to carry on until after the World Final at the Pod. She agreed. Our room at the Travelodge was booked, the car in good shape and we had a full crew, so I was confident of a good result.

To the tunc of 'Happy Wanderer', we set off for the Pod and arrived at five o'clock. The pit area was busy. Trailer parked, I gave Mike the keys. He kept going on about an article in the World's Final official magazine. Brenda said she would read it that night.

Thank goodness we had booked a room. The Travelodge was full, Anita Makale and her crew were staying there, also John Price and Graham Beck-with. Now let's read this article Mike was on about:

BBC 'TOP GEAR' TEST DRIVE

For those of you who missed last weeks edition of BBC Top Gear, here's an insight on what went on!!

We finally did it! We got the famous Tiff Needell, presenter of the BBC's Top Gear TV show, into Peter Lantz's Top Fuel dragster. Understandably it wasn't something he was looking forward to!

The plan was not to throw Tiff in at the deep end but gradually build up his experience of coping with the power and complexities of driving the quarter mile. The first step was to drive Peter Lane's 'Super Gas' Chevy Camaro, which Peter very kindly made available at short notice. After Peter had talked through the controls and various driving techniques, Tiff was ready for his first run of the day. He managed just over 100mph taking it very steady. He was then ready for a full pass after a gentle getaway and achieved a creditable 136mph in 10.77 seconds.

At this stage Tiff was pleased with his results, however, the next step up to Neil Taylor's Chevy Lumina Pro Modified car was going to be a very different story – almost 4 times the power and more levers and buttons to push or pull than anything he's seen before! Neil had installed a passenger seat in the car, so Tiff was strapped in securely and ready to go. This is when Tiff began to realise just how much there was to learn. Neil's run with Tiff on board was just amazing! After a huge long, smoky burnout, the car moved into stage, onto the rev limited and was gone! the time – 7.40 seconds at 188mph!!!! We believe this to be the fastest ever passenger ride down the quarter mile. Tiff's heartbeat monitor had jumped from the normal 68 up to a peak of 202 during the run. It was then that Tiff thanked Neil for the ride as thoughts of actually driving the car disappeared, too much to learn in the short time available. His thoughts of driving the Top Fuel car were that although it was more than twice as powerful as the Pro Mod there was actually far less to do in the cockpit. It was his plan after instructions from Peter Lantz just to slam the throttle down for a couple of seconds. The throttle has to be fully on or off and there's no going back on the throttle once you have lifted or the engine could be seriously damaged, so with the burnout completed he was on the line and ready to go. The tree light had been green for a long time as Tiff prepared himself to 'hit it'. When he did, the sheer violence of noise and acceleration were so great that his foot was forced off the throttle and his heartbeat leapt to 211!! Tiff didn't feel the full force but did go 0 to 60mph in 1.5 seconds. He also now has a very clear understanding of just what it takes. No more 'just a quarter mile straight, what's difficult about that?'

Thanks to Tiff Needell and all the BBC crew for taking the time to do this first in-depth feature. Also a very big thank you to Peter Lane, Neil Taylor, Peter Lantz and their crews.

Yes, true, that's drag racing, we are the G-force boys!

Modified ET were out early and I was paired with Simon Farmer in the first qualifying session, he ran a 10.54 ET, mine was 10.82. The big cars were out next and it would be three hours before our class were to run again.

My wife had gone to see Jens Nybo and the other drivers in the Top Fuel pits so I went over to talk to Gerard Demont who was racing a 23 Ford T Altered called 'Diable'. As it was the first time he had raced at the Pod, I agreed to show him the ropes and race against him in the morning.

Now Mike Ellis was shouting, 'Derek, you are the next out. Hurry or you will miss your turn.' When we got the car to the bottom of the fire-up road and turned into the pairing lanes, Simon Farmer had already burnt out and was reversing back to the start line and ready to pre-stage. I shot through the water with smoke coming from my tyres, Mike running behind me, as I backed up to the start line, where the start line marshall, Ian Marshall, was pointing at me and his watch and then back at the fire-up road. I got the message, 'Watch it or you are out.' I had dived in late and without his permission. It was Simon's win, I broke out. Tomorrow is another day.

Yes it was. Gerard Demont was waiting for me on the start line at 10am. Ian the start line marshall took one look at me and lifted his head to the sky. Gerard had a good launch and we were neck and neck to the eighth mile, then Gerard lost power and slowed – a good time for me, 10.79 on a 10.64 dial-in. When I got back to the pits, my wife said, 'You should have heard John Price and Graham laughing at you because you had dialled in 10.64. They said "He doesn't think the car will go that quick, he must be getting old."'

I soon stopped their laughing, as on the next qualifying run, my ET was 10.66 on a 10.64. Bad luck followed Gerard, his car broke on the line, so no more racing for him. Mike and Brenda were already planning tomorrow's racing. Had we got enough fuel? What tyre pressure to have if it was a hot day? All this preparation was necessary, we were on a 9am call-out.

We had an early meal and as we were finishing, John Price and Graham walked in. John said, 'Some quick times today, Derek, car going well.'

'Thank you, John', and we left them ordering beefburgers and wine.

One thing about staying at a Travelodge is the other guests are quiet and you get a good night's sleep. We had our suitcases packed by 7am and I had a cooked breakfast. Here is Mark Gredzinski's report of the Mod ET finals in *Custom Car*:

Tony Guy took the Mod ET Championship title for the second year running by qualifying number one and going all the way to the finals. Derek Annable was significant in taking number two points man Nigel

Payne, out in the first round, Nigel being three tenths down on his usual reaction times and both cars running 10.82s. Derek's Thunder and Lightning Model T Altered then got past Peter Austin's Pink Cuda when he broke out. Derek bested Ray Guy in a reaction time shoot out 0.553 to 0.664 to go through to the finals against Tony Guy.

In the final Derek and Tony both lit red but Derek by the larger margin thus handing the win to Tony. Double gutting for Derek as Tony went on to break out.

Below this write up was a picture of me and the car on the start line.

Mike and Brenda were pulling their hair out, it should have been my win, Tony Guy was having problems with his car. I knew that to win against Tony, who was always sharp on the lights, I had to pull a near perfect light, 0.560 wouldn't have been good enough to beat him.

Now we had to stay for prize giving. Mike Ellis had gone home leaving Colin to help Brenda and me load the race car onto the trailer. It was too late to drive home, so when I had collected my trophy, we would make a dash to have something to eat at the Little Chef before it closed at ten o'clock.

We made it with ten minutes to spare. I parked the trailer, leaving Brenda sorting a few things out, and ran in to order our food. Five minutes went by, no Brenda, where was she? Then I heard a lady tell one of the staff that someone appeared to be in trouble in the ladies' toilet. After some five minutes, I was asked to help open the door, but as it wouldn't budge I climbed onto a chair and looked over the top of the door. Oh no! It was Brenda, collapsed on the floor. The manageress shouted to us that an ambulance was on its way and after ten minutes it arrived.

The paramedics broke the door hinges and lifted the door off. They didn't move Brenda but pounded her chest and resuscitated her. When she was stable, they carried her to the ambulance and we went to Kettering hospital. What a journey, Brenda kept drifting away and they nearly lost her. I am sure at one stage they injected straight into her heart. Then the ambulance stopped and the driver came to help the other paramedic. After a few minutes they said to me, 'Sir, we are losing her, please talk to her, say anything, your voice may make her respond.'

Then one turned to me and asked, 'how many years have you been married to the lady?'

I replied, 'forty-five years'.

'Good, start shouting at her.'

I thought 'what?' then it came to me, 'Brenda, quick, we have to get the car to the startline, bloody wake up.'

It worked, her arm started twitching, one paramedic whispered, 'keep shouting, I only want her to hear your voice.'

I shouted the same words again and again, the driver said, 'your wife is responding.' He gave me the thumbs up then got back into the cab and drove to the hospital.

What a night. After four hours in the hospital's specialist stroke unit, they had Brenda stable and told me to come back in the morning. After a couple of hours' sleep, I returned. Brenda was quite poorly, she could not speak and was on a drip. The only part of her body she could move were her eyelids. The doctor in charge explained that the next five days were crucial and that I should go home and return with some of my wife's belongings.

Then followed a nightmare of worry and travelling backwards and forwards to Kettering. I would know every inch of that road before my wife was transferred to a Welsh hospital. I phoned our relatives and friends. Colin said he would visit Brenda in hospital at the end of next week. I had cancelled the room that was booked at High View Hotel. When I told the Chinese lady how ill my wife was, she said she would keep a room for me until Brenda left hospital. What a kind woman. Now I could visit Brenda in hospital any day of the week, stay with her all afternoon and evening and return the following morning before I drove home.

Now it was time for Colin's visit. I had warned Brenda he was coming on Saturday morning to see her. She had been in hospital for nearly a fortnight and could grunt a few words and move her hands. When Colin and I arrived, Brenda was upset, the lady in the bed opposite had died during the night. We soon cheered her up, Colin used our camcorder to take pictures of all the get-well cards from the Wild Bunch drivers and their wives. Wendy Talbot and other APIRA officials had sent flowers and other goodies. Brenda was a little more cheerful when we left.

Unknown to Brenda, I was racing her BMW at Santa Pod that weekend. It was a big bracket race for all types of cars which ran times as slow as 19 seconds and as quick as 10 seconds. There were only two things worth reporting that weekend. One was that it rained nearly all the time, the other was that Carla Pittau crashed her car 'Heaven & Hell', putting it out of action well into next year. One or two racers said that it was time for her to give up racing, I soon took them to task. There was a force ten gale blowing and the wind caught the car mid-track and put it into the wall. Added to this, Carla was overworked, trying to look after ETRA business, and unlike me she wouldn't complain about the workload.

Brenda was making good progress, and the doctors at Kettering arranged to transfer her to Llandudno. This was better all round as I could be at the hospital in an hour if need be.

The last round of the Wild Bunch series was on Saturday at the Shakespeare County track and Colin said he would be there if I wanted him to help. I didn't want to go but Brenda insisted I race for the points on offer, and I was to phone the hospital every evening. So I arranged to stay at the Houndshill for the two nights; it would be easier as I could eat in the restaurant and use their telephone to keep in touch with Brenda.

How time flies, it was Friday and I was on my way. When I arrived at the track, I was greeted by Roy Wilding and Angie – questions and more questions about Brenda. By now there were many racers asking the same questions, and they were all pleased she was improving. I thanked them for their cards and flowers. Trailer made safe, I drove to the Houndshill as I wanted to phone the hospital and give Brenda my love. After a good night's sleep and breakfast, I was back at the track for nine o'clock.

Time to sign on, more questions from Wendy Talbot and the club officials about Brenda's progress. I felt humble, these were a great bunch of people. It would be one practice run today. I used my dial-in from the last race. The car ran slow, so I changed it to 10.88 for the afternoon racing. I should have left it as it was, I ran a 10.76 at 122mph. My next run was against Trev Merrett, this time my ET was 10.921 at 122mph, a near perfect average. End of racing for the day, Colin and I put the race car back on the trailer and I drove to the hotel. I phoned the hospital, who said Brenda was improving and starting to sleep through the night – a sign of a good recovery.

No need to rush my breakfast the following morning, it was raining. I checked out of the hotel and drove to the track, thinking, all this way and no racing. Then, as I turned off the main road and into the raceway road, the rain stopped and the sky cleared. It was nearly one o'clock before Bruno and his gang had the track ready for racing.

My first opponent was Wendy Baker driving her car, 'Northern Star'. It was a win for me, ET 10.89 at 123.763mph, the quickest mph I had run. Three o'clock and my last opponent was Roy Wilding in 'Chariots of Fire'. He pulled a good light and crossed the finishing line first. When I got back to the pits, Colin was going mad with joy. 'Derek, look at your timing ticket, ET 10.880 on a dial-in of 10.880. Terminal speed 124.591, a record.'

I collected two awards, closest to dial-in and the winner's trophy, Night of Fire. Because of my wife's illness, this would be my last race with the Wild Bunch and the end of team Thunder and Lightning. I said my last goodbyes to a great gang of racers. On the journey home, I was full of joy and much sadness. It would be late before I arrived at our garage and could phone the hospital. When I did phone, Brenda already knew of my success, Colin had spoken to her on her bedside telephone.

On Monday I drove to the hospital with some presents for Brenda. Her speech had started to come back, a few slurred words came out of the side of her mouth. She was happy to see me and full of emotion. A nurse gave her something to calm the trembling in her body, then came these words, 'Der-r-rek, th-e-e, r-acing.' She managed 'racing' very well. When I told her what had happened, I could see the excitement in her eyes and the tears started to flow down her face, her paralysed mouth was trying to smile. A nurse said, 'Mr Annable, it's time to leave.' I gave my wife a big hug.

Every day that week I visited my wife and took her some goodies, as she hated the hospital food. On one of my visits the Indian doctor in charge of stroke patients explained to me that he was happy with my wife's progress and he would carry out some more tests on her. He was a marvellous doctor. Brenda was being taught how to get out of bed and stand up, and her speech was improving in leaps and bounds.

One visiting day I decided to give the Camaro a test run. Having difficulty finding space for such a big car in the hospital car park, I drove round and round until a space became free. When I walked into the ward my wife was standing up and holding onto the bed. 'Derek, take me to the window, I want to see the Camaro again. It's so long since I have seen our race car.' We sat on her bed talking, then it was time for me to leave. I kissed and hugged her and joined the visitors for the long walk back to the car park.

The Camaro was parked facing the back of the hospital. I fired up the engine. In the distance, I could see three people standing at a window on the second floor. As I drove past I could see it was Brenda, with two nurses holding her up. Tears were streaming down her face, I blipped the engine and roared off.

What to do with our shop? Lynne, our daughter, was standing in for her mother, but this couldn't carry on forever, and in time Brenda would have to decide whether to close the shop for good. Lynne was prepared to carry on until the Christmas sales were over, then she would come in part time.

Now it was time for the meeting at the hospital, with the doctor, the head nurse and an admin lady. Everybody agreed it was a good report and progress was better than normal, my wife's strong will and her determination to get well enough to take charge of the Thunder and Lightning team again was the main factor in her good progress. The big question was, were they going to allow her to have a two-day release from the hospital? Brenda had set her heart on going to the Flame and Thunder meeting on 2/3 November. The doctor said, 'Yes,' but I would have to make special arrangements. The admin lady said, 'No!' There was a standoff.

Brenda was more like her old self, she turned to the admin lady and said, 'If you say no once more, I shall get my husband to take me home this very minute.' There was silence, until the doctor said, 'Mrs Annable, I like your spirit, you can go, but I want you back on Sunday afternoon.'

Success, the Thunder and Lightning team were back in business, and Brenda was over the moon. I had less than a week to arrange everything. I phoned Mike Ellis, who said he would bring his caravan for Brenda and Colin Cripps said he would bring a wheelchair. The hospital were supplying one for her to use at the Travelodge, this would get her to the Little Chef and back. Thus, the disabled room was booked and everything was ready for the trip.

I collected Brenda from the hospital and we had a good journey with little traffic. When we arrived at the Travelodge it was straight to bed for my wife, then I went to get some food for us to eat in the bedroom.

After a good night, it was time to take Brenda to Santa Pod. Colin helped Brenda into the wheelchair and took her to Mike's caravan. Now I could sign on and get in a qualifying run before lunch. After that run it started to rain and it was two o'clock before racing started again. Everybody managed a qualifying run and the eliminations started, a win for me. As the street ET cars finished their first round of eliminations, the rain came back, and the fire-up road was full of race cars. Unable to dry the track, the meeting was cancelled at seven o'clock. There were three club stewards in charge of the meeting, Phil Evans, who was racing, Carol Ismail and Lesley Digby. The points I had gained put me in a strong position in the club championship, so I asked Carol Ismail if the points gained at today's meeting counted towards the championship. She said 'Yes, as all the cars have had at least one qualifying run.'

Mike's friend had looked after Brenda, with Colin providing the food and it was now time to take her back to the Travelodge. This time we ate in the restaurant, and we were very well looked after as one of the staff remembered the night of Brenda's stroke.

I did get Brenda back to the hospital on time and was told that a transfer to Cefni hospital in Llangefni had been arranged and they would be moving her by ambulance in three days' time.

Her stay there was not a pleasant one, so we thought it would be better if she came home. She had spent long enough in hospital. Next week it would be Christmas and it was time to reflect on what could have been.

The results of the Flame and Thunder meeting arrived in the post. They had disallowed all the points at the meeting. This started me on a journey of no return with the club. First through Phil Evans and the RAC, Mike Ellis took up the gauntlet because I was a Rookie Racer. The battle lasted for months. Carol Ismail and Lesley Digby resigned from the club committee and everything rumbled on and on. I made some bitter enemies and they made my future racing at Santa Pod unpleasant to say the least.

Christmas is my favourite time of year. We were celebrating Brenda's sixty-third birthday and I noticed in a magazine that Barry Sheavills had his Top Alcohol dragster, 'Stagecoach', up for sale. I turned to Brenda and said, 'How would you like Barry Sheavills' dragster as a birthday present?'

She replied, 'Pigs will fly.'

'No, Brenda, I am serious, you can't crew any more, the Altered will have to be sold, the Camaro is redundant and I have £15,000 doing nothing.'

She said, 'You? Top Alcohol?'

'Yes, Brenda. Me. Top Alcohol. Why not?'

Race-wise, it had been a good year, and we had achieved the following:

The Altered
6th from 23 in the IHRA Drag Racing Championship
Runner-up in the World Finals
4th in the Wild Bunch series
Winner of the Spring Shakedown
Winner of the Night of Fire trophy
Closest to Dial-in 10.880 on a 10.880

Camaro
20th from 40+ cars in the IHRA Street ET Championship
12th from 30+ cars in the PDRC Championship
Winner of the Santa Pod Dash for Cash
Winner of the third round of the SPRC Divisional Championship
Runner-up in the Finals of the Championship

And the greatest prize of all, my wife was still alive. What more can any man ask? The future looked good for us.

Below: Avon Park, Trailblazer Nationals (© Colin Cripps)

Santa Pod, Easter Meeting, against Pete Austin (© Colin Cripps)

Below: *Avon Park, Roy Wilding's 'Chariot of Fire' (© Wild Bunch);* bottom: *Avon Park, Chris Hartnell's 'Backdraft' – Derek's opponent (© Wild Bunch)*

Inset and below: *Santa Pod, May Meeting*
(© Colin Cripps)

Derek with Brenda, crew and tow car (© Colin Cripps)

Summer Nationals, Avon Park (© Colin Cripps)

Summer Nationals, Avon Park: Mike Ellis taking me back to the start line (© Colin Cripps)

York Dragway (© Derek Annable)

York Dragway
(© Colin Cripps)

Santa Pod: 'Cannonball', start line
with Mike Ellis (© Colin Cripps)

York: Derek lost by ⁶/1000 of a second to Liz (© Colin Catlin)

*York Dragway 1996,
Derek Annable
(© Colin Cripps)*

York: Derek's opponent was Liz Waller (© Colin Catlin)

*Santa Pod, Summer Nationals: Phil Evans racing
his Singer Vogue (© Phillip Evans)*

Avon Park, Hot Rod Drags (© Colin Cripps)

Santa Pod 1996, World Finals: Phil Walker becomes Street ET champion
(© Phil Walker)

Santa Pod: Carla Pittau
(© Carla Pittau)

Avon Park: Brenda
insisted Derek should race
(© Wild Bunch)

Santa Pod, Flame & Thunder: Phil Evans was racing (© Phillip Evans)

Santa Pod: Brenda's BMW, Mike's
caravan, Flame & Thunder
(© Derek Annable)

Cefni hospital, Llangefni
(© Brian Staines)

CHAPTER 6

The Crossroads (1997)

The alterations to my wife's bedroom were now complete. The shower cubicle, grab rails and other aids would make life more comfortable for her.

She had agreed we buy Barry Sheavills' dragster and because I am a soft touch when it comes to buying and selling, she took charge of the negotiations.

Her phone call to Carlton TV Studios in Nottingham was put through to Barry. After twenty minutes of 'Yes, Barry … No, Barry', she turned to me and said, 'It's ours, get your cheque book out. He has agreed to a £5,000 deposit and the balance in March.'

So off went the following letter:

---

5 February 1997

Dear Barry

As agreed with you today, on the phone, I enclose my cheque for £5,000.00 as a deposit on the purchase of your Top Alcohol dragster as per advert in the SPRC Newsletter, Issue 2, Jan 97.

The balance of £20,000.00 to follow next month Mar 97.

Thank you for your offer to help find crew and run through the finer points of racing the car with Derek.

Brenda

Before we had time to take a second breath back came his reply:

Sunday 16 Feb

Hi Brenda & Derek

Hope you are both well.

Just a quick note to keep you in touch with progress my end.

I have spoken to Steve Turner, crew chief of the Turner Racing Top Alcohol dragster. He has agreed to look out for crew members. But, he will also crew chief your car for a couple of meetings, and hopefully train up your own crew. (PS I would be on the look out yourselves for local crew members who could work on the car away from the track.)

I have also enclosed my original For Sale Flyer which gives you some history of the car and parts. Also enclosed is a list of spares I have plus an information sheet and photos.

I am in and out of the office for the next couple of weeks but if you want to ring me try my mobile and leave a message if it's switched off. Steve Turner has given me his mobile number and is expecting a call from you in the near future.

That's it for now.

Regards

Barry

ANGLO AMERICAN RACING STUDIO GARAGE
CARLTON TV STUDIOS NOTTINGHAM

FOR SALE
COMPLETE RACING OPERATION
READY TO FIRE UP & RUN A LOW 6 OR 5sec PASS

275 inch HAUSER DRAGSTER CHASSIS BUILT IN 1994 NEW REAR HALF IN 1995, NEW FRONT HALF IN 1996, ALWAYS HOOKS UP HARD AND RUNS STRAIGHT, 3RD MEMBER OF THE EUROPEAN 5sec CLUB, 1ST ALCOHOL CAR TO RUN A 5sec PASS AT SANTA POD

ENGINE J.P.1. HISTORY
FOR HOCKENHEIM AUGUST 1996 (No 2 QUALIFIER)

BLOCK LINED BORED NEW CAN & LIFTERS, NEW SLEEVES, NEW PISTONS & RINGS, NEW RODS, NEW CRACK, NEW VALVES, NEW OIL PUMP GEARS, RECON BRAD ANDERSON HEADS (NOT FAT HEADS), NEW SPARK PLUG TUBES, NEW MAD LEADS, 2xRECON SUPER MAG 3, NEW FRONT END, CHASSIS COMPLETELY REBUILT, LENCO NEW 34' SLICKS, BLOWER FRESHENED, NEW REAR END, PRO GEARS.

NEW WORLD FINALS SEPT 1996 (SANTA POD)
(STRAIGHT OUT OF TRAILER 5.95 sec)
NEW CLUTCH (CROWER 3 PLATE), NEW HEADERS, NEW CRANK SUPPORT, NEW RINGS, NEW COPPER HEAD GASKETS, NEW BLOWER BELT, NEW BURST PANEL, NEW VALVE SPRINGS, NEW MAINS, NEW ENDS

HISTORY OF OTHER PARTS
NEW REAR END CHASSIS WORLD FINALS 1995
NEW REAR END AXLE COMPETE WORLD FINALS 1995
NEW REAR CENTRELINE WHEELS WORLD FINALS 1995
NEW FRONT CRAGER WHEELS & GOODYEAR TYRES WORLD FINALS 95
NEW FRONT END CHASSIS HOCKENHEIM 1996

CAR IS COMPLETELY SFI LEGAL
CAR ALSO WON ME 3 CONSECUTIVE RAC BRITISH DRAG RACING CHAMPIONSHIPS 1994–1995–1996

(Have ordered a brand new 1997 SFI spec Lakewood Bell Housing, approx 6 weeks delivery from now.)

On his advice we put an advert in the *Hot Rod Gazette* which was the official newsletter of the Pennine Drag Racing Club (PDRC):

THUNDER and LIGHTNING
DRAG RACING TEAM
Wanna Crew?

If you fancy getting involved in some Top Alcohol drag racing but can't afford the wheels, you might be interested in crewing for the Thunder and Lightning team, run by Derek Annable.

The team have Barry Sheavills' old race car and will be campaigning it over the 1997 season. According to Derek, 'Pay will comprise all the vindaloo you can eat. Applicants must be heavy smokers and drinkers between the hours of 11pm and 6am only. Break the rules and your lunch box will be put in the crusher.'

Interested parties can contact Brenda Annable on 01248 852532 (daytime Tuesdays, Wednesdays and Fridays) or any evening on 01407 710615.

Our intentions were to try out the dragster in a couple of Race What You Bring (RWYB) meetings and then enter it in the Summer Nationals at Santa Pod at the beginning of August.

What to do with our free time between now and August? The *Hot Rod Gazette* were holding the Northern Street Car Challenge at York Dragway, which included what they called cruises to Leeds and Preston, and everything carried points.

It was a worrying time on the drag scene in the early part of 1997 for sportsmen racers, as can be seen from Mick's Meanderings:

Mick's Meanderings

Just when you thought it was safe to pick up a magazine ... M.M. returns. For those of you who have just learned to read or were born since 1982, Mick's Meanderings have been around in various forms and various publications *(Ah yes, the Penthouse Days ... Ed)* for the past fifteen years, the only constant factor being that of a complete lack of consistency of format or content. The title is the only pointer to my identity for reasons of legality and personal safety, but I can tell you that I am chairman of PDRC. I love drag racing, Yank cars, hotrods, Boddingtons and small furry mammals.

Okay, okay, enough waffling. I suppose you want to know what's happening in the world of drag racing, or even what in the world is drag racing? Where to start? These are heavy and momentous times and many dark and dirty deeds have taken place over the past five or six months. In a nutshell Santa Pod Racers Club and the promotion team at Santa Pod have cut most of their links with PDRC and York Raceway and come up with lots of reasons why nobody should support our club or venue. The most convincing reasons seem to be that (a) we are a low key bunch of racers who only drag race for fun and therefore an embarrassment in Santa Pod's bid to become dominant in the very, very serious world of European drag racing and (b) we're north of junction 16 of the M1.

Although we work as closely as possible with Avon Park International Racers Club, they appear to be without any dates at Avon Park due to track difficulties and planning problems. So, what are we going to do in 1997? We're going to organise some drag racing and we're going to make it FUN again!

---

and the *Hillbilly Telegraph*'s Racers' News:

HILLBILLY TELEGRAPH – RACERS' NEWS

Big Changes Forced on York Dragway

On the 26 January 1997, representatives from all three UK Racing Clubs met as per usual to decide on the dates and regulations for the 1997 UK National Drag Racing Championship. By a majority vote by those representatives present, it was agreed that the Championship would proceed as per 1996. York Raceway was allocated two rounds and Avon Park, possibly two.

At the subsequent Santa Pod Racers Club, riders and drivers meeting, it was put to the vote and carried that SPRC would withdraw from the National Championship and would run their own Championship, solely at Santa Pod.

On the 12th March we received information that Local Authority to Avon Park had withdrawn planning permission for Avon Park to hold Motorsports events. It is understood from the Planning Department that this decision will only be reversed when Avon Park Raceway management have made a further substantial effort towards fulfilling their planning conditions set some years ago, the cost of which we understand to be around a five figure sum, on top of the 10s of thousands Anthony has already spent so far.

As soon as the PDRC Committee received this devastating news, an offer was made to the APIRC, for the Club to take over or share a number of the traditional dates at the York facility. In making the offer, the PDRC hope that the APIRC will be able to survive, until such time as new finance could be put in place to complete the planning requirements of the Local Authority, so that Avon Park can once again open its gates to drag racing fans.

This means therefore, for the moment, the one venue left to host the UK National Drag Racing Championship, is York Raceway, whether the events be organised by the APIRC or the PDRC or jointly remains to be seen, but you can rest assured that the combined strengths of the two organisations will benefit the drag racing scene immensely. Even without any SPRC involvement at York Dragway, analysis of the numbers of licensed Drag Racing Competitors, registered with the track, exceeds 560, this probably makes the York Dragway facility currently the best supported facility in the UK particularly on the bikers side. Car entries are however now decimated so after 25 years of RAC affiliation, the PDRC have decided, due to the continued escalating costs of RAC affiliation, which the Club feels is strangling the sport at grass roots level, the PDRC has sought and been granted affiliation and authorisation by the IOPD.

This guarantees that the motorsport activity will continue with the same Government Authorisation as issued by the RAC but at a much reduced cost. An RAC spokesman has confirmed that it will take no action against RAC Licence Holders taking part in non-RAC permitted events. The RAC are aware that recent changes brought about by the Office of Fair Trading would preclude any such action on their part.

The 35 RAC Competition Licence holders, living in the York catchment area, are recommended to reapply for their Competition Licences as per normal, as the RAC Licence is recognised by the IOPD and the PDRC. Any racers wishing to race only at the York Raceway venue may apply to the IOPD for an IOPD Competition Licence, cost at £5. These may also be purchased at the strip on race days or from the Pennine Raceway office at the Motorsports Centre, Sandbed, Hebden Bridge, West Yorkshire HX7 6PT. The PDRC will re-apply to the RAC if and when they come competitive and they support a National Championship Series.

Competitors need not register in order to compete at the York Dragway venue and Competitors may retain their Santa Pod Competition Race Numbers when entering York, once again reducing the cost to the competitor.

The *Hot Rod Gazette* gave us HRG 17 as our race number. The first meeting at York Dragway was on the 31 March. Our doctor said my wife should be well enough to travel.

When you start planning your drag racing season, time just flies. It was mid-March and we had promised Barry the balance of the money for his car, but there hadn't been any interest in the Altered, even our price tag of £5,000, including trailer, hadn't worked. Time for my wife to use her charm again on Barry. So she phoned him on his mobile number. He agreed to take the balance in instalments, so off went a cheque for £10,000 and back came his reply:

07/04/97

Hi Brenda and Derek

Many thanks for your cheque received today. Sorry to hear no takers on the Altered.

The new SFI bell housing arrived on Friday and we will be fitting it in the next couple of weeks. So the car will be ready for you as soon as you want it.

Hope you are both well.

Regards

Barry

It would take a further three months to sell the Altered, my last cheque to Barry would be at the end of July – thankfully he was a very patient man. He needed the sale, for without the money from the car his drive in a Top Fuel car may never have been.

The Camaro was ready for the first round of the Northern Street Car Challenge (NSCC) Championship. The cars were to race heads up, first across the line wins, this meant the quickest cars would always win. Ok, I was here to race, let's get on with it and see how we fared. We were to find out there was friction between Steve Murty, the track owner, and Shaun Wilson, who was in charge of the Northern Street Car Challenge. Shaun was always complaining that all the spectators had gone home by the time the HRG cars were allowed to race.

Shaun reported in that month's *Hot Rod Gazette*:

> First out of the bag was Derek 'Grandad' Annable versus Russ Fielding. This was a good bout of Chevy versus Ford, both cars running B&M blown small blocks of nigh on the same displacement. Once again the black Mustang was on and off the throttle fighting for traction, and it was 'Grandad' who took the win with a 14.51 over a 15.10. Russ did lodge a complaint afterwards that 'that old codger is too old to have a driving licence, he should be disqualified', but nobody listened!

In the next round I was taken out by Ian Armitage, 14.6 to Ian's 13.8, and as I have already said, the quickest car wins but I did collect 1250 points which put me in eighth place.

I enjoyed the racing, but was home early as Brenda didn't come with me because it can be very cold at York Dragway in March.

York Drag Racers News reported the following problem they were having:

YORK DRAG RACERS NEWS

York Dragway recognises that if you have £25,000 to spend on a Top Fuel or Top Alcohol car, and you can show an ability in handling and driving the car safely, make three solo passes and have 100% acceptance of your fellow racers, you will be able to run at York events this year. Also all the past masters of drag racing, who maybe don't hold the current necessary RAC Comp licence will be welcomed at York Dragway, without having the humiliation of having to go back to Street Cars for a year in order to drive what they could probably drive in their sleep. Chassis log books are not required at York Raceway, but cars that are well constructed and run straight are required. These 'Hillbilly' racers are simple practical folk!! If your chassis is not right or your car does not run straight, you don't get to race at York Raceway.

The latest news on the Custom Street Eliminator Series, Northern Rounds – there isn't any!!! Why? I don't know, ring the horses mouth, Tim Baggaley. If it is any help, to help you understand the situation, here's what happened in 1996.

January 1996, Steve Murty negotiates with Tim Baggaley for a round, at York Dragway on 10 and 11 August. York Dragway produces 25,000 leaflets carrying the news that the Custom Car Street Eliminator Series is coming to York Dragway.

At the end of May, Steve Murty rings Tim Baggaley, asks for the mailing list so that the racers can all be sent the entry forms for the forthcoming event. Steve Murty is told, 'Ah, the cars are not coming'.
'Why?' asks Steve (Now then folks, hold on to your seats, this is the big problem.)
Tim states, 'Because the road from the entrance gate to the pits is too bumpy.'
'Oh', says Steve. 'Sorry, I didn't know this was a problem for the street cars, but never mind, will you give us thirty days to repair the road?'
'Yes, fine', said Tim, 'but I'll need to come and inspect it.'
'Ok', said Steve, 'shall we say the weekend of the 30 June?'
'Yes', said Tim.
So work parties were organised and three-quarters of a mile of road was improved and subsequently named 'Baggaley's Boulevard'.

The 28 June. Steve Murty calls Tim Baggaley. 'Hi, Tim. Can we make arrangements for you to do the inspection, we've completed the road, you can now drive on it at an average speed of 40mph whilst balancing a cup of coffee on your dashboard.'

'No point', said Tim, 'we are not coming!'
'Why?' said Steve, bewildered.
'Because drivers have been talking to the Super Gas drivers and they reckon the breaking area is shit!'
'Yes, but Tim', Steve replies, 'that's only hearsay, why don't you come and have a look for yourself?'
'Na, we are not coming.'
'But Tim, what about all the Northern fans who want to see the cars? Can't we run an eighth mile? Or if you show us where there is a problem, we'll mend it. Will you please just come and fulfil what we've promised?'

'Na, I'm sorry, Steve, they just won't come.'

All that effort wasted, which could have been put to better use, spending time on the pits and return roads!

For 1997 and beyond we've now got our own Northern Street Car Challenge, for people who drive street cars round town and up hill and down to the cruisers. Also we have got our own Hot Rod Magazine for people who want to read about what's happening in the north.

Roll on the next round of the Northern Street Car Challenge.

Under pressure from my wife, our doctor had agreed it would be good for her to get out of the house and help our daughter in the dress shop for a couple of hours a day. From now on I would go home for lunch, then take Brenda to her shop in Benllech for the afternoon session, returning home with her at five o'clock.

After two weeks of being part time in the shop, Brenda felt stronger and decided she would come with me next time I raced at York Dragway.

So one night was booked at the Travelodge in South Cave, and off we went at a steady 60mph, any quicker and the engine overheats and the inside of the car becomes a hothouse, because the side windows are fixed for racing. It was nice to be back at South Cave, a lovely village, and the friendly staff at the Little Chef added to the enjoyment of a first-class meal and a good night's sleep.

When we arrived at the track, Brenda was greeted by Jean Routhwaite, always a good friend, and within minutes Marjorie Lyons was asking Brenda about her stay in hospital. They all went over to the bar, no alcoholic beverage was sold before 1pm, but it was nice and warm for Brenda. Knowing she was in good hands, I prepared the car for racing.

After a couple of practice runs, it was time for HRG cars to race, but before this happened Shaun Wilson (Ed Gasket) read out a public apology to Tim Baggaley of *Custom Car*:

Apologies to Tim Baggaley whom we misquoted in last month's mag as having been 'bribed', the statement should have read 'blackmailed'.

Speaking from his £1.8 million yacht in Canary Wharf, Tim assured us that he had never been involved in any bribery deal whatsoever, and that his vast collection of automobiles had all been left to him by a rich uncle or anybody shrewd enough to have seen him coming at the time.

Previous evidence suggests that Mr Baggaley is already dramatically overpaid, and would therefore have little use for another wedge of readies.

Given the number of vicious rumours that do rapidly get out of all proportion in our scene, we would like to stamp this one out here and now, it was our mistake, end of story.

That done, let's get back to Shaun's report on the day's racing:

Derek Annable found himself on another first round Ford versus Chevy grudge race, this time pushing his supercharged Camaro to beat HRG 47 Paul Burnley's Mash I. As at the last meeting 'Grandad' Annable could do nothing to stop Steve Naumantas, the jeweller from Brighouse, as he once again ran the coronet down into the mid-twelves second bracket, this put HRG 5 into the lead in the championship.

Yes, I was beaten, but I ran a 14.361 with a top end of track speed of 100 mph. Now I went looking for Brenda, there she was holding court with Dave Allan's wife and children. Dez Brown kept interrupting saying, 'Come on, Brenda, let's go for a drink', and this we all did. One thing about being knocked out early, it wouldn't be midnight when we arrived home.

The Leeds cruise was in a fortnight, but before that I had a letter to write supporting an article Carla Pittau had written:

Let's campaign for our classes, not against others. I think (and mostly hope) that Keith Bartlett wants the drag racing in Britain to be British. If Bartlett needs to put together a class to race in Britain almost exclusively from abroad, perhaps he will look again at how professional, how dedicated, how committed bracket racers are, and think again. International racing, yes, but with a British (hum, I just remembered I'm Italian) presence able to give a good fight for anybody's money. And anyway, I think Comp Eliminator is boring, I always go to the pits when they come on at Pomona, and I only run back when Super Stock line up to race, so there.

There followed my letter to Carla, the editor of *ETRA News*:

28 April 97

Dear Carla

BRACKET RACING: A Stepping Stone

I am adopted Welsh, as you are adopted English, we both live and work away from the country of our birth.

Carla, I hope your wish comes true and Keith Bartlett finds room for

UK bracket racers in his plans for the millennium. Deep down and with all my years in business, I have the gut feeling the answer is 'No'.

You are correct, all bracket racers (cars/bikes) are professionals and show more dedication than most Formula One drivers. Also their cars/bikes have, during the last three years, been turned out to a standard of preparation which the many other forms of motorsport disciplines will find hard to match.

My regards to all ETRA members and keep championing the cause.

Derek (Grandad) Annable

No sooner had I posted my letter, than I received a bombshell in my post. I thought, what more can go wrong with UK drag racing?

AROUND THE CLOCK LOCAL NEWS
AVON PARK UNDER THREAT

Scarcely had poor Alan Martin put the telephone down from explaining to all the world that the Nostalgia Nationals would definitely be going ahead over May Bank Holiday weekend than up pops an officious little twat from the Local Council and slaps a Prohibition Notice on the venue, barring them from running either the Nostalgia Nationals or the two-day meet scheduled for 7 and 8 June.

Lost
Track promoter Antony Hodges is reckoned to have lost in the region of £4,000 in advertising and bookings for the Nostalgia Nationals alone. Alan Martin assured the *Hot Rod Gazette* that none of the monies lost would be from the NSRA funds. Although the NSRA back the event with their name, they did not actually have a financial interest or gain from the event other than for the sale of space for trade stands.

Late
The Local Council explained that their demands to have the approach road widened to include a filter lane, at a cost in excess of £100,000, would not be met in time as the contractors in charge of the work were running behind schedule.

The Prohibition Notice served forbids any vehicle from turning so much as a wheel on the strip, let alone race. The notice was served less than seven days before the Nostalgia Nationals were due to commence, with over £600 having been already spent on spraying the track with Track Bite the weekend before, as part of the customary pre-race preparations.

Bulldog Bash

The Council have also thrown the future of the Bulldog Bash into jeopardy by proclaiming it to be a 'festival' rather than a motorsports event.

This will mean that the organisers will need to approach the Local Authority for an Entertainment Licence before the event could go ahead. What makes you think that the Local Authority would refuse permission???? Here at HRG we would like to see the local council tell ten thousand Hells Angels who've rolled up for the weekend that they can't have their party and see what sort of response they get.

In the meantime we'll keep you fully updated as to how one of our foremost drag strips fares against the Council and if and when events are running.

Keith Bartlett must be some sort of Jonah. Ever since he became involved in UK drag racing things started to go wrong and now this at Avon Park/Shakespeare County Raceway. What else could go wrong in 1997 – Santa Pod Raceway closed for good? This was on the cards, because some contractors who had worked on the track and also APIRA officials were owed money. So this was my letter to *Custom Car*:

I have a story for you.

There was a little old lady with a stick who heard a drag racing club couldn't afford an electronic scoreboard because the Sheriff of Nottingham (Keith Bartlett) was witholding money. Although she had been saving up her weekly pension to buy Christmas presents for all the tiny Tims in our village, this money (£500) was sent to the APIRA (scoreboard fund) instead.

I was double-gutted at the World Finals, Santa Pod – so lads don't triple-gut me. There are eleven honest and true men, get your cheque books out and together match Brenda A's donation.

Derek (Grandad) Annable, Anglesey

The reason I was double-gutted was because my wife nearly died of a stroke after the World Finals at Santa Pod.

Keith Bartlett was quick to reply through *Custom Car:*

I have a little story of mine own.

I am sure many of the readers of Custom Car found the letter from Derek Annable (see last month's mail pages) most amusing in its presentation and I am sure it was written with the intention of benefiting APIRA (Avon Park International Racers Association). However, I am most concerned at its overall meaning and misrepresentations.

Mr Annable, you are entitled to your own opinion of both me personally and my company, Power Racing Communications (PRC), but you must get your facts right. I must make it quite clear PRC does not owe Avon Park Raceway any money whatsoever. The electronic scoreboard fund is being organised by APIRA and Anthony Hodges Ltd (the track owner). It is not the responsibility of PRC to supply, purchase or install electronic scoreboards at Avon Park.

PRC only promoted events at Avon Park in 96 although, in fact, its involvement went much further. PRC organised and contracted for the resurfacing of the track just two weeks prior to Avon Park's biggest race meeting in over ten years. PRC also funded the initial works on the track despite neither owning it, nor having a long-term lease on it. PRC lost around £40,000 promoting that inaugural international Top Fuel meeting at Avon Park so the track could start to become accepted in national and international drag racing circles. Without PRC's investment, the track would have been unusable in 96. May I also remind you that after our one race on the track on 8–9 June, the surface then rapidly deteriorated to the point that two months later racers refused to run on it.

I would love to know what Mr Annable was 'double gutted' about regards to the World Finals last September, as the general opinion was it was the best event at Santa Pod Raceway for many years.

I and my company do not mind any form of criticism, be it constructive or otherwise but to suggest PRC or myself are taking money, witholding money, or worse, not working to further the development of drag racing, is totally incorrect. I think what we have achieved, in less than one year, is already going in the right direction to repair the damage done in the last five years by the various promoters with only one aim – to take the money and run at the expense of the racers.

Keith Bartlett
(Sheriff of Nottingham)
Chief Executive
Power Racing Communications

This was followed up with an APIRA response covering many issues:

As there was been a lot of letters and comments regarding the Hot Rod Drags last September it is time to set the record straight as far as APIRA is concerned. I am sure everyone is aware that APIRA is a completely separate entity to Avon Park Raceway and our primary function as the affiliated club is to run the strip according to the regulations and type of event. We were ready for the traditional Run Wot Ya Brung event and we were aware that there were some Pro Mods turning up as demo cars, but on the Saturday morning we were told that they were running a championship round, which of course could not go ahead since there was no RACMSA permit, as there never has been at these meetings. The track was safe for a burnout and launch as originally planned and this would have entertained the crowds somewhat.

The other problem that weekend was that the track had been prepared for a Run Wot Ya Brung event rather than a race meeting and there was no grip juice available at that time. APIRA had tried to get hold of some but the cost for a barrel (and another of the necessary solvent) was over £1,000, which of course is prohibitive for only two days. Enquiries were made further afield and a superior product was obtained at about a quarter of the price with delivery promised before the ill-fated meeting. Unfortunately the ship was delayed in mid-Atlantic by hurricanes and delivery took seven weeks instead of the two quoted.

We are not saying that we are completely blameless as we realise there are lots of problems, but we are addressing them as best we can on a limited budget. There are a lot of people who are at the track nearly every weekend throughout the year, including the winter, trying to get things right. We are all enthusiasts too and we want the best racing as much as anyone else. We have suffered from a lack of liaison, the same as other parties, but I feel there is nothing to gain in slagging people off left, right and centre. It's better to look to the future and ensure it does not happen again for the good of the sport as a whole.

The good news is that we hope to have the new scoreboards up and running by the first meeting of the season and the finances for this project were almost entirely raised at our AGM in December, so at least some people have faith in the future.

We would like to thank all the people who have supported us in the past and hope they will continue to do so in the future, and thank you to all those people who have already put in a lot of hard work this year.

Richard Warburton
APIRA Committee

In the end I was vindicated, as within six months, Power Racing Communications went into receivership, owing an estimated £70,000. I did a few sums and worked out it was a six-figure sum owed. Soon after the receivership, Keith Bartlett bought his own bankrupt company back and called it Trakbak – very nice. Why are company directors allowed to do this? His former creditors had lost any chance of recovering their money. This was allowed at that time, but the law has been tightened up since.

While this was going on, Brenda and I went on the Leeds cruise, what a waste of money – 350 miles for 500 points. It rained all the way there and back, six hours driving and a beefburger in between. Total cost, petrol and food, £125. I hand you over to Shaun Wilson:

> Heavy rain over the Pennines did nothing to boost the number of cars turning out for this growing monthly meet on the second Saturday of the month, yet still there were more cars out in force than might otherwise have been expected.
>
> All credit to Derek and Brenda Annable who were out on a 330-mile trip in their blown '82 Chevy Camaro. Derek was making an all-important qualifying run for the Northern Street Car Challenge, and had had to make up a shield over the bug catcher to stop the wet elements from attacking the internals of his B&M blower on the American speed specialities-prepped small block. The mid-fourteen second car had average 16mpg on the journey – quite respectable all things equalled. The Camaro was one of fifteen cars out scoring points towards the championship, and once again there was some friendly rivalry for the top position, with Steve Neimantas and Shaun Crowe both out, undeterred by the weather. Amidst the competitors were Dave Rushworth in the Mustang II and Pat Bedford in the Plymouth Sport Fury, both out for the first time and revved up ready for their first eliminator at York later in the month.

The car's next outing would be at York Raceway in the third round of the NSC Challenge and this would be followed by a cruise to Preston – the Riversway.

The doorbell rang. It was the postman with a special delivery for me. The envelope had the House of Commons shield on it. Who had written to me – our local MP? No, it was the deputy prime minister's reply to my letter:

---

22 May 1997

Dear Mr Annable

Thank you for your letter inviting me to one of the meetings of the

Thunder and Lightning Drag Racing Team.

If I get the time I will certainly drop in but this highly unlikely at the moment.

Yours sincerely

Rt Hon John Prescott MP

Deputy Prime Minister

That was a pity, he and his family had lived in Prestatyn before they moved to Hull – not many German bombs fell on the North Wales coast. He and his wife could have been at York Dragway in less than half an hour. Never mind, I shall try again. What was this? Another letter from John Prescott, updated to the 19 June, but carrying the same message as before! No wonder politicians find it hard to govern. Is it because of lack of sleep or boredom listening to debates in the House of Commons all night?

Now back to Shaun Wilson to report on the third round of the NSC Challenge:

Derek Annable posted a new personal best 14.07/100 mph to put him in tenth position. Then Derek went on to eliminate Pat Bedford's HRG 31 Gorgeous Sport Fury. We then came to the final round, despite a feisty 14.16/100mph run from Derek Annable he was unable to compete with the 502 cubic inch Vauxhall of Mark Sherratt, HRG 37, which put in an easy 12.43. That was the end of racing for the old man from Anglesey.

Back home along the M62 motorway two tired people went and were glad to see the lights of their old homestead.

The weather forecast for the Riversway cruise was good, so we left home at 4pm and arrived on what used to be the Preston docks at 7pm. This used to be a busy and thriving dockland area, ships coming up the River Ribble on high tide. Now it has been built over by the big supermarket chains and London money, although they did allow a yacht marina to be part of their great plan.

Morrisons supermarket car park was being used for the cruise, it was long enough for our needs and their customers. We were first to arrive, and feeling hungry, we went into the supermarket café. There was a good choice of food on offer. This was the only plus side to the evening. Brenda, my wife, wasn't a fan of hot rod cruises, so we signed on with Pete Whiteside for the points (300 per cruise) and left for home. As we were driving through Preston, we saw Dave Allan and his family coming towards us in his yellow Ford Mustang; now my wife wished she had stayed, but, too late, once the Camaro is heading for home there is no stopping it.

After we left the Riversway cruise, trouble broke out between the hot rodders and a customer of Morrisons. Why are some people such killjoys and against American cars and their drivers?

AROUND THE CLOCK LOCAL NEWS
Police Intervene
At Riversway Cruise
Good news for rodders!

As you can read elsewhere in this issue, the May Cruise saw the first real intervention by the local police. This followed a complaint of congestion in Morrisons car park from one of their customers. Morrisons, however, were quick to point out that they had no problem with our presence and the four or five officers present simply went on to compile statistics of the number and size of vehicles there.

Following discussions with the local community police, two of the regular Riversway cruisers agreed to meet with both police and Morrisons management to discuss how everybody might benefit in the future.

It's Good To Talk

Although the Riversway Cruise doesn't have any organising body, Pete Whiteside and Shaun Wilson offered to be a liaison point for the authorities.

On 9 June they met with Matthew Hedges, Marketing Manager of Morrisons and WPC Reehaina Saddique, Riversway's Community Police Officer (the cute one). The tone of the meeting was friendly and informal and we even got a cup of coffee.

All parties agreed that the current arrangement which mixes cruisers and shoppers was apt to cause problems and that the time had come to sort things out.

Morrisons have very kindly offered to designate one area of the car park specifically for the cruisers to alleviate the difficulties. The new parking area is situated behind the filling station, where in fact, the cruise used to be held. They have also agreed to extend the car park lighting outside store hours when we are present. Their café will also be open until 9pm on cruise nights.

Reehaina had kindly offered to assist in marshalling a couple of events until everybody is familiar with the new practices.

Behaviour

Also discussed was the behaviour of cruisers, which all parties agreed was excellent. It is well recognised that the local hot-hatch boy racers are not part of our culture or welcome at the cruise. As such the police will ensure that the idiot brigade are kept particularly in check. We have assured the police that none of our cruisers will play loud music or drive in anything other than a sensible manner. By the way, Reehaina did ask that the access road not be used as a drag strip. (Did you know that the local traffic police refer to the cruise as 'Unofficial American Race Day'!) Surely none of our hot rodders could be responsible for such behaviour?

Shop at Morrisons

Obviously we are fortunate to have received such a good response from the local community and would ask you all to support Morrisons and WPC Saddique at the events.

It is possible that in the near future we will be staging a charity event in association with Morrisons and the local police, which we would urge you all to support. More details to follow.

Working in her dress shop was proving too much for Brenda, so we decided to open two days a week, 11am–3pm. Any new stock was to be purchased from the rails which the agents carried inside their vans on their regular visits to Anglesey. If we closed the business down, we still had to pay rent to Pochins, our landlord, but the profit from a few sales would help the bank balance.

There was still friction between Shaun Wilson and Steve Murty. A quick phone call to Shaun and he verified the meeting at York was on. Anglesey is a lovely island but nothing ever happens, the only excitement is when the school bus breaks down on the hill outside Amlwch or the lifeboat is launched from Moelfre because a dog is cut off by the rising tide.

We had a good journey. While I was carrying our luggage into our room in the Travelodge, my wife was reading the Little Chef menu. 'Derek, they have changed it, there are four new items and one is chicken curry.' We had filled in the cards they give us, asking customers what new dishes would they like to have on their next visit. For years we kept writing curry dishes and now we could sample a Little Chef chicken masala. It was good, but the restaurant soon became full of the smell of curry. Somebody must have complained, because within six months the curry was reduced to a mild variety, no more medium hot so now I had to use my own cayenne pepper to hot it up.

This meeting at York Raceway was the main one of the year. Saturday racing and a cruise to Leeds in the evening, Sunday was racing all day. Shaun Wilson was making a list of who was going on the cruise, and we were the only ones who said 'no'. Last time we went on a Leeds cruise, the food was like shaving soap with bits of cat food in it. Leeds, 'no', Riversway, 'yes'! Brenda likes shopping at Morrisons.

I managed six runs on the Saturday, the quickest 14.30/100mph. We were on a pro tree starting light, the tree ambers came on together, then the green. For a bracket racer, this is a new skill to learn and takes time to adapt.

My wife sent me to the chuck wagon for some food and a cup of tea for her. As I waited in the queue, a racer said to me, 'Derek, you like your food, we have watched you. How do you keep so slim, you are five feet nine inches tall, yes?'

I nodded.

'Eleven stone, yes?'

I nodded again.

'Your waist is?'

'Thirty inches', I said. 'Now you can go and tell the undertaker', and I laughed.

Then he said, 'Win or lose, you are always happy. Best of luck, Derek.'

Our last night at the Travelodge passed without problems. My wife slept well and was looking forward to the day's racing.

My first opponent was Mark Freeman, driving a 4-litre Ford Pop, reg. USV 917, which gives you an idea of the car's age. As Shaun Wilson said, 'The Pop was seen off in the first round by Derek Annable's consistently quick supercharged Camaro.'

Yes, it was running quick, 14 seconds for the quarter mile, but what chance would it have against a 13-second car? None, even if I pulled a perfect light. So it was in the next round, when Dave Billadeau, driving his Coronet on treads, ran a 13.10/107mph and crossed the finishing line over a second in front of me. My terminal speed was 102mph, the quickest the car has ever run.

My racing over, we could go home early. Where was Brenda? Dez shouted, 'Derek, she is in the bar with Dave Allan's wife.' My wife must have been celebrating her birthday early, and had had a lovely time with her friends. I didn't mind, it would be peace and quiet all the way home.

The only noise would be from the twin exhausts. My wife had been through sheer hell recently, why shouldn't she have one drink too many?

At the end of the week, things were going to get hectic. On Friday evening it was the Riversway cruise followed by Smax Smith's Aintree Power Festival at 10am on Saturday. In the afternoon we had to be at Drywood Hall in Worsley. To cover all three meant an overnight stay at the Travelodge in Haydock.

The Riversway cruise at Preston was better organised this time and, as Shaun Williams said, 'The top ten were all present to collect their mid-season points at this mid-season event.' Yes, I was. My position was fourth. 'Again, it was Derek Annable who looked likely to have had the longest trip, up from Anglesey and once more in the supercharged Chevy Camaro.'

That over, we drove the short distance to Haydock and booked into the Travelodge for the night.

As we drove into the Aintree complex the next morning, there was Smax Smith with this giant truck – two small block Chevy engines driving the rear wheels, two more engines to drive the front wheels. Engines everywhere, all synchronised to pull together, all 3000hp. Smax shouted to Brenda, 'How are you, love? Nice to see you back in drag racing, you are my favourite lady.'

I parked the Camaro in an area for supercharged Chevys and left my wife talking to Smax and went walkabout. The Liverpool Car Club was holding a sprint and there were many drivers who I had raced against in my youth, including Tony Brooks – not that he was interested in anybody who was involved in drag racing. He had his BRDC badge all over his sprint car; I had mine in my pocket.

It was time to leave Aintree and drive the short distance to Drywood Hall. My wife wanted to stay with Smax Smith and his gang but there were 1000 points for attending Drywood cruise so we left early. Unfortunately we got lost in Worsley – on and off the motorway we went. Then luck was with us, four hot rodders showed us the way to the main gate. After signing on, I pointed the Camaro in the direction of Anglesey and it was 'home James, and don't spare the engine.'

Smax Smith sent a letter to the *Hot Rod Gazette*:

Dear HRG

Just a quick mention about the first Aintree Power Festival – didn't want everyone thinking it was a complete 'washout' as printed. Pity more cruisers didn't come across on the Friday night and stay over. We partied until daybreak!!! True there was a lot of rain Saturday, but true to form we put on a bloody good show. First we fired off a tank (Saladin) which nearly blew off an over enthusiastic photographer's head, then we fired up Desperate Dan's five engine tractor rig to the delight of the crowd. On came Murty's 16 ton wheelie truck; then onto the supercharged Outlaws with a stunning burnout by Steve 'The Lawnmower Man' Nolan in his brown Hemi powered '69 Pontiac GTO. He shot off the track and mowed down a few newly planted trees. The grand finale was everything fired up together revving the bollocks off 10,000 brute horse power, sending the sprint race car drivers scampering for cover, or for ear-plugs!! We lost a little bit of cash due to the rain, but hope to be back next year with an even bigger show. Stay tuned folks. Cheers to those who came and supported us.

Smax (The Mainline Menace)

Preston

Good for you, Smax. Brenda, is one of your fans.

Now it was time to send Barry Sheavills some more money. Off went a cheque for £4,000 and a note saying my wife would send the balance when the car was delivered to York Dragway. Back came Barry's reply:

Wed 9th

Hi Brenda and Derek

Received your cheque for £4,000. Many thanks. Total £19,000, balance £6,000 to be paid on delivery to York. As you know I am currently campaigning the European Top Fuel Championship and find myself very tied up, so I have asked Steve Turner of Turner Racing to keep in touch with you. Steve and Rob will probably deliver the car to York and run thru all the procedure in starting and running a Top Alcohol car. Both are very experienced in Alcohol Racing. If this is the case then please give them the remaining balance. I have also asked them to supply you with spare plugs, Methanol and some oil. Also I will try to put together a small amount of spares for you at no extra cost. Well that's it for now. Good luck if I'm not around.

See you soon.

Barry

We were halfway through the HRG Northern Street Car challenge and I was in fourth position but the cost to date had run into thousands of pounds, mainly on petrol and overnight stays – there were 5,000 extra miles on the car's speedo. The engine would require a rebuild. We decided after the Billing Fun Run we would call it a day and start saving our money for the two meetings the Top Alcohol dragster was planned to race at.

We did attend the Billing Fun Run in the grounds of the Billing Aquadrome, stayed a couple of hours, collected 500 points and drove home.

No sooner had we arrived home, than the phone went. It was Rick Denny. 'Prepare yourself, Derek. I have some bad news. Mike Ellis died of a heart attack at the Cannonball meeting.'

Rick Denny had been brought into drag racing through Mike's Rookie Racers. I thanked Rick for letting us know and sat there stunned. What a sad day. How could I give Brenda the bad news?

Mark Gredzinski wrote the following tribute to Mike Ellis in *Custom Car*:

It is with great regret that *Custom Car* reports the death of Mike Ellis. Mike, aged 52, collapsed and died of a heart attack in the fire-up lane at Santa Pod during the Cannonball meetings. Mike had been involved in drag racing for three years, competing in the Euro Challenge and then in Street ET, in which he finished runner-up in the championship last year. Mike was best known and loved for his involvement with the Rookie Racers, whereby he put up drives in his Pink Panther Capri as raffle prizes for novice racers to encourage them to take up drag racing. He will be greatly missed.

Strangely, the publisher of *Custom Car* died in a motorbike accident:

Justin Sparrow 1970–1997

It is with great regret that *Custom Car* reports the death of its publisher, Justin Sparrow. Justin died at 8.20am on July 22 in an accident on his motorbike on his way to the office.

Justin was not well known by the readers, as his job was behind the scenes, but his death was widely reported in the London area both in the press and on the radio. Unfortunately, it was also misreported that it was the editor of *Custom Car* who had died, adding confusion to a tragic situation.

Justin had been involved with *Custom Car* since the magazine's move to Kelsey Publishing over three and a half years ago but it was just over six months ago that he took on the mantle of publisher. Justin did not have an expert knowledge of hot rodding but he had a flair for the business of publishing and an ability, and inclination, to learn quickly. Indeed, the giveaway car, which features in this issue, was Justin's idea and it is a testament to his organisational skills that he could coordinate the build-up without knowing much about the actual car itself. His limitless energy and boundless enthusiasm was an inspiration to all who knew him. When the rest of us flagged, he seemed to have life to spare.

In the *Custom Car* office, colleagues and friends are much the same thing, but Justin was a particular friend to me. He was a keen motorcyclist and I rode with him often. When we weren't out riding our bikes, we were in the pub talking about them and when we weren't doing that, we were taking them apart in his back garden. What with the beer and swarf and cigarettes, it was hot rodding but with fewer wheels.

My loss, and that of all of us at Kelsey Publishing is, however, dwarfed by that felt by his family and, in particular, his wife Allison and their three young children; Natalie, Joel and Sophie. They have our deepest sympathy. Many thanks to all of you who have written, faxed or phoned in with your condolences.

Tim Baggaley
August 1997

How are we judged? By our peers? By society? Or by our children? No, by ourselves. We judge our success from a feeling deep down inside which weighs good response against hostile response. The good response comes from people who see themselves in us, the hostile response comes from people with a sense of guilt born through jealousy. Money doesn't enter the equation, it is the sense of purpose or lack of it that motivates them. Mike Ellis wanted to succeed but he listened to a hostile response.

A few years later, Graham Beckwith was having coffee with Brenda and myself. I mentioned Mike Ellis's name and his response was, 'I never liked him, there was something not honest in his nature.'

I was lost for words and let it go. Now I shall give my answer to the remarks made that evening about Mike Ellis. I think that Graham was cruel to judge Mike Ellis as he did. It must have been through ignorance of the man. Mike came up with some new ideas for the sport and Graham and many others tried to put him down. This was foolish. The sport of drag racing in the UK is growing through hard times. Graham and John Price were good in the tower, with their endless commentary, but at the end of the day, how many new racers did they bring into drag racing? Mike Ellis went among the crowd who were watching the cars race and sold drag racing to them. They went home, bought race overalls and helmets and started coming to RWYB meetings.

Graham still tends to project an air of 'I raced years ago and you lot are rubbish', and 'There is no car on the track today I couldn't race because of my past experience.' Not a very humble man.

I had my own problems with Mike Ellis. At one meeting I said to Mike, 'Stop sacrificing your own race career for me', and I told him to 'P*** off', then I stormed off. After half an hour Mike came to our trailer and said, 'Derek, I trust you. Everybody else says to me, "Good idea, Mike", and the next day they won't answer the phone when I call them back. You and Brenda always answer the phone and never put it down on me. I don't want your money, just your help.' I felt so humble.

I asked whether some form of memorial could be erected at the Santa Pod track for anyone who had died racing there, but both the club and the track owners rejected the idea.

Tributes kept pouring in for Mike. The *ETRA News* featured the following:

IN MEMORY OF MIKE ELLIS

Following the sad loss of Mike Ellis, ETRA members have offered a lot of different proposals and ideas to both help his family and make sure that his worthy efforts to encourage new racers into the sport live on.

It was our intention, as we did last year, to post any funds not used or needed by the Association as prize money to be won at the World Finals at the Pod, in the same format as last year, ie to the three closest ETs to index or dial-in during eliminations.

However Derek Annable advised us that Mike Ellis, in his effort to run the 'Rookie Racers' operation, cashed in his life insurance, which was there-fore not paid to his wife and family after his tragic death. He suggested that ETRA members could pay their cheques to Mrs Ellis when renewing their membership. Other members thought this was a just cause but thought it may be difficult to organise, and suggested that the association donates the surplus funds to the Ellis family instead.

This can be done easily and without fuss. Unfortunately the ETRA is not rich and total funds amount in the region of £250, however if members renew their subscriptions now and send a donation (whatever they can afford) the ETRA will leave a total of £40 in the bank (no more is required, as stamps, paper, envelopes and photocopying is still provided by our supporters) and donate any amount above this to the Ellis family.

Please call Carla on 01732 761424 during office hours or on 0181 856 5690 in the evening should you disagree or have other suggestions or proposals.

We are also discussing how we can help the Rookie Racers operation to live on, as it proved worthy of praise and successful in encouraging new racers into the sport. We are trying to organise (people, cars and TIME needed, please help) a group of people who could provide, taking turns, as a team or whatever, a car and a crew. We have yet to outline this even on paper, and permission would have to be obtained from Mrs Ellis to use any name associated with Mike Ellis's operation, but we would like to stress in the name used that it is in his memory that the operation is run, and to recognise his worthy contribution to drag racing in general and ET racing in particular.

Again, any suggestion and offer of help is gratefully received.

For money donations outside the ETRA scope, please contact DRAG, the charity specifically formed to provide help to injured drag racers and their families.

Please specify that your donation is to be passed on to the Ellis family.

Having paid Barry Sheavills the balance owing on his car, it was time for us to start to organise our life around the Top Alcohol dragster we now owned. Steve Turner had been paid £130 for a further three months' storage of our car in the Turner workshop. The car and driver had been registered with Dennis Stone who was in charge of all European Top Alcohol dragsters, and our FIA competition certificate had been sent to us.

Before we registered the car with the Santa Pod Racers Club (SPRC), it was decided I should try the car out on the Sunday 3 August Public Test Day at Santa Pod. If it went well, the car would be entered in the Summer Nationals the following Friday. Steve Turner agreed the car would be ready and he would bring a full crew with him, but he suggested I brought my own engine man with us. I phoned Trevor Graves (the Bristol Doorslammer) and he said he would be at the Pod mid-morning.

Brenda had become ill so I travelled down on my own. As I turned into the pit area, there it was, 28ft of pure power parked alongside the Turner rig, with Steve working on the engine. After three hours it was time for me to sit in the driver's seat and go through the controls with Steve. By now my heart was thumping and I felt heady. Trevor, who was on the portable starter motor, shouted, 'We will bring the oil pressure up.' After half a dozen turns of the engine, the oil pressure gauge showed 120lbs. That over, I could give my left leg a rest. The clutch on these cars takes a lot of left leg strength and is tiring, so I was allowed a couple of minutes before we fired the engine. This time, because I was a rookie, Steve switched the mags on and the engine burst into full power. As it did, the kick on the clutch pedal nearly knocked my foot off it. The rear wheels were now spun at tick over, then the second gear button was pressed, the top gear button, clutch out, button released and the gear level was moved into reverse. Release the clutch and spin the rear wheels again. Engine switched off after the fuel line grab switch on the handbrake was engaged.

It was mid-afternoon before the track was cleared for us to make a pass. Alcohol cars require a different fire crew. When alcohol burns, you can't see it, there is a blue haze and the chief fire marshall is the only man who knows when a Top Alcohol car is on fire. Thank God they have the best at Santa Pod. Steve fired the engine up and brought me through the water and gave me the sign. I hit the throttle, and the car shot forward. I don't think it was a good burnout. Finding reverse isn't easy with a lenco box, you have to keep dipping the clutch until the lever moves.

Now I was in pre-stage and bringing the revs up and holding them steady at 5,000. I moved into stage, but I nearly ran through the lights. The amber lights came on and I launched, hitting the throttle; as I did, my head hit the back of the roll cage. The crew had forgotten to put the padding on the vertical bar of the roll cage which was behind my head, causing one hell of a whiplash to my neck. I coasted to the end of the track and I was towed back to the pits. It was a good 60ft, 1.139 and the car had kept straight. This I could build on.

I paid Trevor Graves £50 for helping and Steve Turner £400 to cover his costs. These amounts were going to increase until I was paying the Turner brothers £1,000 a day and Trevor Graves £150 plus before the end of 1998 season.

It was late evening before I arrived home. I gave Brenda a rundown of the day's proceedings. She was feeling better and wanted to come with me when the car was raced at the end of the week. Yes, three days in the Top Alcohol pits would take her mind off her disabled life.

The excitement of the forthcoming weekend, we were racing in the Top Alcohol class, the car was named Brenda's Life Force, what more could one want? A stop at Middlewich for a cup of tea and my wife's toilet needs, then it was the dreaded M6 motorway and the gridlock after the junction with the M56. We made good time and were at the Travelodge, Rushden for teatime. The staff in the Little Chef remembered my wife from that tragic night nearly a year ago and made her welcome, and made sure the food was cooked to her liking.

When we arrived in the Top Alcohol pits, the Turners were busy getting their own car ready. Where was Trevor Graves? Steve said he had phoned to say he wouldn't be up till late tonight. Thank you, Trevor, that meant no racing for me until tomorrow. As the car was out of the rig, John Hackney, the race director, and Stuart Vincent suggested I take my licence personal assessment for Category 'C'. Everything went well, cockpit check, a pass; start verb and prac, a pass; then Vincent started to be difficult – I had to escape from the car in eight seconds. This I did, but without wearing a helmet. He then demanded I do it again, this time wearing a helmet. Barry Sheavills was three inches shorter than me and the roll cage had been made for him. When I sat in the cockpit of the car, my head touched the roll cage, so I slid my legs further forward and more or less lay on my back, therefore an eight-second escape was impossible, but ten seconds, yes.

Vincent turned to Brenda and said, 'If he can't get out of the car in eight seconds, he doesn't race.'

Brenda thought quickly and said, 'Come over here with me, we will have a better view of the car. When I shout "Derek", to my husband, you start your stopwatch.'

Now I could release the harness before my wife shouted my name, which I did, and I was out of the car in under eight seconds. All Vincent could do was huff and puff about how he couldn't see me from where my wife had taken him. Brenda then told him to go and find something else to do and leave her husband alone to concentrate on his racing.

Good money had been paid to the Turners and the car hadn't turned a wheel. Let's hope Trevor Graves turns up as promised. I needed four runs on the track to get my licence. Well, Trevor did turn up late that evening, but it was late on Saturday afternoon before I was given a pass by John Hackney. It was a good launch – so good my head hit the roll cage again and my neck felt terrible. I told Trevor, who was in charge this time, and all he did was shrug his shoulders. What's wrong with these people, don't they want me to race in the Top Alcohol class?!

Brenda and I enjoyed ourselves in the Little Chef that evening. We went through the menu, prawn cocktail for Brenda, pâté for me. Plaice and chips for Brenda, steak and kidney pie for me, followed by two jubilee pancakes and ice cream, coffee and liqueurs (our own liqueur). As we were finishing the meal, John Price walked in and said to Brenda, 'If you paid me £10,000, I wouldn't drive a TA car. Well done, Derek!' Never a compliment like that from Graham Beckwith. He thought it was easy to drive cars like that, even Top Fuel cars, just because he raced a 10-second car twenty years ago! We left John Price eating his beefburger.

Sunday morning dawned, an easy breakfast for me as Top Alcohol wouldn't be racing before noon. When we arrived in our pitting area, there was panic. The Turners didn't have any push rods that fitted our engine. Thank God Barry Sheavills had some in his rig. The car just made the first sessions of the morning trials. I had a half-pass – 4.938/117.47mph for the eighth mile. John Hackney was pleased and signed my licence assessment. No full licence for me this meeting, but I did have my name in the official programme:

Derek Annable (UK) TAD 223

Derek is new to Top Alcohol ranks, having made a huge leap from his previous Modified ET class, where he raced the Altered that used to belong to Fay Fischer. Before that he campaigned a Camaro in Street ET. Apart from our very own Daddy Stone, Derek is a prime candidate for the title of 'Grand old man of Top Alcohol', since he is 67 years old. Before you think 'wow – how can he do this?', bear in mind that Eddie Hill is 61 and still winning Top Fuel races in America – Chris Karameseines was even older when he raced Top Fuel. The car may look familiar, it used to belong to Barry Sheavills.

My racing over, we thanked the Turners, paid them £600 in cash and drove home.

As we drove along the road home, my wife said, 'Derek, what is the matter with your neck? Your head keeps falling to one side.'

Brenda was right. The pain in my neck was driving me mad and there was a clicking noise every time I moved my head. It took over two years before the pain went and I could move my head with ease. I should have had an X-ray to check for any fractures. If I had gone to our doctor and explained what had happened, he would have stopped me racing, so I put up with the pain. Trevor Graves and the Turners should have made certain my position in the cockpit was correct and not a danger for me.

For the type of race licence I needed, the RAC required anybody over 65 years to take a stressed ECG. Dr David Thomas, consultant cardiologist, had tested me at the North Wales Medical Centre. Now it was time to be tested using the Bruce protocol.

When I arrived at the Bangor hospital, they gave me a form to sign. I was taking full responsibility for anything that may go wrong. The hospital were carrying out the test to my orders. Dr Thomas reported:

19 September 1997

Dear Dr King

Mr Derek Annable, d.o.b. 16.12.30
Mount View, Rhosgoch, Amlwch

Further to previous correspondence this gentleman has now attended for exercise testing. He was exercised using the Bruce protocol, his resting 12 lead ECG demonstrated sinus rhythm, heart rate was 95 beats per minute. He exercised in total for 9 minutes 3 seconds achieving a heart rate of 166 beats per minute. During the course of the test there were no significant ECG changes apart from minor non-specific change in the inferior ST segment.

Yours sincerely

Dr D K Thomas, MD, MRCP
Consultant Physician/Cardiologist

It doesn't say that they take your blood pressure up to 200+ and keep it there for two minutes. Then you stop, sit down and if your bodily functions don't return to normal within a set time, you have failed. I passed, but swore never again would I subject my heart to that; it would be foolish at my age. However, the RAC accepted the doctor's report and I would be allowed to race the TA car anywhere in Europe, so it was worth it.

Nothing's simple, however. The Turners were becoming difficult, they wanted to go to the USA. Rob Turner was after the RAC Championship and their car was entered in the World Finals at Santa Pod. Carmel Turner, Rob's wife and crew chief, said to my wife, 'If Derek enters the TA dragster in the World Finals at Santa Pod on 12–14 September, we won't crew for him.'

My wife wasn't pleased but struck a deal with Carmel. If they crewed for me at a Santa Pod meeting on 27–28 September, she would pay the Turners £1,000. They agreed – money talks volumes – and our car would be racing at the end of September for my race licence.

As described in *ETRA News* by Carla Pittau, the bracket racers were having trouble with Keith Bartlett, the owner of Santa Pod Raceway:

So what about Mr Bartlett and his politics? Are they working? Are they beneficial to the sport in general and ET racers in particular? I gave him the benefit of the doubt. I presumed him to be reasonable. I imagined he wanted British racing to be competitive and professional, so as to attract sponsorship and corporate interest. I did not think he wanted to try and squeeze out the grass roots, the less wealthy racers, the beginners.

Perhaps he has advisers who only let him have part of the story, perhaps his long-term plans are indeed fantastically good for all, perhaps … But the story so far appears gloomy, and not just from the point of view of ET racers.

British drag racing is not a native product, it's an import from the USA and we all have to accept that.

So off went my letter:

15 September 97

Dear ETRA News Readers

The admiral at the helm of British drag racing adopts a sinister attitude, stripping all bracket racers of their basic rights to compete. His power will be complete when his final ambition is forced through.

To be, all events promoted and organised by Power Racing Communications Ltd. This will channel entry fees and gate money into one large pot. Then all racers (sorry ladies) will be castrated and completely impotent.

Carla, you and the ETRA Committee have the support of all racers in the future struggle with Goliath. The sling is there and the shot will come in time. History is on our side.

Derek 'Grandad' Annable

TAD 243

Carla replied:

Derek,

Thank you very much for your support. We would be happy to publish a report on your experience so far with the Top Alcohol dragster. Fancy putting pen to paper and tell us?

Regards and all the best to Brenda.

Carla

Time to enter the dragster in the Doorslammers meeting at the Pod but there was a small problem, the car wasn't a doorslammer, it was a dragster. The powers that be within the club agreed I could race for my licence only within the Top Alcohol Funny Car section. Brenda and I still had some friends in drag racing.

Thank goodness the weather was fine when we arrived at Santa Pod. There was a large field of race cars, from Pro Modified to the slow cars in Street ET. This was my last chance to secure the endorsement required for Category 'C' licence.

The car was out of the rig and up on jacks ready for me to fire up. Steve Turner was his usual happy self, smoking cigarettes one after the other,

confident the engine would be on full power for me. John Price was inter-
viewing Barry Sheavills and asking him how he felt about seeing a youthful
OAP driving his old car and what were his plans in Top Fuel for next year.

It was nearly the end of the first day before we were called out for me to
make my first observed full pass. Steve kept saying, 'Derek, only make a
half-pass to get the feel of the car.'

To keep him happy, I said, 'Yes, Steve, a half-pass.' I needed two full
passes this weekend, we were allocated one today. How many tomorrow,
nobody would say. I couldn't see the clerk of the course allowing me track
time for two full passes on Sunday with all the racing which was planned;
it would be now or never.

Down the fire-up road I went, all eyes were on me. Some racers were
shaking their heads, others wishing me luck. Now it was my turn. A good
burnout, Steve brought me back over the new rubber I had laid down and
saw me into pre-stage. This time, if I felt the car was going straight after the
launch, I was going all the way, no lifting off. Yes, it was going straight, so
I pressed the second gear button, now the engine was pulling strong, and
the revs were coming up quick. I pressed the top gear button just before the
finishing line, now I must lift off and pull the shoots. All the way back
through the pits, racers were clapping me. I had never experienced that
before. What I had just done must have looked good.

I thanked the crew and went over to the BMW to show Brenda my
timing ticket – I was an eight-second man:

Reaction	.776
60ft	1.334
330ft	3.401
$\frac{1}{8}$ ET	5.144
$\frac{1}{8}$ mph	134.57
$\frac{1}{4}$ ET	8.232
$\frac{1}{4}$ mph	159.87

I must have reached 100mph in less than three seconds – very satisfactory
for my first full pass. John Hackney gave me a pass tick on my assessment
form. Brenda and I went back to the Travelodge two happy people and full
of hope for Sunday; please let the weather be dry and fine.

Sunday morning was dry and fine. Steve greeted me with the news that
Darren Prentice wanted a low seven-second pass from me if I was to be
allowed to race in Top Alcohol next year. The thought of this got the adren-
aline running through my body. I must put a good show on. I did this, with
a smoky burnout. I brought the car to a stop and selected reverse gear, but

then Steve jumped in front of the car and gave me the cut off engine sign. The car, with me in it, was pushed back to the start line and towed back to the pits for an engine inspection. When the covers were taken off, two rocker arms had broken and there were many bent push rods. I had over-reved the engine in the burnout. No chance of making repairs before the track was shut down. Rob and Carmel Turner kept saying, 'Why did you do it, Derek?'

I thought, do what? I had carried out Steve Turner's instructions to the letter and I was being blamed for the breakage.

It would be three years before I would sit in the driving seat of that car again and run some quick times. I hadn't learned a lot about racing a Top Alcohol dragster in August and September 1997, but I did learn about the people who raced them. They guarded the know-how and would not pass on this information to any new driver. It was as if certain racers didn't want others to succeed, hoping they would run out of money through breakages to the engine and car, then give up. I didn't give up. It took me three years to gain the respect due to me and run a car without breaking it.

I thanked the Turners for bringing out our car and paid our dues. Everything that weekend made my wife angry – me for over-revving the engine and the Turners who had promised to have the car ready for two runs on Saturday, which it wasn't.

The Thunder and Lightning team's racing was over for another year. It was time for me to write to Carla telling her of my experience with the Top Alcohol dragster:

---

4 October 1997

ETRA News

Thank you all for the invitation to share, with you, my experiences (to date) in Top Alcohol.

In the distant days when I was a serious bracket racer, my heart used to sink when TA/TF cars were at the same meeting. More bits on the track, oil on the launch area, delays, delays, loss of track time, bracket racers being forced back down the fire-up road. We could have been out there putting on a show for the public. Damn the big boys and girls!!

How wrong I was. It is a mammoth task to bring a Top Alcohol dragster to the line. Many weeks of planning and arranging crew. The myth is broken. Where, I was told, people would give their right arm to work for free on a TA car, it doesn't happen that way. The few dedicated crew left are in such demand that they are like gold dust.

Now we shall get to the part that matters. Firstly a Top Alcohol dragster is a beast, one hell of a beast. On my first launch (1.17 for the 60ft) my vision had gone. All I could see were two black lines in front of me, these were the side bars of the roll cage. The G-force had forced my eyes back, bringing my side vision to the front. This corrected itself on lift off. This was a burnout and launch. I thought, what the hell is going to happen when I have to do a half-pass tomorrow morning?

Next day dawned. The crew looked more worried than me, even the chief start line marshall had the same expression on his face and was very jittery. This can be very unnerving. I wasn't going into the operating theatre for major surgery, I was racing a brute of a car.

I burn out, crew chief gets me back onto the pre-stage, I then raise the revs to 5000, hold it, hold it, damn, they're falling off, get back to 5000, ease the clutch back and less handbrake, move into stage. The lights come up. Go, release the clutch and handbrake, mash (no half, all full) launch (1.13 for the 60ft), still no vision, thank God vision returned at 330ft, change to second gear, eighth mile coming up, left off, pull chute, we're under the gantry now, cut off fuel, clutch out, slow, slow. stop. Wait for the crew, back to the pits. Time to relax and think, next time Derek we get into that black hole, a full pass.

The human body is a strange and wonderful thing. The full pass we made at the doorslammers although a bit on and off. At least on the positive side we had full vision from launch to the end of the track. It was so relaxing to see out of the corner of your eye the green of the grass bank as you accelerate up to 160mph and one day beyond. This was a 8.2 pass. The RAC require a low/mid 7 next time.

Thank you all

Derek 'Grandad' Annable

TAD 243

PS I am still a bracket racer. My first love, after my wife, is Street ET and always will be.

My wife turned to me and said, 'Derek, you are a member of the British Racing Drivers Club, surely you know somebody who you raced against all those years ago with enough money to help drag racing?' Well, yes, there was. He wasn't rich then but he is now, so off to Bernie Ecclestone of the FOA went the following:

24 November 1997

Dear Bernie Ecclestone

We all in the BRDC and Formula One thank you for your contribution to motorsport. There is an explosive form of motorsport called Drag Racing which in the UK is suffering from lack of funds and men/women of vision and stability to bring it into the twenty-first century. Again the owners of the Santa Pod racetrack, Bedfordshire are in receivership. In 1996 Power Racing Communication Ltd, headed by Keith Bartlett, bought the track from the then official receivers. 18 months on, Keith Bartlett has called in the receivers.

When I retired from racing cars in 1952, never in my wildest dreams did I think at the age of 68 years I would be racing a Top Alcohol dragster with its awesome power in excess of 3000bhp.

Mr Ecclestone, please consider and take up the challenge as UK Drag Racing Supremo. Surely the failure rate by the various owners of the Santa Pod racetrack and land gives the advantage to any future buyer.

All the best for Christmas.

Derek 'Grandad' Annable

TAD 243

Back came the following fax:

Dear Grandad

Thank you for your letter of 24 November. With myself being a Grandad it heartens me to think we are still capable of something, but for your information, behind the scenes I am working very closely with Keith Bartlett in order to see that Drag Racing in general throughout Europe receives the support it deserves. So let's see what is going to happen next year. Do not give up, from another Grandad.

Best regards

Bernie Ecclestone

It was nearly Christmas and the HRG last issue of the year came through my letterbox. The Northern Street Car Challenge final results took up the last eight pages:

16th place HRG 17 Derek Annable 1982 Chevy Camaro 8400 Points 12 Events

Derek started off the NSCC series with some solid performances from his supercharger 350ci-powered Camaro, and by mid-season was travelling some tremendous distances from his Anglesey home in order to attend the cruises and shows to gain maximum points toward the championship. At one point he was running fourth overall, though toward the end of the season he dropped out of the competition. Nicknamed 'Grandad' by his fellow racers, Derek has been an extremely good competitor and sportsman and we hope that we'll see him back in 1998.

Yes, Shaun, the tremendous distances and the strain to my wife's health were the main reasons I had to call it a day midway through the season.

Big decisions were taken, we closed our garage at Moelfre and my wife's shop in Benllech. Both were no longer viable and my wife required more of my time to keep her on the road to recovery. This meant any motorsport would be low key in the forthcoming year. We did have a good Christmas and reflected on what could have been.

CHAPTER 7

1998

Brenda's health wasn't improving and the Turners were being less than helpful. I knew it would be an impossible task to race the TA dragster this year, so I threw my energy into finding a hospital which was able to provide the care my wife required.

During the next six months it was one specialist and pain clinic after another, with still no improvement in her health. First she was having Chinese acupuncture treatment privately and then on the National Health.

Our local hospital had just installed a full body scanner and Brenda was subjected to the frightening experience of going through this machine. The thought of it brought on nightmares for many weeks. The hospital reported back to the doctors what we already knew – her brain had been damaged by the stroke she had suffered. One side of her brain showed massive damage in sections which controlled the feeling and movement in her left leg and arm. She was told that the fall at the time of her stroke could have fractured bones in her ribcage which were trapping nerves, hence the constant pain.

In my spare time I had started to write for sponsorship, but this time for the TA dragster. My first letter was to P&O European Ferries:

---

29 January 1998

Sales Promotion Manager
P&O European Ferries Ltd
Dover

Dear Mr Kevin Taylor

Re: RACMSA British Drag Racing Championship 1998

Two years ago we wrote requesting sponsorship for our drag racing team. At the time your company were unable to help. We are still looking for financial assistance for the 1998 season. We acquired a Top Alcohol dragster in the latter part of last season (photo and specification enclosed) from Barry Sheavills who was the RACMSA champion in 1994/95/96, this gives the car an excellent pedigree.

The Thunder and Lightning team's programme for the 1998 season is to enter the RACMSA British Drag Racing Championship 'Top Alcohol' in which 15-20 cars from the UK, Switzerland, Sweden, Germany and Holland compete. The winner in 1997 was Rob Turner. The Turner brothers prepare our car. We run as a team on race day. This gives us overlap for crews and spares at the meeting. The burden on a crew who have to work overnight on a broken engine is halved, thus a more relaxed driver on race day. The UK Championship will have Sky television coverage and BBC *Top Gear/ motorsport* are also involved.

Two years on from my first letter to your company I have become the oldest, at the age of 67 years, Top Alcohol driver in the world, past or present.

Yours sincerely

Derek Annable

TAD 243

They were quick to reply:

2 February 1998

Mr D Annable
Amlwch, Anglesey

Dear Mr Annable

Thank you for your recent letter dated 29 January, requesting sponsorship for the Thunder and Lightning drag racing team.

You will appreciate that a company with a high consumer profile, such as ours, receives many requests for help and unfortunately, as a result, our budget is allocated for some time to come. Regretfully therefore, we are unable to offer financial assistance on this occasion.

We trust that you will appreciate our position, and we take the opportunity of wishing you every success.

Yours sincerely

Kevin H Taylor

Sales Promotion Manager

Then Bayford Thrust Energy:

---

2 February 1998

Dear Sir

Thank you for your invitation to join Bayford Thrust Energy. We have closed down our garage business (Action's Garage, Llanallgo, Moelfre, Gwynedd LL72 8NZ) and put the freehold property on the market.

Our other activity, drag racing, maybe of interest to a go ahead company like yours.

In 1995 I became UK National Champion in Street ET. Since then we have moved up to Top Alcohol. The car (photo and specification enclosed) is entered in the RACMSA 1998 championship for Top Alcohol dragsters in which 15–20 cars from the UK, Switzerland, Sweden, Germany and Holland compete. The winner in 1997 was Rob Turner. The Turner brothers prepare our car. We run as a team on race day. This gives us overlap for crews and spares at the meeting. The burden on a crew who have to work overnight on a broken engine is halved, thus a more relaxed driver on race day. The UK Championship will have Sky television coverage and BBC *Top Gear/* motorsport are also involved.

To date the car's body, either side of the driver, is available for a main sponsor to take up an option on this advertising space. If your company is interested, please keep the photos, if not please return in enclosed SAE.

Yours sincerely

Derek Annable

TAD 243

They were also quick to reply:

---

4 February 1998

D Annable Esq
Amlwch, Anglesey

Dear Mr Annable

Your letter dated 2 February 1998 addressed to the managing director has been passed to me for attention.

Regrettably, our sponsorship/advertising budget for 1998 has already been allocated and, therefore, we are unable to take your request further. However, I would like to wish you every success in finding suitable sponsors.

I have taken the opportunity of returning your photographs for future use.

Yours sincerely

Jonathan Turner

Marketing Director

This was a repeat of last year's rejections to my appeal for money. I thought I would try one more firm and then call it a day, and this was to Littlewoods:

11 February 1998

Dear Sir

I know your company sponsor the FA Cup. How about a complete new image and sponsor a Top Alcohol dragster (photos and specification enclosed). A couple of thousand pounds will purchase the main area of the car's body for promotion of your company. The RACMSA 1998 UK Championship in which dragsters from Sweden, Germany and Holland compete will have Sky television coverage and BBC *Top Gear*/motorsport are also involved.

If your company is interested please keep the photos, if not please return in enclosed SAE.

Yours sincerely

Derek Annable

TAD 243

Before they replied, I received a letter from Pilkington:

24 February 1998

Dear Mr Annable

Thank you for your letter of 30 December, in which you asked if it would be possible for Pilkington to offer sponsorship for your drag racing team.

Your request was carefully considered, but I have to tell you that we are unable to help on this occasion. I know this will be a disappointment but, sadly, we have had to reduce significantly our grants to individuals and external bodies in recent months, and we are therefore having to turn down requests for help for some very worthwhile causes of which this is clearly one.

I am sorry not to be able to send you a more helpful reply, but I wish you every success with the 1998 season. I am also returning the photographs you enclosed.

Yours sincerely

David Roycroft

Head of Corporate Affairs

For David Roycroft to personally reply to my letter was indeed an honour. I have always treasured that letter.

When Littlewoods did reply to my letter, it was the standard response:

                                                  3 March 1998

Mr D Annable
Anglesey

Dear Mr Annable

Many thanks for your recent letter concerning sponsorship.

As you know, we do sponsor the FA Cup and as such target all our efforts in this direction.

Because football is the mainstay sport of our business, we do not sponsor other events.

Nevertheless, once again many thanks for writing.

Yours sincerely

P A Hughes

Sponsorship Manager

Good news and bad news was being reported on the future of drag racing. First the good news, Terry Gibbs was to be involved again at Avon Park Raceway:

Super Series announced for Avon Park Raceway in 1998

APIRA have been asked to officiate at 4 rounds for Terry and Tina, to be known as 'Avon Park Raceway Super Series Championship'. The dates for these rounds are listed at the end of this letter.

The car classes will consist of Super Comp, Super Gas, Super Street, Pro Bracket, Sportsman, all VWDRC classes and, of course, the Wild Bunch.

In conjunction with the above we shall also be incorporating 4 rounds of the ACU Drag Bike Championship for the following classes: Funny Bike, Pro Stock, Comp Bike, Super Street, all Super Twin classes, and finally 9.90 and 10.90 Bike.

The first of these rounds will also be the raceway's season opener, and to get you all in the mood we have organised a two-day Test 'n' Tune weekend scheduled for April 4/5.

Then the bad news:

SANTA POD LOSE THE PICNIC

The long-standing street racer weekend, Gary's Picnic, will not be staged at Santa Pod Raceway this season, the NASC have revealed.

Since going into bankruptcy Santa Pod have been reluctant to stage events which they cannot guarantee the financial success of. They offered to rent the facility to the NASC for the weekend, but the fees have proved too steep for the club to accept. The event will go ahead but will be held at Avon Park on 16 August.

Winners and losers.

I was still having trouble with the Turners. Steve wouldn't reply to my letters and would only speak to me on the phone. In all my dealings with them, they never signed their names to anything and refused to correspond. Off went another cheque from me for payment of three months' storage in advance.

Unknown to me, Brenda had begun crossing swords with John Wilcox of the BBC at Pebble Mill Studios in Birmingham over some issue on *Top Gear*. His reply was as follows:

12 February 1998

Dear Mrs Annable

Thank you for your letter about *Top Gear*.

Fast cars have a rightful place in a programme about motoring. The question is whether there is too much emphasis on speed.

Top Gear tries, as it should, to mix a whole range of topics. Of course it will include fast cars like the new Porsche 911, but we also do regular items on safety or consumer issues. In the last series, for example, we discovered an alarming problem with the Vauxhall Cavalier and managed to get a major car company to recognise the problem and take major steps to deal with it. This is not the action of a programme obsessed with speed or detached from reality. It does come down to a question of balance and we do spend a great deal of time trying to get that right. That includes using a wide range of presenters, as well as covering many different aspects of the world of cars.

Finally, may I apologise for the delay in replying personally. We have only just emerged from a very busy run of programmes.

John Wilcox

Deputy Editor

Motoring and Leisure Sports Programmes

Off went my wife's reply:

17 February 98

Dear Mr John Wilcox

Top Gear

Your reply to my letter of the 19 December 97 doesn't in any way redress the points I raised in the letter. I do know what *Top Gear* sets out to portray to the viewers, being a fan of the programme from the year dot.

I feel it is a useless exercise for viewers/general public to get involved by letter or other means with any form of the media over the way it portrays itself. Thank you for taking the time to reply to my letter.

Yours sincerely

Brenda Annable

Good for her.

Then there was another lady fighting her corner, Carla, in her editorial in the *ETRA News*:

ETRA News
Issue No. 8 – March 1998
Editorial by Carla Pittau

Happy 1998 racing season to everybody, best wishes for a successful and exciting one!

At the last count, the operating tracks in England were still 3 in total, albeit each with its own peculiarities, problems and faults.

Santa Pod will still be operating in 98, despite Power Racing Communications' demise. PRC went into liquidation last year following insurmountable financial difficulties.

However, a new company has been set up and the racing will go on. Somebody told me that the new set-up was actually composed of 3 different companies, each promoting a different type of event during the coming season. A possible reason for this, my source continues, is to make sure that should one of the companies be less than successful the others could still operate without interruption or disruption. I don't know whether this is the case or if this is good news, bad news, or totally indifferent news to ET racers.

During the recent SPRC Riders and Drivers meeting, Keith Bartlett did not wish to make any statement regarding this or any other matter regarding PRC and the financial details of the liquidation, and this is his right, as the details of the liquidation of a limited company should really only be a concern of shareholders, directors and creditors.

However, this unfortunately leads to all sorts of unconfirmed rumours, and good or bad, popular or unpopular, truth is generally preferable to rumours.

The ones among you who are SPRC members should have received details of the matters discussed at the Riders and Drivers meeting, however I have illustrated the main points of concern to ET racers in the 'News from the Tracks' section.

---

and

STRAIGHT FROM *PRAVDA*?

Towards the end of Lenin's life, rumours have it that Stalin printed a fake copy of *Pravda* and showed it to him, to mislead the dying Bolshevik about current affairs and persuade him to officially back up some of Stalin's less popular measures. So maybe what you are looking at is a fake issue of the *ETRA News*. You wouldn't believe that this publication, biased and full of lies, could possibly publish this article, would you?

Joking apart, this is what the ETRA is about. Opinions may wildly differ (and they do), and different people may report differently perceived truths. It's up to the racers to make their minds up.

However, I couldn't help but notice a couple of misleading statements in Chris's article, and I feel that to put the record straight, the following points should be made:

- Avon Park has not just recently decided to constitute itself as a management committee. This was decided years and years ago, when the club was formed. I don't like it anymore than Chris does, but at least the committee members don't just ignore rules or articles of association when it suits them.

- I'm really glad to hear that Patterson is changing his tune. If Chris says he is, as he meets him regularly, I believe him. This is a positive result and I'm sure a lot of racers are relieved to hear it, especially after the fateful words 'There is no ET racing at Santa Pod in my long-term plans'.

- I felt really sad that Chris decided to call the SPRC committee 'money grabbing bastards'. He seemed to twist some of my statements there and turn them against the committee. I do not think the SPRC are money grabbing bastards at all. I just thought that perhaps they weren't fighting hard enough on behalf of their members. The thought that money was grabbed by anybody never entered my head, after all, none of the money goes to the committee members themselves. (I can't even accuse the promoters of being money grabbers as, at least according to the information officially available, they have not been too efficient at money grabbing.)

- I know Chris did fight for us and perhaps this is the reason why he feels bad about the criticism. But let's be clear about the situation: nobody is accusing anybody. All we want is a fair place to race. And if we have to voice members' complaints, that's what we do. This isn't *Pravda*, it's a debate and discussion forum: check up the ETRA committee's photograph on page 3: do we look like the Politburo? (I'm the tall, beautiful blonde with the stunning body … er … on the right-hand side.)

The ideal situation for ET racers in this country (and indeed for any racers) is many strong, successful racetracks. But if the only even remotely achievable objective in the fairly short term is 3 operating tracks, cooperating with each other, and reasonably successful, this is what we all would like and this is what we strive for.

Carla

One thing I have enjoyed in drag racing is the way the ladies take on an active role, whether it be as a racer or controlling the running of the clubs and the track on race day. I like their no-nonsense approach in the few publications they edit. Unlike other forms of motorsport, drag racing isn't an all-male action sport. It strikes a balance right across the field.

Now it was the fiftieth anniversary of motor racing at Silverstone. Having been a member of the British Racing Drivers Club for forty-six years, it was only right I should attend the anniversary. All members (full and life) are given four free guest passes. Who to ask? My wife suggested I write to John Prescott, the deputy prime minister and invite him and his wife to the British Grand Prix on 9/12 July, so off went my letter:

---

24 March 98

Dear John Prescott

Re: The British Grand Prix, Silverstone, 9/12th July 98

How about a day's relaxation for yourself and your wife at the above. I am not Bernie Ecclestone, no private helicopter and all that, but you are welcome to travel there with us in our BMW 635. My wife has an orange badge so there shouldn't be any problems parking.

My wife keeps going on about you. Our son was in the navy and anybody who has been to sea is tops with her. I have two members' guest passes. Please consider our invitation.

Yours sincerely

Derek Annable

Back came his reply:

21 April 1998

Dear Mr Annable

The deputy prime minister and Mrs Prescott have asked me to thank you for your kind letter of 24 March, inviting them to attend the British Grand Prix, to be held at Silverstone from 9/12 July.

As you may appreciate, the deputy prime minister receives a large number of invitations and, because of his many other responsibilities, cannot accept them all. On this particular occasion, he must regrettably decline your kind invitation.

He really is very sorry. They would have loved to come.

Yours sincerely

Della Armstrong

Private secretary

One day the lad from Hull will come to a motorsport race meeting with us!

Wonders will never cease. Steve Turner sent me a list of parts he required to rebuild the engine and bring the chassis up to date. To keep him sweet, I enclosed a cheque for £340 in the following letter:

22 April 1998

Dear Steve

I have decided, with your approval, a more realistic plan to get Brenda's car to the start line. We aim to have the car ready for the Sportsman Nationals at Santa Pod on 13/14 June 1998 (Professional classes invited to test). Split the repair costs into the three parts.

1) Rods and Bearings (your list 1, 11, 12), order now on my MasterCard, details enclosed.
2) Camshaft etc (your list 2,3,4,5,6,7,8,9,10,13,14,15,16,20) order on 20 April by MasterCard.
3) Pro-gears, harness, chutes (your list 17,18,19), order on 20 May by MasterCard.

This will spread the cost three ways: engine, bottom end, engine top end and then car. Unless you see any problems please put part one of engine repair into full speed ahead while the pound is strong against the dollar.

All the best.

Derek

In the June edition of the *Hot Rod Gazette,* I read:

BRACKET RACERS HEAD TO THE NORTH

Last month we bemoaned the level of support that bracket racers are giving their classes, most notably at York Raceway. Both Mick Bettison of PDRC and the *Hot Rod Gazette* have been in touch with the ETRA and good news! – their newsletter editor, Carla Pittau (of Heaven & Hell Camaro fame) has put out a challenge to try and get some of their racers up to the track for the next round on 19 July.

At present there are just four definites for the journey up north, but hopefully this will soon grow if they get some good old northern hospitality and a decent field of cars to run with.

Bracket racing is open to anybody at York who holds an IOPD licence (price just £5) and there's no reason why you can't run in both the NSCC championship and the brackets on the day.

The ETRA seem like a well-organised bunch and with membership at just £5 with an excellent newsletter included it has to be money well spent. For more details about the ETRA contact Carla on 0181 856 5690.

There are three big bracket meets in the ETRA Championship, the Midsummer Nationals at Santa Pod on 8–9 August, the Super Series at Avon Park on 29 August to 1 September and the European Finals back at the Pod on 11–13 September.

Given a good enough meet, who knows, maybe we could see York back on the calendar for 99? We sure hope so.

When Brenda knew Carla Pittau was going to race at York Dragway, she decided we must race the Camaro there on 19 July. This was more like the Brenda of the good old days of drag racing with our Altered; she was planning everything, such as where to stay and phoning her northern friends – Dave Allan's wife was the first on the list.

Although I had closed down the garage business, the Camaro was still stored there. Time to get John Turner busy again. There was three months left on the MOT so I taxed the car for six months and now I could test the monster on the roads around Anglesey.

Before the meeting at York there was a NSRA meeting at Avon Park Raceway on 4/5 July – the drive there and back would blow the cobwebs out of the motor. I decided York was Brenda's meeting; Avon Park, mine. I could drive down there early Saturday morning, stay one night, returning home early Sunday afternoon. This time the Travelodge, Alcester would be my overnight stay. It was a RWYB-type meeting, no need to send an entry form to Wendy Talbot. I wondered why they were calling it Avon Park Raceway again instead of the new name, Shakespeare County Raceway. Very confusing. When I took it up with the club, the reply was, 'We have a lot of old stationery to use up, Derek.'

Our son Mark was going to keep an eye on his mother and make sure that meals on wheels brought her some food. Since her stroke, my wife was unable to use the cooker, or even boil a kettle. The loss of feeling on her left side meant she was always burning herself and dropping things – very nasty and dangerous.

I was on the loose again, breaking all the speed limits between Anglesey and Stratford-on-Avon. My favourite game was to let an £80,000 Mercedes power up to overtake me, then just as it was one car's length behind me, I would drop the Camaro into second gear and hit the throttle, within a couple of seconds the revs would be up to 7000 and the car was travelling at 100mph. A quick look in the mirror and there it was, £80,000 of car as if the driver had put his brakes on. The rich old man in his German car treated my 20-year-old Camaro with respect and kept his distance from then on. When I told this story to a 20-year-old GTI driver, he said, 'You're a worse hooligan than me.'

It was good to be back on the strip – the sound of all those V8 engines as I drove through the pits, the smell of cooking bacon, Bruno going up and down the track in his tractor, the concrete wall around the start area looking like the walls of Edward's castles in Wales – the whole scene brought tears to my eyes.

There is nothing in motorsport to equal drag racing when it is in full flow – 30,000hp from six Top Fuel cars, the heady feeling from breathing in nitrous fumes from the open headers (exhausts). Cars of all sizes and shapes lined up ready to compete against each other down 440 yards of sticky tarmac. Cars flashing past you every ten seconds, the fastest travelling at over 300mph, the slowest 80mph, and all this happening on the same day. You can walk around the pits, touch the cars and talk to the drivers. There are no barriers holding back the fans. You become part of a big family and all this for £10 at the gate. I have experienced much in my long life, and nothing, but nothing equals being part of the drag racing scene.

Our 500 mile trip to and from Avon Park raceway was rewarded by the Camaro running its best time to date, ET 14.073/101.176mph, plus four wins.

The British Grand Prix at Silverstone was calling all BRDC members to attend. My wife didn't like Formula One cars, calling them dinky cars, but all members should support the main UK Grand Prix, so we booked in at High View Hotel, Wellingborough.

All our luggage and my wife's wheelchair were loaded into the BMW and it was time to leave Anglesey for a couple of days. The journey on the M6 motorway was becoming a nightmare, a 10-mile section north of Birmingham could take more than an hour to cover.

When we arrived at High View, the Chinese lady was glad to see my wife. Because of the early start to drive to Silverstone, she was arranging an early breakfast for us on Saturday and sandwiches for us to take with us on Sunday.

The traffic was light on Saturday morning and we arrived in the BRDC car park without any trouble and were directed past the main stream of traffic – having a BRDC badge on the windscreen helped. On Sunday this journey could take five hours, four hours from the Towcester roundabout. Sheer hell.

I left Brenda in her wheelchair at the entrance to the BRDC suite and went to park the car. When I returned, Kate Scott was being her usual difficult self with my wife. 'Where's your pass? Who are you?'

The other staff at the check-in knew who my wife was, but Kate, the membership secretary, wouldn't listen to them and told my wife, 'You must sit there in your wheelchair until your husband arrives', and she was left outside the entrance door. All this was happening as I was walking towards them. Later in the day, John Fitzpatrick, the BRDC club secretary, took a similar attitude when my wife needed to use the ladies toilets, because they were being cleaned. People in wheelchairs and those who have suffered strokes become incontinent and need a toilet now, not in half an hour's time. I did notice many of the hale and hearty members of our age showed embarrassment when confronted with disabled members and their wives – this speaks volumes.

Brenda soon found something to keep her mind off what had happened. Standing near her wheelchair was a rather confused elderly man with an Australian accent. 'Derek', she said, 'who is that?'

As I have pretty good eyesight, I could see the name on his member's badge. 'It is Sir Jack Brabham.'

'Good', she replied and turning her wheelchair towards him she said, 'You're Sir Jack Brabham.'

'Oh, am I! You are right, young lady, I am Sir Jack Brabham.'

Then my wife fired questions at him about Australia, his years when he raced, where and when. Sir Jack's parting words to my wife were, 'I have never met anyone like you before', and off he went into the bar.

That was excitement enough for one day, I wheeled Brenda to where the car was parked, rested for an hour and drove back to Wellingborough.

We tried a new Indian restaurant that evening, as the Bengal Tiger, our favourite, was at the bottom of the hill from High View. Oh, I could have made it down the hill with Brenda in her wheelchair but not back up. It was a pleasant meal and the waiter service was excellent. Because we had to leave for Silverstone at 5am, we went to bed early.

It was a tiring four-hour journey from the hotel to Silverstone. Thank goodness the BMW had a automatic box. This time I had to park in the main BRDC car park and travel to the BRDC suite in a special shuttle bus for disabled and wheelchair-bound people. We were early enough to join other members and have breakfast in the dining area of the clubhouse. Stirling Moss was holding court in the far corner; his son and Susie, his third wife, were with him. He was giving a demonstration with his right hand of how he used to take the corners. To me, it looked like his hand was a model plane chasing a German bomber over London in the Blitz. David Warwick was sitting at the table next to ours, looking as if he had been up all night at a party Jordan FI had put on for the drivers and crew. As we were leaving, Ken Tyrrell walked in with friends. He was a member of the 500 Club, all those years ago. He turned to my wife and laughingly said, 'Your husband and those cream cakes, how does he keep so slim?!'

We watched the start of the Grand Prix, but after half a dozen laps Brenda felt tired, so we took the shuttle bus to the car park, got into the car and went to sleep. We must have slept a long time, because when we woke the Grand Prix was over and people were starting to go home. Feeling hungry, we went back to the clubhouse and enjoyed sandwiches and tea.

Soon my wife started talking to an elderly man, who turned out to be Hugh Howarth. He had raced his own Jaguar car in 1951 and 1952, winning the William Lyons Trophy for Jaguars, beating Stirling Moss who was driving the works Jaguar at every meeting they raced against each other. I have a picture of Howarth's Jaguar, number 68. Hugh agreed with me that, since his crash, Stirling Moss didn't seem to know people of yesteryear, or was it that he didn't want to know? Many of Stirling's friends say Susie, his wife, and himself are the only things he cares about! So be it.

How is it that a rich man's family always look upon strangers with suspicion? Hugh Howarth's wife had died some time ago from a stroke, or was it cancer? Anyway, he and Brenda were getting on like a house on fire, smiling and laughing. I could sense the daughter and to some extent the son didn't approve of their father talking family, so he was hurriedly taken outside and off home. Brenda and Hugh exchanged Christmas cards and corresponded, but this all stopped when she received a short letter from one of the family. I never did see the contents of the letter.

It was late when we arrived back at High View. We said goodnight to the owner and his wife and retired early. Monday morning on the M6 motorway is like Friday afternoon – murder, stopping and starting in traffic jams – but we discussed the planned trip to York Dragway.

After four days rest we were off again, the Camaro chugging at 60mph along the M62 motorway, and after two stops for petrol, we had arrived in South Cave. Everyone at the Travelodge and Little Chef was glad to see the lady with the stick, but it was a short stay this time, just the one night.

We arrived early at the York track. What a poor turnout – no Carla Pittau and the other ETRA racers. We put in three runs, said goodbye to Jean and Dez and left for home. York Dragway was going through a quiet time. Yes, their RWYB meetings attract hundreds of GTI racers and the Max Power boys, but the drag racers don't bother going. We would give it one more try at the Northern National in August.

More money was sent off to the Turners:

---

21 July 98

Dear Steve

Enclosed cheque for rent (storage) to the end of September 98.

We accept your price of £570 to rebuild the engine and assemble Brenda's dragster, all as per instructions.

Best of luck in the Summer Nationals.

Derek

Then further letters:

---

25 July 98

Dear Steve

Reference the cheque for £180.00 I sent to you on the 17 February to pay the various people involved in the SFI inspection on Brenda's dragster.

My accountants who are in the middle of my self-assessment require from you confirmation in writing that the money was used to inspect:

1) The clutch (£60)
2) Bellhousing (£60)

---

and the final £60 was paid to Geoff Martin who inspected, passed and tagged the chassis of Brenda's dragster TAD 243.

I know it is a bore, but the new tax laws force all of us to supply more in-depth information to the Tax Inspector and in Brenda's and my case where we have three separate businesses, it is mammoth.

All the best.

Derek

---

27 July 98

Dear Steve

I hope you are well. This time last week you asked me for the rent (storage) on Brenda's dragster TAD 243 stored at the Turner Workshop, Santa Pod Raceways compound. Please confirm you have received my cheque for £130.00 which was posted first class to you on Tuesday pm 21 July 98.

At the time of writing I am still awaiting from you the invoices in my name on packages delivered to the UK from the USA for parts ordered from Copperhead, San Clemente, CA Trans 11/06/98 $4555-13 and Midwest Truck and Auto Chicago IL Trans 16/06/08 $690.00 being the only MasterCard purchases authorised by me in June 98.

Please expedite.

Derek Annable

Still no response. I had to phone the suppliers in the USA and put a stop on my MasterCard. Off went another letter to Steve:

---

3 August 98

Dear Steve

My instructions when ordering parts for Brenda's dragster on my MasterCard, were, invoice to us as per MasterCard address details with delivery to a c/o address in Higham Ferrers. I did check with UPS whether imports from the USA could be handled this way and they said yes, and if required the shipped to address could be altered at any time, even if the goods were in transit. I can't understand why Carmel keeps saying, 'Derek, it can't be done that way.'

It was a shock to me the parts were invoiced to Turner Racing and shipped to Steve Turner c/o address.

The photostat copy of Copperhead's documents show a discrepancy between total on page 1 and the amount charged to my MasterCard. Where is page 2? Steve, have all the parts ordered arrived in the UK? Where are the parts being stored? Are they insured? Once fitted to the engine of Brenda's dragster, our insurance on the car and engine would safeguard them against theft.

When this weekend's racing is finished, please sit down with pen and paper and answer my questions in this letter and previous letters.

Brenda's health is paramount to me.

Derek

Carmel kept fobbing us off with one excuse after another; all on the telephone, never in a letter. Why?

The only way to resolve our problems with the Turners was to enter the Camaro in the European Finals at Santa Pod on 11–13 September and confront them face to face. We were told they hadn't touched the car for over a year and in that time it hadn't turned a wheel.

The meeting at York Dragway on the 16 August was much the same as the meeting on 19 July – a waste of petrol. Let's hope the Super Series meeting at Avon Park Raceway would be worth racing at. Yes, it was. There were 100 cars and 100 bikes – that's more like it! Terry Gibbs was offering some good prize money. Well done Terry and Tina, but you will lose money on the meeting, my guess would be £5,000 plus, maybe as much as £10,000.

This time we were booked in at the Travelodge, Alcester, for three nights and looking forward to sampling the cooking at their Little Chef. Brenda suggested we write a gourmet guide because of the dozens of Little Chefs we had eaten at. Now that would be interesting. Granada would sue us for dishonest representation, because we might praise the food more than condemn it!

Being a bank holiday we set off early for Alcester and luckily for us most of the traffic was coming into Wales. Our roads didn't get busy until we reached Shrewsbury, then the main hold-ups were caused by the odd caravan on tow behind a low horsepower car.

Brenda liked the new Travelodge. The disabled room was smart and all the grab rails and so on had been installed to make it easy to get about. Thank God some hotels look after disabled people.

The gang were pleased to see my wife back in drag racing. Angie and Roy Wilding came over to our pit and kept her company while I signed on and had the car scrutineered. Now it was time to check the opposition. I had raced against Sarah Day, Tim Jackson and Rick Denny in the past, but who was this new boy, Chris Hodgkins, with an Audi? He looked nervous, so I went over to his pit and started talking to his father. They lived near Evesham and Mr Hodgkins senior used to circuit race at Clubman events many years ago. He noticed the BRDC badge on my race overalls, and this brought the conversation to who did what and when. I always help a young driver when they start drag racing. A little encouragement goes a long way.

The track was now open, Sportsman first out, followed by Wild Bunch and Super Street, so I lined up with the other cars into the fire-up road. There was poor traction on the start line, I ran a mid-14 second and decided to save the car for qualifying tomorrow morning.

My wife was deep in conversation with a group of racers' wives so I went walkabout. Bertrand Dubet was in the Super Pro pits. He had travelled all the way from France and was working on his car, which had done well in a meeting in France some days ago but he hadn't had time to check the engine before leaving on the ferry from Dover. He remembered me from the days of the Altered.

Wendy Baker's pit was my next stop. There she was with the Stars and Stripes on her Wild Bunch car. All their money was going into a new car, they were building to race in Pro Mod next year and I wished them luck. Then somebody shouted my name. It was another Welshman, Bennett, the track commentator who wanted an update from me on the TA dragster. I explained the problems I was having with the Turners – he wasn't surprised they were being less than helpful. 'Derek, be honest, would you help a new man who one day might take the RAC Championship away from you? It will work out for you, then you can go and break some records, maybe one on this track.'

Brenda came looking for me, she wanted to go back to the Travelodge and have a couple of hours rest before eating.

Sunday was a warm day with good air. Racing was to start at eleven o'clock and Sportsman were out first. My opponent was Martin Isaacs. He dialled in 14.10 and ran a 14.135 making him top qualifier. I dialled in 14.50 and ran a 14.495. I broke out. This put me at the bottom of the qualifiers' list. My second run at three o'clock in the afternoon was even worse, so I would stay bottom of the list. Let's hope I could get a better result tomorrow, as now it was curfew and the end of racing.

Richard Warburton, the race director, made his usual late afternoon tour of the pits with the chief scrutineer, checking that racers hadn't put an extra engine in the car. In the old days, you could race with two engines in the same chassis. He stopped to have a word with my wife, asking about her health and talking about the days when she was crew chief and about our plans for the future.

A bank holiday has the same curfew as a Sunday – no racing before 11am or after 5pm. After a lazy breakfast, we were back on the track for 10am. Who was to be my first opponent in the eliminations? It was Ray Barrow. My wife said, 'Oh no, I don't like that man, he struts around as if he owns the place. You'd better not lose to him.'

How to win? I must risk a dial-in I could break out on so up went 14.58 on the back window of the car. Sportsman had to be in the fire-up road for 11.15am. I just had time to wheel Brenda down to the disabled spectator enclosure halfway down the track, she would then have a good view of the start and finish.

Now I was ready to take on Ray Barrow. He had dialled in 14.00, mine was 14.58 so his light would come down half a second after mine. All weekend I had a reaction time of 0.700–0.800. If I launched on the second amber, I could pull a new perfect light, a 0.500. Every time I had tried this before I pulled a red, 0.400–0.475 – damn it, I will try it. Ray Barrows had all sorts of problems and I crossed the finishing line first, my ET 14.597 on a 14.58, very respectable. My wife was pleased. When Ray got back to the pits, he lifted the bonnet of his car and started playing about with the engine, saying, 'It was a misfire which made me lose.'

My next opponent was Rick Denny, and this time I was doing the chasing not being chased. Rick's car was nearly two seconds slower than mine and he always pulled a good light. I lost this race on the lights. Rick's reaction 0.521, mine 0.685, he crossed the line well ahead of me. Both of us were within $^4\!/\!100$ of a second of our dial-in. It was a good race. End of my day's racing and time to go home. Home was 220 miles away, and it was eight o'clock before we parked the Camaro at Action's Garage and drove home in the BMW. In two weeks' time we would be back at the Pod, then Brenda would get the answers she wanted from Carmel.

We received an invite to a Santa Pod Raceway dinner and disco night at at the Hind Hotel in Wellingborough, so Brenda booked four nights. Off went my cheque to Jenny Catling of Trakbak Racing and the entry form to the SPRC secretary. John and I spent a couple of days checking and testing the Camaro; the engine sounded good and pulled well; now we were ready for the weekend's racing.

Travel on Thursday through Birmingham on the M6 motorway could be murder. Thank goodness we set off early and missed the worst of the hold-up around the junction with the M5. A ground floor room in the annexe had been booked at the Hind Hotel. My wife wouldn't need her wheelchair. The visits she was making to Bangor hospital were paying dividends, her legs were getting stronger, and now my arm and a stick were all she needed to walk with.

The hotel was fully booked with racers from the UK and Europe. No going out to eat this time, we would eat in the hotel dining room. The dinner and disco, the big gala, was in the hotel on Sunday night anyway.

The Santa Pod pits were full to overflowing with race cars when we arrived. Sportsman, with 13, had the biggest field of cars. Top qualifier would have a bye – all to race for.

The international race director was Jon Cross, and his deputy was Darren Prentice. The RAC scrutineers were Stuart Vincent, Amos Meekins and his brother Doug. Who was going to check my car? It was Doug! As soon as he saw me it was, 'Ee bah gum, what's it like up north?'

Why he did this, I don't know. I lived in Wales, not Oldham, Manchester, but he loved taking the mickey out of me, so I just laughed. He was having such fun at my expense that he didn't bother with the car. He tested a couple of wheel nuts and passed the car as A1, OK.

A 13-car field, how many had I beaten before? Most of them I had raced against, Paul Hudson, Gareth Mogford, Rick Denny, Tim Fowler, the two unknowns, David Dony from Belgium and Terri Rogers-Valle from Potters Bar.

Sportsman classes were to have three qualifying sessions today, two on Saturday and their eliminations were to start at 9.30am Sunday.

My first opponent was Alan Didwell. John Price in the tower had already started, 'We have Derek "Grandad" Annable paired against Alan Didwell. Graham, didn't he do well last time, I mean did well!'

Great fun but thank goodness when you are in a race car, you don't hear all this chitchat. Alan didn't do well, I beat him. My time was $^9/_{100}$ of a second on my dial-in. This made me number two qualifier, a position I kept to the end of qualifying.

My next run was against Dave Dony in his blue Buick Skylark, one beautiful car and quicker than mine. I broke out by $^3/_{100}$ of a second. Dave had pulled a bad light, so my wife went over to talk to him. They talked for ten minutes, she explaining where he was going wrong when he was waiting for the start lights. Now it was time to race him again. This time he pulled a better light than mine and won. Thank you Brenda! That was that for the Sportsman classes, the big cars were using the track.

The hotel was very noisy. Thank goodness we were in the annexe away from the many parties being held by the racers in the hotel bars and outside on the street. There were so many Europeans in Wellingborough on a big race day, you would think you were in Paris, France.

On Saturday, without warning, the Sportsman racers were relegated to one qualifying session which was to be late in the afternoon. This gave me a chance to talk to the Turners, Steve and Carmel. Rob never talked to anybody, he hid himself away in the rig. Many things were agreed which they would confirm at the dinner and disco on Sunday evening.

I was paired with Terri Rogers-Valle. Her husband dialled her in on 17.10, she ran a 17.201, a good run and I was again on a breakout 14.342 on a 14.36. Terri had a good reaction time, 0.524.

Every day we took the car back into Wellingborough, which meant it had to be rescrutineered. Amos Meekins had signed my pass on Saturday, but this time his brother Doug saw me driving towards the scrutineering bay. Before I had switched the engine off, he was in full song again, 'Ee bah gum.' This time he wanted to see the MOT certificate, which meant I had to walk back to the pits as Brenda always kept the MOT and insurance certificates with her. When I returned, Doug was laughing his head off. 'Derek, you fell for it. I only wanted to finish my cup of tea before it went cold. Here you are, its signed. Have a good day's racing.'

There is a lot of leg-pulling in drag racing, but it is good clean fun.

Sportsman eliminations didn't start until four o'clock in the afternoon that we were never told why! It didn't make much difference. I broke out by $^7/_{1000}$ of a second, which handed the win to Alan Didwell. The *SPRC News* reported:

SPORTSMAN ET
EUROPEAN FINALS
11–13 September 1998

The European Finals saw the largest field of Sportsman ET cars all year.

Qualifying was headed by Lance Richards who was making only his second appearance at Santa Pod this year with a 13.82 on a 13.80 dial-in from his Capri. Second place went to 'Grandad' Annable in his Camaro.

Round one saw a major upset as Steve Elliott disposed of championship leader Wayne Hiscock who had a very poor reaction time for him (.988). This meant if Rick Denny won the event then he could snatch the title from Wayne's grasp.

Round two saw Rick's chances ended early on as Terri Rogers-Valle (the highest scoring Scrabble name in bracket racing) went on to the semi-finals. Other wins in round two went to Lance Richards over Steve Elliott and David Dony visiting Santa Pod again from Belgium over Alan Didwell.

Terri Rogers-Valle pulled a half second holeshot over Lance Richards to advance to the semi-finals where she would meet the beautifully prepared Buick Skylark of David Dony who had a bye to the final.

The final saw another holeshot from Terri (3 out of 4 round wins) take the win and a respectable third place in the championship.

When my wife came back from her visit to Jens Nybo's pit, she told me what had happened. He and Barry Sheavills were leading the 1998 FIA Top Fuel Championship before this meeting. Jens was having trouble with his car and violent tyre shake had collapsed a wing in qualifying. Brenda had stayed in the pits with some of Nybo's crew when he went out against Barry in the first round of eliminations. Jens had tyre shake, then smoke – it was Barry's win and the title was his. Barry was the FIA Top Fuel Champion for 1998 – it would be some party that evening at the Hind Hotel.

We left the Santa Pod Raceway, which like Silverstone, when the racing finishes, the exit road is one mass of cars. Being hotel guests we had priority over the dinner and disco, thus one small bar was set aside for the few non-racers. Everybody was arriving from the track in minibuses and the hotel was becoming crowded. Tickets in our hands, we went through security, yes there was security against gatecrashers, and were shown to our table which seated eight people. The meal started and we had the table to ourselves. First course over and the Turners arrived and were shown to our table. Rob, Steve, Carmel and three crew. Carmel was carrying an off-licence bag full of wine bottles which she hid under the table. Everybody was enjoying the main course when the managing director of Quaker State Express (he and Keith Bartlett had organised the evening) came over to the Turners. He was angry they had come into the dining area without paying. Carmel had to find £120 to keep the boss man from Sweden happy.

Now Brenda started to talk to Carmel and Steve. When the coffee came, my wife had firm promises from the Turners on the future of her dragster. It is strange how some people have a guardian angel who looks over them. In their worst nightmare, the Turners would never have thought they would have to sit on our table.

Meal over, Brenda and I found a quiet bar away from the main room, where she started talking to a couple from Norway. It turned out he was the Top Fuel biker, Svein Gottenberg, whose ambition in drag racing was the magic 200mph+ pass on his bike. What other form of motorsport has four wheels and two wheels racing on the same track, and then wining and dining together? In my youth, I had a passion to see cars and bikes race against each other, Geoff Duke against Stirling Moss, that would have brought the crowds through the gates. The only reason given that there will never be a race between cars and bikes is the insurance companies wouldn't allow it to happen.

Svien was impressed I still raced at my age and wished me luck when I started racing the TA dragster again. The disco had started so we crossed the hall into the main room. The music was so loud, I suggested we went to our room. At that point I saw someone waving, so with Brenda on my right arm and her stick in her right hand, we walked across the dance floor to applause. Barry Sheavills came over and hugged and started kissing my wife. All she could say was, 'Stop it, I'm old enough to be your mother. Go and find a young girl.'

'No, darling, you made it possible and I thank you.'

Then three racers started pouring champagne all over Barry, A Brit was the Top Fuel European Champion. The car he drove had a power-to-weight ratio of 5000hp to the ton, a Formula One car has between 1200hp and 1500hp to the ton – this man had achieved the ultimate. I wondered why these drivers are excluded from the British Racing Drivers Club. Surely they are at the pinnacle of motorsport and are British. One day I shall take it up with the powers who are in charge of the BRDC.

I found a seat for Brenda away from the dancing and left her talking to Jens Nybo, while I talked to his main sponsor about sponsorship in drag racing. He explained that even in his country top drivers are starved of money which is the reason Jens was retiring from Top Fuel at the end of the year. My thoughts went back to the fax I had received from Bernie Ecclestone. If true, it was time to support Keith Bartlett, not bury him. I didn't know in 1998 that Bernie Ecclestone was planning to pull out of motorsport and become involved in football! I had raced against Bernie many years ago and he bought my Keift, but now he wanted to become a football guru. Ah well, it takes all kinds to make a world.

I could see Brenda was getting tired, so we said goodnight to Barry, who by now was sitting on the floor talking to half a dozen of his fans, and went to our room. My wife went to sleep that night feeling one proud lady. It was common knowledge that nobody had wanted to buy Barry Sheavills' Top Alcohol dragster, and if we hadn't bought it, he wouldn't be racing Top Fuel this year and have become champion.

When I watch *Star Wars* on television, it reminds me of us. We must have a force field around us, many people have tried to bury us, but we are still here shooting back. I say to the people we have met in the Wild Bunch, PDRC, APIRA, SPRC, plus Jon Cross and Amos Meekins, 'Thank you, without your support I would be visiting my wife's grave every weekend, not racing.'

When we arrived home, I was sad to read the following report:

Baggaley Seriously Injured in Bike Smash

Custom Car's editor, Tim Baggaley, was involved in a serious accident a couple of weeks ago, which has left him laid up in hospital for some time to come.

Although the exact circumstances are unconfirmed, Tim is known to have been travelling to work on his motorbike when he was in collision with a car. Tim suffered broken arms and legs, spinal and facial injuries and some internal organ damage. After a time in a 'critical' stage, doctors were able to get his liver and kidneys working again and confirmed that there was no fear of paralysis. Tim is recognised as having brought the magazine back from near extinction and has fought to promote both British drag racing and the 'early' hot rodding styles.

It was several days before he recovered consciousness but he is now believed to be making recovery. During his absence, former deputy editor, Kev Elliott, will be running the magazine.

Any get well cards or messages of sympathy can be passed on to Tim via Kelsey Publishing (address in front cover of CC).

Tim had put up with my letters on various issues and complaints, picked the best out and found a slot for them in *Custom Car*. I don't think I will be able to get on with the new man; Kev Elliott is a different beast and not my kind of a guy. We lose friends all the time.

The *SPRC News* were kind enough to publish two letters, mine and Jeff May's. Mine was first:

Many people have said many things about Keith Bartlett, myself being one.

The 1998 FIA European Drag Racing Championship Finals at Santa Pod on 11–13 September 1998 gives us all an insight into the Keith Bartlett/Bernie Ecclestone future for UK drag racing on the FIA world scene. This can only be made possible by the effort the Santa Pod Racers Club's underpaid and overworked officials from the start line marshal, timekeeper, fire-up lane and pit marshals and many others put into every meeting Santa Pod Raceway (Trakbak Racing Ltd) promote.

I for one have decided to stop making bullets for my wife, Brenda, to fire at Keith Bartlett. When we purchased two tickets for the 1998 European Finals dinner and disco night at the Hind Hotel,

Wellingborough, I thought 'Here is another way for Santa Pod Raceway to take our money and give us little in return.' How wrong I was. There was Jenny Catling trying to bring some order into the occasion, being bombarded in every European language imaginable, she stood there so relaxed and confident. I thought if only that lady, and many of our lady secretaries, Paula Marshall and others, ran drag racing in the UK, we racers would be assured of a future.

My plea from the heart is this. We all give Keith Bartlett one more year to get his act together and show all racers he has the best interest of all sections of drag racing and not just the elite. To close there are two names which stand head and shoulders above all others, Jon Cross and Darren Prentice, thank you both.

Derek (Grandad) Annable

Now Jeff May's:

Dear Drag Racers

I have had the pleasure for many many years of being involved in drag racing on behalf of the RACMSA. I know I've had great enjoyment over those years in meeting many of you and have made many good friends from my attendances at Santa Pod.

At the last FIA-FIM meeting (11–13 September) it became my responsibility to oversee a trainee steward having his first experience of drag racing. This man is very experienced in the 'roundy roundy'(!) racing – T.O.C.A., Formula 3, Formula Vauxhall and MCN Superbikes as well. In fact next year he qualifies to become an international clerk of the course.

There were two things that made his day. The first, I did to him by taking him down to the start line for Barry Sheavills' first run on Saturday – that first four-second run. I watched him (having not warned him of what to expect) and he leapt a foot into the air from that launch – eyes sticking out from his head, deafened, etc – all those problems the inexperienced newcomers who get that close to a 'happening' like that experience!

From that, I took him amongst your good selves, and asked if some of you would explain to him what drag racing is – everyone I asked went out of their way to make him welcome, explained loads of technical knowledge to him – and what so impressed him were you were so friendly and pleased to do so. To me it was the 'norm' that I have experienced over my many pleasant years of association with your good selves – to him it was a fabulous experience and he went off to be clerk of the course the following day for British Formula 3 racing at Thruxton a converted soul – drag racing to him was an experience that he can't wait to be involved in.

Thank you all for your style and standard to this absolute newcomer to your venue and your style of motorsport.

I knew it would be that way – you really opened his eyes for him about drag racing.

Thank you.

Yours sincerely

Jeff May
RACMSA Steward

There is a man who lives and breaths motorsport. His old Porsche car sports the plate MAY 1, he enjoys drag racing, not like some RACMSA stewards I have met and talked to who would prefer to be at a karting race. Most of the time they keep saying, 'Drag racing requires no skill.'

So I ask them, 'In what way?'

They reply, 'No corners. That takes skill.'

It's like converting a beer drinker to wine. They haven't the taste for it.

I received a letter from Carla Pittau:

Dear Derek,

Re: Your comments about PRO ET and Heaven & Hell being over-reported

You are absolutely right, and it is quite embarrassing. The problem is that people will not report on their own class, and it's really difficult to know what goes on in other classes when you are busy racing.

I asked Terri Rogers (and her husband Chris) if they would report on Sportsman ET, but although they said they would, perhaps due to lack of time or whatever else, they never did.

However it is certainly a problem we will need to solve: I would be most grateful for an article on what happened in Sportsman ET in 1998. The same goes for Super Pro, as there really wasn't much about them either.

The reason there was so much about Pro ET is that Rick and I did the reporting, and you will understand that it is easier to report from your own point of view – as well as obviously knowing more about what you are doing and why, than you know about what other racers are doing and why.

Believe me it's really hard work to put together the newsletter. In this issue I forgot to publish somebody's moan and he will probably think the ETRA did it on purpose, and due to an error in printing, a new member's name has been left out. I realised this at 10.30pm, in my office in Sevenoaks, 30 miles from home, after I photocopied both sides of the 300 A3 pages that make up this issue. I felt really bad, but more than anything I felt tired and wanted to go home. So I did.

Help us, and we will gladly publish the reports. More than gladly, they are desperately needed.

Hope you're keeping well, for sure you are prompt with your support, and I welcome the criticism, at least you're right!

My regards to Brenda.

Carla

Then in the December issue of the *ETRA News*, this story caught my eye:

RACING CAPRIS
By Terri Rogers-Valle

It was whilst enjoying my first visit to Santa Pod back in 1995 that the idea of racing my Capri was put to me.

At the time it was sitting forlornly in the garage in bits, having been promised a bare metal respray. The idea appealed and the very next meeting my husband Chris and I were out there racing. We entered the Euro Challenge and raced the car in primer!

During the closed season, the car was sprayed by Catchit Racing in spectacular Ferrari red and the following year we won the Euro Challenge. This year we decided it was about time we went skint along with everybody else, so not only did we get married, we also bought a 400 small block and another Capri to put it in (I like Capris, OK!). As the red one is such a good example (straight, low mileage, no rust etc), we decided to put it back on the road and cherish it (fellow Capri fans will understand this).

The new car has already been sprayed in dazzling fashion by Catchit Racing, so hopefully come next year we'll have a competitive 10.90 race car.

Since becoming involved with drag racing, I seem to have turned into something of a boy racer! When not watching the Grand Prix or the qualifying or the practice, I'm flicking through the satellite channels looking for any form of motorsports.

I have also exchanged the glamorous pages of *Vogue* and *Elle* magazines for the (mostly) unglamorous pages of *Fast Ford*, *Performance Car*, *Top Gear* and of course *Custom Car*.

I even tried Max Power for a while but found them far too testosteroney for me!

I wonder if any other female drag racers have experienced the same strange effect on their normally (good) feminine tastes?

Or is it just me?

See you all next year.

Terri

Good for you, Terri; my wife said, 'Go and win.'

In the same issue was my letter, which was in response to Carla's letter to me:

Dear Members,

I wrote to ETRA pointing out there was an imbalance in reporting the various classes in our ETRA News. Their response was that there were vague promises from racers who would provide some input for the newsletter.

Take one class, Sportsman (Street). Why don't the early casualties in the eliminations make notes of the racing up to and beyond the finals, then hand over their comments to one of the able lady crew members to pass on to the newsletter. This would be a team effort for the benefit of all ETRA members.

The alternative: As I shall be racing in the Sportsman class next year, it's for me to provide the newsletter with the info they require.

GOD FORBID!

Who wants to hear an old fart's ramblings month after month. NO.

You young ones hold the future of UK drag racing.

So, let's see some off-track enthusiasm for our sport with pen and paper!

Derek (Grandad) Annable

Any takers? We would very much like to report on all classes, but some times it's very difficult to know what's going on in your own class, let alone all the others. So, tell us what goes on in your class!

Now it was Christmas and time to cook the turkey and other goodies for my teammate. Her only comment was, 'I could have cooked it better.' There's no answer to that.

Christmas over, Brenda said, 'No more turkey for me' so I prepared a turkey pie for myself. While I was doing this, I was reading a report in *Quick Times Racing News*:

Nybo quits Top Fuel for Touring Cars

Former FIA Top Fuel Champion Jens Nybo has quit the sport he loves so much for a new career in touring cars.

Nybo, who won the FIA Championship in 1996 after some storming runs at Avon Park against Germany's Rico Anthes said, 'I love drag racing, but I cannot afford to continue. There's just not enough competition to attract sponsors'.

'The series needs a radical change', he continued. 'I thought that would happen when the FIA came in, but it hasn't.'

According to Nybo there were in effect only two cars challenging for the 1998 title, himself and Brit Barry Sheavills.

Nybo now looks to a fresh challenge with the Swedish Touring Car Championship in a BMW 320i. The same series which TOCA/BTCC Independent Tommy Rustad won in 1997.

I had just finished reading the article when the phone went. It was Nybo's chief sponsor. Did I want to hire the Top Fuel car for the 1999 season? He offered a very reasonable rate, plus crew for the first meeting. I had to turn the offer down – had it been twenty years ago and I had £100,000 spare cash in the bank, I would have accepted. I knew my limitations and where to exploit the opposition's weakness and it wasn't in Top Fuel in the year 1999. A nice thought, an OAP could race Top Fuel.

It had been a good year, my wife was stronger and thinking of being more active in drag racing. Next year maybe she could ease herself back into the fashion business – we shall see. We were still paying rent to Pochins, our landlord, on an empty shop. Easter would be a good time to reopen. We always bounce back, come what may, and thrive on any challenge thrown us. Time after time, Brenda and I have been written off, but with two deep breaths we come back like a dragon, a Welsh dragon breathing fire, and destroy the opposition.

Last year had been the crossroads. Were we on track? Yes we were. Unknown to us two men would come into our lives and my racing would take off.

CHAPTER 8

1999

The year started off very low key; Kjell Pettersson of Trakbak Racing sent me the following letter:

---

6 January 1999

Dear Derek,

Firstly I would like to take this opportunity to wish you and your team a Happy New Year with the hope that the 1999 season will bring you great success.

I am writing to you in the hope that you can inform me of your racing plans for the new season.

In order to promote and plan each event it would be very much appreciated if you could let me know which events you are planning to take part in here at Santa Pod Raceway during this year.

A prompt return of attached form by post or fax (+44(0)1234 782818) would be very much appreciated. If you have additional information other than what is asked for on the form, please write on the reverse or on additional paper (ie new car, new sponsors, new crew members or other interesting information).

I have also attached a sheet with the 1999 calendar dates as they are at the moment here at Santa Pod Raceway, events may well be added on.

I look forward to hearing from you soon.

Best regards

Kjell Pettersson
General Manager Operations
Trakbak Racing Limited

This I would answer in due course. Then there was the interview with Terry Gibbs of Obsession Motorsport which appeared in *Quick Times Racing News:*

Terry, we have noted with interest – and speaking on behalf of Heaven & Hell and Rat Rage Racing, with enthusiasm – the progress Avon Park Raceway has made during this season. Are you satisfied with the results of your work?

The results have actually exceeded our expectations. I especially value feedback from racers and public. It seems that we are going in the right direction according to both groups, so I am definitely satisfied with this.

We all know Terry Gibbs Super Gas racer. What started Terry Gibbs promoter?

I don't describe myself as a promoter. I much prefer to be seen as a 'co-ordinator' as 'promoter' implies it is all down to me whereas there are a lot of people who have worked hard together to make all this possible. The reason for wanting to have an alternative was mainly frustration with the treatment sportsman racers were receiving, and being a racer myself, that's the point of view I take.

When Trevor Graves asked me to run the 1997 Super Series, I was very pleased that Trevor had faith in me and thought I could organise it. I was also glad to have the opportunity of trying something different and to give an alternative to racers. The event was supposed to be just a 'one-off' for 97 to help the facility survive, but the feedback we received at the time, despite the rain, provided enough inspiration for us to put together a budget for 1998.

So what are your aims for 1999?

Providing we get the support we have enjoyed this year from track owner Anthony Hodges, the APIRA and the racers, we want to continue on the same basis as 1998, mainly consolidating what we have achieved this year. We very much want to keep our feet firmly on the ground, but we are working to bring in more sponsors and we have quite a lot of interest at the moment. We are planning on 6 meetings for the next year, and I would like to stress that all of this can only go ahead if – as in 1998 – we have the same 3-way partnership; Obsession Motorsports: APIRA; and Anthony Hodges.

Anthony has had a key role in ensuring the success of the Super Series, but co-operating with us very closely, literally bending over backwards to help. He has not had a penny from the track apart from the rent, and this has been a very low figure. At the moment he appears to be very keen to continue for next year. But until all details have been agreed, this cannot be finalised.

Which classes will you be including in the events?

The actual number of classes we run will ultimately be determined by the success of the track and the number of racers we have. On the one hand the curfew has almost been useful in terms of discipline. You know you have to finish the meeting by a certain time so you make sure you improve the running of the event to comply. On the other hand it does limit the number of classes you can effectively run. However, we do not have any 'prima donnas' here.

All racers are treated the same. There is no favouritism. We have had the Rover V8 cars back and we will welcome them next year. The Wild Bunch have supported the track over the last few years and they are also welcome, as well the ET classes, and of course the Super classes.

What about an interclub championship; any plans to run it at Avon Park?

An interclub championship has been discussed and we would like four of the six events to be championship rounds. We have had a meeting with the SPRC and Keith Bartlett, together with the APIRA, for a preliminary discussion on this. However, we are awaiting confirmation of several details from SPRC and Trakbak, and at this stage we cannot say yet whether the interclub championship will go ahead.

What about the other events; what format will they take?

Nothing is yet finalised, but talking about our current plans we see the other two meetings as international doorslammer events, as our work is first and foremost aimed at working with the sportsman racers. There is also the possibility of a one-off Top Alcohol event, but this is very much subject to how things develop with sponsors.

There have been a lot of rumours about insurmountable difficulties with planning permission. What is the current situation?

Fortunately we can report that there are no problems with planning. There are some points that will have to be complied with over the next two years, but no complaints have been lodged and therefore we feel confident that all will be well on that side.

So what about beyond 1999?

Our ultimate aim in the next 3 years is to build up a solid future for drag racing, working very closely with Anthony, but our budget is very much down to earth. We want to make sure that what we promise is given and what we aim for is achieved rather than setting goals that are just not achievable. One of the reasons why I don't like to be called a promoter, is that this is not my main line of business. I do not make my living out of promoting Avon Park. I am not looking for short-term gain, fortunately I do not need it. Every penny from race entries has gone back to the racers in prize money and improvements to the facility, with a proportion of the entry money going to the APIRA who have helped to pay for the new timing lights (Portatree) and equipment.

With regard to the timing lights, as you know we have had a few teething problems. The first day (August Bank Holiday) we had quite a few runs with no times or speeds and that is why I wanted to ask racers what they wanted to do, whether to continue with the qualifying with no guarantee that the run would be documented, or stop the racing and wait for everything to be fixed.

The racers voted to continue and that was fine. It's just that I saw a couple of fuel bikes on the line with the tree not counting down, and it really worried me. That's why I wanted to put it to the racers because I am a racer myself and I can see things from the other side of the fence. The problem with the tree did not repeat and the racers were happy to put up with the timing problem which shows how much racers co-operate when they are told what's going on and asked for their opinion. That's what this is about, co-operating for the good of the sport.

Anything else you would like to add?

Just that there are so many people who have helped enormously to make all of this possible; Anthony, Trevor and the APIRA, the FAST team, and many others – including the racers themselves. It's impossible to thank all of them individually, and all played a very big part. You know who you are. A big thank you for what you have done for the sport in 1998.

Good, Terry, we should be racing.

At this time of the year I watch television, and one programme which I enjoyed was Thames Television's *This Is Your Life* when it was Damon Hill's turn. This prompted me to write the following letter:

---

12 January 1999

Dear Sue Green

Re: *This Is Your Life*

Congratulations to yourself and the above programme on Monday 11 Jan 99 and the choice of Damon Hill.

At the end of 1997, hearsay had it that the BBC were considering calling an end to *This Is Your Life* in the early part of 1998. This prompted viewers like myself to write to the BBC with the request to allow you, as a producer, to carry on after a short rethink.

With respect I wish to put forward the following as a future *This is Your Life* person – Ken Gregory. This gentleman is over 70 years old and in many ways the antecedent of Bernie Ecclestone. Ken's vision in 1949 dictated the direction motor racing was to take and paved the way for Bernie Ecclestone to build his billion pound empire. Without Ken Gregory, Formula 1 would have remained a rich gentlemen's sport as it was in the 1930s. Please consider my request. Before making a decision I suggest a copy of *Managing a Legend* (Stirling Moss, Ken Gregory and the British Racing Partnership) by Robert Edwards Haynes F988 is worth perusal.

Yours sincerely

Derek Annable

In February a further letter arrived from Kjell Pettersson, this time about the 1999 FIA European Drag Racing Championships Eurosport Preview.

His invitation to race in the Alcohol class wouldn't be possible as the Turners wouldn't crew for me when they were racing their car on the same programme. People I had spoken to at the end of last season were now unable to crew for us, some of the reasons given were 'my wife is ill' or 'I can't afford the time.' What's time got to do with it when I was prepared to pay an engine man £500 per meeting? These people will remain nameless.

It was decision time for the team Thunder and Lightning; do we race or not? Yes, we do, in the Sportsman Championship at Santa Pod and Avon Park. The Camaro was to be entered, with the BMW as back-up, both cars to be registered with the clubs. The TA dragster, when ready, would be entered in a couple of RWYB meetings, this meant notifying the clubs many weeks ahead so the correct fire crew would be on hand.

I received Sue Green's reply to my letter:

3 March 1999

Derek F Annable
Amlwch

Dear Mr Annable

I am in receipt of your letter dated 12 January 1999 and must apologise for the delay in replying. It is always good to hear from our viewers and I would like to thank you for your support.

Your suggestion of Ken Gregory as a suitable subject for *This Is Your Life* has been placed in our ideas file, which is often referred to by our researchers. As you will appreciate, we get lots of suggestions and it would be impossible for us to feature them all.

Thank you for taking the time to write in to me and for your continued interest in the programme.

Yours sincerely

Sue Green
Producer
This Is Your Life

Yes, Sue, but I won't give up, Ken is perfect for the programme.

We received the championship regulations for 1999. The SPRC Drag Racing Championship Officials were as follows:

Yvonne Tramm, championship coordinator
Amos Meekins, eligibility scrutineer
Philip Evans, Carole Ismail and Kathy Taylor, stewards

Carole Ismail. I had upset her a couple of years ago. The officials in charge of the National Championship were much the same crowd as before, except for one – Tina Gibbs.

It can be cold at the end of March and early April and this year was no exception. When we arrived in the Sportsman pits, 14 cars were already pitted. Paul Hudson with his new car 'Money Hungry', Ian Turnbull with 'Plough Garage II' and Rick Denny with 'Firebird'. Who was this new boy on an observed run? Chris Isaacs. Come on Chris, you raced Modified when I raced the Altered.

Formalities over, I joined the queue of cars waiting to be scrutineered. When Amos saw Brenda sitting in the car, he said, 'Derek isn't allowed a co-pilot when he is racing.' There was much laughing and joking while the car was passed and allowed to race.

I fired up the engine and drove down to the pairing lanes, leaving Brenda in the Pod café; at least she had somewhere warm to sit. My first opponent in qualifying was Terri Rogers-Valle driving her Ford Capri. She ran a 17.277 on a 17.20 dial-in, mine was 14.402 on a 14.31, close racing. It would be late afternoon before Sportsman had their second slot so I went to join Brenda in the Pod café. She was talking to Smax Smith who had brought his Astral Projection all the way down from Preston. Smax had run a 6.857 at 202.52mph and was looking pleased with himself. Brenda was happy so I left and went to Boaters, my favourite chuck wagon, with smoked salmon sandwiches being the order of the day. I had some great grub and felt more relaxed.

Now I was ready to take on Martin Lewis in his Nova 'Blaze'. Martin had dialled in 16.80 and ran a 16.887, mine was a 14.082 on a 14.08 dial-in and that made me top qualifier. Brenda was pleased. I was on a bye in the first round of eliminations. Tomorrow would be interesting as there were 14 other racers trying to outqualify me – $^2/1000$ of a second on your dial-in is hard to beat, but not impossible.

Brenda was now ready for a rest – at home she always had three hour's sleep every afternoon. When we returned to the Travelodge she was too tired to eat, so I washed and changed and left her sleeping while I joined some of the other racers for a meal at the Little Chef. One of the ladies who worked there, who had visited Brenda in Kettering hospital, made some sandwiches for me to take to our room. We had an early night.

It was still dark, what was that noise? I might have known, it was Phil Walker – he had fired up his Pontiac Firebird. I didn't wake Brenda but I got dressed and wandered over to the Little Chef for breakfast. They weren't open, so I walked over to the BP garage, bought a newspaper and three bottles of 7-Up. The price of mineral water at the track was well over the top. Why waste your money?

With breakfast over and Brenda's bits and pieces loaded in the car, off we went to the Pod and straight into the scrutineering bay. Doug Meekins was on holiday, so young Richard Vincent checked my car and signed my pass. He's a nice lad and he wasn't grumpy like his father Stuart. When I returned to the pits, another car had turned up for racing, no bye for me, just top qualifier points and the extra points for number one position.

I was paired against Paul Bishop. In the days when I had raced Modified, Paul was always on hand to help Brenda when she towed me to the start line and had become a close friend. He posted 17.00 and ran a 17.333, I ran a 14.240 on a 14.08, my win on ET posted time.

The last run of the day was against Rick Denny, again a win for me on posted times. Rick was way off his dial-in and his reaction time was 0.701; he usually had a sharp reaction.

It was the end of a day's racing for Sportsman classes and now it was time to join Brenda who was watching Top Alcohol qualifying, but first I must load up the Camaro with our gear for the drive back to the Travelodge.

When I joined Brenda, she told me Smax Smith had crashed his Astral Projection. The car burst an oil hose on the approach to half track which spewed oil under the left slick which sent the car hard across the track, chasing the other car with a couple of nasty rollovers. Smax was uninjured but the car would be out of action for months. Brenda was so upset, we left the track and headed for the Travelodge. That evening we were both going to eat in the Little Chef.

While Brenda was having her early evening rest, I went through my timing tickets – what to dial-in tomorrow? The average was 14.18, so that would be my dial-in.

Time flies and, before we knew it, it was seven o'clock. Sunday nights in the Little Chef are usually quiet nights, but I wanted to finish our meal before John Price and Graham arrived for theirs. Brenda and I were going to enjoy a bottle of wine in our bedroom.

It was an enjoyable meal. Oh no, they were early. It was John Price and Graham and this time they had their wives with them. My wife loves to wind people up and out of the blue she said, 'Graham, you have your girl-friend with you this time.'

Graham stopped dead in his tracks but John Price just laughed. Then my wife put her glasses on. 'Sorry, Graham, I can see it is your wife. I do apologise. You come here on your own with John so many times. I thought your wife stayed at home.'

I couldn't get my wife out of the Little Chef quick enough, she kept saying, 'He has ignored me so many times.'

The next day, Sportsman eliminations didn't start before 11am so I left Brenda sleeping while I had breakfast.

My first opponent was Phil Walker who pulled a poor light and it was my win by $^{18}/_{1000}$ of a second. Who would be next? It was Rick Denny. Now there is a different animal, hungry and out for the championship, he would go for a perfect light, 0.500. It could go either way, he could pull a red. This had happened when racing against other racers but never when he was up against me. I would play safe and try for a 0.600, but this is easier said than done. I have a problem, in that after two o'clock in the afternoon, my blood sugar falls and my reaction times suffer. I can pull a near perfect light in the early morning but late afternoon I struggle.

Rick Denny was trying his usual 'confuse the opponent' trick with his dial-in, changing it as we went down the fire-up road. It didn't bother me, I always put mine on the back window of the car before leaving the pits and it stayed unchanged.

We pre-staged and staged together. Rick is always an honest racer. His start light came down first, no red, he was off. I charged off after him, crossing the finishing line first. Rick's win light came on. I had broken out by $^{5}/_{1000}$ of a second. Brenda was gutted but I did pick up 440 points and was in fourth position in both championships. That's the way I race, wear down the opposition, picking up a steady flow of points at all the meetings, and keeping the opponents guessing.

There was a lull in our racing programme which would give us time to sort out the shop – yes, we were going to reopen. This time my wife had decided to sell other people's junk. No, there were some lovely pieces of furniture and electrical goods and there was no capital outlay for us. We planned to open three days a week and test the market. Did I say test?! After two weeks of the goods on display and our telephone number in the window, we had buyers queuing up waiting for us to open. Some were so eager they were putting £10 notes with details of the article they wanted to buy through the letterbox. The shop was becoming nearly as exciting as drag racing. The people of Benllech were now able to sell all those unwanted presents.

On the days we opened, there would be two to three cars parked outside the shop with their boots open for Brenda to inspect the goods they wanted to sell. Some of the pieces were beautiful, so we started buying the best for ourselves. We now had happy sellers and more than happy customers.

Dreams Come True was more than a ladies dress shop, and word got round so that buyers and sellers were travelling from as far away as Bangor and Caernarfon. The small commission we charged would go a long way towards paying the rent. We realised things could get hectic when the holiday season started so my wife would need someone to help her.

Other shops in Benllech jumped on the bandwagon, but we still had the edge on them. Our shop was in a prime spot and was up and running. Our lease had two years to run so there would be no renewing for us, this new venture should survive that timescale.

It was an exciting time; Brenda's health was improving in leaps and bounds and to see the sparkle in her eyes again was reward indeed. Brenda, the sales lady, was enjoying every moment and was full of energy. This is life being lived to the full and made possible through the many visits to the hospital in Bangor and a complete rest, both physically and mentally, on her days at home.

The Derek and Brenda team, whether it be in the shop or on the drag strip, have tried to give pleasure to those around us. One of my wife's fans was a one-legged man who had followed our racing at York Dragway for the last eight years. When he was told I might not race there any more, he said to my wife, 'When your husband stops racing here, I stop coming.' He had photographs of every car I had raced. Another fan we met at Santa Pod said, 'My children were babies when we first came to watch Grandad Derek race here. They just liked to come and see the old man race in his Camaro.' Such fun.

Somebody once said to me, 'Why do you still race, surely you have made enough money to retire?'

My answer was, 'I enjoy it and there are a few people who enjoy watching me race. When this stops I shall stop racing.'

Here we are at the start of May and down at Shakespeare County Raceway again, hoping the team Thunder and Lightning can improve on the disappointing results we had at Santa Pod. The serious racers for the championships are here, Paul Hudson, Robert Main, Phil Walker, Rick Denny, Ian Turnbull and myself. Two days of qualifying, then we race for those all-important points. With Monday being a bank holiday, there should be a good crowd of spectators which should put some money in the bank for the Gibbs family. Perhaps Tina will let me race without finding fault with my race gear ('No gloves, Derek')!

Having missed the first scrutineering session, Glyn Stockton came over, checked the car and gave it the OK to race. Tim Jackson, seeing my car was ready for racing, wanted to show me how quick his car could run the drag strip. He should have moved up to the next class, the sub-12-second boys. He was happy launching his car in top gear – why argue?

Tim ran a 11.844/116mph and I ran a 14.04/98mph. He'll never run slower than 12 seconds. Now he did show of; on our second run together he ran a 11.568/117mph, with mine 14.070 on a 14.03 dial-in, which put me in the top spot in the qualifying lists for the day and him at the bottom.

Paul Hudson was out again in 'Money Hungry', which was an ex-Super Gas car. Paul had brought the transporter as well. He was becoming a showman as well as a sportsman racer. When we arrived in the mornings, Paul would have the tables and chairs out serving breakfast to the other racers who were Paul Hudson fans. Julie, his girlfriend, would be cooking bacon and eggs, her daughter doing the washing up.

Now it was Sunday morning and time for Sportsman ET to start its first qualifying session. I was against Gerald Cookson. Gerald is two months older than me, making him the oldest competing drag racer in the UK. He pulled a red, it was my win. This gave his son, the track commentator, much to say. He and my old friend, Bennett, do a good job in the tower with their non-stop facts and figures, although sometimes they do go on a bit.

It was time to give the car a clean. Each time I went for clean water, I noticed a couple taking an interest in my car and eventually they came over and started asking questions about the engine and the blower. They lived in Marlborough and introduced themselves as Heidi and John French. This was the start of a friendship that has lasted until today. I finished cleaning the car, leaving Brenda to do all the talking.

Phil Walker shouted, 'You and me, Derek.' Phil dialled in 14.30 and broke out with a 14.110. My run was spot on, a 0.548 reaction with an ET 14.071 on a 14.03; the Camaro was becoming very consistent. When I returned to the pits, Brenda was still talking to Heidi, and John had gone to the bar for drinks.

What would tomorrow bring? Not a lot, I was knocked out in the first round; however, there was one consolation, the car ran its first 13-second pass – 13.977.

Phil Walker was top man, carrying away 740 points, which put him in the lead in the overall championship. My reaction times were letting me down, I would have to go back to basics. The Altered I had been driving launches harder than a street car, so you can pull fives and sixes with ease, but when you return to a street car this becomes sixes and sevens. I must break the mould even if it means pulling red lights.

It was a good meeting and my wife now had somebody to keep her company when I was racing. We took John and Heidi's telephone number as Brenda had arranged to send them crew tickets next time I raced. It would be four weeks before the team were out again so this meant all our time could be put into running the shop.

My wife's health was improving. Her doctor was amazed at the speed of her recovery and agreed she could open the shop four days a week. It was three years since her stroke and Brenda still got tired and her speech would become slurred, but after a good night's sleep she was her old self again and ready for a day in the shop.

The main event at Santa Pod Raceway was looming on the calendar so it was time to make arrangements for the three-day meet. The car was sounding good, our usual room at Rushden Travelodge was booked and spare crew tickets were sent to Heidi and John, plus a vehicle pit pass.

Now let's check the officials: Darren Prentice was both the international race director and FIM (Fédération Internationale de Motocyclisme) clerk of the course – this young man had made a meteoric climb within the MSA ranks; FIA/MSA steward was Jeff May, he would be staying at the Rushden Travelodge; MSA scrutineers were Amos and Doug Meekins and young Richard Vincent. Altogether a well balanced list of officials.

Then it happened. My mother died. We knew she was old, 89, and both blind and deaf, but any death comes as a shock. Because I lived in North Wales, my sister had taken charge of my mother's affairs as she only lived three miles outside Bury St Edmunds and five miles from my mother's house.

We were already packed and ready to leave for Santa Pod Raceway when the funeral arrangements were being made for the body to be transferred to Stockport, therefore with heavy hearts Brenda and I drove to Rushden. The pain of the loss is still with me today – sons are always drawn to their mothers.

When we arrived in the pits, all the main contenders were there and Phil was looking pleased with himself because of his win at Avon Park. The formalities over, it was time for me to make my first qualifying run against Robert Main driving his Ford Punto. There is a dedicated racer; Robert lives in Aberdeen, 400 miles from the Pod. My journey from Anglesey is 200 plus miles – double that, no thank you!

We pulled an equal light, our ETs were close, but my mph over the finishing line was six miles per hour quicker, the blower on my engine giving me that extra thrust where it mattered.

My next opponent was Chris Isaacs, who was driving his Volvo estate car. He pulled a red light, and in eliminations I would have been the winner. This is what happens when you go for a perfect light, there is a 50/50 chance of a red.

That was the end of racing for the day and it rained the following day. Boredom can set in when you are not racing, the weather plays such a crucial part as there is no putting on wet weather tyres for drag racing, as there is in circuit racing. It would be Monday before racing was to resume.

I had a good qualifying run on Monday morning, $^{16}/_{1000}$ of a second on my dial-in.

Now I shall take you over to the report in the *SPRC News* by Spencer Tramm:

Eighteen showed for the largest Sportsman ET field of the year. Rick Denny took top spot with a 9 thousandths over 14.119, Derek Annable took second with a 14.09 (14.08 dial) and Bristol Raider Aiden Kenny took third with a 12.36.

Round one saw Phil Walker take out Graham Stanford. A solid .54 light showed promise for later rounds. Paul Hudson in 'Money Hungry' met Terri Rogers-Valle who after last season's successes is having a lean year, Paul advanced to round two. Gareth Mogford took out newcomer John Ricketts. Other round one wins saw Robert Main, Derek Annable and Paul Bishop advance over their opposition and Ian Turnbull, Chris Hodgkins and Chris Isaacs won through bye runs.

Round two had Paul Hudson continue his rich vein of form over Gareth Mogford. Robert Main too went through over Phil Walker. Paul Bishop made round three with the bye of the round after taking out number one qualifier Rick Denny in the previous round.

Chris Hodgkins won a close battle with Derek Annable and Chris Isaacs pulled a great holeshot to hold off Ian Turnbull.

The quarter finals saw another holeshot aided win for Chris Isaacs in the Slowcoach Volvo Estate to end Robert Main's run. Paul Hudson beat the Cortina of Paul Bishop and Chris Hodgkins ended the round with a bye.

Chris Isaacs used the semi-final bye to test his reactions – a fine .568 showed that you can get good consistent reactions from such a slow/large car. The semi-final pair saw Paul Hudson pull a poor .800, the 12 hundredths holeshot proved enough to let him advance. The final saw that it was Chris Hodgkins' time to fall asleep, a 2 tenths advantage proved too much for the Audi driver to catch up.

Yes, Chris Hodgkins won our round. I broke out by $\frac{1}{1000}$ of a second crossing the finishing line first, a mere $\frac{6}{100}$ of a second in front of him. Unfortunately for young Hodgkins, he was beaten by the other Chris who had come lucky with his reaction times. In qualifying, he had pulled two reds against me, but on the day, after a poor light in the first round, he marched on through the field with mid-fives.

In the championship, Phil Walker was still in the lead with young Chris Hodgkins trailing by a measly 70 points. The next meeting at Avon Park would be interesting, Chris was always good on his home track. I picked up 370 points so it was still all to play for.

I was back in the Sportsman ET class of racing, the grass roots of drag racing. Every driver can relate to the cars which are raced in Sportsman, from the mother who takes her children to school in a Ford Escort to the young man who drives a GTI Gold with a sporty exhaust. That is why touring cars racing around Silverstone generate as much interest as Formula One cars. I am told it is the driver the Formula One fans come to see, not the car.

The time had come for the family to assemble for Reneé Annable's funeral. Relatives from the four corners of the British Isles and the Australian branch waited outside St Thomas' Church, Stockport, while the coffin was carried inside. It was a private service. Now the long journey to the family grave in Failsworth, Manchester. A white marble angel watches over my mother now, with the noise of the new motorway in the distance.

My mother has always had a profound effect on me. She had mystic powers and would tell me about seeing visions of servants dressed in clothes of the period while she was preparing food in the kitchen of the Elizabethan house which was our home. She would stand and watch them prepare food on the old range – the kitchen hadn't been altered from the day the house was built. Sometimes these visions would walk through my mother and appear at the other end of the kitchen.

These weren't just occasional happenings, they were going on week after week and every year. When my father died, my mother moved to Crutched Friars, outside Bury St Edmunds. According to the locals, the house had a tunnel which ran to the town and came up under the cathedral where the monks had hidden to avoid persecution. It was a cruel time in our history. Many nights my mother would phone me, saying she could hear the monks chanting and being ordered to pray silently in the cells which formed part of the house.

We were both Sagittarians and kindred spirits. What my mother couldn't understand was my sister's insistence that she was having delusions and calling the doctor out. Eventually the doctor gave my mother drugs to cure the hallucinations and from then on it was downhill; her mind lost its sparkle and with it the will to live.

During my childhood and later on I experienced many strange happenings, not as vividly as my mother did but nevertheless I had a sense that they were not of this world. Such things as sensing the presence of those other than oneself in an empty room; cold air that shouldn't be there – coming and going in the vacuum of an airtight room; the feeling of being caged, when you are free to leave. I once smelt pipe smoke in an area of woodland that used to be a cottage garden some hundred years ago. Although it was unknown to me at the time, history records that an old man used to work in the beautiful garden and his favourite pipe tobacco was heavy with molasses and produced a sweet-smelling smoke. It was this I could smell!

My mother passed her gift on to me and I treat it with respect and only use it when forced to – it is a heavy burden to carry. Few people understand it and this subjects those so gifted to undue suspicion and much ridicule. Never mind, we are not mad but have a higher sense of pythagoreanism than others.

Now I had received the June issue of the *ETRA News* and Carla Pittau had made a good case in the editorial:

Sportsman Racers Association: Everybody Wants It!

Members may remember an editorial last year launching the idea of a unified association incorporating all sportsman classes. After much debate it seems that the majority of members who bothered to give an opinion (we seem to have extreme difficulty in picking up pen and paper – or even the phone – unless we want to have a moan about something, huh?) were fairly enthusiastic about the idea. Sportsman classes are quite interchangeable, some of us race in the brackets one season and in 'Super' the next, or vice versa, see our Ritchi Smith having a good go at Super Gas after Pro ET, Stuart and Anne Peck racing in Super Street in 99 or even more notably, Spencer Tramm moving from Sportsman ET to Super Gas. How can we have an association that stops catering for members just because they choose a slightly different format? And would it not be better for all involved if we presented a united front, working together to the benefit of all sportsman racers?

So, strong with the approval of a good number of racers, a preliminary meeting was held to discuss the ins and outs of a proposal resulting from the issues raised in discussions among racers who started the ball rolling and collected opinions, which is now detailed on page 2.

In this issue you will also find a form which calls for your input. You will have to tell us if you agree with the proposal as it stands on page 2, if you do not agree – why, and what you would like to propose instead, amendments, etc.

However should you not return the form at all, this will be taken as complete agreement with the terms proposed. This is to prevent the initiative grinding to a halt through procrastination.

Deadline? 31 July meet at Avon Park. Until then all forms can be sent by post to the address on the form – or given to a committee member at Santa Pod on 4 July – or Avon Park on 31 July.

Obviously only current paid up members are eligible to vote (all relevant renewal forms enclosed with this issue). So if you're a little late … make sure you send both forms, and your fiver!

Carla

This was my response:

Dear Carla,

It won't work, you and Ian Turnbull with the help from others have built the ETRA into the formidable force it is today. One question remains unanswered, why does the SGDRA want to join forces with the ETRA? Forget all the usual gloss as per the editorial *ETRA News* issue N° 10, 1999.

We in the ETRA are a success thanks to you and Ian, yes, work with the SGDRA for the good of all in drag racing, but please, no association.

Regards

Derek Annable

The proposal was put to the members and it was carried, I was the only member against the merger. Hearsay has it that the merger didn't work and Carla Pittau resigned from the board of directors.

We were so busy in our shop in Benllech I had forgotten to book a room at the Alcester Travelodge for the weekend's racing; they only had Friday night but we needed Saturday as well. A quick phone call to Mrs Billington and loads of charm from me and we were staying at Bank House in Mickleton.

As Heidi French was going to be my wife's constant companion at the remaining drag race meetings, Brenda thought it would be a nice idea to ask her and John to have a meal with us at the pub next door to Bank House on Saturday evening.

When we arrived in the pits at Avon Park on the Saturday morning, Brenda arranged everything with Heidi while I prepared the Camaro for racing. Heidi was very pleased and went to their camper to tell John, when I heard a racer's wife say to my wife, 'You don't want to get involved with those two!' This upset Brenda and she became very weepy. People who have suffered strokes can't handle emotional upset.

What had happened made me more determined to win through to the finals. Now I was ready for my first opponent in qualifying, Tim Fowler, and I soon disposed of him. A win for me. 'Come on, where is my next opponent?' It was young Chris Hodgkins and I did likewise with him.

That was the end of the day's racing and I was still all fired up and ready for all comers, but it would have to wait until tomorrow.

The meal with Heidi and John went well enough, although one of John's friends was getting noisy, so Brenda told him to go outside and sit in John's car. This he did and was full of apologies the next morning.

After a good night's sleep and one of Mr Billington's perfect cooked breakfasts, I was ready to take on the world. The first round of eliminations was at noon and there was my opponent, Tim Fowler, ready to take me on. He did and broke out; a win for me. Next up was Joseph Little. He broke out; one more win for me. I was through to the semi-finals.

It was mid-afternoon and I was calming down and feeling drowsy, which is when my reaction times suffer. Who was my next opponent? It was Chris Hodgkins, the expression on his face told all. He was about to turn the tables on me for beating him on the lights yesterday. He pulled a near perfect light, 0.514. I had no chance. He won by $\frac{4}{100}$ of a second – it was a good race. There would be another time. Chris and I went through a phase of 'he wins, I win' and we kept coming back at each other. Everybody loved it.

The Cannonball at Santa Pod was the team's next outing. To make life easier for Brenda, we had arranged to buy a caravan through Julie, Paul Hudson's girlfriend. My wife used her charm on Paul and he agreed to tow the caravan from Chesterfield to the Pod, we would meet him in the pits on the Saturday morning.

Now Brenda had somewhere to entertain her friends. The fridge would be well stocked with cans of Budweiser, the 'King of beers'. Paul had parked it near the toilet block which was ideal for my wife. At this meeting Brenda started to take an interest in a Top Methanol team (the cars were called Methanol now, as was some problem with drink driving so the name Alcohol was dropped). Brenda discovered that Doug Bond and Martyn Hannis's car was too heavy to break out of the mid-sixes. Our dragster was in the Turner workshop and had been the quickest TA car in Europe, but as there was no chance of a drive for me, why not sell it on to the Shell team? Brenda did try, but they didn't have the funds.

In qualifying, Doug Bond made a clutch-destroying pass of 6.78/154mph, which meant they were on the trailer and back home on Sunday. Brenda didn't raise the subject again – she thought it would be better to leave it until the European finals in September.

While Brenda and Heidi were enjoying a drink in our new mobile home, I started the first of four qualifying runs. Terri Rogers-Valle was my first opponent. There was not much to report as the Camaro was a bit off tune. It was even worse when I ran against Paul Bishop. I was now bottom of the qualifier list.

After two rounds of smoked salmon sandwiches from Boaters' chuck wagon, I felt better. Did the car? I hoped the cooler air might help. Yes, it did, now I started to break out – $^4/_{100}$ of a second on the run against Paul Bishop and this was followed by $^5/_{100}$ of a second against Chris Hodgkins. A less than happy wanderer drove back to the pits and called it a day.

Brenda had become a very popular lady – the ice-cold Budweisers were attracting attention. I found David Dony and his crewman sitting outside the caravan explaining where they lived in Belgium. My wife always has a soft spot for anybody with an French accent. David came from the southern part of Belgium close to the French border.

I left them while I checked my timing tickets. I had to decide what to dial-in on Sunday morning. One ticket had 'Congratulations 613' written on it. Amos Meekins' granddaughter sometimes helped with the timing tickets. When I started racing at the Pod, she was ten years old, and if I won she always wrote, 'Congratulations 613' on my timing tickets. What a lovely thought. Happy days. Let's try 14.20 and only change it if there is a strong headwind.

It was time to go back to the Travelodge. Heidi was going to keep her eye on the caravan. We had an excellent meal at the Little Chef and left before John Price and Graham arrived back from the Pod.

The weather on Sunday morning was less than helpful and it was late before the track was ready for racing. I hand you over to Spencer Tramm of the *SPRC News:*

Fifteen cars made up the Sportsman ET field, Rick Denny took the top spot with a .022 over 14.23, Ian Turnbull took number two with a .026 over 14.72 and Terri Rogers-Valle was number three.

Round one saw Rick take the bye of the round giving him a round to dial the car in. Robert Main (who deserves an award just for turning up every meeting all the way from Scotland) took out Graham Stanford. Terri Rogers-Valle continued a very bad run of form with a loss to half rally car-half classic Mini of Joseph Lillie. Chris Hodgkins, who must be a contender for 'best newcomer' this year, pulled a .538 out of the bag to take out Championship contender Phil Walker and the 'Royal Ragtop'.

Tim Fowler took out the number two qualifier Ian Turnbull to advance to meet Derek Annable. Derek beat Paul Hudson who had broken his usual Camaro and was racing his ford Maverick People Carrier and dialling in 21 second times!! Chris Isaacs in the Volvo put his deep staging tactic to good use and took two tenths advantage off the tree to 19.42 win over Steven Anderson.

In the final pair of the round David Dony with the excellent Buick Skylark from Belgium took out Paul Bishop in the Cortina.

Round two saw Rick Denny's rich vein of form continue with a win over Robert Main. Joseph Lillie and Chris Hodgkins pulled identical .567 reactions with Joseph taking the line first and winning with a 16.14. Derek Annable was asleep on the line with a .701 but had enough power to drive around Tim Fowler in the Renault 5GT Turbo. David Dony made the final four when Chris Isaacs was heavy on the brakes, but not enough to stop him going under with a 19.296.

The semi's were over too quickly for Joseph Lillie, a .277 ending his day with a blatant red light which allowed Rick Denny to advance to the final.

Derek Annable had another late light, but his consistent near the dial-in runs took him to the final as he beat David Dony. The final was a different matter, as Rick ran another near the dial run and with a good .599 light saw him take all the points.

Yes, Rick had a good light, but my break out by $^2/_{1000}$ of a second secured the win for him.

Custom Car reported, 'Sportsman ET came down to a final between Derek Annable's Camaro and Rick Denny's Pontiac Firebird. Rick prevailed over Derek on a holeshot, a 14.13/93 beating a 14.24/96.' Even Top Methanol only had two short paragraphs in the magazine.

When I arrived home, I sent off the following letter to the *SPRC News:*

---

7 July 1999

SPRC News

Congratulations to Keith Bartlett

In my letter to the SPRC News dated October 1998, last paragraph, 'we all give Keith Bartlett one more year to get his act together and show all racers he had the best interests of all sections of Drag Racing, not just the elite'.

In the calendar of our motorsport we are now mid-season, the Cannonball at the Pod being the high point. This year all the big guns were out again and a good crowd considering the weather. In the quiet moments when we racers in the pairing lanes were held up with track problems (oil and other mishaps) one man was conspicuous, that man was Keith Bartlett rushing here and there to get the sportsman racers moving again.

Darren Prentice with the help of Keith Bartlett has made Santa Pod Raceway sportsman friendly again.

Thank you.

Derek (Grandad) Annable

The phone went and it was Steve Turner saying the dragster was ready for me to race. Carmel had arranged with Santa Pod Raceway and the club for me to test the car on Sunday 18 July at their RWYB meeting.

I would drive down early on Sunday morning, test the car and then drive back home late in the afternoon. It was unbelievable. I was to get back in the cockpit of our dragster. Considering the bad feelings between the Turners and the Annables, I thought it would never happen. I must be pleasant and generous to Carmel and Steve.

As I set off from Anglesey the weather was perfect. At this time in the morning the journey would take less than four hours and I should be down at the Pod for ten o'clock. I made good time and had signed on before the

Turners arrived. There it was, the Turners' rig coming through the main gates with our car inside – the excitement.

While Steve and the crew were checking the car and engine, Carmel was giving me a lecture, 'Don't overdo it, just a launch, then we shall take the car back to the workshop.' A little voice in my head kept saying, 'Softly, softly Derek, be nice to her.'

It was four o'clock in the afternoon before the dragster was ready to be towed to the fire-up road, just in time for one run. A 500-mile journey for one launch. I must be mad but I didn't feel mad.

Then there I was, on the start line, frozen to the spot with my legs shaking. The start lights came down and I just sat there; one second, two seconds, then I launched. The car pulled to the right, I lifted off and 1.541 seconds were recorded for the 60ft. The last time I sat in this car I must have over-revved and it cost me nearly £5,000 to repair the engine damage. It was because of this that I was shaking all over while Steve checked the engine for any damage, but everything was OK. Then they drained the oil and I relaxed.

Steve said he wouldn't charge me for today as he was happy with the money I had paid them to rebuild the engine and rear axle. I asked Steve which weekend he could bring the car out again. Carmel jumped in, 'Derek, you will only break it again, don't think of racing, just sell the car.'

All I said was, 'Yes, Carmel.' She got in her car and drove home. I thanked Steve and said I would phone him before the European finals.

It was late when I arrived home and told Brenda what it was like to sit in the dragster again. We agreed that I should make two more passes in the car this year, if we could get Steve away from Carmel.

The BRDC was in turmoil and their major investments were up for grabs – Silverstone was to lose the British Grand Prix fixture to Brands Hatch. One man in the thick of it was Ken Gregory, so off went my second letter to Thames Television:

---

13 August 1999

Dear Sue Green

Re: *This Is Your Life*

I refer you to my letter of the 12 January 99 and your response of the 3 March 99.

Things have moved on in the life of Ken Gregory. He is now at the age of 74 years in active negotiation on the issue of Nicky Foulston on Brands Hatch Leisure plc's offer to the BRDC for Silverstone Circuits Freehold/Leasehold, under the heading 'A Partnership for the Future of British Motorsport.' A large sum of money is involved with media interest increasing by the month up to a conclusion by the end of the year.

I first met Ken Gregory when we were young drivers in 1950 and think he is worthy of a *This Is Your Life* programme.

Yours sincerely

Derek F. Annable

Back came a reply to my letter:

16/08/99

Dear Mr Annable

Thank you for your letter, which was passed on to me by our producer, Sue Green. The information you provided has been added to our file on Ken Gregory, which is kept with those of other possible subjects.

If we do decide to go ahead with the programme in the future then we will be sure to contact you.

Thank you for writing to us and taking such an interest in the show. We all hope that you will be watching the new series which starts later in the year.

Yours sincerely

Alex Renton

Production Secretary
This Is Your Life

ETRA News carried the verdict of the ballot for the Sportsman Racers Association, and on page three was my letter:

SPORTSMAN ET: The Characters   *By Grandad Derek Annable*

Sportsman ET, the largest car class (nearly!).

We are now past the halfway stage in the National Drag Racing Championship 1999. Five rounds now completed, the points standing is very interesting, which anybody racing at Avon Park on 31 July–1 August in the SS3 will receive an update.

Sportsman ET is grass roots racing open to all. Starting with 17-year-olds, any type of car, whether it runs 12 seconds or 22 and even slower. Instead of results I am going to give you a personal view driver by driver.

Chris Hodgkins: (position No 1) a young man who lives for drag racing. Has worked hard for the last two years in Sportsman, efforts paying off.

Rick Denny: one of Mike Ellis Rookie Racers: very serious racer with a wish to win this year's Championship (Rick try and relax and smile).

Phil Walker and Ian Turnbull: two great racers, championship material.

Chris Isaacs: like myself, he enjoys his racing having raced in other brackets.

Paul Hudson: one of the world's triers, on a good day a winner.

Robert Main: this man puts us all to shame. Every meeting is a 900-mile round trip. Because of the stress of travel, Bob is thinking of calling it a day at the end of this season. We will miss you.

Terri Rogers-Valle: this lady racer I have the greatest of respect for, a real pro. The team are dedicated beyond belief. Crew chief's day starts at 7am, prepare the car, get Terri through qualifying. Track closes at 7pm, drive to place of work, work all night, drive back to Santa Pod, prepare car for racing.

Paul Bishop: one of the most relaxed racers, sleeps in his tent all day, but can still run 17.00 on a 17.00 (shit, why can't I do that).

Martin Lewis: this racer goes back many years, the only racer who has made Carla Pittau runner-up *(Sorry, Grandad – in fact he was runner-up, I remember the race as one of my finest, as it was the finals at the Summer Nationals 94, the race that won me the National Championship that year, and I hit a 13.50 on a 13.50 – after waiting 4.5 seconds for Martin – I waited so long I thought the tree had broken. And … a few others have made me runner-up … or kicked me out in the first round too!).*

Tim Fowler and Joseph Lillie: these racers are what Sportsman ET racing is all about. Young, energetic, will try anything to make their cars go quicker, a real joy to race against.

Aidan Kenny: five years of hard work and all his spare cash brought this car to the track. Money ran out when it came to the windscreen. [This was written before the unfortunate crash at Avon.]

Gary Mogford: a real force to be reckoned with, wins races, then waits for the other racers to catch up on his points, comes out again and wins.

Gerry Cookson: believe it or not this racer is 2 months older than me. Because his wife will not stay away from home at night he only races at Avon Park.

Brian Burrows: a Street VW racer who only races against us when there is a VWDRC Championship round at the Pod.

Tim Jackson is an Avon Park racer from Devon, very quick, break out time 11.70, should be racing Pro ET.

Steven Anderson, 32 Ford B Coupe, 'Tufty' from High Wycombe. My home in 1949, say no more. A good racer.

David Dony from Belgium. That Buick Skylark of his, beautiful and quick (mid-13s).

Graham Stanford. Pontiac Trans AM, you can't miss it. Up goes the Stars and Stripes alongside the Union Flag.

My apologies to Glenn Rees, John Reckolts, Nick Curtis and Paul Martineck.

Yes, Carla, I stand corrected.

Thank goodness the team's next drag race meeting was in the middle of September when the children (not ours) were back at school. The shop was going from strength to strength. Anglesey was busy with people on holiday looking for a bargain and our shop had become a magnet.

There were many charity shops in the area, so to avoid being classed as one of them we had to be very selective in the type of goods passing through our premises. The furniture was too large for car boot sales and other items were too new or too expensive to pass through a second-hand charity shop. Therefore word got round that Dreams Come True was a high-class shop and the lady with the stick would tell sellers what to do with any rubbish. The sales side divided itself into prams and pushchairs; mahogany tables; sideboards and other quality furniture; electrical goods like fridges, electric typewriters; standard lamps; silver coffee sets and Arab tea sets. The other main sellers were Hoovers and children's bikes which ranged in price from £10 to £15. We had a waiting list of customers on holiday who wanted good second-hand children's bikes. Added to the articles which passed through our shop, we kept a list of names and addresses of local people who wanted to sell three-piece suites and larger pieces of furniture. Yes, we filled a niche in the marketplace and were so successful that other retail shops in Anglesey were changing over part of their premises to copy us. I worked out the bubble would burst within two years but by then our lease would be up and we would transfer the business to our garage premises and take our customers with us.

How time flies. It was the European Finals at Santa Pod at the end of next week and the Camaro needed testing. A change of sparking plugs and engine oil were the order of the day, also a new set of points wouldn't come amiss. You would need a back-up truck and a mechanic if you carried out repairs and other work on race day. Brenda and I are old people who enjoy drag racing, no way are we going to turn ourselves into grease monkeys. Even in the days of the Altered, other racers were amazed we never put a spanner to the car. It was prepared by us in our own garage premises and brought to the start line in as near perfect condition as was possible with our limited experience.

This time we were staying at the Rushden Travelodge. Things were hotting up for both championships and Rick Denny was hot favourite for both. I had an outside chance for the national but we must be on track early, thus giving me the edge in the first qualifying session. After a night under canvas, the other racers weren't very sharp.

The club had arranged five qualifying runs for Sportsman ET today and three on Saturday. My first opponent was Robert Main, who ran a 13.922 on a 13.85 dial-in. I broke out with a 14.115 on a 14.26.

Paul Hudson was running 'Money Hungry' this time so now he could say, 'I beat the Camaro.' His car is a 12-second car and mine a 13-second car. I had the satisfaction of forcing him to break out. Not satisfied, Paul Hudson picked me again. Why? I soon found out when Brenda gave me the timing ticket, Paul had run a 13.082 on a 13.08 dial-in that made him top qualifier.

Well done Paul. For some reason he always went well when paired against me. Nobody would get close to his time.

My last run was against Keith Milne, the happy one from the Plough Garage. He pulled a good light and was $\frac{1}{100}$ of a second within his dial-in.

Saturday was much the same as Friday – Paul Hudson stayed top qualifier and I didn't improve on my position on the ladder. This gave Brenda the chance to talk to Doug and Martyn about buying our dragster but the answer was the same, they didn't have the funds. Their sponsors, Shell Oil, wouldn't come up with any extra money and in fact Shell Oil were thinking of pulling out of drag racing. Doug's car had run a 6.595. It would never run better than that.

Over the meal that evening we discussed our future in drag racing. The only way forward was some sort of loose partnership with Doug and Martyn. I had an idea milling about in my head but it was agreed that Brenda would check with them again to see how far they would go. I was sure something could be worked out for the benefit of both parties.

Sunday morning dawned bright and dry and before nine o'clock Sportsman ET were lined up in the fire-up road and ready to go. Chris Hodgkins and myself were out first and Chris dialled in 16.60. Mine was 14.26 – that meant waiting on the start line for over two seconds before I was given the green light. The Audi was going like a bat out of hell; I thought I would never catch it but we crossed the finishing line together. We both broke out, Chris by the greater and it was my win. My better start light secured the win.

Now it was me against Rick Denny; Firebird against Camaro. Rick dialled in 14.07 and I dropped mine to 14.21. We pre-staged and staged together, then the start lights came down together. Rick pulled a better light, edging slightly ahead. We shot down the track together – who would win? The winner's light came on in Rick's lane, I had broken out by $17/1000$ of a second, so it was the end of my day's racing.

It was also the end of Doug Bond's racing. Now there were four people locked in deep discussion. Brenda asked them how much they could afford if we leased the dragster to them. But they didn't want to take the risk.

She then asked how much were they prepared to pay on a 'rent per meeting' basis. This was a possibility with them but I couldn't see that idea taking root after Christmas. There would be this reason and that reason not to take up the offer so it was stalemate.

Now it was my turn to try, and I gave my wife the 'don't interrupt' look. 'Doug and Martyn can have the free use of our dragster, they run it with their engine in at four meetings and, in return, our engine is put into their dragster and they crew for me at two, or maybe three, meetings at Avon Park. I shall pay them £300 expenses for every meeting and they crew for me.'

Brenda said, 'No.' Doug and Martyn said, 'No.' I pulled Brenda to one side and quietly said to her, 'Tell them their car is rubbish and Doug will never win races in it. He should take up my offer, then the Shell Oil team will be among the front runners.'

This is when I went walkabout. I could hear my wife say, 'You two know your car is rubbish and should be put on a scrapheap. Use mine and Doug will be a winner.' At least they agreed to go home and think about it and my wife was to phone them in a month's time.

When Brenda phoned them at the end of October, Doug and Martyn agreed to my proposal. The Turners were to be notified at the end of

November that Martyn would collect our car from the Turners' workshop and take it to their workshop/garage outside Cheltenham. Thus started the Annable/Bond/Hannis drag racing partnership which has been of benefit to all and is still up and running.

At the FIA Euro Finals, Rob Turner ran the team's first five-second pass. Knowing everybody would be in a jubilant mood, I phoned Steve with a request, could they bring Brenda's TA car out for me to practise a half-pass on the Sunday RWYB meeting at the Pod. Steve agreed but he would need to check with Carmel and Rob, which meant it might not happen as they wanted to go to the States before the end of October. The following day Carmel rang me and said, 'Yes, Derek, but it will cost you £1,000 for the day.' I agreed, so Sunday 19 September and Sunday 3 October were booked. My wife was furious, all that money for what? Yes, maybe Brenda, but Smax Smith was charging Darryl Bradford £1,000 per day to practise for his race licence in the 'Mainline Menace', word gets around and suddenly everybody starts charging the same.

No sooner had I arrived home than I was off again to the Pod, both trips on my own, this Sunday and again in a fortnight. I was determined to prove to Carmel I could run the car without breaking the engine.

When I arrived at the Pod, where were the Turners? I waited half an hour and then went looking for them. They were still in the workshop, the car hadn't been loaded into their rig and it took all my self-control not to lose my temper. I forced the issue as far as I could, explaining that for the money being paid to them the car had to be brought to the start line once in the morning and again in the afternoon. Now things started to happen. Steve got on his mobile to the crew and Rob shot off in his car to collect them. The Turners weren't going to pass up £2,000 – it would pay for their holiday in the USA.

I did get two passes in Brenda's dragster on Sunday 19 September and felt more comfortable and relaxed – no breakages.

The next time I saw the Turners was on Sunday 3 October. This time the car was in the pits and ready to race. Surprise, surprise, who else was there but Smax Smith with his TA dragster and Darryl Bradford all kitted up. It was a RWYB meeting, with many young men trying their hand at drag racing in their wives' shopping trolleys. Everybody paid the same money to race so Darryl and I would have to wait our turn.

My first run at 12 noon was a shakedown run for Steve to check the engine and lenco. Now the teams had half an hour's break for lunch – Steve never eats, he just smokes cigarettes.

The club required Darryl and myself to fit into a half-hour slot at 3pm when the track would be cleared of other cars. I was first out. Steve had set the clutch, it was fierce, sending the car towards the side rail when I launched, but I held on, lifting off just before the eighth mile. These cars can be brutes and must be treated with respect, but Darryl and I enjoyed ourselves. Darryl would go on in a few years to drive Top Fuel cars against the best.

The engine and the car were checked over by Steve – no damage and in perfect condition for next year's racing. There you are, Carmel, I didn't break the engine. I had proved what I had set out to do and it cost me £2,000. The car was returned to the Turner workshop and covered up until next year.

My next race was the October National on Saturday and this time the Camaro was entered. There was a quick change of plans. I was to race the BMW instead of the Camaro. Then, racing finished, I could tow the caravan home – the parking fees during the winter weren't cheap.

The main contenders for the championships were Phil Walker and Rick Denny. A good result for me and I would be runner-up in the main championship.

Racing the BMW meant I could tow the caravan to the pits so there was no need to ask Paul Hudson. For some reason known only to her, Julie, Paul Hudson's girlfriend, started to ignore my wife. This was uncalled for and hurtful, my wife had been a good friend to Julie, listening to her going on about Paul and his parents at least once a week over the telephone for over a year.

I parked the caravan next to Brian Huxley's trailer but this turned out to be a big mistake. Brenda needed her rest in the afternoon and this became impossible. The two young children with the Huxleys kept firing plastic pellets on the roof of the caravan and shouting, 'Don't wake the old lady', then they would run away and hide. Two days of this made Brenda a very bad tempered lady.

Sportsman ET had an 11-car field with five qualifying sessions. Paul Hudson picked me again. I pulled a near perfect light 0.538. That's better, now everybody was lining up against me and the white BMW.

Chris Isaacs pulled a holeshot on me, then it was the other Chris in his Audi – two German cars burning the track up. Now it was Gareth Mogford's turn, a policeman with the Wiltshire traffic section. We both pulled good lights, his 0.550, mine 0.591, his win. I broke out by $8/1000$ of a second.

It was end of day's play and all the kids on the block put their race cars away for the night and started drinking their favourite brew, lager and lime, or is it shandy south of Watford gap?

My wife hadn't managed to get any rest during the day's racing – those children with the plastic pellets had enjoyed themselves but you're only young once. It was a quick meal and early to bed. Sportsman ET eliminations were scheduled to start at noon so this would give Brenda an extra hour's rest before we left the Travelodge for the track.

When we arrived on the track the running order was posted and my first opponent was Paul Hudson who was walking about the pits rubbing his hands together and talking to himself. Paul dialled in 13.20 and ran a 13.456, reaction time 0.542. My dial-in was 16.40, my ET 16.617, with a reaction time of 0.523. It was my win by $\frac{5}{100}$ of a second.

Who was next? For the last time this year, it was Chris Hodgkins. Before we raced, he said, 'Derek, I won last time so it is your turn to win', and so it was. I pulled a holeshot on him and it was an easy win. This gave me a bye into the finals against Phil Walker. If I could beat Phil, Rick would be the winner of both championships and I would be runner-up in the main championship. As it turned out, Phil pulled a holeshot on me and became champion. That's drag racing at its best – most races are won on the start line.

Farewells said, caravan hitched up, and it was time to drive home. On the back seat of the car was a runners-up trophy. The car and driver had come good at the last meeting. Now I could start my winter letter writing and there were many issues I wanted to air.

For some time I had been campaigning for a scholarship to be set up to help young up-and-coming racers, so I sent this letter to *Custom Car*:

---

14 October 1999

Dear Sirs

The Future of British Drag Racing

Other forms of motorsport have a fund for the young driver. To date, drag racing UK, to the best of my knowledge, don't have plans to support up-and-coming new young blood.

With respect, I propose the three major clubs and raceways form a trust to promote UK drag racing for the younger driver. A small percentage of their revenues could be channelled through to a registered trust whose trustees would have the power to allocate money to teams who have a programme for younger drivers. The main raceways could set aside track time for the training of these drivers (Junior Dragster to Top Fuel), by qualified instructors from the main clubs.

There must be a reservoir of unused race cars within the UK which are not SFI approved for racing but are more than adequate for a RWYB training session.

Derek (Grandad) Annable

PS Hot rod and drag racing have the same genes.

A similar letter to the *ETRA News* was printed in their mailbag. Carla Pittau's reply came back in the following note:

Derek

Thank you for the article and the kind words – we do (at least I do) appreciate and respect everybody's opinion – I hope you will still be involved in drag racing, in some ways you have been – and are – a great asset to our sport – never afraid to speak up and stand up for yourself, what you believe, and to defend others. Don't give up on us.

Best regards to you and Brenda.

Carla.

Our local newspaper was full of anti-British sentiment. Welsh are Welsh; English don't like the Welsh and so it went on; people shouldn't call themselves British. The following week the subject was back again in yet another newspaper, so off went another letter:

Letters and Comments   3 November 1999
The Mail
Bangor

Dear Sirs

Proud to be British

In a few weeks I shall be 69 years old and for all those years I have taken pride in being British. My life has alternated between Wales and England, the last 35 years being permanent in Wales.

In 1930 my mother was pregnant, who was the unborn baby she was carrying between Wales and England? – me. Christmas 1930 my parents had arranged to spend the holiday with my grandparents in Manchester. Being in a hurry I must have decided Christmas 1930 was going to be my first Christmas, a few days earlier I would have been born in Anglesey, North Wales.

I am an old man proud to be British, I support the British Lions rugby team and everything British. The greatest family on this planet Earth are the Welsh, English, Scots and Irish, whichever order you put them. When working together they are still the greatest.

All success to the Welsh Assembly and UK Parliament. Please allow a few true Brits like me to be British for a little longer.

Yours sincerely

Mr Derek F. Annable

It was December again and nearly the end of another year. What had been achieved? I was third in the SPRC Drag Racing Championship, fifth in the National Drag Racing Championship. Brenda's TA dragster was going to race Top Methanol next year with Doug Bond as number one driver and I was to race his old car at three meetings. The shop had been profitable, when most retail outlets were in decline. My wife's health had improved, she was on the mend and all our bills had been paid on time. What more can anybody want?

The only down was that my mother had left this world for good, but we all come to that in the end. Let's hope 2000 is a good year.

I shall quote the old cliché people hate, 'Life has its ups and downs.' Never mind, how many people have raced a Top Alcohol dragster and lived to tell the tale? Two reasonably old people are up and still fighting their corner, much to the annoyance of the younger generation. Motorsport has no age limit, it is open to all who have the will to race.

Brenda is still alive because of motorsport and her love of it, and I am 100% behind her. Life should be lived to the full – fifty years ago I said in my marriage vows, 'in sickness and in health' and this still holds good today. We will both be up and running next year and for many more years.

Happy Christmas! I do enjoy everything about December including three birthdays – Brenda's and mine, and Jesus Christ's.

*The car Derek and
Brenda bought
(© Custom Car)*

Take from the rich...

I have a story for you.

There was a little old lady with a stick who heard a drag racing club couldn't afford an electronic scoreboard because the other Sheriff of Nottingham (Keith Bartlett) was withholding money. Although she had been saving up her weekly pension to buy Christmas presents for all the tiny Tims in our village, this money (£500) was sent to the APIRA (scoreboard fund) instead.

I was double gutted at the World Finals, Santa Pod – so lads don't triple gut me. There are eleven honest and true men, get your cheque books out and together match Brenda A's donation.

Derek (Grandad) Annable, Anglesey.

(© Custom Car)

*York Dragway: Dave
Allen, Derek's opponent
(© Derek Annable)*

*York Dragway: Derek in Z28
(© Derek Annable)*

Santa Pod, August 1997: TA car, Derek driving
(© Steven F. Moxley)

Santa Pod, August 1997: Derek had a half pass 4.938/117.47 (© Steven F. Moxley)

Mark Coulsell, 'Limited Funz' (© Wild Bunch)

Trev Morrett, 'Adrenalin Overload' (© Wild Bunch)

Bangor hospital
(© Brian Staines)

F. H. Howarth, winner of the Jaguar Trophy (given by Wm Lyons) 1951/52 (© F. H. Howarth)

Carla Pittau fighting her corner (© Carla Pittau)

Avon Park: Nick Pettitt, 'Torture Cab II' (© Wild Bunch)

Steve and Paul Dale,
'Sympathy for the Devil'
(© Wild Bunch)

Avon Park: Rick Denny (© Rick Denny)

Santa Pod: Rick's chances ended early on as Terri Rogers-Valle pulled a holeshot
(© Rick Denny)

Avon Park, Jens Nybo 1997:
Brenda and Jens were soulmates
(© Steven F. Moxley)

Santa Pod: Martin Lewis (© Colin Catlin)

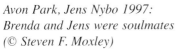

Rick filling tow car (© Carla Pittau)

Santa Pod: Colin Catlin in the pits (© Colin Catlin)

Liz in the pits at Santa Pod (© Colin Catlin)

Smax Smith, Santa Pod crash (© Custom Car)

MSA scrutineers: Amos Meekins (right)
(© Derek Annable)

Avon Park, May 1999: Phil Walker driving 'Royal Ragtop' (© Phil Walker)

Santa Pod, The Main Event, 1999: Brenda (crew chief) and Tracey (Brenda's best friend) (© Phil Walker)

October Meeting 1999: Phil pulled a holeshot on Derek and became champion (© Phil Walker)

Crutched Friars, Derek's mother's house near Bury St Edmunds (© Pam Robinson)

Santa Pod, European Finals 1999: Phil Walker winner (© Phil Walker)

CHAPTER 9

2000

The new year celebrations were over and it was time to start making money to pay for our addiction to the extravagant form of motorsport we enjoyed. While I was cleaning our shop in Benllech, my daughter brought me the *Mail* to read, where I read the following:

Death junction: Ex-racing driver was also a victim *Even Moss crashed*

Even racing driver Stirling Moss crashed at the Llandegai junction with Bangor Road.

That was the surprise revelation from concerned Rev J Aelwyn Roberts about the death junction this week.

The retired vicar from Llandegai has branded the accident spot a 'death' junction and expressed grave concern about traffic incidents.

His comments follow the death of Dr William Beer on December 22 where two elderly women were slightly injured in a car collision.

Mr Roberts said he saw British motorsports champion Stirling Moss crash there 20 years ago.

'Impossible as it may sound, Stirling Moss did crash at the junction.

Some 20 years ago I heard a collision bang and went to investigate and I thought, "I know this chap"'.

He walked out of his Range Rover, which was towing a racing car, and had struck a plumber's van, writing it off.

'He told me that he'd crashed into the van and please could he come in and use the phone.

He explained to his wife that he had crashed his car, at a place called Llandegai, and that it would probably mean he would miss the ferry to Ireland where he would race the following day.'

Meanwhile, Gwynedd Highways Department has met with Llandegai residents and has promised interim safety measures near the junction.

They include rumble strips and altered signs to make drivers more aware of the junction.

Cllr Roy Tindall, who attended a meeting to discuss the danger spot in December, said: 'The Council are beginning to listen at last.

We at Llandegai will be putting constant pressure to ensure they make it safer for residents and motorists.'

Traffic-calming measures are also being addressed with the possibility of a new roundabout being considered.

Mr Roberts, who is involved in the safety campaign, thinks Mr Moss would pledge support.

'It could be that Stirling Moss, if they asked him, would be able to offer good advice', he said, 'as would others living in the village.'

My comment was, 'What the hell', and I sent off the following letter:

Amlwch
Anglesey
7 January 2000

Letters and Comments
The *Bangor and Anglesey Mail*
Bangor

Sirs

FRONT PAGE: Stirling Moss Survived Blackspot
Page 3. Death Junction: Ex-Racing driver was also a victim
EVEN MOSS CRASHED by Barry Ellams (Wednesday Jan 5 2000)

With respect, 'It takes two to tango.' Any accident where two vehicles are involved there is an apportion of blame. Why is it because Stirling Moss was involved in an accident at Llandegai Junction 20 years ago there is something wrong with the road and he (Stirling Moss) could help to improve this so called black spot!

In 1950/52 I raced against the legendary Moss and I can assure you there is nothing superhuman about the man (then boys we were both 21 years old). In those days he stretched the cars he raced beyond what they were built to stand, they broke or crashed (we all had a name for him).

No. The section of road at Llandegai Junction has a bad name. I live in Anglesey and I can assure your readers there are sections of the 5025 which are as bad if not worse. One corner between Pentraeth and Four Crosses has claimed more lives than the Llandegai Junction. Ask the Police, more people have been killed on the 5025 over the last 30 years than any other road in North Wales.

Mr Derek F. Annable

The paper printed my letter in their 19 January edition, with the heading 'Far Worse Blackspots'.

The *Chronicle* were now on the Stirling Moss bandwagon, so off went another letter:

Amlwch
Anglesey

20 January 2000

Letterbox
The *Chronicle*
Bangor

Sirs

In a North Wales Newspaper (5 Jan 2000) there was an article: 'Stirling Moss Survived Blackspot. Death Junction, ex-racing driver was also a victim. Even Moss Crashed.'

With respect any accident where two vehicles are involved there is an apportion of blame. Why is it because Stirling Moss was involved in an accident at Llandegai Junction 20 years ago there is something wrong with the road and he (Stirling Moss) could help to improve this so called black spot.

In 1950/52 I raced against the legendary Moss and I can assure you there is nothing superhuman about the man (then boys we were both 21 years old). In those days he stretched the cars he raced beyond what they were built to stand, many times they broke or crashed (we all had a name for him).

Yes, the section of road at Llandegai Junction has a bad name. I live in Anglesey and I can assure your readers there are sections of the A5025 which are as bad if not worse. One corner between Pentraeth and Four Crosses has claimed more lives than the Llandegai Junction.

When I was a fireman with the then Anglesey Fire Brigade and stationed at Benllech we were called out to road accidents whose horrors still live with me today. A mother and her baby in a pram were crushed to death by a 30-ton road tanker in Benllech. Young men driving back from Bangor killed in a road accident outside Springholme. In recent times bikers killed at Dulas and Penysarn. Young men killed on the section of road between Cemaes and Bull Bay.

David Sutcliffe lives in Bull Bay, when working for the BBC he attended many of the major road accidents in Wales. Please, David, settle the argument. Which road in North Wales is the most dangerous and which has claimed the most lives?

I put forward the A5025 on Anglesey as the front runner.

Mr Derek F. Annable

They printed my response the following week.

The heating turned on and Brenda installed behind the counter, we were ready for business. One of our regular customers left a newspaper for me to read. The motoring section was of interest to both her husband and myself. There it was on page ten, 'Leaded fuel is dead, long live leaded fuel.' At the bottom of the page was the address of the supplier. I thought, 'What's the catch?' The new Labour government had outlawed the sale of leaded fuel through garage forecourt pumps, with a hefty fine in the thousands of pounds, plus the loss of your petrol licence if you were caught. Being too late in the day to phone our local trading standards officer, it would have to wait until tomorrow.

When I phoned the council, they didn't know what I was talking about and said, 'There isn't any leaded fuel in the UK.'

My next phone call was to Bayford Thurst. Jonathan Turner answered the phone, so I asked him, 'Are you able to deliver leaded petrol to my garage in Anglesey, North Wales?'

His answer was, 'When do you want it? Next week?'

'Hold on, Mr Turner, I closed the garage down two years ago and it will take me six weeks to be operational again. Are you able to deliver a thousand gallons on 1 March?'

'Yes, we are. Firstly you need to register with the FBHVC, pay their £50 fee, then it is legal for you to sell leaded petrol BS4040 from your premises.'

Thank goodness they didn't ask me to become one of their outlets. I had been through hell with NWF Fuels Ltd. OK, I could work with their managing director but their agent in Bangor was a different matter. His attitude to Action's Garage brought about heavy sales losses on fuel, and our customers were going to our opposition on the east side of Anglesey.

The drag racing scene was starting to wake up, with the following article in the *SPRC News:*

SFI/FIA CERTIFICATION TOUR

For those of you who need to know:

The SFI/FIA Certification Tour will take place on Tuesday, 13 February 2001 and will be held at MSA House, Riverside Park, Colnbrook, Slough.

The earliest any inspections will start will be from approx 2.00 pm as the team will be coming to the MSA direct from Heathrow Airport. They will be certifying clutches and bellhousings. The team will consist of Arnie Kuhns, Murf McKinney, Tim Hyatt and Mike Baker from the IHRA. Mike Baker's expertise lies with Pro Mod and Pro Stock, so if anyone has any questions for him, try to get to the MSA on 13 February.

Please can you inform Paula Marshall at the SPRC office as soon as possible if you are intending to go, so that she can give an indication to Arnie and his team how many certifications they are likely to be doing. Contact Paula by phone on 01933 313625 or fax 01933 355558 or E-mail paula@sprc.fsnet.co.uk. Thank you.

Doug and Martyn were arranging the inspection of our dragster. My cheque for £180 was posted with urgency. Eurodragster sent me the following:

BOND AND ANNABLE JOIN FORCES

Hot news from the methanol pits is that Doug Bond and Derek Annable are to join forces this year. Doug will be driving Derek's car, previously owned by Barry Sheavills, with Doug's engine and Derek will drive Doug's car with Derek's engine and crew chief Martyn Hannis' old Funny Car Crower auto clutch. Confused! You won't be when the first round of the British Series rolls through the gates of Santa Pod next month because both cars will be decked out in Shell Oil sponsorship. The future looks extremely good for the team.

Drag racing is like a hedgehog, it sleeps all winter, then with the first warm day it comes to life.

I had a deadline to keep as Bayford Thurst would be delivering fuel on 1 March. The garage needed painting, the storage tanks checking out and cleaning. The forecourt and adjacent land we owned was a mess, so there was a lot to do quickly. Thank goodness we were going through a warm spell of weather. I could leave Brenda at the shop and get on with the work.

Bayford Thurst were a family business which started in the coalfields of Yorkshire, hauling coal by road from the many mines in the area. They acquired parcels of land here and there for their haulage business and for the future. The natural step forward from coal was to petroleum, this they took and became a very efficient and large organisation and treated me well.

Now I would have the right fuel for our cars; LRP was causing damage to the Camaro and BMW engines. People with historic/vintage cars had a source of the fuel they needed on their doorstep.

Bayford Thurst made their delivery on time and put our garage on the website. Within a week, people were travelling from all over North Wales for their leaded petrol. Now the usual £5–£10 sale was £40–£50 every time. Our garage was the only outlet in North and mid Wales selling 4-star leaded petrol BS4040 and still is today.

Both businesses were doing well and now it was time to plan the team's racing. The Camaro would be entered in both championships with the BMW as the back-up car. Now I was part of the Shell Oil racing team, it meant preparing myself for the April Test and Tune at Shakespeare County Raceway. The Bond/Hannis dragster was a different beast to ours as it had no clutch pedal. Would I be able to master the semi-automatic two-speed box?

Checking my calendar, it was two weeks to the Test and Tune. A quick phone call to Martin to check the car was ready. Yes it was, our engine was in and ready to go.

Where would we stay? Brenda spoke to Lyn Newbury; her husband would cook us an evening meal and they had a ground-floor bedroom. Perfect, so two nights were booked. My wife was looking forward to getting off the island. Anglesey has its downside, you can feel like a prisoner, like a number in the series, *The Prisoner*.

On arrival at Fosbroke House, the greeting Brenda received was a little cool, 'We never thought we'd see you again.' Never mind, the room had everything she needed and eating there would save using the car in the evenings.

When we woke up in the morning, it was pouring with rain and it was cold. After an enjoyable breakfast we set off for the racetrack. When we entered the pits, nothing moved, everybody was still in bed. All day we sat in the car. Doug, Martyn and the crew sat inside the rig with our car. It rained and rained. The pit area became flooded; would there be any racing tomorrow? It was agreed that if the weather was the same on Sunday morning, everybody would go home and we would meet again the following weekend at the Pod.

Sunday was a reasonable day weather-wise, so the dragster was taken out of the rig and was ready for me to try out by lunchtime. Sitting in the cockpit, I was towed down to the start line. Oh dear, problems with the gearbox; it wouldn't select reverse. Martin worked on it but it was no good, it was jammed. Nothing could be done to the gearbox on the start line to release it. I would have to make my launch without a burnout.

The engine was fired up, I moved forward on the handbrake, damn I wish there was a clutch to release the power to the rear wheels. The gearbox would change from first to second automatically, all I had to do was bring the revs up and release the handbrake as the start light came on. This I did, but the car shot to the right and the track wall came looming up. I lifted off and cut the engine. Very little was proved that weekend. We thanked Doug and Martyn, paid our dues and drove home.

We were glad to be home and sitting in front of a roaring coal fire. You can keep central heating, give me the glow of a real fire. Then there it was, a real gem from the pen of Chris Isaacs in the *Santa Pod Racing Club News*:

YOUR FORTUNES IN 2000
by Chris Isaacs

Let the SPRC's resident clairvoyant Simplistic Meg, cross-eyed pseudoscience garbage-talker to the rich and famous, guide you through the coming year in drag racing.

JANUARY

'Tog' from Eurodragster can't stay away from the track any longer, and files a report from the Pod on New Year's Day. 'It's bloody cold, not a soul in sight and there's sheep everywhere', he reports.

At the Autosport Show, three billion people surround the Drag Racing stand and gaze with awe and wonder at the assembled vehicles. Later, market research will show that twelve of them actually visit a race meeting later in the year, four of which have got lost on the way to Silverstone.

Keith Bartlett announces there will be 'eight Top Fuel cars at the Main Event – at least'.

FEBRUARY

The National Trust slap a Grade II listing on the 'Money Hungry' Camaro, which is bad news for Paul Hudson as he has just had the windshield and side glass replaced with UPVc french windows. 'Those double glazing salesmen just never take no for an answer', protests Paul, but the Trust insists he return to original Camaro glass, 'preferably with diamond-leaded lights'.

Luke Ramage shows his dedication to drag racing as he moves house to be closer to the track. 'I feel like I'm only round the corner', he says from his new home in Carlisle.

Derek Annable casts around for a class he hasn't run in yet.

MARCH

In an effort to finally rid themselves of last year's transmission problems, Carla Pittau and Rick McCann outfit their Camaro with a

Super-Vasco billet everything 'glide, but early RWYB testing doesn't go well. 'I don't believe it', says Carla, 'we've got no third gear now'.

In other testing news, the Moore brothers show with a four foot tall aero scoop on their Triumph Herald, a necessity to cover the carb sitting atop a stack of 14 nitrous places. 'It's really only a stock motor', says Roger after the team's 7.99 checkout pass.

Barry Sheavills unveils his new ride, 'Last year's version was too powerful, so we've decided to fall back on this old donkey', he says as he wheels out Tony Schumacher's 1999 Exide car.

APRIL

'Tog' arrives at the track to upgrade his news page with an Easter report, looks at what still remains on the screen from 1 January and leaves it as it is except for the date.

Chris Isaacs shows for Easter in his new piece, a Trabant. Dialling 42.63 seconds he runs 42.62 in a first round breakout loss. 'I just took a bit too much finish line – it's so difficult to judge you see, these fast cars come at you from nowhere', he says of his race with Spencer's Vauxhall Corsa.

Zane Llewelyn feels he may finally have too much electronic gadgetry on his Super Comp car. 'It cuts 0.400 lights, packs itself away in the trailer afterwards, and tells me the time in Malawi', he reports, 'but it's now so heavy it only runs 9.1s'.

Five hundred cars show in Pro ET and Super Gas.

Both eliminators are abandoned at the semi-final stage on Wednesday afternoon as the UK's supply of C12 is exhausted. Derek Annable sits out Easter after his application for a Junior Dragster is rejected. 'They are just being ageist', he fumes.

MAY

Three Top Fuel cars enter the Main Event, all owned by Barry Sheavills. None of them qualify.

Wayne Saunders debuts his new car. 'I figured, if four cylinders are good, six must be better', he says, pointing to his Mk 2 Zephyr with Raymond Mays cylinder head and three-speed column change. Early checkout passes yield mid 22 second quarter, and Wayne is later seen trying to find some way of plugging his laptop into the triple SU's. 'The power's there somewhere', he claims.

The Nordic Pro Stockers forget about racing and award the winner's trophy to the driver who reaches the highest rpm on the burnout. Entry to the start line grandstands during Pro Stock sessions includes a hard hat and a baseball mitt.

Right at the end of the meeting, Barry Sheavills does a checkout pass in his new Exide/Wynns car and runs 4.60 at 315mph. 'Hmmm … it should have run better', says Rune.

JUNE

The Bug Jam attracts 15 million people, and the roads surrounding the Pod are declared a national disaster area. John Prescott arrives and tells everyone they should have used the train. Meanwhile several racers show up for a novel form of 'testing', which consists of doing one half-pass all weekend and spending the rest of the time ogling the girls in their summer wear.

A week later Barry Sheavills tests the Exide/Wynns car at a RWYB, takes the lane which has been most chewed up by all the front-wheel drive cars, and runs 4.46 at 325. 'I'm unhappy', says Rune. 'It was mixing the cylinders a bit at the top end.'

JULY

Chris Isaacs enters Sportsman ET at the Cannonball in a Sinclair C5, dialling in at 1 minute 37 seconds. 'It's not fair', said one or two racers, 'all he has to do is nail it and it'll run the same number every time'. 'And he can wear that ridiculous extra option clip-on hovercraft lookalike souwester thing if it rains', they added.

Wayne Saunders runs 7.40 in his Mk2 Zephyr. 'We've changed to Zenith carburettors and it's all come good', he explains. 'Now if we can figure out an air shift for the column change, we'll be in the sixes.'

Zane Llewelyn is back running 8.90s again. 'We took some weight out of the car – me'. Zane now 'drives' his dragster from the pit lane using a Tamiya radio control unit, but loses in the final of Super comp when his mobile phone rings and the resulting radio waves override his throttle stop.

AUGUST

The true purpose of the ultimate Street Car weekend is revealed as a neutron bomb is detonated above the track, killing every FWD shopping trolley owner in the universe and giving a new meaning to the term 'hot hatch'.

Keith Bartlett announces, 'there will be eight Top Fuel cars at the Euro Finals – no, really. Trust me'.

SEPTEMBER

Eight Top Fuel cars show at the Euro Finals, seven owned by Barry Sheavills. Six don't qualify, but the Exide/Wynns car nails the top qualifying spot with a 4.39 at 336mph, in the rain. 'Useless', says Rune, 'it turned the tyres between 80 and 100 feet'.

Knut Soderquist has 624 crew members on his Carbon by Design fueller, including Bill Schultz on engine, Al Segrini on clutch, Dale Armstrong on harmonica and Austin Coil making the tea. The car runs big mph but is suffering traction difficulties. 'Perhaps we needed a bit more resin in these carbon tyres', muses Knut.

In the TF final, Alan Jackson runs 4.52 in Knut's car but Sheavills wins with a 3.98 at 360mph. 'That was so-so, I guess', says Rune.

The Pro Stock teams don't make the track at all, instead deciding the outcome in the pits with wallets at ten paces. Kjetil Hauge and Paul Brander are declared the winners because they run Fords.

OCTOBER

Chris Isaacs runs Sportsman at the October meet aboard a Saturn V track transport vehicle. He intends to dial in at eighteen hours but is left off the elimination ladder after only making it halfway down the fire-up road by the end of qualifying Saturday night.

The Moore brothers take the carburettor off their Herald and replace it with an upturned 80lb bottle of nitrous and a BG400 fuel pump aimed into the intake manifold. They run 5.99 with a 0.92 60ft, 'and that's with a ten-inch converter', says Dave.

Street Eliminator co-ordinator, Ian Jackson, debuts his new car, the ex-Jim Oddy '37 Chevy Nitro Coupe featuring a trained chimpanzee strapped to the roof who wipes the windscreen with a chamois if it rains. 'Honest, it's a street car', he proclaims. He qualifies with a 6.30 but fails the cruise after the chimp gets sucked into the injector during a traffic light duel with a Sierra Cosworth.

NOVEMBER

At the Flame and Thunder, Derek Annable debuts his Pro Mod grapefruit and beats the Outspan Orange three straight with mid sixes. 'I've finally found my niche', he claims, before fleeing at the sight of the man from Del Monte.

500 million people pack the bank to watch the fireworks, whilst another 300 million finally figure out that if they park up just outside the main gate they can see them for nothing.

Zane Llewelyn runs his new 'total electronic control' dragster at the Moroso 5 day Bracket Marathon in Florida. The revolutionary car enables Zane to sit at home in Bristol and 'virtual drive' the car via satellite link, but he forgets that American electricity is 110v instead of 240 and runs a 4.40 on his 8.90 dial-in.

DECEMBER

Ian Jackson buys a marmoset. 'There's nothing against it in the

Construction and Use regulations', he states, 'and they've got long fur so you can Evostik them in place'.

Keith Bartlett builds a twenty-storey control tower which includes free hotel suites for all racers and crew, plus one room dedicated exclusively to care of racer's pet hamsters so they don't have to leave them at home. 'He doesn't do enough for us', protests one driver. 'I've got a gerbil'.

In the 2001 New Year Bonanza every one of the 300 new millionaires are racers. This sparks rumours of fifty Top Fuel cars, thirty Fuel Coupes and a hundred Pro Stock cars for the coming season, but at the Easter meeting everyone shows up with the same cars they had last year.

Reading Chris's forecast for the year made me wonder how my readers would understand all this drag racing jargon, so here is a brief glossary of the main terms used. You will find a full version of this at the front of the book.

Alcohol:	methanol when used as fuel in an engine.
Altered:	a car based on a known body type but changed or radically customised.
Blower/supercharger:	a crank drive air-to-fuel moisture compressor. It increases atmospheric pressure in the engine, giving extra horsepower.
Bracket:	the upper and lower ET index limits on a class.
Breakout:	running faster than the index in handicap racing.
Burnout:	spinning the driving wheels in water prior to the run, this heats and cleans them, giving better traction.
Christmas tree:	the starting lights controlled by the timing computer.
Deep stage:	a driver is deep staged when, after staging, he/she rolls forward a few inches further, causing the pre-stage light to go out. The vehicle is nearer the finish line but is dangerously close to a red light. In some classes, the act is illegal.
Dial-in:	in handicap racing, the time the racer considers is the most consistent he can achieve.
Doorslammer:	a full-bodied car with operable doors.
Eliminations:	a tournament-style competition, the losers are eliminated and the winners progress until only one winner remains.
ET:	means elapsed time. The total time taken to travel from start line to finish line.
Flopper/Fuel coupe:	a Funny Car.

Headers:	fine-tuned exhaust system, routing exhaust from engine. Replaces conventional exhaust manifolds.
Heads-up:	non-handicap racing, where both competitors start together.
Hemi:	an engine, which has a hemispherical-shaped cylinder-head chamber.
Holeshot:	an advantage gained by a quicker reaction time on the start line.
In pre-stage:	a racer is in pre-stage when the front wheel has interrupted the first light beam just before the start line. Full stage is only inches ahead.
In stage:	a racer is in stage when the front wheels have interrupted both light beams at the start line (see also Deep stage).
Index:	an elapsed time establishing the limit for a handicap class.
Light up (tyres):	generally too much power is used, causing the tyres to spin in smoke instead of gripping the track.
Reaction time or rt:	the time it takes a racer to react to the green starting light. Measured in thousandths of a second. The rt counter begins when the last amber flashes and stops when the vehicle clears the stage beams.
Slick:	smooth tyres with no tread, giving maximum traction of rubber to track.
Staging lane:	designated assembly area for competitors, also known as the pairing lanes, where competitors are paired prior to racing.
Supercharger:	see Blower/supercharger.
Terminal speed:	the speed through the finish line.
Traction compound or trackbite:	a liquid that is sprayed onto the track, providing added grip or traction when dry.
Wheelie bars:	bars with small wheels protruding from the rear of some vehicles, preventing excessive front wheel lift.

Now it was Easter and the Thunder and Lightning and Shell Oil teams were at the Pod. Saturday and Sunday would be qualifying. Nothing much happened on Saturday, so this gave us the chance to check through the official programme. The press were having a field day:

Doug Bond (UK), the Hannis racing organisation, has been playing musical chairs over the winter. Derek Annable and Doug have swapped, so Doug is now driving the ex-Barry Sheavills chassis built (and freshly updated) by Geoff Hauser that broke all the records a few years back. Crew chief Martyn, fresh off the aeroplane with a retro-blower and clutch, topped off with a new shell paint scheme, is looking for some serious improvements in the performance this year.

Who were my opponents? There were three new racers on observed runs, Simon Chalkly, Robert Main and Alan Platt within a field of 15 cars. The race director was going to have a busy time on Sunday if everybody were to run their quota of qualifying passes.

Sunday morning dawned and the track was ready early. The BMW was running some slow times and didn't settle down until I raced against Paul Bishop, giving me a 17.026 and 17.067. My racing was over for the day so Brenda and I went to the Top Methanol pits to see how things were going for Doug and Martyn. There were problems with the clutch but adjustments would cure this. The blower was also popping burst panels, which was more serious. Let's hope Doug could get through to the semi-final. This being the first round of the MSA Championship, a good show was important.

We had an enjoyable meal that evening and retired to the bedroom with a box of liquorice allsorts and a bottle of wine. This is an acquired taste! When the weather forecast came up on the television, it didn't look good. Bright start followed by rain.

What bright start? It rained on and off all morning. The track marshals battled against the elements all day and the first round of Sportsman ET didn't take place until well into the afternoon, as Spencer Tramm reported in the *SPRC News:*

Ian Turnbull advanced thanks to a red light from Chris Hodgkins in his Audi 80 and finally Derek Annable in his BMW beat the new Firebird of Bob Main.

Round two saw Alan Platt lose on a red light to Paul Hudson, Gareth Mogford advance over a red lighting Simon Chalkly, Ian Turnbull with the round bye and Neil L'Aouette win over Derek Annable.

The semi-finals saw Paul Hudson overcome a reaction deficit against Gareth Mogford in the Moonraker Camaro to meet Ian Turnbull, whose .526 and .05 over 12.15 saw off the challenge of Neil L'Alouette and won Ian the 'Best Package' competition for the bracket classes which is presented by Hauser Race Cars.

The final was unfortunately a victim of the weather.

Neil L'Alouette's win over me was due in part to me breaking out by $\frac{2}{100}$ of a second. Never mind, off home we went with all speed.

Three days' rest at home and we were off again, this time to the Super Series at Shakespeare County Raceway, a three-day meet, where the BMW was entered in the Sportsman class again.

There it was, reported in the Methanol Madness Newsflash!

Bond and Annable join forces full story page 15. 'My name's Bond Annable'. More mad news from the Methanol pits. Doug Bond and Derek Annable are to join forces for the 2000 season. Doug will be driving Derek's car, previously owned by British Top Fuel Ambassador Barry Sheavills.

Derek's car (driven by Doug) will sport Doug's engine and Doug's car (driven by Derek) will be running Derek's engine which will also be carrying crew chief Martyn Hannis' funny old car crower auto clutch.

Confused? You will be as both cars will be resplendent in the bright red and yellow livery of main sponsors Shell Oil! The future is looking good for this team so check 'em out in the pits and give them your support.

We were booked in at the Alcester Travelodge this time and looked forward to sampling the food on offer in their restaurant.

The BMW had run a 16.98 at the Pod, let's leave the dial-in on the back window and enjoy some racing. Rick Denny was my first opponent, which made me determined to pull a good light, which I did – 0.585, my win. Next out of the traps was Paul Hudson, this time saying, 'I'm going to beat the BMW.' No chance there.

Rick Denny was walking about the pits in one of his sulky moods. These came on him every time he lost a race, so I was chosen by his crew chief to be his next opponent. It was all smiles now as I broke out big time – what a difference a win makes to some people.

Racing over for the day, we left Long Marston and headed west to another of our favourite Little Chefs. We made pigs of ourselves, much to the disgust of the family sitting on the next table. I love to finish the meal off with a plate of chips, hot roll and butter, washed down with half a bottle of white wine. Seeing my plate of chips, the children on the next table kept saying, 'Mummy, we want the same as that man is having', although they had already finished their meal. The father swapped places with his children so they couldn't see my chips. Wherever Brenda and I eat we cause pandemonium – oh well, life is to be enjoyed as some Chinese prophet said.

Another day dawned and the weather didn't look good, so we took our time on the short journey to the track. Somebody had taken our spot by the toilet block; it was Paul Hudson's breakfast party, chairs and table out for Paul's guests who were Robert Main, Gareth Mogford and others. Julie was having problems keeping the bacon and eggs hot as she only had one gas ring working.

Qualifying for me was a double header against Alan Platt from Manchester, driving this year's model of the Camaro Z28. He dialled in 14.20, I posted 16.60, Alan pulled a poor light, my win. Back up the return road, we went onto the start line, Alan wanting revenge, which he got. This time I forced him to break out.

My wife's BMW 635 was showing its age, 200,000 miles on the clock, and when under pressure, the plugs oiled up. This was the story in eliminations on Monday; Robert Main knocked me out in the first round – the BMW had let me down, it ran a 17.128 on a 16.64 dial-in.

So we went home with first round points plus qualifying points. This was a poor start to the championship for the Thunder and Lightning team.

Most weeks my wife watched *Top Gear* on BBC2 and in the programme there is a certain lady who irritates her. This evening Brenda turned to me and said, 'Derek, why don't you challenge her to a race in our Top Methanol dragster? You drive Doug's, she drives ours.'

'Yes, good idea. We can ask to use Shakespeare County Raceway.' So I wrote to *Top Gear:*

Thunder and Lightning   May 2000
DRAG RACING TEAM

Brenda & Derek Annable, Amlwch, Anglesey LL66 0AR
Full Member: BDRC/APIRA/PDRC/SPRC/FHVC (British)

Producer, Top Gear, BBC2

Dear John Wilcox

**The Challenge of the Century! Derek (Grandad) Annable -v-
Vicky Henderson of Top Gear**

The challenge is this, we compete at the Silverstone racetrack over 10 laps in a car of her choice and then race over the eighth mile at Shakespeare County Drag Raceway in a Top Methanol dragster under MSA rules.

At the age of 69 years I am still active in drag racing. I raced Allard sports cars at the then Silverstone GP circuit in 1950/51.

I await your response.

Yours sincerely

Derek F. Annable

John Wilcox responded with the following:

Derek Annable
Anglesey   31 May 2000

Dear Derek

Good to hear from you again.

As you know, we are off the air at the moment, but I will certainly put your idea on the list of possibles for next series.

We will be in touch if we're going to follow it up.

Thank you for taking the time and trouble to write.

Yours sincerely

John Wilcox

Producer, Top Gear

It was time for the Main Event meeting at the Pod. The weather that weekend was a repeat of last year, with rain spoiling most attempts of getting any action on the track on Sunday. Tremendous efforts by the track crews were in evidence all weekend and we racers applauded them. The press reported:

> Doug Bond's (UK) performance has been revitalised this year thanks to the chassis swap with Derek Annable and the heavy investment in new parts. The best time for this team is falling every meeting, where will it all end? Personal best 6.409 at 206.28mph.

Because of the weather and the death of Chris Hampson, the Top Fuel Bike rider who was killed in a top end accident, the whole meeting was soured. My heart wasn't in the racing, which showed in my results with the Camaro. Qualifying was poor, my reaction times were mid-sixes.

On race day, I lost to Chris Hodgkins. I pulled a red 0.482 – red lights aren't me. Doug Bond was going well, in qualifying he had his best ever time – 6.11/204. In round one, he scored a 6.15/214 win over a wheel-lifting and shaking Mike Schoefer. Then Doug lost to Bugeja, with a 6.26/221 try to open the quarter-finals.

Chris Hampson's death was such a waste of a life. The track owners should find a way to make the drag strip safer for bikers. This prompted me to write the following letter to the Santa Pod track owners:

At Santa Pod Raceway during the last five years, two bikers have died in competition and one racer (Rookie Racers) by natural causes. With respect, I propose a section of the track should be set aside, where a plaque could be fixed showing their achievements. Further to this a role of honour of all past racers and riders could have a permanent position in the area of the fire-up lane/start line.

Derek Annable

At this time there was open hostility to drag racing in the UK, so I went public with this letter:

Champion of the Case

Derek (Grandad) Annable goes public, wait for it! Here it is! In 1951 I became a member of the British Racing Driver's Club, period. In 1994 I started drag racing at Santa Pod with my 1982 Camaro and enjoyed every minute of it. During the past six years my wife and I have been involved in every form of motorsport that *Custom Car* covers. Drag racing from Sportsman to Top Methanol, Northern Street Car Challenge to NSRA Billing Fun Run, NSRA Hot Rod Super Nats, Knebworth and Avon Park racetrack. Cruises to Preston, Leeds etc.

Brenda and I have promoted our sport to the likes of Ken Tyrell, Sir Frank Williams, Sir Stirling Moss and Lord Hesketh of the BDRC and Formula One by photos, editions of *CC*, Santa Pod guide to Drag Racing – you name it, we have sent it! 'Yes, Derek, very interesting', was their reply.

Sydney Allard (I raced one of his cars in 1949) put on a show of drag racing at Silverstone many years ago as part of a Grand Prix programme. What happened? The tens of thousands of spectators who came to see the Grand Prix were more interested in the Top Fuel etc drag cars than the Dinky car-type Formula One cars. Then Bernie Ecclestone & Co decided drag racing and American hot rods should be suppressed.

I may be a member of the old farts club, but I promise everyone who loves their American race/custom-built car I shall champion our form of motorsport until the day I can't fire up my beloved Camaro.

Derek Annable, Anglesey

Problems with the Camaro meant I had to race the BMW, so we loaded up and set course for Alcester and Shakespeare County Raceway. This time is was the Super Series 2 and our Methanol dragster was entered for a licensing run as a demo car. It would be double duty for me. As Mark Gredzinski reported in *Custom Car*, 'with no fuel or alcohol classes appearing save Derek Annable doing steady runs in the ex-Doug Bond Shell Oils dragster'.

The journey from home taking over four hours, we decided to drive for three hours and stop overnight at Hartlebury Travelodge, then drive to the track in the morning. This worked well and was less tiring for Brenda.

The dragster wouldn't be arriving until late morning, so I got stuck into qualifying the BMW for Sunday's racing. I ran against Tim Jackson, a 12-second car, he would be 5 seconds quicker over the quarter mile than me. My next run was against Alan Platt. This time the BMW plugs oiled up at the top of the track, slowing me to a 18.246 on a 17.00 dial-in. End of my qualifying, now let's concentrate on racing the dragster. Martyn hadn't finished preparing the car, so I went to watch Bill Weston try out his new Pro-Mod car. Bill had spent some time in the USA to get his race licence for that class of car and I wanted to cheer him on. He was one of the first racers I ever raced against and a great guy.

Poor Bill didn't qualify because of a nitrous blowback, which caused his hood scoop to part company with the rest of the bodywork. It shot 15ft up in the air, landing on the side of the track – the end of Bill's racing.

With only an hour to curfew, the dragster was ready for me to be strapped in. Orders were a short burnout followed by a half-pass. The burnout I managed, but as the car had lost reverse, this meant being pushed back to the start line, heavy going for three men. With the engine running, the car wanted to go forwards.

It was a fair launch, with the eighth mile coming up in seven seconds at 100mph. This sort of speed I was used to as the Altered I had raced was capable of this speed. Run over, the car was towed back to the pits for Doug and Martyn to sort out the crower semi-automatic clutch for tomorrow's racing.

For the results of the Sportsman class, I shall pass you over to Mark Gredzinski:

Chris Hodgkins is getting good in the Sportsman class in his Audi 80 Sport. He ran a string of 16s having qualified first, taking out Phil Walker's Pontiac and Rob Main's later Ponco. Meanwhile Derek Annable was taking time off from his dragster and running his BMW Coupe. Derek took out Stephen Anderson's Willys, Alan Platt's Camaro and relaxed with a 17-second bye. In the final Derek ran a 17.31/82 on a 17.15 dial-in but Chris Hodgkins took the spoils with a 16.19/74 on a 16.05 dial-in.

My run in the dragster was slotted in between the Wild Bunch and the Sportsman finals. The clutch worked this time and I was able to reverse back to the start line. It was a good launch, with a lift off just after the eighth mile. Everybody was pleased with the weekend's progress. The car was now ready for its next outing in the Top Methanol class at Super Series 4, or maybe in Super Series 3 if Doug and Martyn were free.

Our next date with the drag strip was 1 July when the BMW was entered in the Cannonball. Both the car and I struggled to make any progress. The best runs were low 17s and the smoke from the exhausts at the top end of the track was becoming an embarrassment. We had to find a new car.

After three poor qualifying runs and losing out to Chris Hodgkins in the first round of eliminations, we loaded up the car and set off for home.

We made good time to Chester so why not stop off at Conwy Honda in Llandudno Junction and see what they had on offer. They had an S2000, but Brenda doesn't like open-top sports cars. Then the salesman showed us a brochure of the Integra Type R. I had heard Honda UK were overstocked with 1999 models and were trying to offload them but it was July so where were the 2000 models? If they could arrange for the import of this year's model, we would buy one. Now the salesman became less than helpful, so we left with the promise that Brenda would phone him in the morning.

There was much soul-searching that evening about looking for a new car, but we couldn't afford the time as the shop and garage plus our drag racing took up every moment of our waking hours.

During breakfast on Monday morning, I said to Brenda, 'If you want the Integra, it is your golden wedding anniversary present. Tell the salesman cash down and the car to be ready for delivery to us before the end of the month.' The salesman agreed. Now the BMW could be retired, becoming our everyday, home to work transport.

As I like to send my entry forms in early, both cars were entered for the Super Series 3, on the offchance that Doug and Martyn would be free to crew. I was shocked when I received Wendy Talbot's letter:

APIRA
DRAG RACING FOR THE SPORTSMAN

Mr D Annable
Anglesey

                                                    10 July 00

Dear Derek,

We have to advise you that it will not be possible to accommodate the running of the methanol car at this event, as there will not be time for observed runs.

The entry level is high and it is just not possible to do this, we do hope you understand as we want to be fair to you.

We do not want to take your entry fee of £55.00 for this and you do not get to do your observed runs.

I have enclosed your cheque of £110.00; you can either send me another cheque for your entry of the Sportsman class or pay on the day for it.

Yours sincerely

Wendy Talbot

I had never in all my years in motorsport had an entry refusal. It was the Gibbs family who had decided the crowd wanted to see a Jet car this time and not our dragster. Now I knew what to expect from them when the Shell team raced both cars. Their dislike of me was to raise its ugly head in 2001 and cause the team much heartache.

At the Super Series 3 meeting, Brenda and I went through the motions and put on a brave face. So many people were asking why we hadn't brought the dragster. One young man said, 'I came today to see you race the red dragster. I have wasted my money. It isn't fair.' He wasn't the only one. There were others who have followed the team's fortunes over the years who felt cheated.

Why are the promoters at the Pod and Shakespeare County Raceway so anti-Annable. When my wife suffered her stroke, they thought that was the end of us! In some ways, when we bought Barry Sheavills' dragster it must have been a slap in the face for them. Plus the age factor comes into it, 'You're too old, Derek, why don't you retire from motorsport? We can't afford an accident on our track, it will cause problems with our insurance company. They don't mind racers being killed, but oh how terrible if a seventy-year-old man had an accident.'

No wonder the gate receipts are falling and the sponsors are pulling out – Fuel and Methanol cars bring the paying crowds in.

The Honda Integra was ready for me to collect from the showrooms and Conwy Honda had pulled many strings so we could have a year 2000 model.

Having replied, as per the following letter, to a BRDC letter I had received, I was awaiting a response.

24 July 2000

The British Racing Drivers Club
West Midlands

Dear Sir Malcolm Guthrie BT

Thank you for the BRDC letter of the 19 July 2000.

Children! The time has come to stop preaching and take some positive action and help them and their parents enjoy motor racing at Silverstone. Millions of pounds have been spent by our club on self and some top people are still on the gravy train.

The Top Methanol dragster I drive on the UK drag racing strips produced 2500+HP (enclosed spec). All children under the age of 14 years have free entry to the meeting and are provided with ear plugs. Great attention is given to babies under three years old and the noise factor is explained to their parents if so required. Our motorsport/clubs are also proud of the way disabled groups are taken care of at all meetings, my wife falls into this category.

Because of the way certain top officials (one male, one female) of the club treated her in the clubhouse and farm, she now refuses to have anything to do with events where the BRDC are involved. If this can happen to an older member (1951), I wonder what sort of treatment the younger driver receives at Silverstone.

Yours respectfully

Derek F. Annable

Sir Malcolm Guthrie came back to me by telephone, Brenda taking the call. This gave her the chance to air her views on the issue of children visiting the BRDC suite on Grand Prix days at Silverstone.

I was so impressed with the Honda Integra that I wrote to the President of Honda UK:

4 August 2000

The President
Honda UK

Dear Hisae Suzuki, Sir

I am the proud owner of a Honda Integra Type R which we purchased from Conwy Honda, North Wales, UK.

I must applaud you and your team who have brought about the outstanding car of our generation (your words). No! The century (my words). The car's development could be unlimited.

The Integra Type R is both our 200hp BMW 635 and 450hp Chevrolet Camaro wrapped in one. The best of German and American cars. Sir, who is the man (woman) who persuaded Honda worldwide to develop the Integra Type R? With respect, that person should be given another challenge. Produce from your factory an engine which will take on and beat the best American engines in Top Alcohol dragsters (enclosed specification sheet and photo of our dragster).

Please for a few weeks forget FI engines and touring cars in which your company reigns supreme and focus the unbeatable Japanese will to win onto the drag racing stage, for which your fellow countrymen are working hard to get worldwide recognition.

The plea comes from a humble racer who is growing old.

Yours sincerely

Derek Annable

Not much joy there. I didn't even receive a reply!

Mileage was needed on the clock if I was going to race the Honda at the Euro Finals at the Pod in September. So off I went to the Ultimate Street Car meeting, which meant driving down early in the morning and returning late that night.

When I arrived at the Pod, the place was teeming with cars, caravans and sideshows. I had never seen it so busy. It took me an hour to find somewhere to park. I then signed on and paid the fee to the club. I managed four timed runs and phoned Brenda with the news that the car was running low 16s and one stripped down Integra was running low 14s. We had made a good choice of car – yes, it was front-wheel drive and I would get a lot of stick from other racers, but it handled well on the road and it was quick. The 500-mile round journey was worth it.

Back in July I had sent Jeremy Clarkson a letter:

Jeremy Clarkson
c/o The *Sun* Newspaper
London

Dear Jeremy

Re: The Dreamer, The *Sun*, Friday July 21 2000

What I am going to say now is no dream, it is for real.

Jeremy Clarkson is going to drive in competition a Top Methanol dragster at Shakespeare County Raceway and race a Honda Integra Type R over 10 laps at Silverstone racetrack against the oldest hooligan in the UK (you have the edge against em at Silverstone, I may have the edge against you at SC Raceway).

We have the Top Methanol dragster and Shakespeare County Raceway is available. Honda UK delivered the Integra Type R to us last week. The BRDC of whom I am a full member would OK Silverstone for the day.

Well Jeremy?

Derek

ps Enclosed photo TM dragster

Now I had his reply:

Mr Derek Annable
Anglesey

23 August 2000

Dear Mr Annable

Jeremy Clarkson has asked me to write and thank you for your kind letter of 24 July 2000, and invitation to blast his cotton socks off at the Shakespeare County Raceway.

Our sincere apologies for not replying to you earlier, but Jeremy has had a hectic summer (he is currently overseas filming a new BBC1 series on speed due to blast its way onto a small screen near you in April 2001) and I'm afraid that time does not permit him to take up your generous offer. However, he has asked me to send you his very best and to wish you and the Thunder and Lightning drag racing team every success in the future.

Yours sincerely

Emma Stanford

(for Jeremy Clarkson)

One day, Jeremy, we shall race against each other, even if I am 80 years old.

Now we had a busy week in front of us. I would be racing Top Methanol against the Turners, Dave Wilson and others. OK, it was a licensing run but with luck and track time, I may be allowed to race at least one round of eliminations. Smax Smith had lent me his FIA overalls, both cars were entered in the final round of the MSA Championship and we couldn't afford any setbacks.

The clerk of the course was G. Greatholder and Tina Gibbs his assistant. Tension was mounting for the Shell team and the crew were put under extreme pressure. It's not easy to bring two cars to the start line in a major meeting. They responded 100% for the results. Now I pass you over to Mark Gredzinski of *Custom Car:*

Top Methanol

Plenty of drama unfolded here as Dave Wilson in the Lucas Oils entry and Rob Turner in the Netcall dragster slugged it out to decide the outcome of the British Championship. In qualifying, Dave Wilson drove through tyre shake to intimidate the opposition with a strong 5.83/236. Doug Bond had the chute out early with a 6.33/136 in the Shell Oils rail while Rob Turner tried to combat the shakes on a 6.71/165 try. Andy Frost in the Canto Racing/Exude Maxima Batteries dragster continued to improve by setting top times on the Saturday and securing the field with a 6.86/198. Derek Annable was on hand to record a ten-second run in the other Shell rail on an observed run.

For the actual race, the scenario was simple. If Dave Wilson took the first round, then the MSA Top Methanol Championship was his. Dave's task was relatively easy, as he had only to overcome class rookie Andy Frost. Dave rose to the task with aplomb but barely a second into the run, his drivetrain self-destructed as the clutch let go, shedding the blower belt, the parachute from its pack and blowing the oil filter and slippery contents across the track. Meanwhile, Andy Frost, having changed the clutch pack in the Lenco, had the slicks literally flapping off the line. Andy shut off then pedalled it again when he saw Dave's plight, taking an ugly but significant race with a 10.08/110. Yes, welcome to the Oildown Nationals! After the clean-up, Rob Turner needed every bit of his holeshot to beat a fast closing Doug Bond, Rob taking the win, 6.52/186 to a 6.58/211. Andy Frost rose to the occasion for the final, using one of his trademark holeshots to record a best yet 6.44/210 but Rob Turner reeled him in to take the race and the Championship with a fine 5.92/239.

Quick Times News paid me a further compliment: 'Derek Annable running a respectable observed run of 10 seconds in the other Shell rail.'

That wasn't the whole story. After the burnout in my second run, Doug was bringing me back to the start line, when I misread a signal he gave to me and touched the throttle, the revs came up and the car did a backward wheelie, scattering the start line marshals. I managed to bring the car under control before it reached the start line. This didn't stop Greatholder coming to the pits to give me a warning. His attitude was so anti-me I knew there was no future in Top Methanol for me while he, assisted by Tina Gibbs, was clerk of the course in the UK. His attitude prompted my wife to say to him, 'My husband will run with Wild Bunch next year, then we shall see whether you are right to condemn him.'

After a long talk with Roy Wilding and Chris Hartnell, it was agreed I could race the Top Methanol dragster with Wild Bunch in the 2001 season. There was a category for rear-engined dragsters, which suited us. I would get some track time with the car. Brenda and I were glad to be back home. It had been an up and down weekend for us and the team.

It would be two weeks before our next race meeting, which gave us a chance to consider the future of the shop and garage. Firstly both would be closed at the end of November for the winter months. Stock had to run down, in the case of the shop to nil. The garage required less planning, any petrol in our underground tanks would be there when we reopened for Easter. Brenda looked tired and needed a complete rest from her shop. The Euro Finals would be the last drag meeting for her, so I must get a good result.

Yes, the Euro Finals. The Honda required many more miles on the road before I used the full rev range, therefore it would be a low-key meeting for us. Doug would be racing the dragster in a 10-car field and the press were on to him:

Doug Bond (UK), any team that can take over half a second off their personal best in one year have got to be given the respect they have so richly earned. No one would deny that they have had their share of troubles in the past, but they have stuck with it and now they are beginning to reap the rewards. The Shell sponsorship is working well for the boys from Cheltenham. Personal best 6.11 at 215mph.

Now the report of the race in *Custom Car:*

Top Methanol
Jarmo Roivas stunned the opposition with a 5.68/247 top qualifying blast, followed by a superb 5.72/242 from Dave Wilson who, like funny car pilot

Gordon Smith, bounced back from terminal damage just two weeks earlier. The Maltese pair John Ellul and Manty Bugeja were next on 5.85/230 and 2.87/234 respectively. Rob Turner was 5th on 5.96/231, Dane Kim Raymond 6th on 6.09/206 followed by Fin, Eero Kilpelainen, 6.09/215, Doug Bond on 6.42/199 and Peter Schoefer with 6.68/211.

In round one, Schoefer shook while Jarmo Roivas fled to a 5.77/243, Andy Frost used 0.436 reaction but rattled to a 14.52 against John Ellul's 5.82/238, Manty Bugeja drilled Kilpelainen 5.98/229 to 19.17, Dave Wilson over Doug Bond's blown burst plate and Kim Raymond covered a shaking Rob Turner 6.42 to 6.64. While Roivas had a 12-second bye, a thin but extensive oil leak put paid to Manty Bugeja while John Ellul soloed to a 5.80/240 and Kim Raymond had an 8.38 single when Dave Wilson couldn't fire. Raymond then ran a 12.30 bye as John Ellul beat Jarmo Roivas 5.76/243 to 6.08/238. Manty Bugeja was unstoppable in the final, a 5.81/241 outpacing a 6.09/228 from Kim Raymond.

It was a disappointment for Doug and Martyn. What to do next year? Everybody agreed any decisions should be left until after Christmas. Four weeks to the next race meeting for Thunder and Lightning. This time Brenda would stay at home as the weather in October could go any way, an Indian summer or rain and more rain. Even I was feeling the strain and looking forward to a Christmas break.

The October meet at the Pod would again decide the winners of both championships. I wasn't in contention but it would be nice to come home with a trophy for Brenda. Knowing the weather, could I get to the finals or would it be rained off? Over to Mark Gredzinski:

Sportsman ET

Simon Chalkly was dominant in his green Corvette, qualifying first and using the quickest reaction times of the eliminator. He beat Ian Turnbull's Camaro 13.69/102 to 12.10/111, had a bye and then left on Chris Hodgkins' Audi, 13.99/100 over a 16.64/75. Facing Simon in the final would be Derek Annable, forsaking his Camaro for a white Honda coupe, Derek beating his opponents off the line in most cases. He got by Martin Lewis' Nova, Jeff Rainbird's Skoda, 17.02/75 to 17.33/80 and lastly, Chris Kirkby's Capri 15.95/87 beating 16.04/81 to reach the final.

Yes, it did rain so no finals and trophy for me and all the other classes. The winner of the SPRC Sportsman Drag Racing Championship 2000 was

Ian Turnbull. He had waited a long time to win the championship (six or more years). I was seventh, more than 1000 points adrift. My position in the National Drag Racing Championship was a respectable fifth place behind Robert Main and Alan Platt.

Now racing was over for the year, it was time to catch up with some letter writing and issues which required resolving. Having been denied results at so many race meetings because of rain and curfews, I sent this letter to *Custom Car:*

---

4 November 2000

Custom Car
Kent

Dear Sirs

Track Curfews/Rain-Offs – Final Rounds

Every race meeting which has progressed to the final round should have a conclusion, one race the winner, the other is runner-up. There is no excuse for the race director to come up with the old clichés – 'The rules this, the weather that, MSA permit doesn't allow.' We racers have given our all, try sitting on the start line in the final round and be told, 'it's raining at the top end, the meeting's cancelled.'

Everybody in the management of drag racing should make one final effort to overcome the problem track curfews and rain-offs have in the final round of championship meetings.

Why not adjudge the winner on the closest total aggregate time nearest to his/her dial-in from all prior eliminations rounds? Reaction times could also enter into the equation. This would also give racers a further target to aim for if they were to go through to the finals.

One further message, I thank *Custom Car* for giving me space in their monthly Mail and Tech section. Over the years they have received many letters from this drag racing nut, some rubbish, others they have published.

Derek (Grandad) Annable

This was followed by my response to Robin Moores' letter in *Custom Car:*

Custom Car
Kent

17 November 2000

Dear Sirs

The letter of Robin Moore, Bad Attitude Racing, Oldbrook in the December 2000 issue has put the relationship of drag racing and *Custom Car* back to the days when I wrote 'The little old lady with a stick' which was some four years ago.

Custom Car were pulling out of their relationships with Avon Park Raceways/APIRA/drag racing and anything not related to hot rods. All those years ago I set out to bridge problems and upsets that had happened and hoped *Custom Car* would again become involved with all drag racing clubs through my letter to the Mail and Tech section of their magazine. Bit by bit Mark Gredzinski began to report drag racing at all venues. Then *Custom Car* said, 'Yes' and Street Eliminator was reborn on the Avon Park Raceway and became the focal point of Street Car racing at both Santa Pod and Avon Park Raceways. Look at the bottom of pages 54 and 55, the names, the firms. Drag news has taken over a big section of the magazine. I say, 'thank you' to the people on page 4.

I have been but a short time in the motorsport of drag racing, my whole energy has been channelled into this sport which brought my wife back from death over four years ago when she nearly died from a stroke (ask any member of the Wild Bunch).

Enough said.

Derek (Grandad) Annable

Then I received a flyer announcing my favourite chuck wagon was being sold:

A FINAL FAREWELL FROM GRAHAM & MARGARET OF BOATERS EVENT CATERING

As many of you already know, Margaret and I have sold our catering business. It was not an easy decision to make but we both felt that as the years increased, we should be taking life a little easier. It was almost ten years ago that we started Boaters with the express intention of providing a healthy and different style of catering. Our success has only been possible because of the support of you the

Santa Pod racers, marshals and spectators. To you all we would like to send our sincere thanks for your business over the years. We will take many happy memories into our retirement and a few that we would rather forget. Who will ever forget the Easter meeting it snowed, with drifts of snow on the cars in the pits or the more recent Easter flooding of a couple of years ago. We have seen the track so cold it was frozen across the full width and sweltered in the sort of temperatures you only get at Santa Pod in (some) summers. Meetings rained off, and events which went on well into the night, this was the special thing about Santa Pod. Catering at Santa Pod was never hard work for us. It was always, or nearly always, a case of meeting friends and acquaintances for a chat while we made a sandwich or roll and provided a drink. It was you, the customers, who made the difference for us. Although we may not be at the track every week next year, we still hope to attend the larger meetings and see old friends. We hope you were pleased with the food, drinks and service we gave and wish you all good luck and fortune in the future, we will miss you!!

We send our best wishes for Christmas and a Happy New Year to you all.

Graham & Margaret Barbutt

I was losing friends of many years and a good eaterie. Time marches on – very sad. The downside about growing old is that you lose family and friends through death and the march of time.

I can't make any predictions for 2001 and beyond, except that we will be back racing at any track where we are welcome, that is York Dragway for one. The size of my bank balance will decide the future of our TA dragster. I am determined to bring Doug Bond into the five-second bracket.

OK, the press and others think the Shell car is Martyn Hannis and Doug Bond's car but this isn't the case. They are having the use of it with Brenda's permission. I pay for all the inspections and chassis tags and any updates. OK, Martyn arranges this and I send him a cheque. If Doug Bond ever runs a five-second pass in our car, it will be made possible with our money and Brenda's authority about where and on what it is to be spent. We still have the MSA logbook dated 24 April 1997 which Barry Sheavills passed onto us when we bought the dragster from him after paying £25,000 in 1997 and had it stamped with change of ownership on 13 October 1997 by the RACMSA.

The engine is the only thing that moves about, one race it is theirs, the next race maybe ours. It is a good working relationship and will benefit both parties.

On the 16 December 2000 I am 70 years old. In 2003 I shall have been sixty years behind the wheel and married fifty years to the same lady. What a landmark.

A thought. Derek, you must write an epilogue for the book now. Others can't finish the book for you, they can't write the epilogue, you are the only person who can do that.

Yes, I did write the epilogue and my head was filled with thoughts going back to my youth, painful thoughts that one can never run away from. Close your eyes and visions of yesteryear come flooding back. The human brain is a wonderful thing. It can store up events that happen over fifty, sixty, even a hundred years. How else could this book have been written?

CHAPTER 10

2001

How time flies. As a friend of mine said, 'The wheels keep turning faster and faster!' What to do with the Top Methanol dragster? Dave Wilson was short of sponsorship money, or so my wife was told, and Doug and Martyn were undecided about their future in drag racing. The team Thunder and Lightning were going to race this year, but with whom? Dave Wilson was eager for Annable money, and Brenda listened to all sorts of proposals, little knowing Wilson was trying to bring Wendy Baker on board. Thank goodness we didn't choose to go in that direction.

TWO-CAR ASSAULT FROM TEAM NEMESIS

After much speculation within the sport, British Top Methanol drag racers, Team Nemesis, confirmed today that they will be expanding to two cars and two crews for the 2001 season. The Krypton name will be back on the scene when Wendy Baker gets behind the wheel of the legendary dragster to compete in the MSA British Championship. The car will be run under the Team Nemesis banner.

The Krypton crew, led by Paul Stubbins, will supply power to Wendy in her rookie season using a motor built for them in the Nemesis workshops. They will campaign with the chassis that was first made famous by Nemesis driver Dave Wilson when he won two NDRC British titles in it in the 1980s. He also ran a best of 6.00 seconds at 229 mph in the car in 1993.

Wendy Baker has been involved in drag racing for many years, most recently competing in the SuperPro category with her police themed Funny Car 'Hot Pursuit' and the retro-styled 'Stars and Stripes' slingshot dragster. These cars were both campaigned with assistance from Dave Wilson and the two teams already work together very effectively.

New Sponsor

Leading specialist vehicle suppliers, American Car Imports, will be joining Team Nemesis for their assault on the British and European Championships during the coming year. The London based company will be supporting the new two-car team with a significant associate sponsorship package for the 2001 season.

American Car Imports are the European market leaders in the sourcing, importation and supply of American vehicles to order. They also specialise in the homologation of American vehicles and as trade experts, even HM Customs and Excise call upon their services in valuing American vehicles entering the UK. With a physical presence in Europe, North America and Canada, plus an unsurpassed reputation for quality service and aftercare, American Car Imports will make the ideal partners for the UK's fastest race team.

Let's wait to see what happens. In drag racing people don't like to be rushed. They run five-second passes at over 200mph, but making financial decisions isn't their strong point. Something would develop.

The APIRA had accepted my registration of both cars which was confirmed by the following letter:

Club & Race Secretary
Mrs Wendy Talbot
Norfolk

Mr D Annable
Anglesey

13 February 02

Dear Derek

Thank you for returning your registration document, your race number will be as you have advised me on your form.

Please find enclosed 1 entry form for Super Series 1 4/6 May 2002.

I hope you're both keeping fairly well, it seems a long winter with all this wet weather around.

Yours sincerely

Wendy Talbot

Also the team had renewed its Wild Bunch membership so now we had some dates to consider. The Top Methanol car could be run in the rear-engined dragster series at Shakespeare County Raceway. The Honda Integra would be entered at the Thunderball at Santa Pod and four rounds of the PDRC championship and at York Dragway.

An agreement had been reached with Doug and Martyn. One car was to be used this season – ours. They would have the use of it for the rounds of the MSA Methanol Championship and two European rounds. In return, they would again crew for me at five Wild Bunch meetings. Each party would use their own engine and be responsible for any breakages on the dragster.

This deal was of benefit to both parties. If the Turners went Top Fuel, Doug was in with a chance to win the MSA Championship. That's if he kept his foot down!

We had six months of the lease on the shop in Benllech to run, but now came the tricky period with our landlord – the dilapidations inspection was looming. Pochin's surveyor would be trying to update the landlord's fixtures and other items at our expense. There are many clauses in the lease which have more than one interpretation but we couldn't afford an army of experts to fight our case through the courts.

The country was now in the grip of the foot and mouth epidemic, many forms of motorsport were having to be cancelled, but luckily Santa Pod Raceways was given the green light by the Ministry of Farming and Fisheries. Then came the good news that York Dragway was to reopen:

York Reopens

York Dragway has reopened after the foot and mouth scare, following guidelines issued by the Ministry of Farming and Fisheries, the Department of Tourism and the National Farmers Union. York Dragway reopened on Easter Monday for a full season of events. Even though only 12 days of notice could be given, a record entry was received and around 3,000 spectators attended the 'Super Street Car Shoot-out' event.

The next event at the venue is on Sunday 20 May *(which if you're quick you'll be able to catch as it's only two days after this issue goes on sale – Ed)*. This will feature round one of the Northern Drag Racing Championship and round two of the Northern Street Car Challenge. Roger Goring will also be providing his famous Flame and Fireball Shows with the Firestorm Jet Funny Car.

The Shell team and the Thunder and Lightning team were racing at the Easter Thunderball, so off Brenda and I went down the M6 motorway in the direction of Rushden and our eaterie. After a good night's sleep, what did Gredzo say about the weather?

It has been said that Santa Pod has its own weather system and this year's Easter Thunderball certainly seemed to bear that out. After some heavy rain showers during Sunday's qualifying, the sky cleared leaving a bright horizon for many miles, which should have left a clear afternoon in which to race. Within two hours however, just as the track was dry, an ominous cloud seemed to appear from nowhere over the tower, and bought with it rain that killed further proceedings. It seems that the wind had changed direction completely and I'd rather not talk about the hailstorms! Despite this, Monday was dry throughout so all eliminators were completed in good time and hats off to the marshals who worked tirelessly throughout, but wouldn't you just know it, when the racing finished, the sun came out! Two new positive things about the Pod this year. One is Halfords is on board as a sponsor and secondly, the road from the main gate has been fully asphalted. Hurrah! No more broken teeth on the way up to the track.

Sportsman ET were lucky on Saturday and we all managed two qualifying runs. Mine were against Simon Chalkly and O'Darren Hulkes. Simon Chalkly is a great racer. His whole family are into drag racing and are so friendly. My wife misses the company of Phil and Tracy Walker, who have put their racing on hold since the birth of their first child.

The Honda Integra, being a front-wheel drive car, was causing me problems, as I am an auto-rear-wheel drive man. My ETs were all over the place, with a 16.51 against Chalkly, followed by a 16.807. Then on Sunday in the only qualifying run we were allowed because of the weather, it was a 15.936 against Alan Platt. Front-wheel drive and a clutch would be a challenge to me, could I succeed?

It was nice to see our Altered, the Ex-Fay Fischer car which we had sold to David Ward, performing well. He had changed the engine over to a big block and was very competitive and he won his class on Monday.

Sunday was a washout, so it would be straight into eliminations on Monday. My first opponent was Rick Denny in his Pontiac 'Firebird'. Why do I always get this man? Can't he find somebody else to race? It was the old story; Rick won, I was $^2/_{10}$ of a second off my dial-in, but Rick was only $^1/_{10}$ of a second – end of my racing.

The Top Methanol class as reported by Gredzo went as follows:

Top Methanol

David Wilson was impressive, qualifying his American Car Imports back Nemesis dragster with a fine 6.01/228. Rob Turner was next with a 6.87/167 in the Net Call rail with Doug Bond only having one chance to shake the cobwebs out on a 7.37/141 in the Shell Oils car. Of the other runners, the Canto Racing dragster didn't make it out of the pits having discovered a cracked chassis. Wendy Baker only had a short try in the Krypton device and Stephanie Milam ran a pair of nines and a good eight second pass in the She Devil Daytona Funny Car. Maybe not impressive on paper, but new clutch and engine parts meant the car was arrow straight and will be now on the right track for some seven and six second passes. In the race, Dave Wilson had a 20 second bye run, while Rob Turner poured on the power to take out Doug Bond's decent 6.48/197 with a 5.93/216 for low ET of the meet. The final was excellent, with Dave Wilson setting top speed with a 6.01/235. He left the line with a 0.501 reaction time but Rob Turner had a 0.500 reaction and coupled with his 5.99/227, Rob took the win. But boy was it close at the top end!

Things could only get better for both teams. I would be racing at Shakespeare County Raceway in five days' time.

Back home, my wife had turned the shop over to sportswear and wet suits which would take up the last six months of our lease. We had chosen JAG International as our suppliers. They had a colourful range which we could retail at a price below the opposition, ruffling some feathers.

We didn't unpack our suitcase, just filled the petrol tank on the Honda and headed south to the reunion with our dragster. When we arrived at the track, most of the Wild Bunch had already pitted and we were greeted by Claire Meaddows. Roy Wilding had his new car down for some engine testing. It looked a mean machine.

Right on time, the blue-coloured rig came through the main gate. Doug was behind the wheel with Martyn following in the crew car. Within an hour the dragster was ready for me to get in the cockpit and go through the pre-race procedure. When Martyn blipped the throttle, the clutch pedal kicked hard on my left foot. This was like old times and I was filled with excitement.

Brenda didn't like watching me race the dragster, considering it too powerful, so off to Heidi's camper she went leaving the boy racer enjoying himself. The pit marshall called us out and within minutes I was under the concrete sound wall and looking down the track. In the distance, a good mile away, is a tree which I always aim for. Martyn fired up the engine, I released the clutch and moved ever so slowly forward, as the front wheels went through the water I pressed the second and top gear buttons, brought up the revs to 5,000 and did a long smokey burnout to the applause of the crowd. I was halfway back down the track before Doug caught up with me and brought me back over the rubber I had laid down – boy, was he out of breath and red-faced – sorry Doug!

Easy does it, forward I went, bringing the car into pre-stage, a quick blip on the throttle to loosen the butterflies on the air intake, hold the revs at 3,500, lift the clutch and move into stage, mash the throttle and it was go, man, go – ET 10.592/140mph. My next run in late afternoon was a 9.492 and everybody in the team was pleased with that run. Martyn made a slight adjustment to the throttle for my next run. Brenda wanted me to have a quick eighth mile; this time she was going to watch her car run. The track curfew was now on. Doug and Martyn went home and Brenda and I to the Travelodge, Alcester.

The team managed one run on Sunday and it was quick. The ET at the eighth mile was 5.864, speed 134.73mph. That was the end of the weekend's racing. Next time the car came to Shakespeare County Raceway, Doug would be the pilot in the Super Series I on 5–7 May.

Yes, Doug did well in the Super Series I, as was reported by Gredzo:

Top Methanol

Some good runs by the blown alky burners started with Dave Wilson who headed the field with an unchallenged and very strong 5.89/235 in the 463ci Nemesis dragster. Rob Turner was suffering from tyre shake all weekend in the Net Call rail, mustering a 6.11/201 for second place. Doug Bond was on form with a 6.34/210 in the Shell Oils car while in fourth spot came Darryl Bradford completing his observed runs with aplomb on a 7.57/137 in the Canto Consultancy machine. Finally, also in observed mode was Wendy Baker who handled the Krypton dragster well on a 8.52/104, while Lindsay Deuchar retired with a torched block. In the race, Dave Wilson had a 7.88/120 bye and Doug Bond beat Darryl Bradford 6.45/211 over a 6.72/185. Darryl did well with a good holeshot but lost the motor in the traps with resultant oilspill. Then Rob Turner made short work of Wendy Baker's 14.25/48 with a 6.04/233 blast. In round two, Dave Wilson had the pace despite not burning out due to a broken reverser, but his 6.01/225 was burdened with a red-light as Doug Bond took the win on a 6.93/142.

The Shell team were starting to come good and stamping their authority in the Methanol class.

Monday 21 May was the grand opening of our shop with its new range of sportswear, but before that we had a journey to York Dragway to support the club's first meeting since the foot and mouth close-down.

The Honda engine was near its peak, with 10,000 miles on the clock, and this showed in qualifying – 14.952/95mph on the first run, followed by a string of mid-15s. Graham Beckwith was giving me some stick over the public address. He doesn't like front-wheel drive drag cars, maybe German, but Japanese – no!

I went through to the semi-finals. A good day's racing – everybody was glad to see Brenda back at York Dragway – and then racing was over for the weekend.

Monday morning was the big day, so we arrived early at the shop to set up the display of wet suits and accessories. Even before we opened there was a lot of interest in the children's wet suits as many on their way to school had stopped and pointed at them. In the afternoon the shop was full of school children and their mothers, asking about prices and when could they come back and try the suits on.

The interest was there all week and the sales on Saturday were beyond our dreams – six children's wet suits were sold, plus many pairs of slip ons. Even JAG were surprised at the response when we phoned through our re-order on the Monday morning.

The wet suits and accessories sales gave us a steady income all through the summer, thanks to the people on holiday who had motorboats and jet skis. Yes, we would transfer the business to our garage next year.

While we were busy selling wet suits, Doug was racing Annable/Bond rail in the Main Event at Santa Pod; I'll hand you over to Gredzo:

Top Methanol Dragster

Rob Turner stamped his authority with a top qualifying 5.90/239, followed by 2000 winner Manty Bugeja in the Mr Whippy car from Malta, tuned by England's Charlie Draper, on 5.90/233. Dave Wilson was next with 6.01/235 followed by Doug bond, 6.45/206 and newcomers to the class, Wendy Baker in the other team Nemesis car, 7.10/191 and Darryl Bradford in the Canto dragster on 7.19/129.

In eliminations, crew chief John Wright turned up the wick and driver Darryl Bradford surprised everyone by leaving on Rob Turner and recording an excellent 6.29/210 but Rob powered ahead for the win with a 5.87/232. Doug Bond was down on power as Dave Wilson beat him, 5.93/231 to 6.79/181.

In the next round Rob Turner had a 5.86/239 bye while Manty Bugeja left on Dave Wilson – 5.84/235 beating 5.86/234. In the final Rob Turner had the power with a 5.88/235 but it was ice creams all round as Manty Bugeja cut a demon 0.430 reaction, taking the trophy home to Malta with a 5.90/211 winner.

There would be a quick change of engines. I needed the dragster to race with the Wild Bunch in their rear-engined dragster championship on

Saturday. This rapid engine changeover was putting pressure on the crew; if the partnership went into next year, there would have to be a rethink on who were to crew.

When Brenda and I arrived at Shakespeare County Raceway, the dragster hadn't arrived in the pits. Martyn had a full-time job and worked nights. This meant Doug had to load up the rig on his own, leaving Martyn to follow on in the crew car. Let's find Claire and pay my £5 registration fee for the day. Fee paid, she went on to explain that as it was a public test day, the Wild Bunch were allowed three slots. If the car wasn't ready I would miss the first one, but please let her know if there were any problems.

Our dragster arrived in the pits at lunchtime but because of problems with the compatibility with the engines and modification that had been made, the car wouldn't be ready for me until mid-afternoon. Never mind, I was to have one run today and, with luck, two tomorrow.

Because the car is a methanol burner, the fire crew had to be notified well in advance of the time we would be racing because special equipment is needed to put out a methanol fire which you can't see. Bruno is the only man qualified to fight these fires and he is respected in the UK and Europe as one of the best firefighters.

It was time to get kitted up and take the car down the fire-up road. My first run was a simple launch and shut off just past the eighth mile, then a tow back to the pits for Doug and Martyn to check over the car and set up the engine for racing tomorrow. I needed two runs to keep up with Harvey who was after the championship.

It was important that I didn't damage the chassis – Doug was up with the front runners in the MSA Championship and we didn't have a second car – so no clever stuff from me in tomorrow's racing.

Sunday morning was a perfect day for racing, with good air and the track warm and sticky. The Wild Bunch were the first out. I was to be the last car down the track, then the public test and tune would start again. The big cars attracted attention, and the drivers have to get used to the flashbulbs going off, because if the camera is forward of you, you can get blinded and not see the start light coming down.

My instructions were a full pass this time. After a short burnout, Doug brought me back to the start line. This time the front wheels lifted a 1.200 for the 60ft, 5.312 at the eighth mile and 8.422/147.06mph at the quarter mile – all very satisfactory. The clerk of the course was happy with my control of the car. That should give me some peace from Mr Greatholder and others. My wife asked him, 'Can my husband take his L plates off now?' There was no response.

Doug and his brother decided to give the engine a leak down test and check valve clearances. Our short stroke engine was producing plenty of power, maybe more than Doug's own. Here's Paul Bland for the press report on my second run:

> Derek Annable was over from sunny Anglesey in the Shell sponsored Top Alcohol car and with Doug Bond overseeing things Derek got the low ET prize with a 8.214 run, a later run looked like a seven but a red light put paid to any times, and all this from a seventy-year-old!

Yes, my eighth mile was a 5.193 at 132.74mph, the quickest any of the Wild Bunch had run.

Paul Harvey took top points in the rear-engined dragster series with myself in second place. Brenda and I thanked Doug, his brother and Martyn. It would be over a month before the dragster would be raced again here at Shakespeare County Raceway. We wished Doug luck at the Cannonball and hoped the Shell team had a win.

I had waited many years to get back in the cockpit of the ex-Barry Sheavills Top Methanol dragster and patience had paid off. Today I ran my quickest time ever, 8.214 seconds. I wasn't going to blow it and break anything. My track time in the car hinged on Doug having a ride at the MSA and European meetings. He was number one driver in the team and I was held in reserve for the future. Cost-wise, both parties weren't overstretched; the partnership could go forward and there would be silverware for both drivers.

Although the shop and garage businesses were busy, Brenda liked York Dragway. There were three meetings we could attend, one this month, followed by one in July and again in August, all on a Sunday. This meant closing the shop early on Saturday afternoon and arriving at the South Cave Travelodge by tea time for an overnight stay.

The Midsummer Nationals was the first meeting. When we arrived at the track, all the HRG boys were already there. Shaun Wilson had fallen out with Steve Munty and the PDRC but many HRG racers, being members of the club, still turned up and supported the club.

It was time to sign on and Cathy was in charge. Marjorie Lyons soon took charge of Brenda, arranging for a chair to be placed at the end of the fire-up road so she could watch the racing.

Qualifying was a bit hit and miss for me; I managed two runs and both of my passes were low 16s. Then it was straight into eliminations. I dialled in 16.10 and ran a 15.743. That's what I call breaking out big time. My opponent HRG also broke out, but by less – his win. Brenda enjoyed the day out from the shop and had seen her Honda car run on her favourite track.

The Shell team had a poor day at the Cannonball, as Gredzo said:

Top Methanol Dragster

Rob Turner in the Net Call dragster was again the class of the field in Top Methanol. He qualified first with a fine 5.87/240 and was followed by Lindsay Deuchar's decent 6.16/193, both cars with more top end in reserve. Doug Bond paced out a 6.42/208 and the field was secured by Wendy Baker and Dave Wilson with off pace runs.

Things picked up in round one, with Dave Wilson pounding out a 5.85/224 as Rob Turner left with him, running an identical 5.85 but at 241 mph for the win. Lindsay Deuchar covered an improving Wendy Baker, 6.29/176 to a 7.37/189 while Darryl Bradford's car reported broken. Rob Turner had an unassailable points lead and so took the British Championship, as well as the race with a great 5.82/241 while Lindsay Deuchar bounced his dragster through the staging beams with no times recorded.

My next outing with the Honda was a BRDC track day at Oulton Park circuit. The British Racing Drivers Club (BRDC) had been in turmoil following Brands Hatch Leisure's offer to buy the Silverstone circuit. Nicki Foulston was only trying to fulfil her late father's wish to own Silverstone and run the British Grand Prix. Some of our club members were downright hostile to her and the offer on the table and didn't mind how they showed it. Now Octagon was the major player, as their letter shows:

SECRETARY'S LETTER

With the start of a new season of motorsport almost upon us the sense of expectation is as keen as ever.

There is much to look forward to on the racing scene: Bentley back at Le Mans, David Coulthard challenging for the F1 crown (is this his year?), Jenson Button at Benetton, the British Grand Prix back in July, and a full programme of national and international races at Silverstone, including the popular night races. The Silverstone programme has just been finalised and you will find the Clubhouse Opening dates on the back cover of this Bulletin.

The new season will coincide with the start of a new era for the BRDC and Silverstone. It is now over two months since the EGM on 18 December 2000 when the Membership voted in favour of the Agreement between the BRDC and the Octagon Group of Companies. The Agreement was completed on 20 December. Since then we have been making the necessary arrangements for implementing the Agreement by the end of the Transition period on 31 March 2001.

You will appreciate that by leasing the circuit and selling the assets of SCL the BRDC now consists of a Member's Club and a Race Department, and is landlord to Octagon as well as retaining some significant areas of the property, which we will need to develop and manage.

Thus we have spent the last two months making the Club 'self-sufficient'. We have examined every aspect of how we run the Club and its businesses, particularly as we now have to undertake many of the functions and services carried out previously by Silverstone Circuits on our behalf.

You will find articles from Jackie Stewart and Martin Brundle in this Bulletin, looking at the underlying approach to future development of the Club and Silverstone. By now you will have received the President's letter (24 Jan) explaining the vision for Silverstone and an explanation of why Government funds are a necessary part of the package.

I have had many calls since December, and included in this issue is a page that addresses the most frequently asked questions with answers (page 4).

The regions are ever active (reports pages 10/11). The Regional Co-ordinators have met and we have had 3 regional dinners already this year. Peter Procter has taken over as the North East Co-ordinator, following the sad loss of Bob Staples.

We have lost some highly respected and influential Members over the winter months: Bob Staples, John Cooper, Walter Hayes, David Benson, Anthony Marsh, Sir Nicholas Williamson and John Smith (obituaries page 15). The world of racing has also sadly lost Dale Earnhardt, and was shocked at the tragedy of the helicopter crash that resulted in the death of Bertie Fisher and members of his family.

There are several inserts included with this Bulletin: an Annual Dinner Survey Form, a Members' Health Insurance offer, details on the Silverstone Bypass (work has started in earnest), an AGM supper application form (please book now as the Clubhouse maximum dining number is 120), and a list of candidates for membership.

The Bulletin heralds a busy year for the BRDC and an exciting season of racing. I look forward to seeing many of you at Silverstone during the months ahead.

Roger Lane-Nott

Then Martin Brundle's:

We have achieved much, we have much to do

The most important part of ensuring success is in preparation and planning towards very clear and focused objectives. We all know what that means. It is what makes the difference between winning and losing.

When we sat down last year in the January Forum, and then at the June EGM, it was with the intention of laying out the framework for the future of the BRDC, our priorities and our objectives. At the December EGM we went through these again. It is worth repeating what we wanted to achieve and how to judge future success in reaching our goals.

What we set out to do in 2000

We had a list of key criteria that summed up how the BRDC hoped to move forward.

- To secure a minimum risk income to enable the Club to serve its members
- To ensure that the Grand Prix is retained at Silverstone on the best available terms
- To provide increased financial security for all older members
- To provide major finance for young driver development and for the benevolent fund
- To secure the investment necessary to maintain the Circuit to FIA/FIM standards
- To keep pace with change and opportunities provided by big sport promoters
- To finalise a structure for the Club and its commercial affairs, which will safeguard the future of the Club and its assets
- Start separating Club issues from the Club's commercial affairs, while leaving the BRDC in ultimate control in accordance with the Key Criteria
- Empower the newly separated commercial company to progress talks to as wide an audience as possible to endeavour to secure the British Grand Prix at Silverstone on acceptable terms
- Progress and refine ideas for support to members in need, motorsport development pensions and/or dividends
- Reopen the Club to new members who qualify under the current criteria
- Consider amendments to the joining criteria with particular

emphasis to make it possible for younger drivers in a wider range of premier facing formulae to become eligible to join as Full Members.

What we achieved in 2000

The Agreement with Octagon has secured a stable income for the BRDC. The agreement allows us to focus on non-commercial affairs while ensuring ownership of Silverstone Circuit remains with the BRDC. We have secured the British Grand Prix at Silverstone, the home of British racing. The 2007 Concorde and 2010 European Union regulations mean that the Grand Prix is guaranteed until at least 2007, but the agreement with Octagon, with the support of FOM, is for 15 years to 2015.

Octagon is committed contractually to a full repairing lease, so there will be no deterioration of the Circuit over the 15 year lease period. We have secured considerable investment in the Circuit (£40 million over the first 5 years) and considerably reduced our commercial risk. The agreement gives Octagon use of the name Silverstone Circuit, and obliges Octagon to keep Silverstone in the name of the Circuit at all times. The agreement does not permit Octagon to use the BRDC name under any circumstances.

The BRDC remains the ultimate owner of Silverstone Circuit and, within the agreement with Octagon, retains over 100 acres outside the lease. This includes the Clubhouse, Club Grandstand, farm, farmyard, farm grandstand and campsite, and an area set aside for the Advanced Technology Park and the Business Park.

All members' benefits are protected and enhanced within the Agreement and are extended through arrangements for entry to circuit days at all BHL tracks. From the end of 2001 the Dividend paid to eligible members is expected to be higher than we had anticipated before the Octagon Agreement.

More Progress in 2000

It would be wrong to think that in reaching the agreement with Octagon nothing else was achieved in 2000. Over the past year we have ensured that the Guardians are in place, that the process is in place for the Board to be reduced in number, that arrangements for the Benevolent fund are complete, and that the Rising Stars membership category has been established. We have also started the search for a Chief Executive for the BRDC and will be seeking to strengthen the Silverstone Estates (SEL) Board once we have a CEO in place.

There is still lots to do

It would also be wrong to believe that our work is over and we can rest on our laurels. Since 18 December we have been working within what we would regard as a three-month transition plan, where the Silverstone Circuits Staff continue to support the BRDC. By the end of March we hope to have the structures in place to operate the BRDC entirely separately from the commercial business of the Circuit. This will sort out the practical day to day issues of managing our estate; Clubhouse and Farm maintenance, gardening, cleaning, and all the other contracts to keep our Club facilities in top condition.

Part of the Octagon agreement, and clearly in the interest of the BRDC, is our agreement to support the planning and development process for Silverstone over the next five years. We have a fairly tight schedule to gain the necessary planning permissions that will ensure the first phase of development is completed in time for the 2002 Grand Prix. First stage is the development of a master plan, which needs to be ready for planning application by the beginning of June 2001. We then need to work to have planning permission agreed by the end of December 2001, to allow implementation to begin in January 2002.

We have strong foundations on which to build an exciting and beneficial future

Jackie has already written to you recently, explaining the need to think beyond the immediate requirements of the Circuit as a racetrack and why Government support will be essential in making our vision a reality. I will endeavour to keep you in touch with the practical matters relating to the Club, as well as keeping you abreast of the wider site developments as we settle into partnership with Octagon.

There will be no slacking in 2001 as we build on the foundations that hard work and dedication delivered over the past year. Our Advanced Technology and Business Parks need to be developed. Our Club needs to gain from its freedom from commercial management and to further focus on developing membership benefits and services. The BRDC has an unrivalled heritage. We must ensure we make the most of the exciting prospects that the future now offers.

To complete the picture, here are the comments of Jackie Stewart:

THE BRDC IS THE CHAMPION OF BRITISH MOTORSPORT

Our Club uniquely combines the memories and heritage of a great past, but holds the promise and ambitions of future success. Members, young and old, share a desire to see the very best of British sportsmanship lead the world. The British Racing Drivers Club is not about being a collection of champions of the past. We all want to be champions for the future of the sport we all love.

From the Forum and EGMs of last year we have tried to summarise all our thoughts in a number of simple statements that best express our underlying principles. At the Annual Dinner I outlined the Mission of the BRDC, a summary four points that capture the essence of all we are setting out to achieve for our sport in particular, and for the industry in general. In a single phrase, we see the BRDC as Champion of British motorsport.

Through the Club:

- We will champion excellence, integrity and sportsmanship in British motorsport.
- We will champion the development of the highest standards of technical excellence and safety.
- We will champion and encourage young British talent up a staircase of excellence, while caring for those who have given their best to the sport.
- We will champion and invest in Silverstone to develop it to the very highest international standards, to generate income for future investment in British motorsport for the benefit of customers, spectators, drivers, teams and our members.

The future of our motorsport and the motorsport are intertwined

The passion for motorsport in Britain has generated an industry of over 5,000 companies and over 125,000 full and part-time employees. Modern motorsport runs on high-technology every bit as much as high-adrenaline. Yet it cannot be assured that the Great British success story that is British motorsport will always remain so. Our shipbuilding and motorcycle industries didn't have to compete within the global, fast-moving and mobile media world that we have today, and where are they now?

Our sport and industry has many and varied interests, and there is the ever present danger of complacency. That is why we believe that Silverstone must become a Centre of Excellence, a showcase of

British motorsport that will champion and nurture the very best of British sport and engineering, expertise and skill.

We are competing against foreign Governments taking a strategic interest in motorsport

We know why the governments of other countries have invested in Grand Prix circuits. The Malaysians, the French, Germans and Australians, the Spanish and Hungarians have all recognised the value of motorsport to the wider economy and have invested accordingly. Yet also we know from looking at the past experience of others that it is not enough to simply invest to keep pace with the rest, to be among the best. That is why the plans for Silverstone as a Centre of Excellence represent more than just the next step in the development of the Circuit. Instead we have acknowledged the need to take a great leap into the future and be second to none.

We would not be going to Government if we as a sport had not already committed ourselves to spending £40 million on improving racing facilities at Silverstone. Over the past couple of months I am pleased to report that we are not knocking at closed doors in our approaches to Government and our discussions with public officials. Kate Hoey, Minister for Sport, who attended our Annual Dinner, has been a firm believer in strategic support to sport – and we know the success of that approach from the victories of the British team at the Sydney Olympics in shooting, rowing and boxing. The additional investment we are seeking for the future of our sport pales beside what is being considered for the new Wembley Stadium.

We need a world class resource that will nurture the next generation of drivers, mechanics and technologists on which the success of our sport depends

The BRDC may be Champion of motorsport, but we are not chasing medals. The BRDC is chasing a far greater prize of more enduring benefit to our sport. Our sport generates the drive for new technology that leads the world, and nourishes the unique engineering skills that create wealth and an international pride of place for Britain.

There is a window of opportunity

The BRDC has a window of opportunity to provide motorsport with a Centre of Excellence that will keep a focus on the future and on the potential that is forever possible through imagination, ambition and drive. The personal dedication in time and resource spent by Ron Dennis, Sir Frank Williams, Denys Roham and Martin Brundle has set a tremendous example of commitment to our Club and our sport.

However, our Club is so much more than individuals. Our Club is a meeting place for all those who share the thrill and passion of racing, and who want to see Silverstone as a showcase for our sport and industry, open and accessible to everyone who shares our love of motorsport.

Our mission is clearly defined and simply stated

To achieve our objectives we will always be willing to work with others who share our vision of Silverstone as a Centre of Excellence. As Champion of British motorsport the BRDC will work in partnership with Octagon and with Government, and with all others in industry who also wish to secure a great British future for a great British sport.

The winter of 2000/2001 saw many members pass away. One, John Cooper, built my first pure race car in 1950. He and his father produced an affordable circuit race car for young drivers like me. Some achievement, as World War Two had only finished five years earlier. In the obituaries, one man stood out above others, Bob 'Sideways' Staples. In his lifetime, he projected what the BRDC stands for, as James Beckett wrote:

On our first meeting Bob Staples told me, 'Life is about having a laugh and a giggle.'

During many happy meetings, Bob often relived his racing days to me on days at Silverstone, and with a boyish twinkle in his eye once told me how he became known as 'Sideways'.

Always one to stand out in a crowd, Bob had wished for a racing nick-name. During the late fifties, 'Fireball Roberts' was a successful Stockcar driver in the United States, and Bob thought that to have a name like 'Fire-ball' was rather 'fun'.

On returning to the factory with his car one evening, after a frantic weekend of racing, he found a signwriter present, packing up his brushes and about to leave. Bob encouraged him to stay, and after a few minutes work, and a series of swift brush strokes, 'Sideways Staples' was born.

Having started Club Rallying in 1956, Bob found that 'The trees always seemed to be running out into the middle of the lanes,' – and decided that circuit racing may be a better bet.

Purchasing a Triumph TR2, Bob was sixth on his debut at Mallory Park, but he didn't care for the TR2 and quickly switched to a Lotus 11 – although the 1172cc engined didn't allow him to drift the car in the style that he liked.

Money was tight, and Bob had to miss the last two rounds of the 1957 Ford 1172 series after cash ran out while leading, but by 1958 Bob was back and running in BARC Marque races for road going production cars. Great racing at circuits such as Aintree, Goodwood and Mallory followed, and Bob purchased an AC-powered Ace that he drove for the first time in the Grand Touring and Production Sports Car race at Brands Hatch on Boxing Day – qualifying fourth behind Colin Chapman, Mike Costin and Jim Clark.

Bob purchased the famous VPL 442 AC car in February 1960, and an early drama with the car saw him practically drive into the lake at Oulton Park to avoid the upturned Ace-Bristol of Paul Fletcher.

Richard Shepherd-Barron recalls, 'All those who were involved with his entry of the AC Bristol VPL 442 at the Nurburgring 1000kms in 1960 will, I am certain, never forget the hilarious week. How he and I finished that race after practice problems that included a broken half-shaft, a leaking fuel tank, a cracked chassis and during the race, a disappearing hard-top, I will never know.'

Continuing, 'The next week saw continuing hilarity in the Grand Prix de Spa Sports and Touring Car race. Bob's AC Ace broke a piston in practice and my mechanic, Tom Southon, managed to effect a temporary welded repair to the top of it (technically impossible!), thus enabling Bob to struggle round for two more laps and collect his starting money!'

Bob's motor racing dream was to race at Le Mans. He hoped for a 'works' AC drive in 1959, but was listed as reserve, and he was again on the reserve list in 1960 for Mike Salmon's Aston Martin Zagato entry.

During 1961 Bob was again a major force in Marque racing, winning the Freddie Dixon Trophy for the Marque sports Championship – scoring victory in each of the eight series rounds. During twenty five races that season, Bob totalled fourteen wins, five seconds and two thirds – all this after missing two months of the campaign due to an accident while acting as a passenger to brother, Barry, in the Ace at Brands Hatch.

Before hanging up his helmet and goggles, Bob moved on to race in Formula Junior single-seater events, and then spent a while enjoying hill-climbing and sprinting with a Jaguar E-type.

Richard Shepherd-Barron recalls, 'He never gave up trying – that was Bob Staples. He never gave up laughing either.'

The last time I had the pleasure of Bob's company was at the BRDC Annual Dinner and Dance at the Grosvenor House last November – an event at which Bob was in his element – supping 'ribena' and generally having a 'fablington' time.

To his wife, Sue, all at the BRDC send their deepest sympathies.

I had to report to Oulton Park by 9am Monday morning on 2 July. The track was open for BRDC members to use from 11am to 4pm, the clubhouse was open for refreshments and a meal was laid on for free. There are many perks members of our club receive during any one year, the most valuable being the Grand Prix pass for each member and three of their guests. This pass covers the four days and is worth £600 plus. Then there is free entry to every race held at Silverstone, plus other circuits. I couldn't put a value on that.

At Oulton Park, first our cars were checked for exhaust noise then we were allowed out on the circuit. Having never raced there before I had an instructor as passenger. He talked me through the corners, but on the second lap at Denton's Cascades, a left hand, he grabbed the steering wheel and stopped me turning it. The car was heading towards Forsters, but it was closed off with steel drums, also the driver's side wheels were now on the grass verge. Then he let go and the car shot round the corner onto the Lakelands Straight: 'That's how you take that corner', he said. Was I glad, after four laps, to stop and let the brakes cool. He was a clever sod.

When the brakes had cooled, I went out again but this time on my own, so I could learn the circuit my way. Clay Hill was the most scary. It is like a humpback bridge where you can't see what's on the other side. OK, there are flag marshals around the circuit, but when I passed the Clay Hill one he was reading a newspaper with his head down. Before the end of the day, I was relaxed enough to pass this section at 110mph. I also enjoyed powering through Deers Leap. By now I didn't see the point of wearing my brakes and tyres out and called it a day. I thanked the BRDC officials who had travelled up from Silverstone and drove home.

On the journey home, I kept thinking, do I want to start circuit racing again? If I did, a race car was needed, but I was heavily involved in drag racing and it would be foolish to put that at risk. This is when I was caught in a speed trap, doing 50mph in a 40mph area.

This shock took me back to when I was eight years old and the family lived on the top of a steep hill. At the bottom of the hill the road crossed the main road and then went into a builder's yard. That Christmas my mother bought me a bicycle with a speedo which ran off the front wheel. When I went to school in the mornings, it was a joy to know how fast I was travelling, some mornings it was 35mph and that was quick.

One of the local boys challenged me to a race down the hill. We set off together, picking up speed all the time, then he started to move ahead. I wasn't having this, so I peddled like hell and passed him. My speedo was showing 50mph and rising. Now I needed to stop before the main road. Suddenly, the rear wheel locked, sending me across the main road and into the builder's yard. Luckily for me, I went headfirst into a mound of building sand and survived. I was cut and bruised and the builder took pity on me and drove me home. There was no school for me that day.

My mother played hell with me; the bicycle was a wreck and I would be off school for a week. Now I would have to walk to school every day. Luckily, grandmother decided that if I wanted to race, she would buy me a racing bike with eight gears, but I would have to wait until next Christmas. When the big day dawned, I couldn't wait to try my new bike but this time on the straight, flat roads of Cheshire – no more hills for me.

It was quick, so quick you could get into the slipstream of passing motorcars and read their speedos through the back window. In those days, very few drivers ever looked in their mirrors so you could have a tow for miles. This stopped when I was sent to Wrekin College in Shropshire and petrol went on ration.

The second round of the Wild Bunch rear-engine series was at the Mini Nationals on 14/15 July at Shakespeare County Raceway. Now I could sit in the dragster again and feel its power, with the blower pushing in all that fuel. The acceleration when you hit the second gear button is a joy to one's senses – ask anybody who has driven a Top Methanol dragster.

The journey down including our usual stopover at Hartlebury Travelodge followed by one night at Alcester. Prices double around Stratford-on-Avon when a few American tourists and others arrive to look at our beautiful country. The summer price increase at the Alcester Travelodge would buy enough petrol to travel the extra miles from Hartlebury every day.

Brenda and I had breakfast in Hartlebury and were on track before the dragster arrived. When it did arrive, Doug Bond and the crew soon had the car ready for me to race. Heidi and John had arrived to keep Brenda company while I was racing. This allowed me to relax. At any time during the day or night my wife could become ill and require swift medical treatment. Brenda is crew chief and my greatest fan – thank God she is still alive.

Doug decided I should make the first pass and get used to the feel of the car again, which I did. Late afternoon just before curfew, I put down a

8.220 pass which repaid the crew for all their hard work. Let's see what tomorrow would bring. Bruno was to spray the track with trackbite so this would give everybody some quick times. It was good to see some respect being shown to the up-and-coming Wild Bunch cars, usually trackbite is only put down for five and six-second cars.

Sunday morning was warm with a cool breeze and Bruno was already out with his tractor towing the sprayer. Wild Bunch were told to be ready for a noon start. I was to run on my own in the left-hand lane for both passes.

We joined the other cars in the fire-up road. Now it was my turn. Martyn and Doug fired up the engine and I slowly drove the car round to the start line and took it through the water. Martyn gave me the sign and I hit the throttle, it was a good burnout and long, nearly to the eighth mile. The engine sounded good so I selected reverse. By now Doug was in front of me and out of breath; I had made him run halfway down the track.

A quick check of the car by the start line marshal and I moved into pre-stage. The start lights came on, I hit the throttle and let the clutch go. The car suddenly had tyre shake on the start line and didn't move, and then when it did, it went like a rocket; at the eighth mile, my speed was 157.34 and increasing across the finishing line. Martyn and Doug's faces said it all as they towed the car back to the pits: I had run my first seven-second pass – a 7.548 at 178.57mph.

When I checked the timing ticket, my 60ft was down by $\frac{3}{10}$ of a second. Clearly, the tyre shake caused this and without it the car would have reached the eighth mile in 4.700, so a six-second pass was within my grasp.

My second pass in the afternoon was a 7.722 at 177.17mph. This had backed up my first run. I had set a new track record and Claire Meaddows was jumping with joy when I gave her my timing ticket. Also Brenda and the team were over the moon. It would be celebrations when everybody arrived home.

This was a milestone for the Wild Bunch. The track owners and promoters were being shown a new standard of excellence by the Wild Bunch teams. Teams like 'Backdraft', Ian Hanson's red 'Blown Altered', Paul Harvey with 'Ex-locomotion' and Tony Froome (a racer from way back) in 'Sundance III' who was in the eight-second bracket. I was part of it and proud to be.

Brenda and I said our goodbyes to everybody and thanked Martyn and Doug for their total commitment and encouragement to an old man of racing. We went home very pleased with the weekend's results with one more trophy to add to the collection. I wouldn't be driving the dragster again until the Super Series 5 at the end of September. The Honda would be my race car at York Dragway in two weeks' time, and again on 11/12 August.

How time flies, the season was past midway, and Christmas was round the corner.

The first York meeting was a test and tune for the Honda, and I ran three passes, with the last two a respectable 16.169 and 16.143. The August meeting was much the same, with all four passes close to my dial-in of 16 seconds. I did run a 15.660 pass. Roll on September when I would be running the dragster again with the Wild Bunch.

Now it was the August bank holiday weekend and Doug Bond would be out with the Shell car, our car, in the Super Series 4 at Shakespeare County Raceway. It was to prove a marvellous weekend for the partnership. Over to Mark Gredzinski first:

Top Methanol Dragster

On Saturday, Rob Turner showed why he's the perennial British Champion of late, coming off the trailer with a 5.77/245 new track record to head the field. Dave Wilson was next with a similarly strong 5.86/238 and he was followed by Lindsay Deuchar's 6.51/163, though a previous quicker looking run didn't receive a time. Doug Bond was in fourth spot with a 6.64/203 with Darryl Bradford in the Canto Consultancy machine on a 7.45/124 half pass. A subsequent try ended in disaster, as severe tyre shake split the Lenco, bent the axle, damaged the chassis and caused two rods to exit the block, oiling down the track extensively. Finally, the field was secured by the licensing runs of the Funny Cars belonging to Doug Ripley and Stephanie Milam on 8.20/144 and 8.74/152 respectively.

In the race Rob Turner ran a 5.89/231 bye but terminated some drivetrain components, putting him out. With Darryl Bradford out, Doug Bond had a 10.40/74 bye and Dave Wilson was rather too long on the revs in stage waiting for Stephanie Milam, going up in smoke but winning with a 8.29/114 to Steph's 8.91/162. Doug Ripley was into the sevens with a 7.80/162 but a 5.90/213 stormer from Lindsay Deuchar eclipsed this. In the semis, Doug Bond had a 9.13/97 bye while Lindsay Deuchar left before the green, receiving no times as Dave Wilson won with a mortally wounding 5.90/204. With Dave unable to show for the final, all Doug Bond had to do was break the staging beams in the Shell Oils rail to take an easy win!

Now the report in *Quick Times Racing News:*

Our first introduction to the hunger of our competitors came with the British MSA Top Methanol Championship where Darryl Bradford and Doug Bond paired up. On launch Darryl clearly had the holeshot on Doug, but it was Doug who would eventually pass Darryl's out of shape tyre shaking run, forcing him to shut down early, before shutting himself down with a semi respectable 6.827s @ 144.69mph. Fresh from a personal best in Norway of 5.73s Rob Turner showed us what it was all about and stormed up the track, clocking a run of 5.771s @ 245.90mph with Dave Wilson hot on his slicks running 5.869s @ 238.10mph during that qualifying session. Sadly Lindsay Deuchar's run didn't record any times or speeds, but the run was strong and on form.

Given half a chance during the next session Lindsay, after his clutch had cooled down, went on to run a very out of shape 6.516s @ 163.64mph securing the 3rd qualifying position. Also in this session we saw another tyre shaking destroying run from Darryl Bradford shredding the Lenco casing, dropping two rods, bending the rear axle and damaging the chassis. Doug Bond in the Shell sponsored car had an easy drive up the track with a run of 7.769s @ 141.07mph.

The team were now in a strong position to take the championship. Well done Doug. To celebrate, Brenda opened a bottle of bubbly and we toasted the team's success on into the next morning.

It was a quiet period in the drag racing scene, but no rest for us. The shop and garage were very busy; being the last two weeks of the holiday season, business was brisk.

The warm water off the coast of Anglesey had brought the jellyfish in shore to spawn. Every day children were being stung, which brought them to us with their parents to buy wet suits, and soon our stock of children's suits was sold. One lady said to my wife, 'Does your husband feed the jelly-fish?' My wife said, 'Why should he do that?'

Then it happened. While I was watching *Top Gear* on TV, there was Vicki Butler Henderson racing at Santa Pod Raceway. Before the programme had finished, I had written this letter:

Producer – *Top Gear*
Birmingham

30 August 2001

Dear John Wilcox

Top Gear, **Thursday 30 August 2001**

Vicki Butler Henderson racing at Santa Pod. Naughty, John!! My ideas poached by your programme or is she in training for the big one against me in the Top Methanol dragsters at Shakespeare County Raceway?

I am old enough to be one of *Top Gear's* first viewers. I have had great respect for the format over those years which the fledgling programme set out to project. Against all odds you and your predecessors turning it into the force it is today.

Please don't lose sight of all our (you and me) humble beginnings.

Derek F. Annable

This had happened to me before – my ideas had been used by Yorkshire Television and Granada Television. This after the producer said he would contact me if he intended to use the theme.

Doug Bond's last outing in the Shell dragster (when he races the car, it is the Shell car, when I race the car it is Thunder and Lightning III) was coming up in a fortnight's time. Unable to be there, we wished him luck by telephone.

This is the report of what happened:

Euro Finals 2001

There is nothing like a good drag race to get a motorsport crowd whipped up and the many thousands who attended the Euro Finals had a great time. There were plenty of reasons to get them cheering too, with burnouts, wheelies, darn close racing and international needle, with the Brits on top for a change! Formula One is visually poor in comparison and at just 20 quid, it was great value for a day's racing, compared to say 25 nicker at your average Premiership footie match for 90 minutes in a cramped plastic seat. The track was trainer-removing sticky but not all cars found it to their liking and a crosswind didn't help either.

Top Methanol Dragster

Qualifying had the most excitement on Sunday as Dave Wilson in the Nemesis dragster nipped Manty Bugeja for top slot with a fine 5.78/233. Later in the afternoon, Maltese Manty came out again in the Shark energy drink rail and regained honours with a 5.77/245 but then came Rob Turner, out to take the European championship and he lopped another hundredth off, to record a remarkable 5.76/242 from the Net Call machine! Brilliant stuff that the crowd really responded to. Lindsay Deuchar was fourth with a 6.11/213 and he was followed by Doug Bond on 6.34/213, Darryl Bradford with a 7.79/125 half pass in Rob Turner's old car and Wendy Baker on a 7.89/170.

In round one, the Turners elected to run hard on their first round bye but it cost them a motor, Rob slowing to a 5.93/199. Dave Wilson now had a shot at the title and dispatched Darryl Bradford's 11.35/71 with a solid 5.84/237. Then, Lindsay Deuchar drove around Doug Bond's relit 6.30/197 with a 5.94/223 and Manty Bugeja similarly beat a well-early Wendy Baker, 5.87/243 to a 7.55/181. The semis were depleted when Rob Turner was broken and both Dave Wilson and Lindsay Deuchar ran out of time. Manty Bugeja therefore ran a solo 6.25 and then closed the eliminator with a winning 5.80/241.

Doug did end the season runner-up and would carry number 2 on the car next year. Now the car would have an engine, our engine, which would go back in for the remaining races, my races.

To make sure of a race with the dragster at Super Series 5, I had sent my entry to Wendy Talbot, the APIRA secretary, on the 18 August, with the following letter:

18/08/2001

Dear Wendy

Super Series Round 5, Sept 01

As Wild Bunch will be in an ET bracket situation I shall dial-in 8.50 or slower in eliminations.

Derek

My entry was duly accepted and tickets and so on were sent to my home address. Arrangements were made with Martyn and Doug to have the car ready for the 21 September race meeting.

During that week I was in Rochdale on business. Tuesday morning my mobile rang. It was Brenda. 'Derek', she said, 'Tina Gibbs will not allow you to race in the Super Series 5 at the end of the week.'

'Why not?'

'I don't know. You will have to come home and phone her before five o'clock.' Thank goodness it was only a two-hour journey. I made it with half an hour to spare.

'Hello, Tina, this is Derek from Anglesey. What's the problem?'

'Listen, Derek, you didn't ask my permission to race, and I only received the entry list from Wendy today.'

'Yes maybe, Tina, but I posted my entry to Wendy on the 18 August, which was before the Super Series 4 meeting, giving the club and yourself ample time to consider whether I race a TM dragster in Wild Bunch in Super Series 5.'

'That's the point, Derek. It is a TM dragster and I am not happy it races in Wild Bunch, a six-second car among all those slower cars.'

'Tina, at the time of my entry, I enclosed a letter to Wendy saying I shall run 8.50 or slower and it would be up to you to set the bracket.'

'Yes, Derek, but you haven't got a MSA licence to race a TM dragster.'

'Tina, the car stopped being a TM dragster at the Pod last weekend. The car is owned by my wife, Brenda, and we don't have any intentions for me to race Top Methanol.'

'OK, Derek, what licence have you got?'

I went into a long, lengthy explanation of the type of car I had raced, what grades I had been given, on and on it went. In the end Tina Gibbs agreed I could race no quicker than 9.50, but she still kept complaining that I had got in through the back door and shouldn't be racing.

Race day arrived and we booked into the Alcester Travelodge. It was a tiring journey for Brenda, so it was straight to bed for her when we arrived. A couple of hours sleep would refresh her.

With haste I drove to the track to meet Doug Bond who was going to leave the rig and car in the pits overnight, having arranged with a friend to be on guard duty. He and Martyn gave me the bad news that they and the crew wouldn't be on track before eleven o'clock in the morning.

Key in hand, off I went looking for the chap who was going to be on guard duty. As I was talking to him about the arrangements for the morning, Terry Gibbs drove up, got out of his car and said to me, 'I hear you intend to leave someone else to arrange for the scrutineering of your car in the morning. Also you are leaving the car unattended in the pits?'

'Yes, Terry, that's right.'

'Do that, Derek, and you won't race.' Then Terry said, 'In my days as a racer, I had to be with my car when it was to be scrutineered.' Then he got in his car and drove off.

Does a promoter have the right to dictate to an entrant? No, they don't, only the race club has the power to do that. What have we done to the Gibbs family for them to be so vindictive? What Terry demanded meant leaving Brenda at the Travelodge and me being in the pits before 7am.

Then when Doug and Martyn arrived, I could go back to the Travelodge for Brenda. Thank you Terry and Tina Gibbs. This made for a very miserable evening and what turned out to be an unpleasant weekend.

Well, I was in the pits for 7am, but where was the scrutineer Terry said would be checking my car? Martyn and Doug arrived, so I left them to take charge of everything and now I could go back to Alcester for Brenda. No I couldn't. Suddenly I was called to a meeting in the central tower by the Gibbs family.

Tina Gibbs was waiting for me with an ultimatum. 'Derek, if you go quicker than 9.50 even by $\frac{1}{1000}$ of a second, you can put the car back in the trailer and go home.'

'Yes, Tina, I understand. Is that all? I am sure you know my wife had a massive stroke some years ago. She is waiting for me at the Alcester Travelodge and will be worrying.' No answer from our lady clerk of the course. Brenda was in a terrible state and very upset having been left so long on her own.

Now it was time for my first qualifying run (observed run) – 9.50 dialled in, I launched, lifting off before the eighth mile and then coasted through the finishing line at 70mph. At this speed, I managed to turn off the track at the first exit. Martyn said the run was well controlled. As I was getting out of the car, the pit marshall came over and said I was required in the control tower.

Tina Gibbs greeted me with a face like thunder. 'Sorry, Derek, I am not happy your car is racing with Wild Bunch. I can't allow you to race.'

'Tina, I don't believe what you are saying. I have done everything you have told me to do. I pulled off track at the first exit and it was a controlled run. What more do you want me to do?'

Then Bruno pipes up, 'It is a TM dragster, Derek.'

'Yes, Bruno, but I am not racing in the TM dragster class. I am racing with Wild Bunch and being restricted to 9.50.'

To this Tina said, 'I shall allow you one more run today, then come back and see me at the end of racing.'

My second run was at five o'clock. This time I powered it to the eighth mile. Time 5.404 at 120mph, lifted off at three-quarters distance, crossing the line at 90mph, ET 9.696. That clinched it; Tina now allowed me to race eliminations on a 9.00 dial-in, but no quicker.

Now I shall pass you over to the press reports. Firstly from Paul Bland:

Derek Annable was running his Top Methanol Dragster, 'Thunder and Lightning' and was limited firstly to 9.50 and then to 9.00 by officials at this MSA event. He put in a 12-second checkout pass, followed by a great well-calculated and controlled 9.696, thus qualifying 11th in the ladder of the 16-car field.

Round 1

Tony Smith also progressed with a 12.507 on a 12.20 dial-in by virtue of a quicker reaction time up against Derek Annable who ran an excellent 9.200 @ 151.01mph (Fastest MPH Spot Prize) which was very good on a 9.00 dial-in in a Top Methanol Dragster.

Now the report from Gredzo of *Custom Car:*

Wild Bunch

Top qualifier Chris Hartnell showed how he has dominated Wild Bunch competition this year, pulling the wheels up on every run in his injected methanol Chevy slingshot. He beat Colin Aldred's slingshot, 9.51/131 to a 10.31/124 and Paul Croston's bright yellow B Sting Topolino 9.69/128 over a 12.49/100. Then, in the semis, he covered Sarah Howell's Ramraider slingshot, which broke out of its dial-in, 9.35/134 over a 10.48/127. Taking a march up to the final was Mark Coulsell in his Limited Funz slingshot. He beat Darryl Howells 11.20/116 to 12.19/107, Ian Roddy's dragster, 11.11/111 over a 10.55/124 and Andrew Gosling in the Nutcracker sling-shot, 11.12/97 to a 14.62/95. In the final, Mark Coulsell stepped up to an 11.06/114 but Chris Hartnell was up for taking the win, with a 9.45/131.

One interesting race was Derek Annable who lost to Tony Smith's Chrysler motored Mini van. Tony ran a 12.50/98 while Derek lost with a 9.20/151 driving the Shell-backed Top Methanol dragster he shared with Doug Bond.

The outcome of the weekend's racing was that I was barred from racing Brenda's TM dragster at any future race meetings in which Terry and Tina Gibbs are involved, so no more Super Series for me. History is still on my side. The Gibbs family are promoters no more, having given up at the end of 2002. The people who took over as promoters at the Shakespeare County Raceway for 2003 said, 'Everybody is welcome.' Brenda's car will race there next year in the main championship.

One race meeting I was looking forward to was the October Finals at Santa Pod. All summer I had been training myself to drag race a front-wheel drive car. Brenda was staying home this time. It would be an early morning drive down to the Pod on Saturday, race and stay overnight, race again Sunday then return home.

Over to Gredzo for his report on the meeting:

The 2001 Santa Pod October Finals bore quite a resemblance to the previous year's event in that it was cut short by rain. Most eliminators got as far as determining which cars would run in the later rounds, but no actual final rounds were run. The threat of inclement weather unfortunately kept the crowds away but hats off to the racers and track crew for battling through testing conditions.

Sportsman ET

Derek Annable parked his Top Methanol dragster for this meeting and turned to his four pot Honda with some success. Derek had to face a pair of Skodas to reach the semis, beating the Estelle of Phillip Cowdrey and the redlit Rapide of Chevy Llewelyn 16.32/78 to a 13.48/99. Also in the 13s was Al Plass whose Camaro beat Martin Lewis' Nova and then had a 13.78/102 bye. Meanwhile, Simon Chalkly's Corvette also had a 13 second bye and shut down Lance Richard's Capri, 13.77/101 to a 12.44/100. Either Simon or Al Platt would've had to face Derek Annable in the final.

The weather had spoilt the racing. This prompted me to check my race records. They showed that I had had a few wins, many runners-up and other placings in my nine years in drag racing. One thing stood out in all those years. I had reached the finals at 18 race meetings where the finals had been rained off. This meant 18 wins or runners-up or a mixture of both. This was a revelation.

Now for the last race of the year – the Wild Bunch meeting on the 27/28 October in Brenda's TM dragster. Saturday was rained off but Sunday allowed everybody two passes, against A. Gosling and Ian Roddy. As Paul Bland reported:

Derek Annable was in the 'Thunder and Lightning' Top Methanol rear engine dragster and dialled in 9.50, adjusting the car to a cooler track and weather conditions. He did not register a time for round one, but ran a good 9.398 in round two.

The next time the Wild Bunch gang met it would be the annual dinner and prize giving at Drayton Manor on 17 November. Before this happened, I received sad news from the BRDC that Ken Tyrrell had died of cancer. There was also some good news in the secretary's letter:

First, I am sure that you will all wish to join me in offering out deepest sympathy to Norah and her family on the great loss of our former President, Ken Tyrrell. There is an extensive obituary in this issue and I hope that many of you will have seen the BRDC web site and the full appreciation there.

There will be a Memorial Service on Thursday 15 November at 2.00pm at Guildford Cathedral and a formal announcement is on page 3.

The details are not finalised as I write but there will be a special area in the Cathedral reserved for BRDC members. It would be most helpful if you could let me know if you wish to attend, and then I can send you the full details.

You will also have received the good news that the Secretary of State for Trade and Industry accepted the findings of the Competition Commission and cleared the BRDC/Octagon Agreement. You will also have seen the interim accounts.

Over the last week, the BRDC staff have moved from the portacabins next to the Clubhouse and we are all (Club and Race) now accommodated at the Farm. James Beckett is now located in the office on top of the Shower Block. The facilities for Members are unchanged except that the Dining Room is now occupied by the Race Department. We hope you will come and see us when you are at Silverstone or in the area. Updated contact details are on page 23.

The racing scene has been dominated by Michael Schumacher's retention of the World Championship and surpassing Alain Prost's record number of F1 wins. We have also seen the first CART race at Rockingham and the dreadful accident that Alex Zanardi suffered in Germany the week before. All this against a background of the events in New York and Washington on 11 September.

This issue also includes reports on the British Grand Prix and the Historic Festival. I must apologise again for the standard fare available at the Grand Prix dinner and to let you know that steps have been taken to ensure there is no repetition. Thank you for your comments on both that dinner and the Historic Party and I am pleased that you enjoyed the latter, including the new band.

There have been several regional events and I know that you are keen to continue these. Many thanks to the co-ordinators for all their hard work in making the arrangements. There are plenty of suggestions for next year but if you have any ideas please let us know.

The Annual Dinner is only two months away and we hope that you will try to attend. There is a booking form inserted in this Bulletin and the closing date is 14 November. Also included is a list of hotels we have managed to find with good deals. I expect that this will probably be the last dinner at the Grosvenor House and we are aiming to make it a good party.

Roger Lane-Nott

The Annable/Bond/Hannis partnership had achieved runner-up in the MSA Top Methanol Drag Racing Championship, a result that should please the team's sponsor, Shell Oil.

My own achievements were mostly with the Wild Bunch:

Rear Engine Series	2nd Derek Annable, 'Thunder and Lightning' $^{TMD}/WB$ 243
Daddy Cool (Soap) Trophy (Personal Achievement)	Derek Annable, 'Thunder and Lightning' $^{TMD}/WB$ 243
* Quickest ET for 2001	Derek Annable, 'Thunder and Lightning' 7.548
* Fastest MPH for 2001	Derek Annable, 'Thunder and Lightning' 178.57mph

(* Times must be backed up within 5%)

Now for the big one:

Track Records, Shakespeare County Raceway
7.548 – Derek Annable (426 CIKB Dragster) 15.07.01
178.57mph – Derek Annable (426 CIKB Dragster) 15.07.01

Added to this, my wife collected an award at the Drayton Manor dinner dance for the wives of the successful racers, in recognition of their patience over the long season.

The year 2001 records show there were further achievements with Wild Bunch for me:

14th in Wild Bunch Series, out of 40 participants
29th in Custom Chrome Series of 38 participants
15th in Super Series, of 22 participants (raced one event)
26th in Roy Wilding NRC series, 33 participants

What a year! Was this my best year? If it wasn't, it would take some beating. Doug and Martyn were undecided whether to become involved in further drag racing at the level of previous years. Shell Oil had withdrawn their sponsorship and money was tight. Let's see what the new year would bring.

Brenda said, 'Derek, you can race my Honda in the Sportsman class!'

To this I said, 'Thank you darling, but where are you going to sit when I am racing?'

Like a flash came back her reply, 'In the bar with a bottle of wine!' This was my Brenda of old.

Next week it is Christmas, then on 29 December it is Brenda's birthday. Also, don't forget to send Christmas cards to the team, family and friends. Friends. That reminds me of the famous quote by Winston Churchill, 'I know where the opposition are, they are in front of me, but friends and enemies are behind me.'

CHAPTER 11

2002

During 2001, I had become a member of the Caernarvonshire and Anglesey Motor Club. In the Christmas edition of the club magazine *Control* there was a price list and details of the Anglesey Performance Driving Centre's introductory course. The one which interested me was Formula Race Car Trials (FRCT) 4, price £285, with a club members' discount of 15%. Being one who never passes over a special offer, I filled in the application form, paid by Mastercard and booked the track day for the 23 March.

Why choose FRCT 4? Well, FRCT 1 was tuition plus 10 laps, price £130. For £285, less 15% discount, FRCT 4 included advanced tuition and – wait for it – 37 laps.

During the first two months of 2002, Brenda and I worked hard to make sure the dragster would be ready for Doug Bond to race at the first meeting at Santa Pod. Our investment of nearly £4,000 on a Whipple supercharger to bring the car into the five-second class would have been wasted if the car wasn't prepared in a way to take the extra horsepower. It was entered in the MSA Championship – one round at Santa Pod, the Easter Thunderball, and two rounds of the Super Series at Shakespeare County Raceway.

The older you get, the quicker time goes! Could it be a sense of being wanted elsewhere, somewhere not of this world? Anyway, instructions arrived for the track day on Saturday 23 March: report at 9.30am for a 10am start. I must be honest, although we had lived on Anglesey for forty years I didn't know the precise location of this track. To describe my experience, I shall quote from my letter, which our local newspaper printed on 4 April 2002:

Letters to the Editor
Chronicle, Bangor

25 March 2002

Dear Sir,

Whinge and Jewel

We in Anglesey are always whingeing about lack of tourists, money and being last in line for handouts from central government.

Wake up, there is an asset on our west coast which given more local support could generate revenue for all on our beautiful island, I mean all. Anglesey Circuit, Trac Môn runs a Performance Driving Centre with course prices which are the envy of all other UK Driving Centres. Sandwiched between spectator events and track days you can take part in Formula Race car trials in single-seater cars with a power-to-weight ratio equal to the best £150,000+ sports cars. The cost of tuition is less than £8 per lap.

For me, who is nearly old enough to get a free TV licence and lives half an hour's drive to the track near Ty Croes, I was greeted on arrival by some of the most amazing characters, of which our island is full. We all had a briefing, then were taken out in a saloon car to assess our individual capability. This over, we were fitted into a single-seater race car. I challenge any boy racer to have the nerve for what was to follow, nothing can prepare you for the G forces through the faster bends, and the terror on braking when the front wheels lock (no ABS brakes) and you go home, in guess what? After 5 to 6 hours of intensive instruction, you wait for the final prize, a certificate (if you have passed) signed by one of the MSA licensed instructors, your relief at this point is far greater than when you passed your first driving test.

You all ask, shall I be going back? My answer is yes. The MSA/ARDS Competition licence course (Racing National B) is my next goal.

Yours

Derek Annable

Now it was the start of the Thunder and Lightning drag racing season. Overheating problems with the Camaro meant I had to race my wife's Honda Integra at the York Dragway in their Super Street Shoot-out. Brenda never likes me racing her beloved Honda, so I endured some nagging on the way to our overnight stay in Goole. Forty-nine years of marriage has programmed my ears to switch off to vocal noises in the car while driving; what you do is grunt now and again, with the odd 'Yes' and 'No' thrown in to keep the peace.

Thankfully, the weather was kind on Easter Monday, with a cold wind blowing down the track. No moisture – we would have good grip. The car was checked out by young Murty, the track owner's son, and I signed on and paid my money. Looking around, I wondered where all the other racers were. There were just half a dozen cars present, so we had a couple of runs down the eighth mile to dial-in our own car. The meeting was a Mini v Beetle shoot-out, plus our championship for PDRC members and a RWYB meeting which started at 10.30am.

Then, from nowhere, cars were arriving in droves and the RWYB meeting exploded. All kinds of hot hatches, sports cars and saloon cars were being parked in the pits. There must have been nearly 300 cars, and the fire-up lane was crowded, with a queue stretching back into the distance. Public participation race days can get like the M25 at 8am on weekdays. I don't agree with the police and the media's criticism of young men who spend thousands of pounds on kits for their cars and want to race them. They controlled themselves like a regiment of the Queen's Guard.

The first round of eliminations had me racing against an American muscle car which was having misfire problems at low revs. I must pull a good light. This I did and off we went, my VETEC came in and I won by $3/100$ of a second. The next round went my way, followed by a bye for me in the semi-finals.

The finals would be close as the car in the other lane ran 15 seconds against my 15.40. He was much quicker than me to the eighth mile, reaction times would be all important. My light came down $4/10$ of a second before his, I had a good launch and kept ahead of my opponent. Then disaster struck at the eighth mile – I couldn't find third gear, and when I did, he had passed me. I piled on the revs, hitting the rev limiter. Now I was in fourth gear and the VETEC responded well. Fifty feet from the finish line we were level but as we crossed, he pulled away. He had won, so I thought, and that missed gear cost me the race.

In drag racing anything can happen, this is what makes it so exciting. My opponent had run his quickest time ever by $8/100$ of a second and had broken out by that amount. I was the winner of the spring shoot-out. On reflection, if I had found third gear in the normal way, I would have broken out and lost. The next championship round at York Dragway is on 26 May, the Camaro should be ready, and we will be running 13s not 15s.

Now the history of Pennine Raceway Ltd:

Pennine Raceway Ltd

This was formed by Steve Murty and others in the 1970s. They moved from venue to venue when the landowners kept increasing the rent. I forget how many times this happened but in the end the partnership closed down.

Then Steve Murty and his family took control. They pumped their own money into what is now Pennine Raceway Ltd. On and on they fought with courage. The venture to bring drag racing to the north of England was bleeding them dry. Luck was with them. By chance they found a successful local pig farmer in Melbourne who owned part of a disused wartime airfield.

Thus was born a relationship which was to bring about 'York Dragway'. It wasn't a relationship where money ruled, but more a passion both men had to give the public the best whether it be roast pork on your table or a spectator sport.

Today York Dragway is a stable base for drag racing in the north of England. With the help of the Pennine Drag Racing Club, York Dragway is a magnet for young men to try their road cars against the clock in the RWYBs (Run What You Bring).

The club officials help the Murty family prepare the Dragway in the winter months, thus costs are held down to within the budget set by the track owner, PR Ltd and PDRC. There is a saying, 'Yorkshire men watch their brass'.

I have raced the northern track for the last nine years, and never mind which car I am in, year after year, my best times, ETs and mphs have been achieved at York Dragway. Some racers refuse to race this strip, saying it is dangerous, the track is this and that. Could this be a convenient smoke screen to hide their inadequacies?

Out of the blue, I had a call from Desmond Hammill. He explained he was writing a book on the history of the Kieft race car and the life of the man they are named after, and could I help? With pleasure, sir, fire away. Our conversation lasted over an hour. Many questions I answered with ease, others would require many days of thought. That phone call opened the flood gates and Desmond kept coming back with questions about Stirling Moss and our racing years in the early 1950s. It took many months of telephone calls to answer all Desmond's questions.

During this time, the man who was restoring my 1950 Kieft wanted information from me, such as the colour, the modifications that had been made to the car and how many times Stirling had raced it. Suddenly, after around fifty years, my race car was becoming a part of history – I was flattered to say the least.

Then I came down to earth with a bang. Doug Bond had broken our Top Methanol dragster at the Thunderball meeting. Brenda was fuming at the bad news. Martyn Hannis promised the car would be ready for me to race at Shakespeare County Raceway on the 20/21 April and the Whipple supercharger would be on the engine.

Having enjoyed my outing at the Anglesey track, I decided to reinstate my racing licence with the RAC. The Sprint and Hill Climb Championship 2002, which the Association of North West Car Clubs was running, would give me a springboard for my race licence. I registered with the ANWCC through their championship secretary Dave Thomas. Then I entered my wife's Honda Integra in the first sprint of the season at the Aintree circuit, sending off my cheque for £75 to the Liverpool Motor Club, who returned my race number and details for 27 April meeting.

The season's opener for the Wild Bunch was in a couple of days. On Martyn Hannis's promise that the car would be ready to race, we booked our usual room at the Alcester Travelodge and prepared ourselves for the journey south.

It was nice to be back at Shakespeare County Raceway. The car didn't make the first practice run, but when it did, I had a good burnout, stopping just short of the eighth mile. Halfway back to the start line, there was a fuel surge and the revs went up to 7500. I switched off.

Back to the pits we went, the blower had broken away, stripping the holding down bolts. One nut was missing. Where was it? This meant taking the heads off. It had gone on a journey through the engine, ending up in pot number four, or what was left of it.

Martyn Hannis's only comment was, 'In all my years in drag racing, I have never seen a blower break loose in burnout.'

I replied, 'Stay with me long enough and anything can happen.'

The crew worked hard to restore the engine ready for racing on Sunday. Let's hope our problems were over.

The weather on Sunday was perfect for some good times – dry and warm. Now I was under Martyn and Doug's instruction: 'Derek get into the driver's seat and we will fire up the engine.' When the engine was fired up, everybody within 10ft of the car was sprayed with methanol fuel. On tickover, the fuel pump was delivering full pressure, forcing fuel back through the induction. After two hours, Martyn Hannis called it a day. Nothing could be done to rectify the fault in the fuel pump.

We said our farewells and drove home. It would be three months before I could race the dragster again as Doug Bond had priority over me. The team was after the MSA Top Methanol Championship and had our full support.

The disappointment of not racing the dragster behind me, Saturday was the big day – my first sprint meeting in all my years in motorsport. This was to be at the Aintree GP race circuit where Stirling Moss and others raced in the mid-1950s. They would enter Beechers at 135mph and reach 185mph down the Railway Straight; let's see what my wife's Honda could do.

The weather was cold with heavy showers. There were 110 cars entered and my class, Road Modified Saloon and Sports Cars 1400cc to 2000cc, had the largest number of cars – 21.

Everybody had two practice runs followed by four timed runs. This was a friendly venue with good grub at a reasonable price in the golf centre.

Cars leave the start line singly at 25-second intervals, thus three cars are always on the track, the starter, finisher and a mid-track car. For the information of the driver, there is an electronic scoreboard which gives you your time and terminal speed, which is 35 yards past the finishing line. My best of the day was 63.29 seconds/106mph.

My wife's humble Honda created interest from the highly modified brigade. 'Yours is a standard road car and it went through the speed trap at 106mph. Our cars are out and out cars and we could only manage an extra two mph.'

Most drivers liked the two corners up to Valentines Way but not me, Beechers was my favourite. On reflection, if I could increase my exit speed out of Village Corner, my time for the 1.64 mile sprint would be below 60 seconds. The next meeting at Aintree was on 29 June with the final on 7 September.

I did make some friends, Mark Le Riche for one and David Barrow who raced a Saab Sonnett II.

Our Top Methanol dragster was entered in the Super Series, Spring Nationals at Shakespeare County Raceway on 4–6 May, Doug Bond being the pilot. I shall pass you over to Mark Gredzinski of *Custom Car:*

> The Shell team arrived sporting the Annable engine this time, having destroyed their own at the Pod. Martyn Hannis was confident Doug would run a 5 second pass, the new fuel pump would give them the boost they required.

The problems of the car's last outing at Shakespeare County Raceway when the blower lifted on burnout had been solved. But no, no five-second pass for Doug and the Shell team, just rods making windows in the block.

Yes, Doug destroyed the engine, so that's two engines destroyed, one at the Pod, now this one. One day, Martyn and the crew will get it right and the car will be a winner. Brenda was less than pleased with the Shell team's showing, so we were both happy that at least her Honda was showing reliability.

Forget drag racing, the Honda was entered in the New Brighton Trophy Sprint. I had received the final instructions from the Wallasey Motor Club who were running the meeting. There was a field of 100 cars, 18 in my class, and we had to report to race control at 8.30am, which meant leaving home at 6am.

Saturday morning dawned, the heavens had opened and it was heavy rain all the way to the seafront at New Brighton. There it was across the Mersey, Liverpool docks with the odd wind turbine spoiling the view and the larger ships queuing up for high tide.

We were being called to the drivers' meeting. One hundred drivers stood there in the pouring rain listening to the clerk of the course, who warned us there would be a delay because of the weather. A convoy run would take place even in the rain in half an hour. This would be followed by a practice when the rain eased. Everybody went back to their cars to sit it out and prepare themselves for the convoy run.

One hundred cars lined up down the main road alongside the sea wall and slowly moved off for the convoy run; luckily, when it came to my turn, the rain stopped. The marshals became active, sweepers went out to clear the ponds in the roads. We slower cars were sent out for our first practice run but sadly it had started to rain again, which brought my time down, or rather up, to 81 seconds.

While the faster cars were still in the pits, the slower cars were sent out for their second practice run. My turn came. Off I went with the windscreen wipers going full blast. My time, 74.84 seconds. A lunch break was called, hoping the weather would improve. My mobile phone went off and it was Brenda asking me how I was doing. When I told her my times, she suggested that perhaps I should come home as they weren't very good. I said I would think about it over some food.

I enjoyed a chicken tikka roll, with a large portion of chips. By now, the track was drying, and so I thought I should try my drag racing tactics, bang the throttle down and hope for the best. It worked. My first timed run was 71.85 seconds, followed by a 68.75-second pass – not too bad I thought, until one of the drivers told me the track record was 46.66 seconds. I was the slowest car of the day. Well not quite, Mark Le Riche and I tied for slowest car of the day.

The New Brighton Trophy Sprint is run on the seafront road, which is closed off for the day and there is a heavy police presence. Many race cars come to grief when they hit the 6 inch high road kerbs. These can be intimidating. My wife's Honda is our only car and is needed to keep her mobile, so I best not hit a concrete kerb.

I came away from my second sprint meeting knowing there is a lot to learn and my times would come down with practice. Drag racing is won on your start light (reaction time). Sprints and hill climbs require far greater skill, also you have to remember every corner and its camber. I had set myself quite a challenge.

The following week we did travel the 200-plus miles to York Dragway and entered the PDRC UK Open Nationals, but it isn't worth a mention. The meeting was rained off and some of the people were less than friendly.

Now we come to the big one, the Main Event at Santa Pod on 1–3 June 2002, the Queen's Golden Jubilee: European round I of the FIA Top Fuel dragsters, Top Methanol dragsters and Funny Cars, Pro-Stock plus all the FIM/VEM bike rounds, the list goes on and on with 21 classes in total. Where else can you watch 250 cars and bikes compete for the highest honours in European drag racing. I am not a fan of Keith Bartlet, and many who have tried to work with him will know what I mean. But this time Keith got it right. Santa Pod Raceway and the SPRC who looked after the entrants did a really good job.

My wife's Honda Integra, Thunder and Lightning IV, was entered in Sportsman ET class. This gave us three days of good racing and a chance to sort out the many problems we were having with Martyn Hannis and Doug Bond who were using our Top Methanol dragster in the UK and European Championship. At earlier Shakespeare County Raceway meetings, both our engine and their engine had been destroyed, so several questions had to be answered. Racing cars and motorsport aren't a hobby to me and never have been. Good money had been invested to produce results and, with luck, win championships, but this year it wasn't happening.

Martyn and Doug had spent many days and nights prior to the meeting rebuilding our engine so it could use the extra power the Whipple super-charger was capable of delivering. On the first day of Top Methanol quali-fying, Doug's half-pass was impressive. A complete engine checkover showed no damage, thank goodness, so no parts to replace. The car was now ready to race. It was agreed not to run the car again until eliminations on Monday. Here's hoping for some good racing.

The dragster sorted, it was time for me to enjoy racing the Honda. In all my years competing in drag racing, I had never tried launching on the second amber, so why not at this meeting? When one is after champi-onship points, the risk of pulling a red is too great.

My first run of the day was against Richard Hillier driving his Ford Mustang – I pulled a red (.391). My second run was against Martin Batsford and his Ford Capri and off I went on the second amber – .510 was recorded, a win for me. It had worked. More practice was needed before I would try the second amber again. But now was the end of Saturday's racing, time to go back to the Travelodge, have a meal and a good night's sleep.

Sunday morning dawned, a quick 7am breakfast for me, toast for Brenda to eat in the bedroom and off we went to the racetrack. There was Amos Meekins enjoying a cup of tea.

'You again Derek?'

'Yes Amos. Sorry, am I spoiling your cuppa?'

'Yes, Derek. There's your car pass.'

For eight years Amos Meekins has had to put up with me going off site every evening, returning the next morning for him to scrutineer my car. Amos and his wife, also his brother Doug, are gems and the drag racing scene would be the poorer without them.

The pit marshal was calling out Sportsman ET, so down the fire-up road we went. My first opponent was Paul Voyce driving his Ford Escort Nexus, but I pulled a red (.440). In round two I had Simon Chalkly and his Chevrolet Corvette. This time, my reaction time was .507, just .007 of a second outside a perfect light and a £50 prize. We would be in race situation on Monday, so it was time to give the car a rest, call it a day and return to the Travelodge and a slap-up meal in the Little Chef.

As we were finishing our coffee and liqueurs, John Price walked in. This man is 'Mr Drag Racing'. Forget Murray Walker, John's commentary is far better. He greeted us with a cheerful, 'Evening Derek and Brenda, good lights today, a couple of fives. I hear you are going for your Formula Ford race licence.'

I said, 'Yes I am. Didn't your late father work at the Ford Motor Company in the 1950s, in their engine department?'

'Yes, that's right Derek. At the time we lived in Kent, as did a lot of engine men, but then he was transferred to South Wales.'

'John, the Formula Ford car I shall be driving one day has a Kent engine in it, named after the men from Kent who worked on the first engines all those years ago.'

Rarely have I left John Price speechless, but this did.

Monday morning dawned with clear blue sky. Brenda looked tired. The extra medication was having its effect and there is a limit to the number of painkillers people can take in any 24-hour period. This weekend she had exceeded the allowed dose and was showing signs of stress – let's hope the TM dragster runs some good times.

Sportsman ET are always first out on race day as we lay rubber down for the big cars. My first opponent was Al Platt, last year's championship winner, with number one on his car. This should be an interesting race – the 1995 champion, me, against the 2001 champion, Al Platt, in his Chevrolet Camaro, with its 346ci engine. John Price was having a field day giving the details to the large crowd of spectators.

Al Platt knew I had been trying a second amber launch in practice with good results – .510 or 520 and he would lose the race. Being bracket racing, I left the line first. He had to wait over two seconds before his start light came on. I was watching his every move in my mirrors as I shot the track; Al Platt had a perfect launch and came pounding down the track after me, like a bat out of hell. Then I noticed my scoreboard had all the white lights on. Al Platt had pulled a red .479, and I was the winner. John Price was delirious, giving the thousands of spectators my life history.

Now the Top Methanol dragsters were lining up to race. Doug Bond against Rob Turner, great burnouts by both racers – high tension. Turner staged first, Doug was cool and he held back, trying to unnerve Rob. The start light came on, bang, over 6000hp exploded. Doug was ahead at the 60ft (timing ticket showed .87, the best of the day); at the eighth mile it was neck and neck, then suddenly Doug lost ground – his foot had been vibrated off the throttle. The Shell team and Brenda were gutted, although there was one consolation – the engine and the car were in one piece for me to race in July.

As was reported by the press, Doug Bond was definitely making more power as evidenced by a best ever mph and ET, 6.17/220. On the next round, Rob Turner had Doug Bond beaten on a 5.77/238 to 6.38/176. Doug was on a real flyer 'til the motor went away, which could have been a five'. This is why Brenda and I bought the Whipple supercharger for the car so Doug could run a five.

Young Nick Griffin knocked me out in the next round of Sportsman ET. I broke out by $\frac{5}{100}$ of a second. Brenda and I watched Barry Sheavills set a new European speed record of 304mph. We said our farewells and returned to the Travelodge for Brenda to rest before supper.

We discussed the future of our Top Methanol dragster, whether we should carry on or sell, and also the forthcoming double header sprint at the Anglesey track in two weeks' time. There was no travelling back home until the morning, as Brenda didn't feel too good. So it was to bed and a good night's sleep. We would be home tomorrow.

Over the years I have met many interesting people, and high on the list is Jon Cross. In a conversation we had at Santa Pod, during the Main Event meeting, I mentioned that it had been agreed Brenda's Honda would be raced in sprints and hill climbs and I was to be the driver.

Jon's response was 'Derek, I always thought of you as a sprint man.'

'Why is that?', I asked.

His reply was a revelation, 'I race karts for charity, unlike you Derek, I couldn't race full time. I hate it. But, when I get into the race kart, my whole being changes. I become aggressive and try to force the other drivers off the circuit.'

'Well, Jon, that is your will to win.'

'No Derek, I was black flagged one time and pulled into the pits, then when the clerk of the course came over to me, I jumped out of the kart and said, "I am an international race director, you can't black flag me." Things got heated. If I didn't calm down I would lose my international race director's licence.'

'Jon, all drivers get like that during the pressure of racing. When the fear factor comes in, the brain produces hormones which heighten our reflexes and our will to live, thus we become very aggressive.'

He wasn't convinced and still thought he was some sort of monster. A kinder man you could never meet, and race meetings under his control ran like clockwork. There were never any raised voices, instead it was all smiles and everything was calm.

Our garage in Moelfre, Anglesey was now open most weekends, as the vintage car boys were back on the road and needed 4-star leaded fuel BS 4040. This prompted my wife to join me on the days when the weather was warm and dry and start again selling wet suits to the locals and holiday families. She would sit in her BMW 635, reading novels and drinking wine.

The third sprint meeting of the year was organised by the Chester Motor Club at Anglesey circuit on 15/16 June. The length of the course is approximately 3000 yards, which is one and a half laps of the circuit. Being a club full of humour, the chain gangsters for the Basil Davenport Memorial Trophy sprint on Saturday were Peter Cobb, James Bareter and Anne Berrisford – their words not mine.

Thank goodness I only lived 15 miles from the circuit. Scrutineering started at 8am and was in class order, with practising for my class starting at 10am.

I arrived at the circuit with twenty minutes to spare, just enough time to fit the timing strut to the front of the car and the race number to the side windows before George Smith and the other scrutineers started checking that the cars were to MSA rules and specification for their class. My wife's Honda passed that test. Now it was my turn: race licence, car insurance, overalls, helmet, shoes, gloves, followed by bend down and touch your toes, open your mouth to check whether you had false teeth, (they must be taken out when racing), all for safety against injury in an accident.

That over, now I could put into practice what I was told by a Formula Ford driver when I was at Aintree circuit. 'Derek, you must drive over the cobbles on every corner if you want a quick time, but make sure you keep one wheel on the tarmac. If you don't, the corner marshal will give you a penalty.'

My first practice run was 128.00 seconds, but I can't come to terms with the hammering the car's suspension takes when you drive over the cobbles on the corners. Luckily for me I was pitted next to George Povey, a veteran of thirty years of speed sprints.

Before we began, he said, 'Derek, why have you started speed sprints at your age? I'm fifteen years younger than you and I'm retiring from the sport this year.'

'Well George, if you are retiring at the end of the year, I won't be a threat to your position in the championship next year! Do you mind talking me through the circuit?'

'OK, I'll watch your next practice run, then we can talk.'

A quick check of the scoreboard showed George's time in his Rover Mini Cooper was 117.73 seconds, 10 seconds quicker than me. This would give me a target to aim for. Out on the circuit I went. This time I managed a 124.31-second practice run, still nearly seven seconds slower than most of the roadgoing cars. Now for George's comments on my performance, and so I went in search of him.

After five minutes I found him under Bob Jones's Seat Ibiza looking at the car's rear brakes, muttering something about how the brake cable was sticking and should be taken off. Seeing me, Bob said, 'George, Derek's here'.

The veteran had plenty to say: 'Derek, you are showing promise. The long right-hand corner up to Abbotts should be taken further out and then when you come into Abbotts, you are braking. Keep your foot off the brake pedal, just let the front wheels dig in, only lift off slightly if the car starts to understeer. Then you must snap it over quicker and later at Radar, which will give you more speed down the straight.'

'Right! And what about the hairpin, George?'

'Take the hairpin like all hairpin corners, leave it as late as possible. I liked the way you came out of Douglas, you were on the correct line and quick. Now go and work on what I have told you, and good luck.'

'Thank you very much, I'll do my best.'

Laughing, he said, 'I'll never forgive you Derek, if you go quicker than me!'

The clerk of the course was calling everybody out for their first timed runs. George said, let the car dig in. I tried this and ran out of road between Abbotts and Radar and couldn't get the car settled down for the rest of the lap. My time for that run was 121.84 seconds, I was pleased with myself, over two seconds quicker than practice. My joy was short-lived; George had run a 110.56-second pass, 11 seconds quicker than mine. I kept telling myself he is an expert, I am a novice.

Racing stopped as it was time for a fly-past of a wartime Spitfire. It came in from the east, made a long sweep, dived over the circuit, pulling up into the blue sky, real Battle of Britain stuff. Its next pass was at 100ft; we were deafened by the noise of the Merlin engine. The Chester Motor Club has strong connections with the RAF, past and present.

Fly-past over, the call out came for the second timed run. I followed George's instruction to the letter and had less dig in this time but I couldn't get below 120.00. After a half-hour break, I was lining up for the third and final timed run. This time I could see the car in front and was starting to catch it, which spurred me on. It meant the challenge was there; I left the breaking late, powered out of the corners and there was a good feeling about that run. Yes, I had broken through the 120-second barrier. There on the noticeboard was my time, 118.90 seconds – success.

I thanked George Povey for his help, took the numbers off the side of the car and drove home. Tomorrow it was the Dave Moore Memorial Trophy Sprint, with the promise of six timed runs.

My wife was pleased her car was still in one piece and had run a sub-120. I asked her to come with me to the race on Sunday. 'No thank you Derek, I like drag racing. Any other form of motorsport is boring.'

Sunday morning dawned, blue skies and a cool breeze, no need to take the car to the scrutineer or sign on. There was another Honda in my class, driven by Dave Baines, who I was told is quick, having been a racing driver for the last five years. One practice run for everybody; Dave's Honda time 118.70, mine 121.63. I had managed a 118.90 yesterday, so we would have some close racing, I thought. How foolish one can be.

The first timed run by Dave Baines was 112.82, while mine was 120.98; the second timed run, Baines 112.56 and mine 118.75. If my opponent had run those times in practice, he would have been placed in a higher class. I was finding out the hard way how things worked in speed sprints. The key is to run a slow time in practice, at least in the first practice run, check the opposition's time, then gear your times to be no more than half a second quicker. This gives you a five to six-second cushion, as you know your car is capable of quicker times.

The outcome was that Dave Baines won the class with a 110.37 second timed run against my best of 118.19 seconds. During a conversation with Alan Clarke, who races a Lotus Elise, he said, 'The Honda which Baines was racing had raced last year and had been in a higher class. Baines wasn't the driver. He must have borrowed it for this meeting.'

I said, 'That's not the point Alan. Baines must have known the car was too quick for the class he had entered it in.'

'Maybe he didn't Derek.'

'Somebody knew and its too late to make a complaint', was my reply.

Alan Clarke's girlfriend Karen Williams was in second position for the Novice Championship, only two points behind me. I must concentrate on my points for the championship, not who wins what race in a car which may not be legal. Roll on the next sprint at Aintree in two weeks' time. Before that I was entered to race the Camaro at York Dragway in round three of the Northern Drag Racing Championship which I was leading on points.

The last round of the championship was rained off. Disaster struck again. The Camaro broke in the first round of elimination and required a transporter to take it back to Anglesey. This meant the end of my dreams of winning the championship.

No sooner had we returned from York Dragway than it was time to race the Honda in the Liverpool Motor Club sprint meeting at Aintree circuit. When Brenda and I arrived, the pits were full of every type of race car, old Austin 7 Ulsters and specials, MG Midgets, Westfields, Caterhams, Lotus, Van Diemens and, last but not least, the RBS 5c race car driven by the one and only Barry Whitehead with his grey hair and two new hip joints, fitted some months earlier by the NHS. Motorsport has no age limit.

With Brenda installed in the golf clubhouse, it was time for my first practice run. The four slowest cars in Class 1B, all 50+ second sprinters, were competing for who would be closest to 60 seconds. First practice run I managed a 62.37, followed by a 62.04. Stephen Norton had improved to a 62.50, a full second quicker than his first run. David Kelly was third with a time of 65.07, followed by Mark Le Riche on a 65.83. The quickest time in our class 54.57 seconds.

Time for lunch in the clubhouse; two bacon baps for me, a ham roll for Brenda. For all of half an hour we talked tactics in my timed runs. Brenda wanted me to go all out, even if it meant breaking the car. This took me back to the days of Stirling Moss, the win-at-all-costs man who would break the car for a win. The middle road was agreed – go quick and remember we needed the car to drive back to Anglesey.

My first timed run was slower than my best practice run. Brenda was giving me a hard time, saying, 'Stephen is getting quicker every run, but you aren't.' This fired me up, so that my second timed run was 61.92, quicker by $\frac{2}{10}$ of a second than Stephen. After a short rest, everybody was called out for the final timed run of the day. Stephen went off before me and it looked quick. Now it was my turn, a good launch, no wheel spin, at the first corner I hit the rev limiter in second gear. After a short straight, it was the second corner and a voice in my head said, 'Derek hold the throttle down and aim for the cinder path'. Now a quick turn into the corner. Damn, the car has gone into understeer and I was running out of road. Quick lift of the throttle, then bang it down again, and off down the straight I went, 90mph coming up, now 95mph. Brake and swing through the fast right-hand bend, keep the throttle down, 80mph coming up, now 95mph, change into fourth gear, crossed the finish line at 110mph, my time 61.73 seconds. Success, I had beaten Stephen's time by $^{37}/_{100}$ of a second.

As I drove back to the pits, there was Brenda, all smiles and thumbs up; I was 9th in my class and 96th overall. An improvement on the April results. Karen Williams, my main opposition in the Novice Championship, was on holiday, which could cost her the championship. Many years ago Paul Hudson lost a winner's trophy because of a holiday in Kenya; one can never make up the lost points.

True to form, when we arrived home, I cooked the best curry this side of India, washed down with some wine. I would be teetotal for the rest of the week because in six days the Honda was contesting the Lancashire and Cheshire Car Club and MG Car Club (NW) Ty Croes Weekend Sprint.

The final instruction and the entry list showed a field of 93 cars, with Class 2 first out. My number was 14 which meant I would be leading the cars out of the pits with Dave Baines, No.17, second behind me, or so I thought.

It was a perfect day for racing; dry and warm with a sea breeze. Drivers' briefing over, now it was time to line up for the first practice run. As per instructions, I took first spot in the line-up of race cars, then a Renault Clio No.12 dived in front of me – it must be a late entry. No it wasn't, the driver was Andy Davies who was down to drive a Subaru Impreza in Class 3 Standard Saloon and Sports Cars 2001cc and over, but had changed cars to be in my class. Never mind, Dave Baines driving a Honda Civic would be the quickest.

The two practice runs completed, now it was time for the first timed run. Again I followed the Renault Clio to the start line and watched it launch. This wasn't a standard saloon, let's wait for the timing tickets to be posted. When posted, Andy Davies had run a 107.82, Dave Baines 112.15, Nigel Dodds 118.09, Chris Cole 118.14, myself 120.06 – this meant there were two non-standard cars in my class, so I must try for third place. The second timed run moved me up one place to fourth position – .34 of a second slower than the third placed man, Nigel Dodds, who was going faster as the day progressed. The hairpin corner was still causing me problems. I must exit quicker.

Now it was call-out for the final timed run. While I was sitting in the fire-up road, Mark Le Riche came over to me and said, 'Derek you look worried.'

'Yes I am, the hairpin is slowing my times by at least one second, maybe more. The change from fourth through the gears is taking too long.'

'Derek, your Honda Integra has a race box, one of the best gearboxes in production. Come from fourth to second in one shift.'

Mark's advice gave me my best time of the day, 117.47, giving me third position and 17 points for the Novice Championship. This was the end of Saturday's racing. I thanked Mark and drove home, feeling well pleased.

Sunday was a bright day. This time there was no drivers' briefing and practice runs, it was straight into timed runs. Andy Davies was going quicker and this time I decided to take the matter up with the secretary of the meeting. Martin Nield's response was, 'Sorry Derek, the scrutineer passed the car for your class, you must take the matter up with him.'

I must be careful how I handled my complaints from now on. Sitting in the car, I remembered all those years ago when I made a protest to the SPRC. The people I upset ostracised me; there was no way would I put my wife through that again.

The chief scrutineer Chris Mansley came over to me and asked, 'What's your problem, Derek?' I explained the way Andy Davies' Renault Clio was set up, it couldn't be standard, surely it was a rally car.

'OK, I wasn't the scrutineer who passed the car, but I will check with my colleagues. Come over to the scrutineer's bay in ten minutes.'

This I did. Chris said, 'Derek, we didn't find any modifications to the car in question. It is a standard model.'

'Sorry, it isn't, the car is a Renault Clio rally car and should have been racing against rally cars.'

'Derek, the choice is yours. I shall impound the car, strip it down, including the engine, and make a report to the MSA. You know what the Blue Book states in Clause 0.5 about protests.'

'Chris, that isn't fair. I have brought the facts as I see them to you. How can I race in today's meeting if I am to fulfil Clause 0.5?'

Yes, of course I know what Clause 0.5 says:

'Every protest shall be in writing stating the grounds of the protest, be signed by the party making the protest and be accompanied by the fee laid down in Section 2. It must be lodged with the Secretary of the Meeting, or the Clerk of the Course or their deputies within the appropriate time limit as before stated.'

I didn't have my cheque book with me or paper to write on. I would have to leave the race meeting, thus foregoing my timed runs, to go home and prepare the protest. As Chris said, the choice was mine. I had to 'shut up or put up'. The next sprint meeting I attend, writing paper and cheque book will come with me.

Two hours of politics had caused me to go off the boil and my timed run was 120.15. Maybe I should call it a day and go home. This is when a man in a raincoat came over to me and asked, 'Are you Derek Annable?'

'Yes I am, who are you?'

'I am Dave Thomas, the ANWCC championship secretary. Sorry to hear of your problem. You should have raised the matter of the Renault Clio on Saturday. Run a sub-120.00 in the final timed run and you will be leading the Novice Championship.'

This fired me up so I raced again. This time the Honda did me proud – 116.96, the quickest it had ever run at Anglesey track. Now I was leading the Novice Sprint Championship with a cushion of points over Karen Williams. The day finished on a happy note for me and Brenda was pleased, so pleased she said, 'The next sprint meeting is at Anglesey track and I shall be your crew chief.'

I wasn't happy with Chris Mansley's answers and the handling of my complaint by the Lancs and Cheshire Car Club, so off went a letter to Dave Thomas:

ANWCC
Championship Secretary
LLandudno Junction

8 July 2002

Dear Dave Thomas

Re: Ty Croes Weekend Sprint 6 & 7 July 2002 organised jointly by the Lancashire and Cheshire Car Club Ltd and North Western Centre of the MG Car Club

I am still not happy Andy Davies was allowed to run a Renault Clio Rally Car in Class 2 Standard Saloon & Sports 1401 to 2000. The entry list given to me on signing on 8.30 am Saturday morning the 6 July put Andy Davies in Class 3 with a Subaru 2000cc Impreza No 20, my number was 14 in Class 2. At some point on Saturday morning, before practice session, he changed the car he was to drive to a Renault Clio Rally Car and the clubs in charge of the meeting placed him in Class 2 and gave him No. 12. It was plain for anyone to see from his practice times he was too quick for that class, still he was allowed to carry onto timed runs. The outcome was he won the class, this was repeated on Sunday 7 July.

Being a member of Caernarvonshire and Anglesey Motor Club Ltd. I paid my registration fee to the ANWCC because I wished to enter their Sprints and Hill Climbs Championship with the hope they would have some control over the meetings organised by the various motor clubs within the association, perhaps I was misinformed.

Having taken part as a competitor since 1948 in many different motorsport disciplines I know mistakes can be made to keep everything rolling along to the satisfaction of the majority. My points in the ANWCC championship 2002 were affected by what happened at Ty Croes weekend sprint and cannot be rectified. Motorsport isn't a hobby to me, it is a very serious business and costly. I hope there isn't a repeat of what was an oversight by all concerned at last weekend's meeting.

Yours sincerely

Derek Annable

Rec No: 02 298

and back came his very prompt reply:

ANWCC
Association of North Western Car Clubs
Llandudno Junction

9 July 2002

Dear Derek

Thank you for your letter received this morning.

After Sunday's event I had a 'chat' with Alan Walker, the owner of Car 12 Renault Clio. As you will note from the original entry list, he and Alan Davies had originally intended using Alan W's road car, the Subaru Impreza. For various reasons, they decided that Alan D would use the Clio, which is Alan W's rally car and is taxed and insured for road use.

The Clio is standard in terms of engine modifications, but does have revised suspension for rallying, therefore in the terms of the regulation 'Standard Saloon' it does not qualify, and Alan W acknowledged this during our discussions. Alan D had assumed, incorrectly, that Standard Saloon meant roadgoing and this had not been picked up by the organisers as it was a change of car from that originally intended.

In view of the above, I have recalculated the points for Class 2 by excluding Competitor number 12 Alan Davies for championship purposes. He is not registered with me this year, although has been in the past when he used a Honda Civic in the same class. Alan W is registered with me but is not affected by these calculations.

This means that you have gained 0.78 points for the Saturday event and 0.71 for the Sunday event, also one point each day in the novice series, to that which I originally calculated on Sunday evening!

I enclose the corrected championship chart, and also a copy of Sunday's results as I promised, and hope that you agree with my actions.

I can only apologise for the upset, and assure you that Chris Mansley is now aware of the situation, which seems to have been caused by the interpretation of what is and is not 'Standard'. It is unfortunate that pressure had not been put on the organisers earlier, as they already reclassified Alan W who was amalgamated with Class 4 on Saturday, but running with Class 6 on Sunday.

Congratulations on leading both championships, the main and the novice, and wishing you the best of sprinting for the rest of the season, and beyond!

Kind regards,

Dave Thomas

Championship Secretary

For me, this brought a satisfactory conclusion to the episode, which never repeated itself, as the class structure was improved.

I did receive a mention in the Caernarvonshire and Anglesey Motor Club official publication *Control:*

NEW MEMBER SPRINTS AWAY!
Derek Annable who was at one point leading the ANWCC sprint championship is now in a very good 8th O/A, second in class B2 in his roadgoing Honda, all to play for. Good Luck.

There was a two-week lull in the Annables' racing. Brenda and I enjoyed some pleasant days at our garage on the road to Moelfre, selling wet suits and being lazy. The island of Anglesey is a picture during the summer months and has few equals; sitting in the hot sunshine, we talked about the next Wild Bunch meeting, the weekend of 13/14 July. We hoped I would get some track time.

As it turned out, it was a less than happy weekend. I did make a checkout pass in round one on Saturday, then in round two I ran a brilliant (as others said, not me!) 7.732 at 172.41mph.

Sunday was an altogether different story. The blower popped on burnout and the car caught fire. Bruno and his fire crew pulled me out of the cockpit with such speed my right leg became trapped for a fraction of a second, causing torn muscles.

I was lucky I only received a sore leg, it could have been worse. Methanol burns with a near invisible blue flame, no smoke, you could be alight and not know it until the heat melts the cockpit. Thank God Brenda was in the pits and didn't see the controlled panic on the start line.

It was four weeks to the next race meeting, which would give us time to prepare the Camaro for the big one at York Raceway.

The weeks flew by and now it was time to leave for York Dragway. The Honda would be contesting the Northern Drag Racing Championship and the Hot Rod Challenge, while the Camaro was entered in the American Super Stock Series on the Sunday. John Turner had agreed to drive the car up from Wales early on race morning and in time for the first round in qualifying. The Travel Inn at Goole had been chosen for our two-night stay as it had better access for Brenda's wheelchair, also the restaurant was in the main building, so now she could join me for breakfast.

Saturday consisted of two sessions of qualifying. The Honda settled down to mid-15 seconds, with my reaction times .623. End of day's racing, goodbyes said, it was back to the Travel Inn for an early evening meal. As we were finishing our meal, the Murtys and Graham walked in. They didn't see us, being deeply engrossed in their conversation. Never mind, my wife was feeling tired and wanted to retire for the night.

The weather was kind to us on Sunday and John Turner arrived on time with the Camaro. Ten minutes later, Super Stock were called out. My first run with the Camaro was a 14.548/94mph. Now I had to change cars, it was the Hot Rod Challenge, and the Honda performed well. Time for lunch, during which time there was a show and shine parade by custom cars.

Everybody was now ready for some serious racing, first out were Street ET, eight cars in all. The Honda was on a flyer, a win for me. No time to go to the pits, the cars were lining up for the Hot Rod Challenge, which was a heads up race, the quickest car wins. With a 15-second car against a 12-second car, I lost.

After a bit of a breather, I was called out with the Camaro for the first round of the Super Stock. But there was no win for me as the car broke on the line, having thrown a blower belt. The spare belt was fitted, then John Turner drove the car back to Anglesey.

The second round of elimination for Street ET with the Honda was a breakout, marking the end of my racing for the weekend – a very expensive weekend. Two cars entered, petrol for 1000 miles, 500 miles for each car, plus hotel expenses, total cost £600. That's what motorsport is about, if you can't afford it, don't get involved.

My disappointment was overcome by my excitement, because on Saturday I was going to take part in my first ever hillclimb at Scammonden Dam. Now I shall pass you over to the Pendle District Motor Club:

WELCOME
Welcome to Pendle District Motor Club's annual Hillclimb at Scammonden Dam, a counter in 2002 for 3 regional and 1 motorsport group Hillclimb/ sprint championships.

May we wish you a safe and enjoyable days motorsport, and as with all 'Pendle' events, if you have a query/question, please do not hesitate to contact an event official, and we will endeavour to sort the problem.

This is a sensitive venue for both noise and access. We would request that you park your vehicle/trailer as directed and try to keep all access ways free for non motorsport users of the area. Thank you for being considerate. Please ensure that your vehicle(s) are locked at all times with valuables out of sight.

Please remember to take your litter home.

Scammonden Dam Hillclimb
2002 represents the 37th anniversary of the opening of Scammonden Dam as a speed Hillclimb venue. The short but tricky hill has long been regarded by competitors as a significant challenge where a good time depends on achieving the perfect balance of car control to maximise use of power. Indeed, until the early 80s, the hill was regarded as sufficiently difficult to be included in one of the National Hillclimb Championships, and was regularly visited by the top British Hillclimbers. Now it is mainly

used for club level events, many of which are rounds in a number of Northern Championships for the club competitor.

Over the years, Scammonden has seen many exciting incidents, not the least being the 1975 outright hill record setting of Roy Lane, many times winner of the British Hill Climb Championship. In his five-litre Chevrolet powered McRae GM1 single-seater racing car, he achieved a time of 21.97 seconds, this represents an average speed of more than 50mph – no mean feat from a standing start, despite spinning just after the finish and narrowly missing his own and other tow vehicles parked in the paddock! Even though none of the cars here can match the awesome 500+bhp Roy had in 1975, chassis development, particularly the use of high power, low weight motorcycle engines, modern materials, such as carbon fibre, Kevlar etc and much improved racing tyres has led to cars with a power-to-weight ratio greater than 500bhp/ton. They have a much greater capability to transfer the power to the road.

Although no one here today will match the time of Roy Lane, some of the faster cars should be able to get within one or two seconds.

(reprinted by kind permission of Mid Cheshire Motor Racing Club).

The weather was very hot, it being August. Because there were only 27 cars competing, Rod Brereton, the secretary of the meeting, had arranged for everybody to have eight timed runs. Off we went in convoy down the hill (track), all 27 of us. I soon found out what a speed hill climb is! My turn came and went. I got massive wheel spin on the start line, selected all the wrong gears and crossed the finishing line bottom of my class. The only way to improve my times was to find an expert and flatter him.

Luck was with me. Bernard Collins was sitting in his Mallock U2 MK20 single-seater race car and he was excited with his last timed run. This gave me the opportunity to say, 'You went very quick around the first corner. It was so skilful.'

Bernard replied, 'Do you think so?'

'Yes, I do. I'm a novice. I shall never master this short track, I might as well go home.'

'What are you driving Derek?'

'A Honda Integra', I replied.

Now Bernard started talking me through the corners, you do this, then that, don't lift off on the last corner, hold your revs and power through. Thank you sir, I have enjoyed talking with an expert.

My second timed run was two seconds quicker. All afternoon I worked on what Bernard had told me and in the last timed run I managed a 30.97. This made me the winner of Class 2 for standard production cars over 1400cc to 2000cc. The whole day had been enjoyable and worth every penny. I took the trophy home and showed it to Brenda, who was also pleased.

My wife's mind was on her TM dragster. Doug Bond would be racing it in the Falls Nationals at Shakespeare County Raceway at the end of the week. We had decided to stay home and hope for the best, and let Heidi and John keep us informed of the results.

Back came the results: Doug Bond left the line well in the dragster, but unfortunately a rod exited the block, slowing down to a 9.10/90 – another engine gone. When would Martin and Doug get it together and start to pay back the money spent? They had one more chance left this season, the European Finals at Santa Pod, then they had to hand the car back to Brenda – the end of their use of the TM dragster.

Well, here I am back at Anglesey track to compete in the Lancs and Cheshire/MG Car Club sprint, with the troubles of the last meeting behind us. At this point I was leading both Novice and Overall Championships.

A quick look at the entry list, I should have a win on Saturday and runner-up on Sunday. The only man who could stop me winning the Novice Championship was Bob Beadon who was racing his Vauxhall Astra in Class 5. For some reason, before racing, he was moved to Class 17. On reflection, the move from Class 5 to 17 made it hard for Bob to get maximum points.

Saturday morning was perfect for racing; warm with a slight breeze which stopped the tarmac overheating. The drivers' briefing over, everybody was looking forward to a good day's racing; we all went through the two practices with ease. My times were 123.60 and 121.63. This wasn't good enough, I was becoming lazy; Karen Williams had run some good times and was within a second of mine. Although she was in a different class to me, our times counted towards extra points.

Now we were into timed runs – I won my class with a 119.42 run, Karen Williams came third in her class with a 121.54.

The meeting over for the day, the secretary of the meeting came over to me and apologised for the cockup (his words) at the last meeting, when they had allowed a rally car in my class. This was new to me; in drag racing, no one ever makes a public apology for club and track mistakes. The band of brothers I was racing with are gentlemen and will always have my respect.

Being a late start on Sunday, Brenda was coming to watch me race, so she said. But being a drag racing nut, I doubt she will watch me race! Today, my class would be dominated by Dave Hensley, who was driving a Peugeot XSI, and would win the class. It would be better for me to try and improve my times.

During the lunch break, I left my wife sitting in the café having some lunch and went walkabout. There he was standing by the Porsche May 1 – Jeff May, the MSA steward of my Santa Pod days; he was in charge of the sprint for the MSA. This man has been Mr Drag Racing for nearly thirty years, from the early days when the American teams came over to race at Santa Pod. We talked drag racing for nearly half an hour, then came, 'Derek, your dragster with Doug Bond as pilot has had a bad year, what is your problem?'

'The Whipple blower Brenda and I bought for the car has destroyed three engines', I told him. 'I hope Martyn Hannis can set up the engine to take the extra power. A good result at the European Finals at the Pod will make up for a bad year.'

'Derek, I wish you luck today with your wife's Honda and with the dragster next week.'

'Thank you Jeff, I have enjoyed talking drag racing with you, and when you retire from the MSA, I wish you a happy and long life.'

Out I went for the last timed run, my quickest of the day at 118.07, which kept me ahead of Karen Williams with a cushion of eight points. Bob Beadon was three points ahead of me. The Aintree sprint in six days' time would be the decider, all to play for. Brenda and I left the track and headed home.

The Liverpool Motor Club was in charge of this sprint which was marking 100 years of northern motorsport and the club's centenary year. They were all there, Ron Hunt, John Harden, Bob Chester, the secretary of the meeting Jim Bebby, chief scrutineer Chris Mansley, medical officer Rick Bate, also Ian Johnson, Alan Smith, Lawrence and April Powell, with back-up provided by RAF Rescue and St John's Ambulance.

Last but not least the man with the microphone, Mark Richardson. At signing on, you leave a note with comments for Mark, this was mine: 'Liverpool MC 100 years! Murray Walker may be Mr Formula One, you Mark Richardson are our Mr Aintree Sprint. Thank you for all the kind words during the 2002 spring season. Please return next year.'

Now I shall talk you through the circuit. Leaving the start, preferably without too much wheel spin, there is a 250-metre straight before the first corner, a sharp left-hander called Country Corner. 230 metres further on is Village Corner, a banked right-hander which, I am told, has to be taken just right to get a slingshot out along the 450-metre long Valentine's Way. Beechers is next and can be very intimidating as it starts quite tightly but quickly opens up. It lasts for nearly 450 metres, and even the slowest cars exit at 75mph, myself in excess of 90mph. If one gets it right, you gain extra speed to take you on the Railway Straight; the finish line is halfway along the straight; by now you have reached 110mph plus. Total length – 1847 metres from start to finish.

Brenda wasn't with me, having broken her arm. Our son Mark was looking after her. I travelled down early, leaving home at 6am. Driving into the pits I could see George Povey and Bob Jones were already pitted. Before I could switch the engine off, Mark Le Riche opened the driver's door, 'Derek I have made modifications to my Toyota MR2 MK1; you will see some quick times from me today.'

'I will come and look at your car Mark, but first I must have my car passed by the scrutineer.'

I fixed the timing strut, now where were the race numbers I made last night? Oh no, they were on the kitchen table at home. Panic, I can't race. Up and down the pits I went, asking the other drivers if they had any spare numbers – none had.

Sitting on the bonnet of my car, eyes looking down to the ground, I was in complete despair. The driver pitted next to me was Stephen Crawley and he was on his mobile phone. Turning to me, he said, 'Derek I have got my wife out of bed, she has agreed to go to our workshop in Bolton and in half an hour there will be numbers for your car. Why don't you go and have some breakfast?'

'Thank you Stephen.'

'That's OK Derek, we young ones have to look after old drivers like you', he said laughing.

While eating, I checked the entry list. There were 12 cars in my class, all quicker than me except Mark Le Riche and Karen Williams. Although Bob Beadon wasn't racing, I needed seven points or more to take number one position in the Novice Championship.

On returning to my car I saw Stephen Crawley had fixed on the numbers. Now it was call-out for the practice run. A good launch, everything felt good and there it was on the finish line timing board – 62.08. Now I had to wait for the results to be posted – good, I was fourth fastest. Second practice run, I had dropped to seventh fastest. What could I do? The other drivers were improving on their times but not me.

It was lunch break, so I homed in on George Povey and Bob Jones who were running nearly four seconds quicker than me and started asking questions. What speeds were they reaching? How do you take Beechers Bend? They said they were having the same problem at Beechers, not able to sight the entry to the corner. How do they take Village Corner? George said he didn't lift off and went round it at 85–90mph. I said I braked, and didn't increase my speed before the exit.

Both said, 'You are doing it wrong Derek, aim for the cinder path on the left-hand side of the corner, keep your speed up, the camber at mid-corner will stop you sliding onto the grass.'

The call-out came for everybody's timed runs, three in all. It would take a brave man to power through Village, but following George and Bob's advice, I tried it. Success! My time was 59.46 secs, 110mph – I had broken the 60-second barrier. This placed me fifth fastest, but still the others were going faster every time. I ended the day in seventh position and with it the points needed to win the Novice Championship. The only person who could confirm this was Dave Thomas, our championship secretary.

While checking the times of various cars, one factor stood out way above others and this was the timing differences in shared cars. Take the Lotus Elise, for example, shared by Alan Clarke and Karen Williams. Alan's time was a new class record of 52.26 secs, while Karen could only manage a slow 63.34 secs. Given an expert sprint driver, my Honda Integra was capable of a 55-second pass.

I said farewell to George Povey and Bob Jones, who had made my sub-60-second pass possible. Stephen Crawley waved as he left for home. The many modifications Mark Le Riche had made to his car gave him his best time to date – 64.08 secs. David Barrow thanked me for my support all year, he would stick at it with his Saab Sonnet MK2 850cc road car. Now I must phone Brenda and let her know I would be home in a couple of hours. As I switched the phone off, a gentleman came over to me. 'Are you Derek Annable?'

'Yes', I said.

'I'm Mark Richards, thank you for your comment sheet. Yours and one other were the only ones worth reading.'

He then asked how long I had been racing and other questions. He was surprised by my answers.

I then made reference to the Whiteheads, Barry and Eve, who race an RBS 5c (1074cc) car. When I said the other drivers called him the reverend, Mark spluttered, 'What? The reverend? Well Derek that's news to me, I don't think Barry knows he has a nickname.'

Mark's last words to me were, 'It has been an honour talking to one of the older drivers who is still active in every type of motorsport.'

As I left the Aintree track, I could see Alan Clarke and Karen Williams holding hands. Would it be a husband and wife team next year? Two hours' driving along the A55, and I should be home. It had been one hell of a year in the Sprint and Hill Climb Championship, with some new friends made.

At long last, there was some good news. Our car, with Doug Bond behind the wheel, had repaid us in kind. *Custom Car* reported on the FIA Finals at Santa Pod Raceway, with the following for the Top Methanol dragster class:

> Doug ran some quick times all day, showing the new Whipple super-charger was producing the power the team had promised all year.
>
> In the Shell team's race against Dave Wilson, Doug pulled all the stops out and ran his first five-second pass (5.97).

Brenda and I say well done Martyn and Doug.

That was the good news, now the bad news. Dave Wilson had lent Martyn Hannis a set of rods for our engine, now he wanted them back, which meant I didn't have a car to race at the next Wild Bunch meeting. I had made one pass in our car. That wasn't good enough. They had had the use of it and blown away three engines. A quick check of the VAT receipts for the year 1997/98, and there it was, the invoice from GP1 of Denver, Colorado and the details of the rods required to rebuild the engine.

Now it was up to me. As it was 8pm UK time, GP1's office would be open for orders. A very helpful gentleman in Denver took the order, said it would take one week to make the rods, then delivery by UPS express an extra three days. The parts would be in Martyn Hannis's workshop one week before the Wild Bunch meeting at the Pod. My MasterCard had worked wonders plus half an hour on the phone.

To take my mind off the dragster, I decided the Northern National at York Dragway was worth the journey. It was a low-key meeting, Brenda stayed at home, and I had a miserable day and wished I'd stayed home. Surely things can only get better.

It was two weeks to the Wild Bunch fall shoot-out at Santa Pod. I would be leaving Brenda at home. Martyn Hannis should have the new rods for the engine next week. I'll phone him and check. These were my thoughts as I was reading an article about something which happened in September 1943. I cleared my head and wrote the following letter to the SPRC secretary:

Dear Sir,

I have a formal request. Could you ask the Committee of the SPRC and Santa Pod Raceway if two minutes could be set aside on Sunday 29 September at the National Finals to honour all the pilots of the P51 Mustang fighter plane which protected the US Bombers based at Poddington Air Base during 1943/45 on their raids over Germany.

The plane was American, the engine British, the combination produced a decisive weapon. In the USA there are many bomber pilots who owe their life to the courage of the P51 Mustang fighter plane pilots.

The National Finals at Santa Pod 28/29 September 2002 could be our part and the bomber pilots' thanks to their comrades who are long gone but not forgotten.

Yours sincerely

Derek

The boys from Cheltenham phoned, the dragster was ready to race and would be at Santa Pod Friday evening. Good. Thank you both. I should have some track time at this meeting. I said farewell to Brenda and drove off in the direction of Wellingborough.

Thank goodness the weather on Saturday morning was dry. Amos Meekins passed the dragster for racing. Now there was a call from the tower. The race director wanted me to sort out the times I was to run with the car. I asked Darren Prentice what times he was going to allow me to run. He was generous, 'Derek you know the car, whatever time you are comfortable with'. So we agreed that I would keep to an eight second.

Who was at the bottom of the control tower stairs, but Jon Cross who I hadn't seen for months. We talked about the minute's silence to be held on Sunday for the USAF squadron who were based at the village of Poddington – this track was one of their runways.

In the Wild Bunch call-out, there were only six cars. Because of problems with the track, we were held up in the fire-up road. This brought the fans around the dragster and for half an hour I answered their questions. Now the cars were moving forward.

I was paired with Connor. For some reason known only to him, he shot into the lane I was going to stage in. I had good burnout and started to reverse back to the start line, but, oh dear, Connor had staged. The rules state, you wait for your opponent to complete his burnout before moving forward into pre-stage. Why don't the young racers read the rule book?

Down came the start lights, amber, amber, amber, green. Off Connor went, he pulled a good light, .506, mine was .700. Never mind, I passed him at the 60ft, my eighth mile was 5.277/141.91 with an ET 8.189/156.66, Connor's was 10.496/126.40 – the end of the first session. I left the crew checking the engine and went to get something to eat.

Lunch over, it was time for my second qualifying run. Oh dear, my opponent was Connor again. This time I managed to take the right-hand lane. A good burnout. Doug brought me back over the rubber I had laid down. Connor had staged again. When will the young man learn some restraint and wait for the faster cars to go through the set of rules of engagement? I had dialled in 8.00 and run a 8.294/167.83, which was 42mph quicker than Connor. Martyn was pleased with the eighth mile times on both runs, an average 5.30/140mph.

End of day's racing and now the short drive back to the Travelodge and my favourite meal, pâté and toast, plaice and chips, half a bottle of white wine. The phone went, it was Brenda, 'How quick did you go today Derek?' I gave her all the results and told her about Connor. She said, 'Stop whingeing Derek, go out tomorrow and run a seven-second pass. It will be a record for a Wild Bunch car at Santa Pod. It should stand for years.'

Sunday morning dawned damp and cold, with overcast skies. After a quick breakfast, I changed into my race gear and went off to the Pod. The running order showed Wild Bunch were out at 1.01pm, after the one minute's silence. The club had agreed to my request.

The first round of eliminations showed my opponent was Paul Murphy, a real gentleman from Rochdale. This would be a real challenge. As his car was a 12.40 second/103mph, I would be waiting on the start line for nearly four seconds before I could launch, and he would be a third of the way down the track. To catch and pass him, I would have to better my existing eighth mile record of 5.120/150mph which I had set at Shakespeare County Raceway.

Now John Price read out my letter to the thousands of spectators, as if he had written it. Then the one minute's silence. That over, the Wild Bunch cars started to move off down the fire-up road. Paul Murphy chose the right-hand lane and we would be the last of the Wild Bunch cars to race.

After a short burnout, Doug brought me back to the start line with his usual smile and gave me the thumbs up. Paul Murphy showed what a pro he is, we pre-staged and staged together, the go light came up and off he went. I started counting, one, two, three, four, all the time concentrating on the lights. On came the green, I hit the throttle and side-stepped the clutch, 8000 revs, hit the second gear button, bloody hell did the speed pick up, the vibration, had I got tyre shake? Keep the throttle down, now the car was pulling to the right and towards the other car which was 50 yards in front of me, so now I hit third gear, and the car went straight again. As I passed Paul, I lifted off and we crossed the finish line together.

It seemed ages before the crew car came down for me, and when it did

Martyn had a big smile from ear to ear, a 7.732 pass. Brenda would be pleased! Also my timing ticket showed I had broken my previous record for the eighth mile, with a 5.013/157mph – no other car except Dave Wilson had bettered that today.

This was reported in *Drag Racing News:*

> Derek ran 8 second passes all day, then in his last run threw his dial-in out of the window, blasting a 7.732-second pass. When will this old man of motorsport calm down.

I also picked up the Best Dragster/Radical sport prize for my efforts and the whole team were pleased with the runs I had made.

I thanked Martyn Hannis, Doug Bond, Chris and Claire, and left for home before the meeting finished. When I arrived home, Brenda was over-joyed at the way the car had run.

We all get surprises and ours was a letter from Claire and Chris:

> Dear Derek and Brenda,
>
> Just writing to say we hope Brenda's arm will soon be better and that she will be feeling well!
>
> Also, congratulations on the trophy and the 7.73 run, Derek! Very well done!
>
> The good news for us was that Chris won the event (he beat B-Sting in the final when Paul broke out!). He also got a trophy from SPRC which was really nice, and was selected 'Best slingshot' (only 2 there!) plus 'Best Appearing Team', so we had a very good weekend and enjoyed it. So hopefully they'll invite us back next year!
>
> Bye for now, and take care.
>
> Best wishes
>
> Claire and Chris

This really touched us both. Chris and Claire are lovely people. They seem to relate to Brenda's problems with her health and pain. Maybe their parents went through what Brenda is suffering.

True to form, I had set my sights on the All-rounders Championship. This required three disciplines, sprints, hill climbs and autotests. The Bury Auto-mobile Club were running one on 27 October, so I entered, and back came my final instructions and race number.

Luck was with me, as having travelled from North Wales on Saturday evening, I missed the gales which closed both bridges from Anglesey early on Sunday morning. This meant I was the only member of the Caernarvonshire and Anglesey Motor Club as Lee Matthews and others were unable to drive off Anglesey.

Eve Fisher was in charge of signing on; that over, I was given my Class D2 timing card and test area sheet. The club marshals were having problems setting out the marker cones. Strong gusts of wind kept blowing them around the car park. Also the rain was lashing down. Being new to autotests, I couldn't make sense of test area A. There must have been 20 red cones in that area, and over the hedge in test area B, a further 15 cones.

The Minis of Goodlad, Griffiths and Preston were off first, followed by an assortment of Fiestas and Novas. I held back, trying to remember which cones were driven around first and then the order from then on. I had made the mistake of not walking the course, very few did as the rain was bucketing down. Now it was my turn. I went off from the start in first gear at about 5mph. I was around the first three cones, then it was up to and around the next two, carry on into the garage, reverse out – I was gaining confidence. Then it happened. After driving around the island at the top of the car park, what met me was unbelievable, a mass of red cones. Which was the first cone I had to drive around? My mind went blank, so up went my arm and I drove straight across the course to the start line. WT was written on my timing ticket.

There were still tests B and C to go through. I would never master this autotest so time to call it a day and go home. After a talk with Gordon Holmes, who was an expert and drove a Westfield, it was agreed with the clerk of the course that I would be allowed to use test area A until I mastered it, then they would allow me to go home.

As my first run was a WT, I needed a time. This time, after watching the other drivers for half an hour, out I went. Slowly around every cone I drove, no mistakes this time; stopping across the finishing line, the starter gave me my time – 104.4 seconds. My next run was 98.4, which gave me the confidence I needed so now let's join the queue of other drivers waiting at the start line.

My turn. Off I went, sliding the car around the cones, up and into the garage, reverse out, faster and faster I went, now in second gear, shot around the last cone and over the finishing line. The timekeeper said, 'It makes all the difference when you know where you are going', and gave me my time – 93.6 seconds – very respectable. It was now the end of the day's racing. After thanking Mr Bray, the clerk of the course, and Eve Fisher for an enjoyable couple of hours, I went racing off back home to Anglesey, well pleased with the results.

When I told Brenda about my day at the Bury autotest, she said, 'No more autotests for you and the Honda. A special car is required.' My wife was right. You need to build a special car for autotests or alter a small car to take the course, if you want quick times.

It was the end of October so no more racing for me. Brenda and I had bought the Barry Sheavills' winning Top Alcohol dragster in 1996 so I could race Top Alcohol in the UK. This didn't happen until five years later when my patience was rewarded, thanks to Martyn Hannis and Doug Bond. My dream in 1996 had been to run a six in the ex-Sheavills' car. Maybe in 2003 this would come true.

Looking back on my years in motorsport, I have competed in twelve disciplines. How many other drivers have achieved that? I wish to explode the myth that motorsport is a rich man's sport. My income in 1950 was £500 per year, and by 2003 it was £15,000, so I am no rich boy. Every year Brenda and I set aside £3,000 for our joint venture in motorsport, and we try to keep to this budget. We control our spending, never take holidays, because motorsport is our holiday. This people can't understand.

One evening during 2002, Brenda was having coffee with Graham Beckwith, when he said, 'We in drag racing can't understand what Derek is trying to prove racing the dragster. It would be easier for me to race the car. He'll never run a six or seven.' Maybe, but Brenda and I have a passion for motorsport and will help anybody to go quicker than me. Some years ago, one racer gleefully said to his wife, 'I have beaten the Camaro!' Good for him, I had brought out the will to win in him, and so to me his remark was a compliment.

When I was at the Santa Pod meeting on 28/29 September 2002, Claire Meaddows was over the moon because of the way the Wild Bunch were treated at the Festival of Speed at Goodwood.

'Derek, I thought of you all those years ago. Chris and I were treated like royalty, we were taken to the big house, and Lord Marsh came over to talk to us!'

'Fifty years ago his father would have brought you a cup of China tea.'

'Stop it Derek, the whole scene was marvellous, the cars, the people of yesteryear. Jenson Button had all the girls around him.'

'Claire, one day drag racing will be like that. What would you say if all the girls were around Chris?'

'Derek, I wouldn't like it.'

Thank you Lord Marsh and others for asking the Wild Bunch to the Festival. Sidney Allard would have been pleased that his work to bring drag racing to the UK all those years ago was being rewarded.

The year 2002 was my most successful year in motorsport, far eclipsing any of the years I raced Allard sports cars and Kieft single-seaters back in the early 1950s. This year I raced in four disciplines and gained many trophies – the challenge was there. Meanwhile, the voices around me were saying, 'What the hell does that fool think he is playing at.' I didn't go out and race to silence these jibes, I went out to enjoy myself, win or lose.

One racer's father came over to me and said, 'Derek, you haven't brought the TM dragster out many times this year.'

'No, I haven't. Martyn and Doug have had problems with the engine set-up because of the Whipple supercharger.'

Then he paid me the greatest compliment ever, saying, 'When Doug drives your Shell dragster, I carry on working on my son's car. Then at the end of Doug's run, I check his time and speed, end of story. But when you are driving the car, I stop work, go up into the stands and watch you from the time the engine is fired up until you cross the finishing line.'

I said, 'I don't believe it. Why?'

'Derek, I shall tell you why. I know your age, but you are in complete control of the car, not like some drivers. When you reach top speed, it's as if you're saying, "There you are gentlemen, you will never stop me racing."'

I stood there, looked him straight in the eyes, took his hand and said, 'Thank you'. To have praise from one's peers makes all the effort and disappointments worthwhile. We are judged by our gentle kindness to others and any pleasure that comes from it. The car has 2500hp in the engine behind me. I handle it with kindness, it rewards me and the spectators welcome this, saying to themselves, if he can do it, so can we.

I was well satisfied with the year 2002. One more to go, then it would be time for me to fade away and leave it to others to please the many followers of motorsport.

The year's results:

ANWCC Novice Sprint Championship	– 1st overall
ANWCC Novice Sprint Championship Class B2	– winner
ANWCC Newcomer Sprint Championship	– 1st overall
ANWCC Sprint Championship	– 2nd in class
Basil Davenport Memorial Trophy	– 1st in class
Chester MC Sprint 16 June 2002	– Runner up Class A2
MGCC (NW centre)Ty Croes Sprint 1 September	– 1st in class
Pendle MC Hillclimb	– 1st in class
York Dragway, Street Shoot-out	– winner

Wild Bunch Trophies

Fastest MPH	– 172.41mph backed up with 167.83mph
Best ET	– 7.732 backed up with exactly 7.732 again!

Wild Bunch Meeting, Santa Pod (Record)

Fastest MPH	– 167.83mph
Best ET	– 7.732

also Best Dragster: 'One hell of a year!'

Chris Hartnell, seen here with his team, collecting the Don Garlits Spirit of Drag Racing trophy (© Wild Bunch)

'Crazy Chris' Hartnell and Roy Wilding on the start line (© Derek Annable)

Carla and Rick, Heaven & Hell (© Derek Annable)

Santa Pod, Main Event: Smax (© Custom Car)

Avon Park: Bill Weston with his 632ci Mustang Pro Mod (© Custom Car)

Avon Park: Wild Bunch entrants Martin Holgate in 'Paranoia' and Steve Goode in 'Wobble' in an all-Jag Altered final (© Custom Car)

Avon Park: Angie Wilding in a rear-engined dragster (© Roy Wilding)

'Crazy Chris' (© Custom Car)

Santa Pod: The winner –
Malta's Manty Bugeja went
home with the island's first
major trophy in Top Methanol
Dragster (© Custom Car)

Santa Pod 2001: Doug
(© Martyn Hannis)

Above and right: *Tim*
Blakemore, Funny Bike
(© Derek Annable)

Avon Park 2001: Doug
(© Martyn Hannis)

Avon Park 2001: Brenda
never liked Derek driving this
car – a 70-year-old man in a
3000 hp car!
(© Martyn Hannis)

Neil Midgley, Funny Bike
(© Derek Annable)

*Derek and Brenda's old Altered 'Rampage', sold to Dave Ward with a
full body fitted (© Derek Annable)*

*Avon Park: Derek Annable
(© Bill Sly)*

*2001: Chris and Claire's
car and bus
(© Wild Bunch)*

Avon Park: Angie and her dragster (© Wild Bunch)

Derek collecting awards (© Wild Bunch)

Avon Park 2002: Derek Annable, Top Methanol Dragster. The engine now produced 3000+ hp (© Martyn Hannis)

Santa Pod, 2002,
Doug at FIA Finals:
The burnout
(© Martyn Hannis)

Ray Debben
(Pro Stock Bike)
(© Derek Annable)

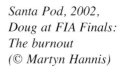

Scammonden Dam, August 2002: Hill
climb (© Steve Wilkinson)

Not Brenda's favourite dragster! She thought it
would make a widow of her. Derek was pulling 4-G
on launch, reaching 200 mph in 7 seconds from a
standing start (© Martyn Hannis)

Avon Park *(all © Bill Sly)*
Above: *Derek waiting in the fire-up road*
Right: *Burnout*
Below: *Derek*
Below right: *Derek – the launch*

Right: *Derek collecting a Wild Bunch trophy*
(© Wild Bunch)

The Anglesey track
(© Martin P. Ruddick)

CHAPTER 12

Last Chapter

This is the last chapter of my life in motorsport, or it should be. Age has nothing to do with my retirement but there is a time when we must hand over to the young ones.

The year 2003 started with the BRDC function at Nuthurst Grange. I had decided to attend the regional dinner with much apprehension; never in my fifty-plus years as a member of the club had I got this close to my contemporaries. Using the Auto Sport Show at the NEC as an excuse, I sent my cheque off to Michael Ostrournoff, the regional director of the BRDC.

Brenda said, 'Derek, you are a mountain man from Wales, you won't fit in.' Maybe I am, but when I first became a member of the BRDC, we lived in Marlow, and there are no mountains there.

It was a long haul from Anglesey, so to avoid the hold-ups on the M6 motorway I took the Chester–Shrewsbury route through Kidderminster, and then on to the M42 to Hockley Heath. I made good time and arrived at Nuthurst Grange at 12 noon. The hotel reception said my room wouldn't be ready until 2pm, so I left my luggage with them and travelled on to the NEC. Here I spent a couple of hours in the drag racing section, had some lunch and then went back to my hotel.

As the BRDC function started at 7.30pm and I am never late on the start line, I was in the bar for 7.31pm. The barman gave me a free drink and I sat there alone for over half an hour. The first to arrive weren't my generation but then things started to liven up – some older people arrived; now I could have a meaningful conversation. We talked about the first Mini car that was built and where they raced it. The bar was soon full of BRDC members and guests, most of whom had raced in the 1970s and 1980 – there wasn't one who had raced in the 1940s/50s. Michael Ostrournoff came over and introduced himself and thanked me for attending.

It was now time to go into the dining room. From the seating plan in the bar, we all found our allotted places. My fellow diners were John and Judy Morris from Berkswell, Coventry, Bob and Carol Meacham and Joan Douglas and her husband.

The meal started and I discovered I was as hungry as a horse. The little morsels put in front of me didn't fill a mountain man's appetite but I struggled on and the food was acceptable. I turned my attention to the conversation – I don't know why Carol Meacham took a liking to me; it was as if we had known each other for a lifetime. Her sister was suffering from an incurable disease and, like my wife, she was losing control of her bodily functions. My conversation switched between Carol Meacham on my left and Joan Douglas to my right. Many years ago, Joan had been a timekeeper. Now timekeepers are important people in motorsport and for a woman to be a timekeeper in the 1950s and 60s was unusual. When her husband said she had had to go through some sort of ritual and other exams because she was a woman, my response was, 'That's discrimination'. The men in charge of the RAC motorsport section were being superior – this is the way I see things.

The main course over, now it was time for the coffee and petits fours. Now the guest of honour launched into his speech with regard to the club's profit and loss account. When the debate was handed over to the members, one gentleman came up with an idea close to my heart; he rumbled on saying that Silverstone could become Disneyland.

Bob Meacham and I discussed the pros and cons of the Welsh's hatred of the English throughout history. He agreed the language should be supported by all, but some Welsh speakers' vindictive attitude didn't further their cause. By this time everybody had left the dining room, so I said goodbye to Bob and Carol, thanked Michael Ostrournoff for a most enjoyable evening and returned to my room.

Both the room and the hotel were sumptuous; a room for one night usually cost £150, but having booked every room in the hotel, the BRDC's cost to us members was only £48 including breakfast – a pretty good deal.

Breakfast the next morning was perfect. I had the dining room to myself as the other guests were still in bed. I thanked the hotel staff and drove home without stopping, being completely satisfied with my stay at the hotel.

The next day Brenda asked, 'Did you enjoy meeting the other members of the BRDC?' I said 'Yes and no. Captains of industry aren't my type. These people are politically correct all the time, give me a man or woman who uses a four-letter word from time to time and challenges me to a joust at dawn – winner takes all – and for the ladies, a dual with pistols!'

My life was being ruled by motor club functions; the ANWCC presentation of awards for the 2002 championship was to take place at the Holiday Inn in Runcorn on Saturday evening, 8 February, so I booked a single room again as Brenda wasn't well enough to attend. This was the second of three functions I would be attending on my own; it was lonely without Brenda, my crew chief.

Since crossing the borders from drag racing to compete in speed sprints and hill climbs, I had settled in and was up for two awards: winner of the ANWCC Novice Sprint Championship and 2nd Class B2 in the ANWCC Sprint Championship – now I was classed as an expert!

The evening was to commence with a buffet at 7.30pm prompt. The awards covered stage and forest rally, road and historic rally, autotests, trails, sprints and hill climbs. My disciplines were only a small part of the whole and I would be a lone ranger on the night. The Caernarvonshire and Anglesey MC (my club) were overall club champions, but all the members were rally drivers and none I knew. Never mind, I found a large unoccupied table on the fringe of the dance floor and sat down to eat.

A young man came over and asked if he and his friends could share my table; if I had known who he was I wouldn't have been so quick to say 'Yes'. It was Kevin Roberts and the prizewinners from Bala Motor Club. Our table turned into a Max Boyce comedy show, with jokes flying backwards and forwards. When I told them I lived in Anglesey, one elderly gentleman said he knew my daughter – did he heck, all he knew about Anglesey was the Amlwch roundabout. Then the jokes turned to Russian tractors as one of the party was a young farmer – why did the farmers buy them as nobody in North Wales knew how to repair them? The sport of drag racing also came under fire; 'Do you drag race, Derek?' Then his friend said, 'What sort of clothes do you wear?' and the table rocked with laughter.

The trophies on our table were a sight to behold and became the focus of the evening. The ANWCC Club Championship was a close call, the C&AMC winning by seven points. My points from sprints and hill climbs were the deciding factor and because of this Lee Mathews, the club vice-chairman (who had received an engraved glass crystal decanter with a set of goblets on behalf of the club), came over and added a goblet to my collection. This was a very nice thought. I had a very enjoyable evening, which was followed some days later with the following insert in the *ANWCC News* of the 2002 Championship rundown:

It was a close call. Young at heart Derek Annable gave the Club valuable points from his sprints and hill climbs which tipped the balance in our favour.

Unfortunately, Brenda wasn't well enough to enjoy my report on the weekend's merrymaking. In fact, the rest of the month was very low key except for the PDRC dinner and AGM at the Bradford Novatel Hotel on the 22 February. This weekend was important to me, as arrangements had to be made with the hotel for our forthcoming golden wedding anniversary party on 4 July. Marjorie Lyons had provided me with much needed information which would help keep the cost of the function to budget.

The AGM started on time with only a few stalwarts in attendance. In my opinion, considering the hard work the committee put into the club, attendance was poor. The meeting was chaired by Alan Perkins and, much to his credit, all business was completed on time.

It was a shame Brenda wasn't well enough to travel; this meant I had two tickets for the dinner! Never mind, it gave me the chance to sample the full menu on offer, which would allow me to choose the best for our party.

When the meal was over, I retired to the lounge with my bottle of wine. The prize giving was well underway when suddenly Ian Armatage came into the bar, grabbed my hand and said, 'Derek, you are wanted.' He led me back to the dining room where Graham Beckwith announced that I had won an award for Services to Motorsport – the Rescue Unit Award for 2002. Past winners included John Ledster, 1993; Phil Evans, 1996; Steve Horne, 1997; and others including Mick Bettison and Graham Beckwith. Roy and Angie Wilding presented the award to me; it was a great honour and marked the end of a smashing weekend.

My mailbag was becoming full of entry forms for this year's racing. Our Honda Integra would have a heavy workload; it was good to know the car makers in Japan made reliable cars.

Although I hate autotests, these are needed to enter the ANWCC Allrounder Championship. You must have results from three disciplines, so I entered our car in the Jon Mackenzie Autotest at Curborough sprint course on Sunday 9 March.

With high expectations, I left home at five o'clock on Sunday morning, with a 150-mile journey ahead of me – Lichfield being my target. I made good time, due more to the roads being quiet than my navigation – having made a left turn instead of a right, I was heading north towards Derby, however a local farmer came to my rescue.

The pit area was empty when I arrived and this gave me time to walk the course before I took the car to the scrutineers and signed on. It was an exhausting day, I couldn't master the many tests and our Honda wasn't built to take part in autotests. The clerk of the course, seeing I was a novice, agreed that if I completed 8 of the 16 tests and mastered tests A and B, there wouldn't be any penalty points against me.

By late afternoon, I had mastered tests A and B – the driving side of the test – but my times were outside the limit allowed. This put me in last place, 54th, and third in my class, which had three cars competing in it.

No more autotests for me, or so I thought, but being a foolish man (which my wife reminded me!), I had entered the car in the Thistlethwaite Tyres Autotest at the end of April in Bolton. Never mind, things could be worse.

At this time, the war in the Middle East was happening and I felt compelled to write the following letter to our prime minister, Tony Blair:

Dear Prime Minister   24-03-03

Stand firm, your course is right and we the older generation give you our support.

If it takes a thousand years evil will be defeated, your destiny was to lead the British people into the twenty-first century and show faint hearts the world must be cleansed of despots who destroy the fabric of God's given life in the family.

Sir, be patient, our cousins the other side of the pond will follow your lead when the conflict is over and you, Sir, will balance and unite our European partners through your leadership as their president. This will galvanize the north Atlantic treaty into a force for the good of all on this planet.

Yours sincerely

Derek Annable

This was quickly followed by my second letter, both of which were acknowledged by his secretary:

Dear Prime Minister   28-03-03

Here we are, a week on in the conflict our troops (British) have given their lives to rid the world of the despot Saddam Hussein.

History repeats itself; I refer you to an article in the *Daily Mail*, Saturday March 1, 2003. 'Master of Genocide' by Christopher Hudson.

The world was lucky Laureni Beria who was in charge of the Soviet Union atomic programme held back on the first test of the hydrogen bomb in 1952 (before the Americans could test theirs).

This demonic figure (Josef Stalin) who ruled the Soviet Union from 1924 to 1953 wouldn't have hesitated in using his weapon of mass destruction, neither would Saddam Hussein when the time was right.

Isn't it strange there was a forecast of the coming of the second Messiah and it would be two thousand years after the first? No, Prime Minister, you aren't the second Jesus, but God in someway has channelled his will for the human race through a man as humble as the young Tony Blair and set him on a course to rid the world of evil and Anti Christ (Mohammed and Jesus Christ are equal prophets).

This burden weighs heavily on you, but all around you is a divine light, few people can see it, but it is there. I am seventy two years old, which is only a second in cosmic time, but in my short life I have met and followed the fortunes of many great men and women. You, Sir, are unusual having seen through the mist and been chosen to lead from the front and set the American and British people on a crusade not equalled in history and beyond.

This is the beginning of a new enlightenment with the fusions of all religions to bring about a peaceful time for the world in which many will look back and say I was prepared to give my life knowing right will prevail.

Sir, if you read my letter from the heart I shall rejoice, God be with you.

Yours sincerely

Derek Annable

Letters despatched, now it was time to return to my destiny in racing and prepare the Honda Integra for my next race meeting. This was a round of the ANWCC Championship and the Chester Motor Club's Championship at the Three Sisters racing circuit, Wigan. These were being staged by the Longton and District Motor Club.

I must be mad. My class had to be ready for scrutineering at 7.30am, which meant leaving home at 5am. Last year I was allowed to race as a novice but having won this championship, I was now classed as an expert! However, as I was still running novice times, I had to work hard to improve my times.

The Three Sisters racing circuit is a national kart track with a restricted width. It took me back to the days when I raced Coopers and Kieft single-seaters at Brands Hatch in the early 1950s.

Our class record is held by Alan Clarke driving a Lotus Elise 1800cc, time 50.83. This young man had spent megabucks to improve the performance of his Lotus. If I had carried out this upgrade on my Honda, it would have been moved up a class, so why hadn't Alan's Lotus? The answer is because within the MSA Blue Book the modifications were allowed for his Lotus but not my Honda. Make the best of it, Alan, one day the rules will be changed and the Lotus Elise will have to race in a class of its own. This will give out-and-out road cars a chance to have some tight racing.

The final results showed I was placed 13th out of 16 in my class, with a time of 56.80. With more practice, this time should come down to mid-53 seconds.

I thanked the club officials and drove home, realising that my first love was drag racing and always will be, forget all this FI stuff – I'm a G-force man.

The weeks passed by quickly. This year I would be racing our Honda, except for two outings in the dragster, which was currently up for sale, Martyn Hannis being the salesman. Brenda was still in charge of my racing and reminded me I had a busy weekend ahead. On Sunday 27 April there was an autotest near Bolton which followed the Liverpool Motor Club's Bridge-stone Aintree Spring Sprint on the Saturday. This was another round of the ANWCC's sprint championship and required my full attention.

With my overalls duly washed and my helmet cleaned, I drove to Liver-pool. On arrival all the main contenders had already pitted; formalities over and it was straight into the first practice session. I ran a 59.10 second; Karen Williams, whom I beat for last year's Novice Championship, came back at me with a 59.71 – the young lady was out for revenge.

After the lunch break the serious racing started. The Lotus Elises of Alan Clark and Dave Coveney were running mid-56 and 57 respectively. Me? I lost to Mark Pocklington's Renault C110 by $^{15}/_{100}$ of a second – 58.07 to my 58.23 and I didn't beat this time all day. One consolation was that I went quicker than George Povey and Stuart Tranter.

Karen Williams had a good day, she pulled a 58.63, her best ever time at Aintree. However, she lost heart when I bettered it with a 58.23. This lady had set her heart on the 2002 Novice Championship, then I came along and in my first year became champion.

The final results showed my position, 9th in Class 1B and 65th from a field of 100 cars from Minis to single-seaters. To give you an idea of the field of cars, the fastest time of the day was 44.68 seconds; that was Stephen Miles driving a Van Diemen RF96M.

Why I bothered to drive back home to Anglesey when I had to be in Bolton at 7am on Sunday for the Thistlethwaite Tyres Autotest, I don't know. Sunday morning was gale force winds and heavy rain so it was a less than pleasant journey to Bolton. When I arrived everybody was sitting in their cars, with a few club officials marking out the various tests with cones.

I soon realised this MSA autotest was for the professionals with special Minis and other cars they had built. Some competitors had driven up from London and the Midlands. The cones were set too close for my Honda so there were no handbrake turns for me. I withdrew my entry and prepared to drive home.

Although the weekend had been very stressful– the Aintree sprint on Saturday with the autotest today – I did meet some interesting people. John

Symes, the MSA's safety and environmental executive was one – he gave me Jeff May's telephone number.

There was a three-week lull in my motorsport activities and this gave me time to bring our garage on the Moelfre roundabout back to selling petrol and wet suits. My wife's health wasn't improving and she spent most of the day in bed, but she was determined nothing would spoil our fiftieth wedding anniversary party on 4 July; she was really looking forward to it. Our children rallied round helping with her needs while I was away racing the dragster in another round of the Wild Bunch Championship – the Classic American Nationals on 17/18 May 2003 which was for rear-engined cars only.

The commentary came from the ladies of the Wild Bunch:

There were two Wild Bunch rear-engined dragsters taking part, Welcome Break 40 Dennis Hawkins in the 'Wicked Lady' and Welcome Break 243 Derek Annable in the re-named 'Brenda's Life Force' Top Methanol Dragster.

After sitting out the rain on Saturday, Dennis's dragster suffered from a broken starter motor and he had to pack up and leave early Sunday. Derek was raring to go Sunday, with the support of Martyn Hannis and Dougie Bond as crew. He dialled in blind at 8.00 seconds, and put in a good burnout and launched into the run. The engine started to smoke at half-track, but Derek ran a good 8.643 @ 166.05. Sadly though, 3 rods exited the engine at the end of the run, making a window right through the block, curtailing Derek's fun for the day.

Being the only driver running on Sunday, Derek took home ALL the Spot Prizes for the weekend: with a 'Best Reaction' of .803, a 'Quickest E.T.' of 8.643, which was the 'Closest to Dial-in' at .643 off, and the car was 'Best Rear-engined dragster'! Derek and the team hope to be back out later in the season!

Wild Bunch Results – Classic American NATS – 17–18 May 2003

Best Reaction	Derek Annable	WB243	'Brenda's Life Force'	.803
Closest to Dial-in	Derek Annable	WB243	'Brenda's Life Force'	.643 off
Quickest E.T.	Derek Annable	WB243	'Brenda's Life Force'	8.643
Best Rear-Engine Dragster	Derek Annable	WB243	'Brenda's Life Force'	

This weekend was the first half of the two-part round of Wild Bunch Series Rounds 2, Roy Wilding Nostalgia Race Cars Series Round 1 and Real Steel

Series Round 3 (for rear-engine dragsters); with the second half (for the rest of 'the bunch') to be held at the Nostalgia Nationals. There was a field of 2 Wild Bunch Rear-engine dragsters taking part, as follows:

WB40 Dennis Hawkins	'Wicked Lady'	rear-engine dragster
WB243 Derek Annable	'Brenda's Life Force'	rear-engine dragster

The weather was very poor on Saturday and the event was almost rained off. Only about an hour's worth of street-treaded tyred cars ran, but the rain returned mid-afternoon and no slick-tyred vehicles were able to make runs. Sunday started off wet but dried out a bit and racing started about noon. By about 2.00ish the track had been sprayed ready for slick-tyred vehicles and racing then carried on until a late rain shower at quarter to five.

We will have to wait until the Nostalgia Nationals at the end of June to see how Derek fares amongst the other results, so it will be quite a wait! And we have the UK Open Nationals May Bank Holiday weekend at York, and the Power Nationals in mid June before then, so looking forward to all those events!'

John Turner was preparing our Honda for its next meeting at Ty Croes sprint weekend on 24/25 May. This meeting was another round of the ANWCC Championship and I needed the points on offer to improve my position within my class.

On arrival at the track I pitted and wondered where all my opponents were. Our Honda was the only car racing in Class 2 Standard Saloon and Sports Cars 1401cc to 2000cc. All day I raced against myself trying to improve the car's times. I ended the day with a respectable 116.95 seconds.

Sunday was a dry warm day and this time I had an opponent, Dave Hensley, driving a Peugeot 306 XSI. This was the rally driver I crossed swords with last year. He was too quick for me so I settled for second place with a time of 117.42.

The weekend proved fruitful as it gave me some valuable points towards the Sprint and Hill Climb Championship. My wife was well pleased with the weekend's results which gave me a higher position within my class.

I have been asked what has given me the most pleasure in motorsport over the last sixty years. Well, many things have, but one memorable pleasure was in the last years of my racing, but not on the track. When I had finished racing at Aintree and it was time to drive home, I had reached a set of traffic lights just before the motorway and this Ginetta sports car drew up alongside.

Although the day's racing was finished, the driver wanted to race against my Honda Integra and me. We waited for the lights to turn green; when they did, the two hooligans left the traffic lights with smoke coming from their tyres.

John Francis, you made my day and I would like to say 'thank you my friend', and also to your son who was in the car with you. I have raced against Stirling Moss and others, but for sheer pleasure, you and me at those traffic lights takes the biscuit. I am sorry we can't repeat it. Good luck with your charity track days at Three Sisters, Wigan. See you one day in the distant future, God bless you.

There are two names in motorsport – Basil Davenport and Dave Moore – that stand high above us juniors, great men who achieved the ultimate – something I could never do, and my respect for them knows no bounds. Stirling Moss, are you listening? These men achieved their greatness through sheer true grit and the input of their wives. My book is about husbands and wives who, through heaven and hell, worked together to fulfil a dream in motorsport, be it Clubman events, rallies or – my own love – drag racing.

I say this to my friends of the 1950/60 period, drag racing – my passion which only came to me in 1990 – is the only form of motorsport where Joe Public can compete for £100 outlay and race against world champions. My book is about a man's passion for motorsport, grass roots motorsport where you race within your means. I live on a state pension. My wife and I have some small investments which keep us out of the poorhouse. Life can be hard for us. Our friends in drag racing know what I mean as they, like us, have to put their racing on hold for one, maybe two, years when money is short. This sets me aside from my fellow BRDC members whom I respect, but some of them don't live in the real world. (Derek, that comment will cost you at least a thousand book sales!) These people organise a visit to an FI factory, a tour de France costing £1,000+ and seats at the Monte Carlo Grand Prix which costs £10,000+ for the weekend.

Gentlemen, we are the elite in motorsport, so in this book I distance myself from you (Derek, that comment has cost you a further 10,000 sales!). The public think that because I am a member of the BRDC, I am mega-rich and my motorsport costs are just petty cash to me.

Forward to the Bridgestone Anglesey Sprint on 14/15 June, which was the Chester Motor Club's big weekend – on Saturday, the Basil Davenport Memorial Trophy meeting, followed on Sunday by the Dave Moore Memorial Sprint. When I arrived the weather was sunny, with a cool breeze coming off the sea. There were eight cars in my class and four were Lotus Elises – no chance of a win for me today. Then there he was, Mark le Riche and his Toyota MR2 MKI. The smile on his face said it all, 'Derek, I have fitted a special gear shift. The car will go quick this weekend.'

I looked him straight in the eyes and said, 'Mark, I have only known you for two years but to me you are a true racer.'

His reply was, 'Derek, from a pro like you that was some compliment.'

'Mark, you work hard to improve your car to bring results and go quick.'

There was a new face in our section of the pits, Helen Harper with her BMW Mini Cooper. Sorry, a BMW Cooper. John Cooper and his father would turn in their graves – a BMW Cooper – what next?

The only driver who could stop a Lotus whitewash was David Marshall with his Peugeot 205 1900cc. We slower drivers converged on him with this message, 'we lesser beings have chosen you to eclipse the Lotus Elise cars'.

When the practice over, because of an overlarge field of cars, the club decided there would be two timed runs instead of the normal three. This was a bad omen for the slower cars as we required at least three timed runs to achieve a good result.

The timed runs began, and Alan Clarke (Lotus) recorded a 98.57-second run and took top slot in our class. Our champion David Marshall came second with a 105.47 followed by Dave Coveney (Lotus) 106.79, Simon Lawrence (Lotus) 109.39 and – wait for it – Karen Williams (Lotus) with a 110.74. This lady had got her revenge on me. I was four seconds slower with a 114.86. I didn't better this all day.

The final results showed me in sixth place, a poor position in the points table. Mark Le Riche managed a 119.91 so the new gear shift he had fitted to the car hadn't improved his times. His parting words to me were, 'Derek, next year I shall fit a turbo to the engine, which should make the car go quicker.'

'Yes Mark, a good idea but the turbo will put you in a higher class.'

'Derek, you have all the answers.'

He could win his class next year. Why fit a turbo which would mean racing against Ford Cosworths?

Now it was Sunday and the Dave Moore Memorial Sprint. The weather was a repeat of Saturday but warmer. My class had a strong field – ten cars with a newcomer, Stewart Lobley, driving a TVR Vixen S4; Paul Waters was also back driving a Ford Fiesta XR2. It was a repeat of Saturday, with Alan Clark (Lotus) the winner and David Marshall (Peugeot) as the runner-up.

Again there were only two timed runs (maybe the club should restrict the entry, so allowing three timed runs and give value for money.)

At the moment, you pay your money, sign on, and agree to abide by the rules of motorsport as set out by the people in charge (MSA). One day the young up-and-coming drivers will rebel against the Blazer Boys in charge of motorsport. Then there will be no motorsport or, with luck, a sport for everybody. I say move over the old men of motorsport for the future of British motorsport and give the young blood a chance to run a forward-looking sport for all.

The two only timed runs worked to my advantage. Karen Williams (Lotus) in her first timed run got all crossed up and spun, putting her down to tenth place (last). The lady was all shook up, recording a 117.73 on her second run, seven seconds down on Saturday's time.

My time of 116.17 gave me sixth place and equal points to add to Saturday's. Karen Williams would be under pressure next time we raced in two weeks' time at Aintree.

Monday morning dawned and it was time for my overdue appointment with the nurse at Amlwch Clinic. The days of seeing your doctor are over, Sister Linda and her team are in charge of people's health in Amlwch. This visit to the clinic taught me a lesson. During the last three months I had suffered from night cramps in my left leg. Even during the day I had problems climbing the stairs. I tried to explain this to the nurse in charge and her response was, 'Mr Annable, we require a blood test.'

'Sorry, nurse, every time you take a blood test my left elbow becomes inflamed to the point that I am unable to move my arm,' I replied.

'Mr Annable, I am not interested in the problems you have with your arm, we require a blood test. Furthermore, if you don't agree to take a blood test, I shall refer you to a doctor.'

OK, all the lady wanted was my blood. She thought the problems with my leg and arm could wait until my next visit to the clinic. So I left the clinic one angry old man – they could wait until my next visit for my blood; two can play at that game.

I walked out of the clinic and crossed the road to Hefin's the greengrocers and purchased two bundles of asparagus to buck me up. Brenda and I liked this sexy vegetable. Many a night we would eat a bundle each, then sit and watch television, our bodies full of passion.

Never mind the passion, a week after eating the asparagus my right knee relaxed and I could walk up the stairs and my sex life was restored. There must be a lesson here somewhere but it doesn't come to mind!

It was now time for John to prepare the Honda for the last race meeting before our party on July 4. I needed points for the ANWCC and Chester MC Championships and the Aintree Summer Sprint should provide them. This would be my last race at Aintree as their next meeting clashed with the double header at Ty Croes on 6/7 September where I could pick up maximum points.

It was an early start for me. There was very little traffic on the A55.

Coming out of Colwyn Bay, the Holyhead to London Express train passed me at the point where the railway and road run alongside each other. Now here was a challenge. The time on my clock was 6.30am; it was going to be Honda Integra 'R' versus Virgin train. The train entered the tunnel and I was determined to be ahead of it when it came out of the tunnel. 100 mph came up on my speedo, then 120 mph and rising. Bingo, I was ahead of the train. The engine driver and I stayed alongside each other at what must have been over 100 mph until the point where the train follows the coast to Rhyl and goes inland. The train driver gave me a blast on his horn and we parted company.

Maybe the chief constable of North Wales police will buy my book and then fine me for speeding! To my readers I must stress there were no other vehicles on either carriageway at the time and also there are no junctions on that stretch of road.

This took me back to a time when I took delivery of the red Allard. Soon after that I was driving along the Staines to Windsor road. That morning I kept to the various 30mph speed limits in Staines, but used the car's full power whenever I could. When entering Windsor I was stopped by a Wolseley police car which was ringing its bell. I thought, 'Oh no, this is all I need.' The two police officers came over to me and asked me to get out the car. They then said, 'Sir, we have been trying to catch up with you for more than ten miles. Please can we have a look at the engine you have under the bonnet of this monster car.'

A pleasant ten minutes was spent talking about American engines. They wished me luck, got back in their police car and returned to Chertsey. In those days we were all boy racers and children at heart and the police drivers loved us.

Now I was crossing the Melling Road and entering the pits. Class 1B had a full house of 22 cars: five Lotus Elises, seven Peugeot 205s, and a couple of Fords, Tony Anderson with his Citroen Saxo VTS, Helen Harper with her BMW Mini Cooper and others.

The order of the day was two practice runs and three timed runs. Let battle commence – you know which battle, Karen Lotus Elise and Derek Honda Integra!

I was now running sub-60 seconds at Aintree; could I improve on this with a sub-58 seconds? Last year a Civic Type R had run sub-56 seconds. The morning practice went well with a 59.41 and a 59.29. If I was going to improve my placing, a 57-second pass was required.

When the lunch break was over, the timed runs started. My best was 59.59 and I had one timed run left. Karen Williams was within half a second of my time and getting quicker, the pressure was really on. Now it was time for the last timed run of the day. A Lotus 756 went out before me and not knowing the result, I went for it. When I crossed the finishing line, there it was on the electric scoreboard – 58.98, had the lady in the Lotus bettered that? I had to wait half an hour before the final results were posted. My position was 13th, Karen's was 16th, our duel was over and we never raced against each other in the same class of car again.

The journey back home was very relaxed, never exceeding 70mph on the motorway. It was mid-point in my racing season and Brenda being unable to be crew chief left me feeling sad. Let's hope she would be well enough to come to York Raceway in August when, with luck, I would be racing the TM dragster with the Wild Bunch.

Golden Wedding Anniversary Party
March/April 2003

With the venue agreed, I now had to find a Glen Miller-type band. The Manchester Yellow Pages were a great help and Orchestral Creations fitted the bill with their Starduster band.

My next task was the cake. It had to be five tiers, one for every ten years – and fruit, not sponge. I made a visit to Rhyl first where I found Celebrate in Style where Carol and Andrew took the details of the cake and we agreed the price.

Now I set about the guest list. The three major drag racing clubs had kindly supplied me with a list of members, and from this Brenda and I started to choose the guest names.

May/June 2003

The printers did a good job and the invitation cards were ready for me to collect at the end of the first week in May. All the invitation cards were posted by 15 May but the response was slow. By the second week in June, we only had fifty replies. The hotel required a firm booking from me with a list of bedrooms required, plus the menu choices and a table seating plan.

Every evening was spent phoning the many guests who hadn't replied; from this a further ten confirmed they were coming. Now I had reached the deadline of the 24 June. My final request went out, 'Please respond within 48 hours or I will withdraw the invite.' It was a shame but in the end we had to settle for fewer guests than planned. None of my wife's family could make our party, giving one reason or another. My relatives had prior engagements and even two of our children stayed home. This spoke volumes and my wife became upset, while I was angry.

We had been married for fifty years which is a landmark occasion. I was footing the bill for our anniversary party when usually people's family and relatives would arrange a surprise Golden Wedding party for an old couple. This disappointment was in some way made up for when nearly a hundred friends from the world of motor sport said YES. Some went back over fifty years – like Ken Gregory who plays a big role in Chapter 2 and is our eldest daughter's godfather. Then there are our new friends in motorsport – those that I compete against in sprints and hill climbs, and the larger family of racers from the drag racing world.

Thus 94 guests would be seated at 13 round tables plus the top table. Thirty-five bedrooms were booked and the following announcement appeared in the Marlow edition of the *Bucks Free Press* on 3 July 2003:

Austin–Annable, Brenda and Derek
Celebrate their wedding of 4 July 1953 in High Wycombe at 11am or was it 11.30am.

This Great Marlow girl, who has been exiled to Anglesey North Wales for most of the last 50 years, sends greetings to family and friends in Marlow.

Derek takes a back seat this time and says, 'Why did I visit the Odeon Cinema, Marlow to watch High Noon? And get drunk in the Marlow Donkey all those years ago – thanks Cyril!

4 July 2003

The great day dawned. The cake was loaded in the boot of the Honda and I set off for Bradford. Brenda, her wheelchair and luggage were to follow in our son Mark's car. All afternoon I worked with the hotel's functions lady and her staff arranging the seating. The cake was to take pride of place on the end of the top table. Every table had a bottle of red and white wine with a jug of pure fruit juice for the children and non-drinkers. (See table plan on next page.)

It was now four o'clock and the guests started to arrive, some having travelled more than 300 miles. Then there were the London and Home Counties brigade, followed by many who lived south of the River Thames. The pace was hotting up with guests from Bristol, Birmingham, now North Wales, Lancs and Cheshire, the northeast counties, Hull, Doncaster and the local racers, Leeds and Bradford and north and south of the M62.

The car park was full of American cars. The party, like our wedding, had a 4 July American theme.

At the stroke of six thirty, the cocktail pianist started to tinkle the ivories and the guests made their way to the tables. Brenda now entered the room,

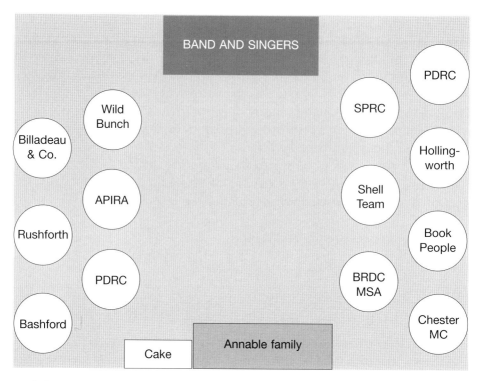

Table seating

Billadeau & Co: David, Annetta, Bill, Scott, Margaret. Dave and Richard Smith, John Turner.

Rushforth: Dave, Julie, Ben, Bethany. Richard, Joan Cole and Crystal.

Bashford: Nick, Claire, John, Patricia. Steven and Sheila Cawley.

Wild Bunch: Chris, Claire, Mark. Nikki Denton, Bruno and Sophie, Gerald, and Joan Cookson.

APIRA: Wendy and Richard, Frank and Maureen, Tracey and Jim, Colin and Liz.

PDRC: Richard and Marjorie, Andrew and Christine, John and Cheryl, Graham and Carolyn.

SPRC: Ian, Paula and Holley, Jon Cross, John Hackney, Steve and Julie Moxley.

Shell Team: Martyn and Lou, Doug and Jayne, Carla and Rick. Darren Prentice.

BRDC/MSA: Ken and Julie, Michael and Elizabeth, Philip and Beverly, Amos and Lydia.

PDRC: Dez and Pearl, David and Cath, Alan and Angela, Kayleigh and Abbie.

Hollingworth: Jon, Joanne, Janet, Stephen. Tim Holmes and Wendy. Jon and Michelle.

Book People: Richard, Annabel, Chelsea, Lucy, Sharley, Jenny. Wilf and Audrey.

Chester MC: Bob and Jan, Ian and Frances. Martin and Janice, a lovely child!

accompanied by our son Mark and daughter Lynne. Slowly, she made her way to the centre of the top table to the applause of the guests – the sound was deafening.

The room became a hive of activity with staff everywhere and in complete order; nobody had to wait more than five minutes for the first course. Brenda had decided on Washington corn cream, myself mushroom and asparagus parcels, sheer excellence. The man on the piano played all the old tunes from the 1950s and 60s. I kept watching the many tables; yes my choice of seating was spot on, everybody was engaged in intense conversation – nobody looked left out, even the children were relaxed.

Brenda and I were married on American Independence Day fifty years ago. In those days 4 July meant a great deal to most Americans and to Brenda and I it still does. The room vibrated with pure American zeal.

The staff were working wonders; the main course was on the table in front of us – American-style chicken for me and Brenda had chosen beef tenderloin. The chicken was perfect but the voice next to me said, 'Derek, I don't want the beef, can I have your chicken?'

'Yes, darling.' was my reply and we exchanged the main course.

At this point in my writing I must apologise to my readers for food taking priority over all else. Many years ago, I was in a room with an old gentleman who had only weeks to live and do you know what brought a sparkle to his eyes? When his wife said, 'A cup of tea and a round of toast Frank?' The smile on his face said it all – he did enjoy his toast and tea. The following week he was dead.

The function room was now bubbling with laughter. The main course was over and, as arranged, the band and singer burst into life with a Glenn Miller favourite 'American Patrol'. All through dessert and coffee they went through their typical programme. When they played 'In the Mood', the older guests took to the dance floor and jived; now the party was really swinging. Then came, 'Little Brown Jug', 'Tuxedo Junction', 'String of Pearls' followed by the Miller hallmark, 'Moonlight Serenade'.

It was time for Jon Cross to say a few words about the Annables. Standing there with a glass of wine in his shaking hand, he launched into an unprepared speech; this from an international race director. Sorry Jon but never in your life have you ever had to address Derek, Brenda and their guests. To him, on race day at Santa Pod, 250 racers and bikers were less intimidating. That evening in front of your peers, your hand didn't stop shaking until you sat down and finished the bottle of red wine. Brenda and I thank you Jon.

Now everybody was in a party mood and the non-smokers stayed and danced. Because of my wife's poor health, we had made the dining room a no-smoking area, so when the speech was over, the smokers rushed to the bar and lit up. I can imagine what was said. 'That bastard Derek gave up smoking ten years ago, then he does this to us!' Sorry lads, my wife's stroke was brought on by smoking and now she needs clean air.

The clock ticked away and then it was time for 'Land of Hope and Glory', not once, not twice, but three times. I think it was a good party, and everyone enjoyed themselves. Brenda and I went to bed early, leaving our many guests in the hotel bar.

Breakfast next morning was a revelation. Having had my breakfast early, I wheeled my wife into the silent dining room. Looking to the left and right, I said, 'Brenda, say good morning to everybody', while swinging her wheelchair in the direction of the many tables. Then people responded with 'Good morning, Brenda', and other platitudes. Some saw the joke and laughed.

Goodbyes were said and we loaded three cars with the fabulous presents we had received and headed west along the M62. A very tired Brenda went to bed that night knowing the Annable family had put on a good show. This was confirmed when we received the photos taken by family and friends. As well as this, many thank you cards arrived the following week, some of the words written brought tears to Brenda's eyes. Word got around and many who were unable to attend the party phoned with their congratulations. I was later asked if I would do it again. And my answer was – I think not, it would be better to pay an agent to organise this type of function. It had taken a great deal of organising, but had been well worth the effort.

Now the party was over, it was time to prepare for a round of the Chester Motor Club's championship and all those points on offer.

It was the Three Sisters National 'B' Sprint meeting on Sunday 13 July. Having entered and received my final instructions, I drove down to Wigan thinking that this circuit wasn't really for me and our road car – never mind I raced for points not pleasure.

As the day progressed, the corners were difficult to take. Once you were off the racing line, you were on what are called marbles (dirt/small chippings) and your grip was lost. Many cars were spinning and bringing more rubbish onto the tarmac surface. I wondered why the people in charge didn't pay for sweepers to clean the track.

After two practice runs and an equal number of timed runs, I called it a day and drove home. Never mind, next week I would be in the high ground of Yorkshire again at Scammonden Dam, where the locals say the Pendle witches visit the water to gain strength. This area of Yorkshire and Lancs is full of folk stories. Thus Sunday 20 July dawned.

The Westfield Sports Car Club were in charge of this hill climb and they are a great crowd of drivers. In my batch was Steven Gillot from Huddersfield with his Sierra 4x4 and Bernard Mooney with his Porsche 914. Our batch was split into three groups of three.

Everybody was to have two practice runs and four timed runs – this was value for money. The morning practice was very slick and my times were reasonable, considering the rev limiter always came in as the car crossed the finishing line. Bernard Mooney had the same problem with his Porsche and he had considered removing it. 'Bernard, it is there to save your engine from over-revving. Ok, your times may improve but at the cost of a new engine.'

One good thing about Scam Dam is that they have the best chuck wagon this side of the Rocky Mountains. But now it was time for some serious racing. My first timed run of 30.96 was followed by a 30.86 and the winning time of 30.67, which I then backed up with a 30.68. A good result for an old man driving an old man's car, a Honda!

Brenda was pleased with the result and she reminded me that next Sunday would be a 5am start for me with a drive to Shrewsbury and the Liverpool Motor Club and Hagley & District Light Car Club Hill Climb, Loton Park. This is the big one. The meeting is held in Sir Michael Leighton's deer park. When I was at Wrekin College, Sir Michael's family owned all the farms from the great house to Criggon Mountain and beyond, which is a vast estate. Now they are down to a few tenant farmers who work hard to make a living. One's private life can cost you dearly. His lordship's young teenage daughter will inherit what is left of a once great estate.

The narrow tarmac road we race on through the deer park is 1475 yards long with an average gradient of 1 in 25 (4%); the steepest part is 1 in 7 (14%). The supplementary regulations state, 'It is strongly recommended that all competitors, in particular those on their first visit to Loton Park, walk the hill before commencement of the practice session.' I made the walk, just – my legs were giving up on me.

Who was this arriving? It was Stuart Tranter towing a trailer with his Rover 216 GTI on it, the same trailer which had broken down on the Oswestry–Shrewsbury road when I passed it over an hour before. Unfortunately worse was to befall Stuart and his car, as I shall explain later.

After my car had been passed by the club scrutineer and his team, I went for a walk to inspect the Leighton family church and the gatehouse which were across the other side of the main road. Status symbols today are Rolls-Royce or Ferrari cars, but 150 years ago it was the family church with its own vicar. This is what my late father strove for all his life. He managed to achieve the ownership of a large Tudor house which had a long drive with a gatehouse at its end, but never a family church with its own vicar!

After my first practice run, I went looking for John Harden and Ron Hunt so I could give them boxes of anniversary cake as they were unable to make our 4 July party. Ron is a big man – twenty plus stone and over six feet tall – for him there were four boxes, only three boxes for John. Later I saw Ron sitting in the timekeeper's cabin enjoying the iced fruit cake I had given him.

With the 5am start and the long journey, it was time to find the chuck wagon. The order of the day was chicken tikka and chips with a large hot dog to follow. First-class food, well worth the money and the 120-mile drive.

Twenty classes of cars took some shifting. The start line was manned by some old friends of mine from the MG Car Club. They had us rolling through with some true northern grit. If you were two seconds late, you were given a red card, which would end the day's racing for the offender.

Pitted opposite me was one lady racing driver, Tricia Davis who was sharing the drive with Terry Davis. The car was a TDK 903 and it was quick, and it should win the class. Their opponents were Tony and Jocelyn Adams driving a Jedi Honda MK4 race car. These lady drivers were top rate and you could see they didn't approve of an old person racing hill climbs. Never mind, I weathered the storm, knowing Bernard Mooney, whom I had raced against, thought I was quick in both hill climbs and sprints.

During a quiet period in my day's racing I sat with the spectators, watching the Ferrari Club racers take their 550 Maranellos, Mondial T, 380s, F335 and F40 up through the corners. The winner's time was 60.65 seconds; these cars were valued at £100,000–200,000. A humble Lotus 7 Caterham recorded 56.12 seconds; even my Honda recorded a 63-second pass. Tony Willis driving his Ferrari 330 GTC proved money can't buy success.

As promised I will relay the fortunes of Stuart Tranter driving his Rover 216 GTI. Having not walked the course, he was caught out on the last bend (a point where you can lose sight of it) and went straight into the banking, breaking the front end of his car. Poor Stuart put the broken car on the trailer and drove back to Lancs. Surprise, surprise, who repaired the car? A firm in Holyhead, Anglesey.

There were ten cars in my class and no production cars this time, only modified road saloons. The only pure road cars were mine, David Goodlad's Ford Sierra and Bernard Mooney's Porsche 914. We had some good and happy racing, leaving Bob Jones to take fourth spot with his Seat Ibiza, well done Bob.

This meeting was filled with many of my friends like Steven Crawley with his BMW M535I; Bob Beadon with his Vauxhall Astra; the Westfield lads, Newstman, Hawker and Morris; the Formula Ford racers, Worsley and Jackson; the classic car people, De Rycke, Glasbey and Brown; and don't forget those two ladies Tricia Davis and Jocelyn Adams.

The results for this most enjoyable day were that I did run quicker times than David Goodlad and Bernard Mooney, who said to me, 'You are an animal, Derek, and are quick.'

'Thank you, Bernard; it has been a pleasure to race against you. But don't take the rev limiter off the engine of your Porsche 914.'

The journey home was full of fond and happy memories. This would be the last time I would race at Loton. Although I entered the next meeting, I never arrived, the clutch on the Honda having broken when driving down so I slowly made my way back from Chester to Anglesey.

That clutch had taken some punishment during the last three years, with meeting after meeting at Santa Pod and other drag racing venues and then sprints and hill climbs most weekends throughout 2002 and 2003.

Why is my life in motorsport, which has been so exciting, going so quickly in its last year? Looking at the calendar, I saw I had four more meetings racing my wife's Honda and one with our TM dragster car. I had promised Brenda that 2003 would be my final year on the track.

Deep in thought, I heard a voice shouting, 'The Honda's MOT has run out. I have booked it to be at Eric Jones's workshop at ten o'clock this morning.'

'Where is his workshop, Brenda?' I shouted back.

'The top of Parys Mountain and remember to take your cheque book with you, Eric is a cash only man!'

Women, what is it about them? We men have to 'remember this' and 'don't forget that'. My mother always gave me a list of things and facts I had to remember before I set off for school in the morning – and that was before I had learnt to read (*The Beano* and *Dandy* were my only reading matter)!

Eric passed the Honda and I returned home, gave Brenda the certificate, sat down and started to read about Doug Bond's exploits in *Custom Car*. There it was – our dragster, the Shell car painted all red, which I would be racing at the end of next week along the York Raceway quarter mile, Brenda's favourite drag strip, with the Wild Bunch on Saturday and Sunday 9/10 August.

This time Doug Bond had double duties as Martyn Hannis had to attend a funeral. My crew would be Doug, his wife Jayne and daughter Millie, with help from the Wild Bunch.

Brenda booked a room for the Bond family at the Hotel and Steak House in Evington and ourselves at the Travel Inn at Goole. To our excitement, we were going to race the dragster at York Raceway. A dream of ours was coming true. This showed during the meal on Friday night at the hotel when Brenda never stopped talking.

We had an early breakfast on Saturday morning, my wife's wheelchair was loaded into the car and I drove with all speed to the track. To our surprise, the rig and car were in the pits. Doug had left Cheltenham at midnight and a very tired Bond family greeted us.

Within an hour Doug had the car ready to race so we joined the other Wild Bunch cars in the fire-up lane. As the engine was new, my instructions were, 'Only a half-pass, Derek.' This I did to the letter, then back to the pits I went for Doug to check over the engine for any damage.

While the engine was being checked over, I drove Jayne and Millie to the hotel in Evington, leaving Brenda with her friends. On our return the news was good – the dragster's engine was OK and ready to race on Sunday. We secured the race car and called it a day. When we returned to our hotel in Goole, we had a good meal that night and went to bed early.

Sunday was a perfect day for racing, except for the wind which blew dust around the pit area, blinding everybody. Shit! I hope the blower didn't suck in too much and damage the teflons. Now it was call-out time for the Wild Bunch cars – all 17 of them. I had to run on my own but it was a good run with an eighth mile speed of 145.09. I lifted off at three-quarter track, crossing the line at 125.80, with an ET of 8.453 on a dial-in of 8.50. That run could have been a mid-7/180mph if I had kept the power on but my brief was to run in the engine for Doug who would be out in the Allstars Nationals at the end of August. I must remember that the car was up for sale; why break it to prove to the York racers I could run a low seven?

It would be one o'clock before the Wild Bunch had their second slot. Brenda was feeling hungry so off I went for some food; while I was away, a deal was struck with the Bond family that they would buy the rolling chassis for Joe to race next year. Unfortunately, this deal was overruled by Martyn Hannis on their return to Cheltenham. His actions caused much friction between my wife, who was the owner of the car, and the Hannis/Bond partnership. I was glad I was retiring from the motorsport scene at the end of the year.

It was now time for my second run of the day. This should have been a solo run but in drag racing anything can happen. I had burnt out so Roy Wilding had brought me back to the start line where I had just moved forward into pre-stage when this lunatic called Daddy Cool came rushing into stage in the lane to the right of me.

The start light came on as Sag (his name) shot off at least $^2/_{10}$ of a second ahead of me. I hauled him by the eighth mile and powered away to a 1.386-second win. To this day Daddy Cool calls it his greatest race. When he knew it was my last race with the dragster, he said, 'Derek, I am honoured to have been part of it.'

One's life is full of highs and lows and the Wild Bunch meeting on the 9/10 August 2003 was a high and my race against Sag was the greatest.

Brenda and I returned home well pleased with the weekend's results, knowing that very few wife and husband teams had achieved what we had (and none of our age) in the UK.

Tuesday night was spent, among other things, checking timing tickets, when out of the blue, the phone rang. It was Dez from York Raceway, and he fired questions at me about the track. To these, I said, 'My friend, if I had known how good it was, I would have dialled in a 7.50 not a 8.50 and been the quickest car of the weekend.'

Dez came back at me, 'What else, Derek, what else.'

I responded, 'With minor improvement, it should be possible to run a five-second pass at York Raceway, this means Top Fuel could run. To me, your track is the safest in the UK.'

Dez shouted back over the phone, 'Thank you, Derek, thank you.'

Many racers criticize the only drag strip in the north of England and I think this is unfair. OK, the approach road is only a farm track which requires a driver to take his car down it at 5–10mph, but the PDRC officials work hard over the winter months filling in potholes. A special fund was set up for a new toilet block which is now up and working. The eighth mile strip had been improved either side of the start line which gives the cars a better launch. The street legal cars with standard road tyres have a special grip surface of their own on a launch pad by the start lights. Spectators are safe behind steel barriers on their section of the strip. After the eighth mile, either side of the drag strip there are open fields, which gives us racers (when in trouble) a run off onto grass which slows us down and not a concrete wall like at Santa Pod.

I must now return to recording my racing. The next race was on 15 August, a charity track day at the Three Sisters in Wigan. I had received a letter from John Francis, the chairman of Dayz of Funder Motorsport Ltd, who invited me to enter their charity track day. I sat there enjoying a glass of wine and considered the invite. My wife, seeing the look on my face, said, 'Derek, you don't like the Three Sisters race circuit.' She had a point, I didn't like that race circuit. I looked at the letter again, his address was Jericho, and in my opinion anybody who lives in Jericho deserves my support before the walls came tumbling down! So off went my cheque for £50, and by return post my tickets arrived.

The M6 would be murder on a Friday, so I left home mid-morning, arriving on the M6 when the business traffic was long gone, and I could follow the heavy trucks north at a steady 60mph. I reached junction 25 on the M6 in good time and turned off for the A49 and right at the roundabout in Bryn. There was the kart circuit. Thank goodness I was wearing my race overalls because the man on the gate said, 'Sir, it is a fun day for children, not an OAP picnic!' Then he said, 'Nice to see you now.'

As promised, everything was there for the children, including a heli-copter from the Ministry of Defence Helicopter Flying School, Shawbury. (In 1940 when I was a pupil at Wrekin College we in the ATC visited Shaw-bury and were trained to fly their Avro Anson twin-engined flying machine.) There were bouncy castles for the young children and a small number of fairground stalls and rides. John and his team were putting on a great family fun day – it should go from strength to strength.

In a section of its own there were autotest cars and if you really liked being scared there were passenger rides in the race cars doing three laps of the circuit. The mayor of Wigan was invited to don a crash helmet and sit in an open sports car, then, as the local newspaper cameras flashed, the car shot forward at full speed, taking Cowards Summit at nearly 100mph. By now the mayor's face had turned green, so had his chain of office! He would have a tale to tell at the next council meeting.

Everybody was enjoying themselves. I think my £50 donation and other drivers' money was going towards a good charity. That said, I am a competitor who races for points and maybe when I retire my energy can be channelled into this type of event.

Driving home, I reviewed the day's events and what worried me in particular was how dangerous it was to allow members of the public to be taken at race speed around a circuit like the Three Sisters. What would happen if a young child or adult was killed while a passenger in a sprint car at the Three Sisters circuit?

During the afternoon when I took to the circuit in my car, there were idiots passing me with members of the public as passengers. Some cars were spinning off at corners like the Luna Bend. The promoter must tighten up safety on the fun days and expel these idiots.

This said, the meeting was a success and everybody I spoke to enjoyed the charity day and would be coming back in 2004. Good luck.

It is said that old men start wars and young men fight them. In my case, old men start wars and this old man fights them also, thus the world will prosper because one old man will be the victim of the war he started.

My next war/race was at Scammonden Dam on Sunday 17 August 2003. Having received the final instructions from Rodney Brereton, the Pendle District Motor Club entries secretary, I fired up the Honda and headed east in the direction of the M62.

Scam Dam is my favourite hill climb and this short course (550 yards) suited my wife's Honda. If one has the bottle to take the last bend without lifting off, quick times could be recorded.

When I reached the highest part of the motorway, the sun was blinding my vision. Oh dear, there was a police speed trap, had I hit the brakes in time? Surely they had caught me doing nearly 90mph. It would be six weeks of misery waiting for that dreaded letter which would be delivered to me at Brookfield School, sorry Mount View.

The night before I had watched 'Goodbye Mr Chips' on the television. When asked on his deathbed whether he had any family, this quiet man answered, 'I have many boys, they come and visit me every year.'

You ask, did I receive a speeding fine? Thank God, no. Mr Chips must have been my guardian angel.

There were three cars in my class or so I thought. Jim Wright with a Peugeot 306 XSI, Steve Courts with his Peugeot 205 GTI and happy David Goodlad's Ford Sierra. This man is an autotest nutter, there is no stopping him, even a broken gearbox in his Mini doesn't stop him. He takes it out and fits a straight-through drive or takes the course in reverse using the handbrake to steer the car, grinning from ear to ear. To watch this man drive is a joy indeed and the memory will stay with me for years.

Let's get back to the hill climb. There were to be two practice runs and eight timed runs, now there is value for money. After the five o'clock start this morning I was hungry, so off I went looking for the Travel 'N' Bite chuck wagon. There was a lovely lady in charge called Pauline, and the other half of the team, Brian, spent most of the day sleeping in their Ranger Rover tow car. Their bacon bap was the size of a dinner plate filled with four slices of bacon. Pauline, seeing me, had a bacon bap and a hot dog ready for me, she must have read my thoughts.

Fully refreshed, I returned to the racing. We went in convoy down the hill to the start line; this is when a drag racer called Steve Mementos came striding through the long grass, 'Derek, I didn't know you were a hill climb racer.'

'Yes, Steve, I started this type of motorsport last year.' It turned out that the Brighouse jeweller's father lived in the valley below the hill climb track.

The results of the Scam Dam hill climb were as follows; I came second in Class 2. A maverick came late with his ex-rally car and race tyres and took the winner's cup. His time was a 30.26. He paid the same entry fee as me and the scrutineer Jack Neal okayed his car – except for the tyres. This man had had a major hip replacement weeks before and without him we racers would have had our entry money returned and there would have been no meeting.

Most years I write letters to our local newspaper on various issues and some of them go to print. This one headed 'Pride in the greatest nation of all time' appeared in the 20 August 2003 edition of the *Mail*:

'QUESTION: Why do the Welsh hate the English?

ANSWER: Because the Welsh are a nation of dreamers!

Throughout their history they have had great leaders (Prince Llewelyn and others).

What happens? These men of vision were undermined by petty squabbles within the tribes.

The Welsh nation could have been the greatest nation since the Romans if they could have united as a force. Mercia was the beginning of what could have been.

What Happened? Jealousy among the leaders of the many factions stopped the progress forward with the result the great Welshmen of the time spread out through the known world.

These men made great fortunes because they were free, not of the English yoke, but the jealousy of their own countrymen.

I am an English man who has lived in North Wales for nearly 50 years. If my mother hadn't gone back to Manchester 73 years ago, I would have been born Welsh.

Did I say Welsh, the purists say you are not Welsh if you were born in Wales. One can only be pure Welsh if your ancestors were born in Wales hundreds of years ago.

What was this country of Wales before the Romans? It wasn't Wales.

In my youth I once heard a great Welshman and professor say 'There was no Welsh nation before the Romans, this means we are all Roman b******s.'

That statement sums up our history. We are the product of the greatest nation of all time and should be proud of it. Yes, you ask why? Just look around you, this nation of Wales has produced some of the greatest scholars and men and women of words and religion.

For hundreds of years English children, whether they lived in London or York were taught by Welsh men and women. Even today, a Welshman is the head of the English church, what more do you want.

Instead of the Welsh hating the English, why not say to the English: 'The Welsh are the greatest scholars of the first magnitude, without them you would never have been a great nation.'

The time has come to repay us, not through handouts to the Welsh

Assembly or a Prince of Wales who visits once or twice a year.

Gentlemen, allow the Welsh dragon to be part of the Union Flag. Then all men and women will be equal.

Derek Annable

Rhosgoch

September 2003 – Cyril Kieft

The phone rang, 'Is that Derek Annable?' a voice asked. 'Yes, who wants to speak to him?' I replied.

'I am Brian Jenkins.' Then he started asking questions about the days when I raced Kieft race cars, in the early 1950s. Following our phone conversation, I wrote him a letter.

Some weeks later, a Peter Tutthill phoned me. He had written a book called *Kieft Racing Cars*. Both he and Brian Jenkins had been fans of mine when, as teenagers, they followed the fortunes of the Kieft 500 cars. He wanted to know if I would autograph a copy of his book. Also he was in daily contact with Cyril Kieft who lived in Spain.

Now I was receiving regular phone calls from Brian, Peter and Cyril. One Thursday evening Cyril phoned and we had a very interesting conversation about the old days and my drag racing with our TM dragster. When I said this car could be bought for £25,000, Cyril said, 'I built a F1 car for £6,000 in the mid-1950s which had a Coventry Climax engine as its power unit. How much would it be worth today, Derek?'

'All of £250,000 Cyril,' I replied.

'Well, Derek, the car has been rebuilt and raced at Silverstone and the Festival of Speed at Goodwood.'

We talked for a good twenty minutes, then Cyril said, 'I haven't bored you, Derek?'

'No, you haven't, please keep in touch and we can ramble on about the good years.'

Having put the phone down, I wondered if Cyril was a member of the BRDC. Checking the yearbook showed that he wasn't, but not why he had been passed over. I shall propose him if the family in Spain will allow it.

Peter Tutthill agreed to put the question to Cyril as I didn't have his number. Cyril agreed, but kept saying to me, 'Derek, I have never raced a car. How can I become a member of a racing drivers' club like the BRDC?'

'Don't worry, Cyril, I will phone Ken Gregory tonight and ask him if he will second you.'

Ken agreed, so off went my letter to the club secretary:

BRDC Club Secretary   24 November 2003
British Racing Drivers' Club
Silverstone Circuit
Towcester
Northants

Dear Roger Lane-Nott

In my active circuit motor racing years (1949–53) there was one
name which, through his contribution to motorsport, fulfilled all the
principles of our club, the BRDC. This name is Cyril Kieft. He is
unique, firstly through his love of motorsport, and secondly his age,
having just celebrated his ninety second birthday.

Therefore I propose Cyril Kieft become an Associate Member of
the British Racing Drivers Club and his name be put forward at the
next meeting of the directors of our Club.

Mr Ken Gregory, a life member of the club, is prepared to second
my proposal.

Cyril has been known to me for over fifty years, even at his age he
takes an interest in the type of car I now race, a Top Methanol
dragster. The other night on the phone he said, 'Derek, I would
love to build one of those dragsters.' What more can I say about
the man.

Yours sincerely

Derek F. Annable

Full Member

It was followed the next day by Ken Gregory's letter. Within a week,
Roger, the club secretary, was on the phone to me, 'Derek, thank you for
your letter but there is more to membership of our club than just one letter.
There is a proposal form to be filled in and other criterion.'

'Roger, please send the form to Ken Gregory.'

It would be four months before Cyril's name went before the board of
directors and a further month before he became a member. Ken had been
working hard behind the scenes, stressing to everybody Cyril's age. Time is
against us after we reach eighty, then we are living on borrowed time.
Many of the directors had expressed disbelief that Cyril Kieft wasn't a
member of the club, saying, 'Why has it taken so long?'

Without Ken Gregory's help, Cyril's application for membership would have been dealt with in order, and it would have taken a great deal longer.

In November I received a lovely letter from Brian Jenkins of Swansea with a great deal of historical info, plus three photos of the Stirling Moss Kieft, the restored prototype.

Chris Hartnell and Claire Meaddows of the Wild Bunch, who were showing their slingshot 'Backdraft' in the NASC section of the classic car show at the NEC, had seen the Stirling Moss car. Like Brian, they sent me photos of the car.

Monday 10 May 2004 turned out to be a sad day. The phone rang and a voice said, 'Derek, this is Peter.'

'Yes, Peter?'

'Cyril Kieft died this morning.' Through the subsequent silence, my mind went back fifty years to visions of Cyril and the race cars he built in the Bridgend factory with the Kieft badge on the nose. I could hear Cyril say, 'Derek, this is your car.' Yes, one of the first production race cars.

Then the voice on the phone said, 'Derek, are you still there?'

I replied, 'Yes, Peter, sorry it is a shock. Cyril was so happy last time I spoke to him.'

'Derek, he was going through a painful shingles attack which brought on an infection of his water works and spread to his kidneys.'

I thanked Peter and sat there in a daze. In less than six months, two motorsport giants had died, Jeff May and Cyril Kieft. Both deaths were sudden and I couldn't help but wonder who would be next. This spurred me on to finish this book but not for reasons of vanity. The characters I have met along the way and thus recorded deserve recognition for their unselfish input to the various forms of motorsport they were involved in.

You don't have to drive an F1 race car and win races to be important. The lady who cleans the toilets plays her part. Many a race meeting I thanked God the toilets were open and my overalls would stay clean – 4G-force can play havoc with one's stomach!

All that week my mind kept going back to the days I raced Kieft 500s and to the great man himself. I decided to reread Peter Tutthill's *Kieft Racing Cars*. Yes, everything was there about the Kieft family history and the man – Cyril. I can recommend this book (and also the sequel to it). The pages are full of one man's driving force to produce a racing car with Welsh roots and his dream to have the Kieft badge carried on the front of sports racing cars, then the ultimate – Formula Grand Prix cars. These books can be purchased from Peter J. Tutthill, 'Woodcott', Trevanion Road, Wade Bridge, Cornwall PL27 7PA (Tel: 01208 812358).

To the best of my knowledge, although Cyril Kieft was in hospital before he died and mail wasn't reaching him, he did know the directors had approved him to be a member of the BRDC and his name would go on the register.

Cyril's life was motorsport and mine still is, and it continued at the Anglesey track with a double header, the Lancs and Cheshire Car Club and MG Car Club in charge of the action.

This meeting would be the last sprint in my career and it was on my home track. I was retiring, but there wouldn't be a clock – not even a 'Derek, good luck on your retirement' from the club officials or other drivers. To me, this reflects today's attitudes where longevity means nothing to people. The human touch has been lost and money has taken over – or is kindness seen as a weakness?

There was only one man who, like me, understood the old values and that man was Martin Platt, the MSA environmental scrutineer. He and I were both ageing and getting a little ragged around the edges. Jeff May came from the same mould as Martin, and both these men were relaxed and knowledgeable. They had seen it all happen before and didn't need to prove anything to anybody.

The weekend went well for me, giving me the uplift I needed in the ANWCC Sprint and Hill Climb Championship and also the All-rounders Championship in which I finished fourth. This was against the great rally drivers of the time – Gwawr Hughes and Barry Green who were first and runner-up respectively. They were followed by David Goodlad, the autotest nutter, then myself. Only 19 points separated first and fourth. That is what I call close racing. Yes nine months of racing and that was the high point of my time competing in the ANWCC Championship.

On reflection, older drivers like Stirling Moss and myself had in our youth to master all forms of motorsport – rally, road and circuit racing – which involved applying skills in any car be it a pure race car, sports car or rally car, the list is endless.

The Battle of Britain was won by Spitfire and Hurricane pilots who had to adapt to every challenge; thus were born young men in motorsport who followed these values.

In the late 1940s and early 50s (my era), drivers in motorsport were being killed weekly. We all knew the dangers involved in racing cars – there were no seatbelts or helmets (except a polo hat) and no roll bars to save us. Many of my friends were killed. When this happened we would drink a toast, knowing next week it could be our turn.

Remember, men survived a war in which tens of millions had been killed, life was cheap. If we had an accident, we didn't look for millions of pounds in compensation. No, every driver lived his life to the full. If you don't believe what I have said, ask Stirling Moss, who is recorded in the early chapter of my book and he will tell you, 'Safety has gone too far. Without fear of death, today's drivers know in any accident they will survive. Millions of pounds worth of car is destroyed to save them because of, in most cases, human error.'

In my youth I was told stories of the Zulu wars in which a few hundred British (mostly Welsh) soldiers fought thousands of Zulus and died with honour. Even Napoleon said to his troops, 'We shall fight with honour.' Like my father, I am a man of my time and for both of us honour ruled our lives. These values can still be found in motorsport today. There is a new breed of young drivers bringing back the values of the 1930s to our sport.

Enough said. I shall return to my last race, the Flame and Thunder at Santa Pod in which I drove the Honda. But before that I must tell you about my letter to Jeremy Clarkson (journalist) who, in the *Sun* newspaper of Saturday 27 September 2003, was giving a radical diet in his article to some people he was trying to provoke.

Dear Jeremy Clarkson

Here's a radical diet – try eating less.

Come off it, Jeremy! In your case the challenge has gone out of life. It is nothing to do with eating.

In your youth all those years ago when you wrote articles for 'Max Power' and nine out of ten were rejected, it got you so steamed up with aggression you lost 8lbs off your waistline in two days. This after drinking your favourite tipple and eating six of your mother's paddington bears, after spitting out the glass eyes.

My parents were successful, your parents were also successful, neither you nor I were starved of life's necessities. When all that ended we were thrown to the wolves and had to make our own way in life, things changed. In my case, yes, I don't know about you?

One day we shall meet, then we can compare notes. You and I go back a long way.

Please put a squirt of nitrous oxide into 'On Saturday Clarkson' and give us (your fans of many years) the Clarkson we all respect and love to hate.

Don't let us down.

Derek Annable

The year 2003 was an emotional time for the team Thunder and Light-ning. My wife's health was in further decline; a small stroke she suffered after our golden wedding anniversary party put an end to her days of being able to move her legs and she needed a wheelchair to move about the house.

Brenda, being her unstoppable self, decided we should race her Honda Integra in the big bracket at Santa Pod on the 1 November. She said, 'Derek, ten years ago you started in drag racing at the Pod. Let's finish it at the Pod.'

'Yes, Brenda, but what do I do after that?'

'Finish your bloody book – and it had better be a success. You have enough people helping you!'

Now the last piece of the jigsaw could be taken out and put away. No more motorsport for me. Team Thunder and Lightning would be relegated to the pages of history. Then this old man of motorsport could finish his years looking after the lady who made it all possible. The best crew chief any team could ask for – we must have travelled halfway to the moon and back to race our cars so let's enjoy the final weekend.

The Travelodge was booked and a phone call was made to Heidi and John who said they would meet us in the Santa Pod pits early Saturday morning.

I loaded the car with my wife's wheelchair, walker and other luggage and we set off due east in the direction of England – Tony Blair having given us a visa to travel out of Wales. After two hours, we reached checkpoint Chester, where our passport was inspected and stamped and my luggage was searched for any illegal Welsh whisky! We were lucky, three days earlier Max Boyce had been refused entry having made a joke about New Labour on Welsh television.

This reminded me of something that happened some years ago. We were racing at Avon Park drag strip and one of the racers was wearing ear plugs. At the time there was a curfew, so there was complete silence. I tapped him on the shoulder and asked him why he was wearing the ear plugs. After he took one out, I repeated my question to him. He answered, 'Derek, when you start talking about Wales and the Welsh you don't know when to stop.' He put the earplug back in and shook my hand saying, 'We all love hearing you talk, please never stop.'

The journey over and luggage deposited in our room, it was time to have some food. I installed Brenda in her wheelchair and we went to the Little Chef and ordered our meal. Halfway through, John Price and his family walked in. Seeing Brenda, he came over to us, gave her a kiss and asked, 'How are you, love?' Brenda explained that she would have to spend the rest of her life in a wheelchair and I was retiring from all forms of motorsport.

John turned to me and said, 'You will come and see us from time to time?'

'Sorry John, but no, Brenda is too ill. This meeting will be the last. It all started at the Pod and we shall end it at the Pod.'

John said, 'Derek, you and Brenda will be missed.' We thanked John, finished our meal and left as we had decided to have an early night.

Dawn broke and with the rain clouds moving away, everybody should have a good day's racing. Over the years the Flame and Thunder meetings had been dogged with bad weather. Driving through the pits you could see the track crew drying out nearly one mile of tarmac road – Jon Cross was in charge of a great bunch of underpaid helpers. We racers could win trophies and money but they got little thanks.

Amos Meekins passed the car fit to race, gave Brenda a kiss and put an MSA pass on her wheelchair. We would miss Amos, his brother and the other MSA officials – and you, Vincent's senior and junior.

I left Brenda with Heidi and John and joined the cars in the fire-up road. After two practice runs I returned to the pits. I was amazed to see who was pitted opposite me. It was none other than Smax Smith, this year's European Top Fuel Champion; the television people were all over him, watching his every gesture.

When Smax saw Brenda, he came running over to give her a bear hug and a kiss, saying 'I have been in Canada for two weeks, it was my parents' golden wedding anniversary last week – like you two. I am sorry to have missed your party.' The television people needed a shoot of Smax with a junior dragster, so he left after giving Brenda another kiss.

The pit marshall was calling out the cars for the big bracket, so off down the fire-up road I went to be paired. My opponent, car 654, chose the right-hand lane. Before we moved forward towards the start line, John Price and Darren Prentice came over and spoke to my opponent. The junior dragsters were moving forward to complete their runs, now it was 654 and my turn to race.

I don't burn out when I drive the Honda but my opponent, an 11-second car with slicks, always did. I wondered why he was holding back while I moved forward to the start line. Without warning, the chief start line marshall gave me the sign to move back and cut the engine. I wondered what was wrong with my car, then John Price walked to the side of my car and I opened the door. 'Please, Derek, get out of the car.'

To this day, I don't believe what happened. John Price produced a microphone from nowhere, turned to the thousands of spectators, and told them how long he had known Brenda and me, that I lived and breathed drag racing and had championed the sport for many long years. He told them

I was the oldest drag racer in the UK, maybe even anywhere in the world. When he had finished, I asked, 'Can I go and race now, John?'

'No', he said, 'Stay there, Derek.'

I was presented with a bottle of bubbly and a bouquet of flowers for Brenda. Then John said to the crowd, 'This great racer is retiring to look after his wife who has been through a long illness. He deserves your applause, come on, give him a farewell he will remember.'

I thanked John Price and Jon Cross and got back in the car. Then car 654 made his burnout and we raced, he won by virtue of a better light at the start line. My ET was $\frac{1}{100}$ of a second the right side of my dial-in of 16.18, a 16.19 – that was satisfaction indeed on my last ever dial-in.

Brenda and I said our farewells and drove off into the setting sun, knowing motorsport has no equal.

Now it was time to relax and enjoy a few home comforts. I started looking at photos which reminded me of all my dreams and what could have been. Could we recover from the march of time which nearly took my beloved wife away from me all those years ago? Could we rebuild a future for ourselves?

Yes, we could. Today the grass grows through the tarmac of what was once a prosperous garage forecourt, where hundreds of cars a day stopped for petrol. Those were the golden days of Action's Garage – the central point of the Thunder and Lightning drag racing team: the Camaro, the ex-Fay Fischer Altered, the ex-Barry Sheavills TA dragster and the Honda Integra Type.

How many racers can look back on fifty years of marriage and a husband/wife partnership in business and motorsport – few have equalled our achievements.

Now our future is in a West African country – the Gambia. There are challenges out there for two old people to channel their energy into – education, health and village welfare.

Suddenly, on 20 November 2003, a very unpleasant situation occurred. My wife took a phone call from John Turner who said, 'Come to Action's Garage as quickly as possible. Somebody has broken into the BMW and moved it to try and steal one of the caravans.'

Off I went with all speed, wondering what the hell had I done to deserve this. All summer I checked and double-checked the caravans in our compound, then in the middle of November at nine o'clock in the morning someone decides to try and steal a caravan.

All the way to Llanallgo, my mind played tricks. Was there somebody trying to close us down? No, it would be some young family man trying to up his income to provide his children with a few extra goodies. I thought to myself, Derek, you were young once, don't be too critical, poverty can be hard. Don't forget you started married life in a caravan all those years ago. Yes, I did, but I didn't go out and try to steal somebody else's property.

When I arrived at the garage forecourt, what greeted me was unbelievable. My wife's BMW had been pushed into a ditch, the driver's window was smashed and there was broken glass everywhere and the passenger door was wide open. Also one of the better caravans had its nose in the ground – it was sheer chaos.

It took John and me two hours to put our security system back in order. Next time the thieves would require a bulldozer.

My mother's birthday was on 23 November (born 1909, died May 1999) and it was time to visit the family grave. Off I set on a cold and frosty morning towards a brilliant sunrise. There was black ice on the roads but, being Sunday, the council hadn't started gritting. On the approach to every corner I had to tap, tap the car brakes to check for ice.

I was travelling along the North Wales expressway at a steady 70mph when a black Mercedes car passed me at speed in excess of 100mph. My wife's Integra could easily outpace this car. No, Derek, your mother's spirit awaits you and in the back of the car are two majestic holly wreaths for the family grave. There will be no racing today – you are on a mission.

Thank goodness the sun wasn't blinding my vision any more and I started to reflect on my youth which had been hard on me as I was sensitive boy. Many a morning I would say to my mother, 'Why was I born a boy?'

'No tears, Derek', she replied, 'Go to school and play rugby and football.'

'Mother, please can I stay with you? The boys at school bully and hit me. Please send me to a girls' school.'

'Derek, it is a good job your father is away fighting in North Africa, he wants you to be a man. Now, my son, take a deep breath, put your satchel over your shoulder and go to school, we'll have no more of this crying.'

Shit! I nearly ran into the back of a German trucker on his way home.

Now the fog was rolling across the M56 and I must slow down. Some idiots were passing me at full speed and driving through the fog without a care and to a certain meeting with their maker.

I had arrived at Failsworth Cemetery and as I drove through the open gates, I was met with a sight of complete destruction. Every gravestone had been broken and lay flat on the graves. For all of five minutes I sat in the car, not daring to open the door. Air-raid sirens filled my head and I was back in 1943 not 2003 – were the Germans bombing Manchester?

No, they weren't. The local council had decided that because a young boy was killed in Salford by a falling gravestone, all gravestones should be flattened. This was bureaucracy gone mad. It was nothing short of vandalism by authority. Where will it end?

Thank God my mother's grave didn't have a blue cross on it. If it had, the white angel which looks over her would have been sent crashing to the ground and the marble would have been broken beyond repair. No wonder the Hindus burn their dead and scatter the ashes on the River Ganges.

Here comes the bottom line: all headstones with a blue cross on must be reset by council employees at a cost of £300–£800, subject to size and weight, with a local stonemason in charge. Added to this cost is an insurance charge which the council arrange to cover public liability at a cost of £50 per ten-year period.

My mission was completed – two holly wreaths and a message lay on the soil which covered the bones of my deceased family: my mother, father and my baby brother, who died at the age of two months. Peace be with them. Let's get back home to Wales. The drive along the coast road will calm my angry thoughts.

I shall now record team Thunder and Lightning's achievements:

FINAL RESULTS 2003

Dragster
Winners Cups SCR 18 May
Winners Cups York 9/10 August

Honda Integra Type R

Winner class	Hill Climb Scam Dam 20 July
Runner-up class	Hill Climb Scam Dam 17 August
Winner class	Ty Croes Sprint 24 May
Runner-up class	Ty Croes Sprint 25 May
Winner class	Ty Croes Sprint 6 September
Runner-up class	Ty Croes Sprint 7 September

ANWCC Championships:
2nd class Sprints
1st class Hill Climbs
All-rounders:	4th
Sprints:	10th
Hill Climbs:	5th
Hill Climbs (Novice):	6th

Autotests: last behind Fiona Maxwell
Drivers class 'C', again last behind Fiona Maxwell
Novice driver – overall 10th
Novice driver – Class 'C' 8th

The All-rounders Championship:
I was ahead of great drivers like Gordon Holmes, Damen Garrod, Peter Bryson, Bob Beadon and Medwyn Jones.

The Sprint Championship:
Again ahead of Roger Fish, Tony Anderson, George Povey, Karen Williams and Bob Beadon.

Hill Climb Championship:
Ahead of drivers like Dave Coveney, Dave Goodlad, Bernard Mooney, Stuart Tranter, Steven Cowley and Bob Jones.

Wild Bunch Trophy Presentation:
1. Derek and Brenda were awarded the Lifetime Dedication to Motorsport award.
2. The Derek and Brenda Annable Trophy was won by Roy and Angie Wilding.

Final Thoughts

In July 1999, Nicky Foulston came into my life at a troubled time within the BRDC. Being a gallant man, and a white knight who had devotion to women and their wellbeing, old Derek was woken from his slumbers.

This lady was receiving a hostile response from the British Racing Drivers Club, so I took up the challenge to help her fulfil her late father's dream of owning and holding the British Grand Prix. His dream was cut short when he was killed racing around the Silverstone Circuit in 1987.

Nicky was only 19 years old when this happened; even at that tender age she put aside the loss of her beloved father and set about turning Brands Hatch Leisure into a successful company. The driving force being her late father's dream and the family will to win.

What happened is history, but Derek Annable applauds the spunk of a 31-year-old lady who took on the big players of this world.

Nicky Foulston, you are one of the greats of my time in motorsport. Please take a second breath and come back fighting to fulfil your father's dream.

Derek Annable

Epilogue

The book has taken nearly three years to write. Every moment has been a pleasure and I thank my family for their generous support, for without them I would have backed off and thrown my scribblings away, never to be found.

In the early 1940s, when I had succumbed to an unknown virus, the matron of York, my house at Wrekin College, sent me to the school sickbay. Though feverish, I heard on the radio a young singer, Frank Sinatra, sing his first UK number one, 'I'll Be Seeing You'. I was impressed with these words:

> I'll be seeing you in every lovely summer's day,
> and everything that's bright and gay.
> I'll always think of you that way.

Now, nearly sixty years on, I still rejoice in the great man through his music from the album New York, New York, side 1, track No 8, 'My Way', which best expresses my life. His rendering fills me with emotion. We are all children and deep down look for our mothers' forgiveness:

To quote his words:

> And now, the end is near … for what is a man, what has he got?
> If not himself, then he has naught.
> … I did what I had to do … I did it my way.

If this has upset some along the way, I say 'Sorry, but it had to be done.' Would they have thought less of me if I had not done it my way? Judgement day comes to us all, and when that day comes I shall stand there with head bowed and accept my lot.

I sit here looking at a room full of trophies and ask myself if it was worth it. My answer is 'Yes'. Given my time over again, I would not change a minute of it. My destiny was written long before I was born and the passage of time has fulfilled it. There have been a few hiccups along the way but generally it has run its planned course.

As a baby I suffered from bronchial complaints which, in 1930, should have killed me. Then I went through hard labour at boarding school – being rejected by one's mother and sent away is difficult for a ten-year-old to bear. Many others of my age suffered emotions and torments far worse than mine, but we are stronger for it.

I have travelled a long road through life and the one thing which has nearly broken me is rejection by others, but I can only be myself. People can be so cruel.

As I have said before, 'I did it my way', and to the few friends that have survived me I say, 'Thank you and God bless you.'

THE END

NEC January 2003: Restored Kieft. From left, Stirling, Peter Tutthill, Brian Jenkins and the man who restored the car (© Brian Jenkins)

Cyril Kieft (© Cyril Kieft)

Left: *Avon Park 2003, Doug's first five (© Martyn Hannis)*
Below: *Avon Park 2004, May Day weekend (© Martyn Hannis)*

Santa Pod 2003, May Day
meet: Joe Bond, Junior
Dragster
(© Martyn Hannis)

Nuthurst Grange Hotel:
BRDC dinner, January
2003

Avon Park: Derek and
Brenda's TM Dragster with
Derek racing
(© Martyn Hannis)

Anglesey Racing Circuit, June 2003:
Derek and Brenda's Honda
Left: *On the line*
Below: *Exiting Douglas*
(© Steve Wilkinson)

Three Sisters, August 2003:
Derek and Brenda's Honda
Above: *Into Lunar*
Right: *Apexing Lunar*
(© Steve Wilkinson)

50th wedding anniversary,
4 July 2003

Left: *Brenda and Derek,*
cutting the cake
(© Brian Staines)

Below: *Invitation and*
menu

Golden Wedding Anniversary

Venue: The Novotel, Bradford 01274 683683

Date: 4th July 2003

Dinner: 6.30 for 7.00pm until approx. 11.00pm

Please select from the menu with a tick for each course and mark W for Wine or FJ for Fruit Juice after your name.

Music will be provided by The Star Dusters and Singers with an interlude Cocktail Pianist.

If you have an American Muscle Car, please bring it - an area of the hotel car park is set aside.

Smart Dress please style: 40's, 50's, 60's. 70's and on.

With respect, we request no smoking in the dining area.

Thank You

Menu

Starters

Washington Corn Cream

Mushroom & Asparagus Parcels
filo pastry parcels filled with
mushroom & asparagus

Main Courses

Beef Tenderloin
with fresh asparagus and
a grain mustard sauce

Salmon Parcels & Sesame Seeds
dressed with a mushroom & ginger sauce

Mushroom Risotto

American Style Chicken
stuffed with mozzarella cheese
and wrapped with bacon

Desserts

Blueberry Pie

Key Lime Pie

Glace Fruit & Coffee

The anniversary cake – some cake! Only the best for Brenda…
(© Brian Staines)

Jon Cross making his speech
(© Steven F. Moxley)

Anniversary celebrations US style – on 4 July! (© Steven F. Moxley)

Derek and Brenda's family and friends enjoying the party (© Derek Annable)

Derek reflects on his marriage and wonders at all that he and Brenda have been through together … and survived! (© Derek Annable)

Mark Fisher 2004:
First Super Street bike
into 8.0 seconds, Avon
Park. He was Brenda's
biker friend from the
early days (1995)
(© Steven F. Moxley)

Left: *Svein Gottenberg*
(Norway) 2004 at
Santa Pod – another
of Brenda's biker
friends, this time from
1997
(© Steven F. Moxley)

Loton Hill Climb
2003
(© Derek Hibbert)

Derek's farewell (© Eurodragster)

European Drag Racing News
recorded Derek and Brenda's
retirement from the sport

Swift snippets.
4th November: At 73 Europe's oldest competing drag racer, UK Wild Bunch and Sportsman ET racer **Derek Annable**, made his last competitive run at the Flame and Thunder Show at Santa Pod Raceway on Saturday. Derek announced his retirement before qualifying for the Car bracket and finished his career in the first round of eliminations just after track announcer John Price presented him with a bottle of bubbly and a bunch of flowers for wife Brenda. We are sure that everyone will join Sharkman and Tog in wishing Derek and Brenda all the very best for the future, which we hope includes visits to the track to spectate.
©Eurodragster.com

Roy and Angie receiving the Derek
and Brenda Annable Trophy,
January/February 2004
(© Wild Bunch)

Drayton Manor 2004:
Derek receiving the gift
(© Wild Bunch)